The Nigeria–Biafra war and the making of a humanitarian crisis (1967–70)

Manchester University Press

HUMANITARIANISM

SERIES EDITOR: BERTRAND TAITHE

SERIES EDITORS: BERTRAND TAITHE, REBECCA GILL

This series offers a new interdisciplinary reflection on one of the most important and yet understudied areas in history, politics and cultural practices: humanitarian aid and its responses to crises and conflicts. The series seeks to define afresh the boundaries and methodologies applied to the study of humanitarian relief and so-called 'humanitarian events'. The series includes monographs and carefully selected thematic edited collections which cross disciplinary boundaries and bring fresh perspectives to the historical, political and cultural understanding of the rationale and impact of humanitarian relief work.

To buy or to find out more about the books currently available in this series, please go to: https://manchesteruniversitypress.co.uk/series/humanitarianism-key-debates-and-new-approaches/

The Nigeria–Biafra war and the making of a humanitarian crisis (1967–70)

Marie-Luce Desgrandchamps

Translated by

Monica Biberson

Manchester University Press

Published by Presses Universitaires de Rennes 2018
First English-language edition published in 2026 by
Manchester University Press
Oxford Road, Manchester, M13 9PL

www.manchesteruniversitypress.co.uk

British Library Cataloguing-in-Publication Data
A catalogue record for this book is available from the British Library

ISBN 978 1 5261 9024 6 hardback

First published 2026

EU authorised representative for GPSR:
Easy Access System Europe, Mustamäe tee 50, 10621
Tallinn, Estonia
gpsr.requests@easproject.com

Typeset by Newgen Publishing UK

Contents

Figures

Tables

Introduction

In the summer of 1968 images of emaciated children suffering from malnutrition-related illnesses flooded the Western media. They were taken in the south-eastern region of the Federation of Nigeria, which had declared its independence a year earlier under the name of the Republic of Biafra. Surrounded by the Nigerian army which sought to recapture it, the province was in the grip of war and famine. This conflict, which could have gone largely unnoticed in the West, was now on European and American agendas. It marked the beginning of a lasting association between "Africa" and "humanitarian crisis" in collective representations. The emotion aroused by the famine led to the mobilisation of various humanitarian and charitable organisations wishing to help the civilian population. Directed by the International Red Cross Movement as well as Catholic and Protestant aid organisations, international relief operations were set up in support of the Biafran-controlled region and the areas that were gradually retaken by Nigerian troops. This book traces the making of this humanitarian crisis and explores why it has been seen as a major turning point in the history of humanitarianism.

The Biafra moment: an important crisis in the history of humanitarianism

"New Solferino",[1] the birthplace of the "modern humanitarian movement",[2] the end of the "first century of humanitarianism",[3] or the beginning of the "twenty glorious years of humanitarianism"[4] – French-language scholarship offers plenty of expressions highlighting the significance of this conflict. Its special place has long been closely linked to the creation in 1971 of one of the most emblematic French NGOs: Médecins Sans Frontières (MSF). The war has been identified as the moment when the future founders of the organisation broke with the International Committee of the Red Cross (ICRC), for which they were working at the time. Considering the

ICRC as too conservative to act without the agreement of the belligerents and too neutral to denounce the violence it witnesses, MSF founders are said to have broken up with the Swiss organisation. They soon became a symbol of a new kind of humanitarianism characterised by the practice of "speaking out" and "*sans-frontiérisme*". This interpretation of the Biafran moment, which was first put forward by some of the actors of the time,[5] has had a lasting impact on humanitarian studies in France, and the decision of the doctors in Biafra to break away has gradually been portrayed as a major turning point in the history of humanitarianism.

It is only in the 1990s and 2000s, that this view started to be contested in France. Gradually, some practitioners presented a more nuanced reading of the events which no longer saw the war simply as the place where a small group of French doctors invented a new kind of humanitarianism, but as an episode that illustrated the complexity of aid.[6] For Rony Brauman, their stances thus attested to the "dangerous links between speaking out and political propaganda".[7] In a book about Médecins Sans Frontières, Anne Vallaeys revisits the role played by these actors, presenting a broader picture of relief operations. She highlights the political context of France's support for Biafran independence in which their actions took place.[8] Showing the ambiguities of the positions taken by the doctors may well have something to do with the internal quarrels within the French humanitarian community,[9] but it does have the merit of widening the scope of the analysis. Such works joined a more Anglo-Saxon tradition which is less marked by the birth of *sans-frontiérisme* and uses the Nigeria–Biafra crisis as a case study that illustrates the "perverse effects" of aid, its instrumentalisation by the belligerents and its role in prolonging the hostilities and the blockade.[10]

These two traditions have gradually converged, as shown by the work of authors who have proposed general histories of humanitarianism. For Philippe Ryfman, the end of the 1960s and the Biafran war still mark the beginning of a "second century". However, this moment is no longer characterised solely by the creation of MSF and the invention of *sans-frontiérisme*, but more broadly by "the rise in power of the NGOs [non-governmental organisations] born during the previous four decades and the emergence of new ones, the change in practices, the repositioning of the Red Cross, and the assertiveness of international organisations".[11] As for Johannes Paulmann, he has put forward a history punctuated by four junctures (the second half of the nineteenth century, the First World War, the 1960s–1970s, and the early 1990s) and considers Biafra as one of the events of the third juncture which he calls the "moment of postcolonial mobilisation".[12] Finally, for Michael Barnett, the history of humanitarianism has been shaped by the evolution and combination of three structural factors: the "forces" of destruction, production and compassion. He distinguishes three ages of humanitarianism: the first from the early nineteenth century to the Second World War, the second from the Second World War to the fall of the Berlin Wall, and the third from the end of the Cold War to the twenty-first century.[13] The late 1960s and Biafra are, however, a central episode of the second period, "The age of neo-humanitarianism", which is defined in particular by the broadening of the spectrum of potential beneficiaries of humanitarian aid and the growing role played by non-governmental and international organisations in decolonised territories. For Kevin O'Sullivan, Matthew Hilton and Juliano Fiori, it is partly for these reasons that the period from 1968 to 1985, which began with Biafra, was a "moment of acceleration" in the history of humanitarianism.[14] According to O'Sullivan, Biafra "set the tone for the NGO moment", during which a Westernised, NGO-led model of compassion became the dominant global expression of solidarity with the Third World.[15] Thus, although it is not systematically thought of as a turning point, the conflict remains an important milestone in the history of humanitarianism and human rights.[16]

For a long time, these analyses were essentially based on two types of publications. There were either memoirs or accounts by actors of the time, sometimes supplemented by extensive documentary research.[17] Academic studies on the conflict, mostly dating from the 1970s, provided the second type of resource available. In addition to the works on the civil war and its internationalisation, which looked at the role of the humanitarian crisis in this process,[18] two doctoral theses in political science written in the early 1970s had paved the way for an analysis of relief operations.[19] Since the 2010s the conflict has been the subject of a major historiographical renewal,[20] in which human-rights and humanitarian-aid questions have received particular attention. For instance, the special issues and volume published by Dirk Moses and Lasse Heerten in 2014 and 2017 question the use of the notion of genocide at the time of the conflict and in its memory.[21] By bringing together contributions from numerous researchers, these publications have put the analysis of primary sources back at the heart of the production of knowledge on this conflict. In the same vein, Lasse Heerten's work on the conflict and the importance of humanitarian issues and representations in its internationalisation is now an authoritative study on the subject. Heerten shows, in particular, how this conflict resonated in Western societies – German, French, British and American – and was a decisive step in the reimagination of the Third World within a postcolonial world order.[22] As for Arua Omaka's book, it offers a different perspective insofar as it looks at the mobilisation of churches and the deployment of humanitarian aid from religious organisations in the conflict (Joint Church Aid).[23] Kevin O'Sullivan has shown that Biafra provided new opportunities of "access to those in need" for British, Canadian and Irish humanitarian networks that mobilised during the crisis.

A transnational history of the postcolonial humanitarian field

Written at the same time as these books and published in French in 2018, the study translated in this book is part of the new historical approach to the conflict which re-evaluates its place in the history of humanitarianism. It offers an analysis of the relief action that was deployed there, which fits into what analysts of 1990s humanitarianism refer to as a "humanitarian action". The following definition put forward by Philippe Ryfman helps grasp its essential characteristics:

> assistance provided by a single actor or a group of actors as part of various levels of an international aid system, governed by a certain number of principles and implemented (in the name of values considered to be universal) for the benefit of populations whose living conditions have been disrupted by nature (disasters) or by the actions of other people (internal or international armed conflicts), and whose physical integrity has been affected, or even whose very survival has been compromised.[24]

Studying humanitarian action therefore involves looking at the mechanisms by which this assistance is developed, the actors who deploy it (organisations, states, but also individuals), the principles that underpin it, its implementation, as well as the way in which it is perceived by the populations for whom it is intended.

The history of humanitarianism in general, and of the Biafran crisis in particular, has long provided only a partial view of these multiple dimensions. Indeed, the essentially positive connotations of humanitarian aid due to the values of generosity, sacrifice and altruism towards "victims" which are associated with it, and which particularly resonated in Western societies in the second half of the twentieth century, have produced a polarised literature on the subject.[25] On the one hand, the latter consists of benevolent, even complacent narratives which interpret the evolution and expansion of humanitarianism as a sign of moral progress.[26] The first volunteers, for example, were portrayed as secular saints, before becoming the new heroes of modern times. On the other hand, a critical literature has developed which often chooses to highlight the disjunction between practices that have harmful consequences or are undertaken for the "wrong reasons", and the values that are supposed to drive humanitarianism. These ways of looking at the phenomenon, whether in terms of a "euphoric celebration" or a criticism of its "perverse effects", can be seen as two sides of the same coin and ultimately say little about humanitarianism as such.[27]

Furthermore, many studies focus on a single organisation. Whether it be academic studies, institutional histories or hagiographies, such a perspective has certain limitations. Firstly, it fails to reflect the complexity of humanitarian action, which often involves a multitude of actors from different backgrounds and cultures. Thus, not enough research has been done on the otherwise formative relationships between humanitarian agencies and between them and states. Secondly, the institutional focus has emphasised the (legal and moral) principles that are supposed to guide organisations in order to justify their existence and their practices, or to establish their specificity and identity in the humanitarian field.[28] This latter preoccupation has had the effect of obscuring the continuities or similarities between these actors, who often present themselves as the source of a new form of humanitarian action.[29] On the other hand, their functioning and internal workings in terms of decision making, funding or staffing are sometimes not studied enough.[30] Finally, the contexts in which their activities take place, in terms of both their development and deployment, have often been barely looked at. Indeed, the entry into the history of humanitarianism through these predominantly Western organisations leaves little room for reflections on the way in which aid is perceived in the places where it is delivered, most of the time its beneficiaries being seen as mere recipients.

This book addresses these different dimensions. Drawing on first-hand sources and documentation, it analyses how the situation in the ground became an object of interest in Western societies, and how this mobilisation gave rise to a vast and complex relief operation in Nigeria and Biafra. Following these processes empirically requires adopting various points of view, whether it be scales of observation (international, national, local), ways of observing actors (at headquarters or in the field), or geographical areas (Nigeria/Western Europe).[31] This approach first of all allows us to see who the humanitarian actors were at the time (individuals, institutions, but also governments), and the contexts and traditions in which they evolved. Moreover, by shedding light on the relationship between principles and practices, it invites us to think in terms other than moral ones about the impact of relief operations on the conflict. Finally, it examines the perceptions and relationships between "beneficiaries" and Western actors. The major new historiographical insights which humanitarianism has benefited from in recent years provide conceptual tools for paying particular attention to these three dimensions which are at the centre of this study.

In the wake of the developments in transnational and global history,[32] various authors have revisited the role played by international organisations and NGOs during the long decolonisation process.[33] Examining the way they interact and position themselves in relation to one another often provides keys to understanding how they make their decisions or set their agendas.[34] The same is true of the way in which the individuals who make them up move between local, national and international spheres.[35] The aim is therefore to provide an analysis of the relief operations developed in Nigeria and Biafra which takes into account the multiplicity of the humanitarian actors involved, their diversity and their interactions.[36] More generally, focusing on the backgrounds of the individuals working in the field and on the problems they faced on the ground sheds light on the porosity between different humanitarian traditions.[37]

Taking these actors into account does not mean neglecting the role played by states, who remain fundamental to understanding the development of humanitarian aid in the twentieth century, its institutionalisation and its entry into the industrial era.[38] Nor are they strangers to the proliferation of NGOs from the 1970s on.[39] In the Nigeria–Biafra case, examining the workings of non-governmental actors and the resources available to them illuminates how the European governments most involved in the conflict – British and French – viewed the humanitarian crisis and the ways in which they attempted to respond to it. The relationship that states had with relief agencies also provides an insight into the political dimensions of humanitarianism.

In the literature, the attitude of the relief organisations during the Nigeria–Biafra war is presented in different ways. On the one hand, some authors stress humanitarian organisations' failure to respect international law and the principle of neutrality. They thus point out that the ICRC exceeded its prerogatives in the Biafran conflict, did not respect the provisions of international law and went beyond the principle of neutrality that was supposed to guide its actions.[40] On the other hand, the historical accounts centred on the French doctors' break with the ICRC emphasise the latter's overly legalistic character as it prioritised obtaining the agreement of the parties over the effectiveness of its action and was too attached to its neutrality to denounce the Nigerian government's treatment of the Biafrans. They thus highlight the limitations of this type of humanitarianism.[41]

These two ways of looking at this crisis echo the moral debates that regularly occur in the humanitarian world on the duty or lack thereof to intervene or denounce a given situation.[42] Underlying these questions is the failure of the ICRC and the wider international community to protect Jewish populations from the Nazi regime's extermination policy.[43] As noted by Sébastien Farré, focusing on the concrete aspects of humanitarian actions makes it possible to approach these debates from a different angle than the normative one.[44] Such an approach leads us to qualify interpretations that focus too closely on the legal or moral frameworks within which organisations operate and underestimate the rooms for manoeuvre they allow themselves. This book analyses how actors linked up their practices with these normative considerations depending on other constraints imposed by the situation on the ground and the emergency they were faced with. By showing how they concretely positioned themselves in relation to the media coverage of the crisis and the sovereignty of the Nigerian government, we can grasp differently the invention of the "media hype" or the "right to interfere" by the French doctors.

Looking at the relationship between humanitarians and the societies in which they operate means reintegrating local issues into a history long dominated by a Western perspective. Little attention has been paid to recipients, particularly because of the difficulty in accessing sources, but also because such an approach requires adopting a ground-level perspective and not seeing beneficiaries merely as passive victims.[45] This trend was reinforced by the fact that beginning with the 1960s humanitarian aid became essentially a phenomenon that went from the North to the South.

In the Biafran case, while the consequences of relief operations on the prolongation of the conflict have been clearly highlighted, other aspects have remained little studied, such as the situation after the departure of Western organisations, or the impact of the latter on the balance of power between local actors. And there has also been very little work done on the role played by Nigerian humanitarian institutions in the conflict.[46] This book does not aim to fill these gaps which would merit further research. Nevertheless, to the extent that the sources consulted have allowed, it pays attention to the role played by Nigerian and Biafran actors in the processes concerning the media coverage, deployment and reappropriation of humanitarian aid. A key question is: What was their relationship with this "assistance" from abroad, mostly from the West? Restoring their perception of relief operations and comparing it with how Western actors viewed their African interlocutors reveals the importance of the postcolonial context in the tensions that ran through their relations. The complexity of these phenomena finally makes it possible to go beyond a binary vision that portrays Western humanitarians as either new colonists or benefactors, and African societies as either passive victims needing to be saved or irresponsible entities instrumentalising humanitarian aid.

Outline of the book

The book is divided into three parts. In order to examine the relationship between the places where humanitarian responses were elaborated and those where they were deployed, Parts I and II follow this crisis as it shifted from the local to the international scale, and then the responses that came from the West to Nigeria. Part III revisits both the issue of the perverse effects of aid and that of the emergence of a new kind of humanitarianism in the late 1960s.

More specifically, Part I examines how a civil war that unfolded on the African continent and could have gone largely unnoticed became the "first televised famine".[47] This was not a given, since in the late 1960s there were so many galvanising issues of concern in the world (the Vietnam War, May 1968, the repression of the Prague Spring). Looking at the relationship between the media and humanitarianism thirty years on, Rony Brauman identified four (necessary but not sufficient) conditions for a local tragedy to become an international event. The first is the "image tap", that is, the availability of a continuous flow of images of the crisis. The second prerequisite is that similar situations should not occur at the same time, otherwise they may crowd each other out. The presence of a "mediating" actor on the ground able to establish a link between "spectators" and victims, and to authenticate the latter, is the third condition. Fourthly, the innocence of the victims should be beyond doubt.[48] By underlining the importance of images, "mediating" actors and the representation of victims, this analytical framework makes it possible to identify the constituent elements of the media coverage of humanitarian crises.

The work of Lasse Heerten has shown that different concepts (human rights, genocide, self-determination, sovereignty as well as the larger field of humanitarian practice) interacted to shape the new forms of politics and activism that characterised the Biafran campaign.[49] I adopt a slightly different perspective by following how Biafra, which was initially associated with a struggle for independence, gradually became synonymous with famine. Starting from the controversies that still exist in historiography on the extent of the famine or the use of the term genocide,[50] Chapter 1 retraces how the events were portrayed in belligerents' discourses and how these discourses fuelled contradictory interpretations during the conflict. In order to understand Biafra's emergence in Western newspapers, Chapter 2 focuses on the moments and actors of the media coverage. Whilst the role of the Igbo diaspora, Markpress agency and missionaries is well known, I also shed light on the influence of the French and British governments. Chapter 3 studies the dissemination and impact of a certain type of representations of the crisis to explain the emotion stirred by this African civil war at the end of the 1960s and examine its repercussions on Western government policies. I argue that the iconography used during the conflict left a lasting impression on the Western imagination of Africa. The way in which the situation was presented led above all to "humanitarian" reactions, which question the link between humanitarianism and politics in the postcolonial era.

Part II analyses the concrete responses of different humanitarian actors. In response to the emotion aroused by the situation in Nigeria–Biafra, various Western charities were galvanised into dealing with the humanitarian crisis by sending food, medicines and volunteers on the ground. The setting up, deployment and reception of the relief operations during the three years of conflict provide an interesting laboratory for studying the composition and functioning of the humanitarian field in the late 1960s. Although many NGOs, especially in the 1960s, turned to "development" activities in postcolonial countries, not all of them had the means and capacity to provide emergency aid in a civil war. Moreover, their deployment in a relatively limited area raises questions about the relationship between these various organisations and with the governments that often provided them with resources for their actions. Finally, studying the reception on the ground and by the Nigerian government of the international humanitarian action show the influence of the late-1960s postcolonial context on the behaviours of the various actors and their perceptions of each other.

The discussion of these issues is structured around the two main moments that marked the action in Nigeria–Biafra, namely the summer of 1968 and the summer of 1969. The difficulties encountered by non-governmental actors in mounting a "humanitarian intervention" were most felt in the period from May 1967, when independence was declared, to September 1968. Focusing on this period, Chapter 4 unpacks the decision-making processes that led many non-governmental organisations to intervene in Biafra without the formal agreement of the Nigerian government, raising the more general question of the relationship between humanitarian actors and the sovereignty of the states in which they intervene. From then on, the establishment by the churches and ICRC of regular airlifts to Biafra marked the beginning of a large-scale operation in the breakaway province without the formal agreement of the Nigerian government. Dedicated to the deployment of relief operations on the ground between the summer of 1968 and the summer of 1969, Chapter 5 sheds light on the knowledge and resources mobilised by humanitarian actors in the late 1960s and analyses the problems associated with deploying relief in the federal and Biafran areas, namely the questions of efficiency and collaboration between disparate organisations. The Nigerian government's taking over the co-ordination of international aid in the federal area and its formal ban on night flights to Biafra in June 1969 marked the beginning of the last period of the humanitarian action. This was characterised by a hardening of the Nigerian attitude towards foreign actors, which was confirmed at the end of the conflict in January 1970. Chapter 6 examines the ways in which the relief operations were perceived and received in Nigeria to understand the ambiguities of such an evolution.

Part III of this book revisits two aspects that have been mobilised to explain why Biafra is an important moment in the history of humanitarianism, namely, the instrumentalisation of humanitarian aid by various actors for political purposes, and the birth during this conflict of "modern humanitarianism" which was characterised by speaking out and *sans-frontiérisme*. These two aspects are not unrelated since the invention of a new humanitarianism, as claimed by the founders of Médecins Sans Frontières, took place in the context of the instrumentalisation of the humanitarian crisis by the secessionist authorities, but also by the French government, which raises the broader question of the relationship between "humanitarianism" and "politics", whether in terms of the practice of bearing witness or the impact of sending aid into a conflict situation. Chapter 7 looks at this last dimension and the basis on which, already during the war, the conviction was formed that the relief operations prolonged the Biafran resistance. The focus is not so much on attempting to quantify this phenomenon as on examining the way in which this issue emerged and the reactions it produced among humanitarians. The aim is to gain a better understanding of how relief activities were perceived by those who carried them out in the late 1960s. In this context, the specific positions taken by the French doctors and their break with the ICRC during the conflict is analysed in Chapter 8. The issue of bearing witness is addressed from the broader perspective of denouncing violations of human rights and humanitarian law, and is linked to the evolution of the ICRC's practice in this respect. Whilst the opposition between the founders of Médecins Sans Frontières and the Geneva-based organisation proves to be less dramatic than it has been depicted in retrospective accounts, it is nevertheless part of a more general trend of challenging the Committee. Chapter 9 focuses on the ICRC, which was the object of much criticism during the conflict. The difficulties it encountered in managing the relief operations prompted it to question itself and particularly underscored the need for introducing reforms. Moving away from exclusively concentrating on the French doctors and the creation of MSF in 1971 makes it possible to take a different approach to the question of the birth of modern humanitarianism at the time of Biafra.

The archives of humanitarian actors are the first type of sources used in this work. As these organisations were structured into three main groups during the conflict – Red Cross, Protestant and Catholic networks – the choice was made to consult documentary collections that could shed light on each of these groups. Since many organisations within these groups were involved at very different levels (fundraising, sending staff, field work), the focus has been on the archives of those who centralised the various initiatives and acted directly on the ground. As regards the Red Cross Movement, the archives of the International Committee of the Red Cross have been the main resource due to the central role the organisation played in relief operations in Biafra, as well as in co-ordinating international aid in the federal area. These particularly rich collections include documents belonging to the ICRC's decision-making bodies, correspondence between headquarters and the field, as well as numerous delegates' reports which provide an insight into the situation on the ground. This documentation has been supplemented by the archives of the International Federation of the Red Cross, which is the other "international" component of the movement. Although they are less extensive, they nevertheless provide some additional information on the different ways in which the conflict may have been viewed by some National Societies. The archives of the French Red Cross are the third collection consulted specifically for this group, and were chosen for two reasons. On the one hand, this National Society is an interesting interface for studying the relationship between humanitarianism and politics given its role in mediating the French government's policy of support for Biafra; and on the other hand, it is among its teams sent on the ground that we find the French volunteers who would later found Médecins Sans Frontières.

As Caritas Internationalis, which co-ordinated Catholic responses to the humanitarian crisis, did not grant access to its archives, other resources had to be found to be able to grasp this point of view. To fill this gap, the trail of the Congregation of the Holy Spirit missionaries, whose special role in awakening European interest in Biafra and the relief operations is well known, proved particularly fruitful. Their archives in Chevilly-Larue have preserved important correspondence between the missionaries on the ground and the Vatican, but also documents issued by Caritas Internationalis and Joint Church Aid, as well as extensive documentation on the conflict. A collection of documents belonging to the Catholic Secretariat of Nigeria, stored in the National Archives of Nigeria in Ibadan, provided additional information on the role of religious organisations at the end of the conflict and the Nigerian authorities' positioning in relation to them.

The archives of the World Council of Churches (WCC) held in Geneva made it possible to reconstruct some of the Protestant activities in response to the conflict. The holdings of the General Secretariat, of the Commission of the Churches on International Affairs, and of the Division of Inter-Church Aid, Refugee and World Service contain documents that show the diversity of the Protestant response. Once again, correspondence, reports and internal notes show the links between the various organisations involved in the relief effort in Nigeria and Biafra. As the WCC was less present in field operations, having acted mainly as a provider of resources for other organisations, it has been possible to gain an insight into this dimension through the personal papers of one of those in charge of the Protestant operations in Biafra. The letters of Reverend Alexander Somerville and his wife to friends and family in Scotland and to the Church of Scotland's missions office, which are held at the National Library of Scotland in Edinburgh, have proved useful in understanding the concrete problems faced by humanitarians on a daily basis.

This corpus provided the material necessary to study the relationships between the various organisations, between the wider groups to which they belonged, as well as the links between headquarters and the field, between raising funds and implementing relief efforts. Moreover, the internal documents of these organisations, which are less suspect than their public statements intended to raise the alarm and funds, provide an insight into the situation of the Biafran and Nigerian populations during the war. Finally, the United Nations (UN) archives and the personal papers of the co-ordinator of the Nigeria–Biafra relief effort appointed by the US government, Clarence Clyde Ferguson, have helped illuminate the choices of actors who decided not to become directly involved in the relief effort but to support it in one way or another.

The second major category of archives consulted emanated from governments. The Civil War collections held at the National Archives of Nigeria in Ibadan were consulted during a trip to the country in 2011. Consisting mainly of pamphlets published by the federal and Biafran authorities during the war, these holdings provide information on official discourses but say little about attitudes towards humanitarians and relief operations. As the archives concerning the conflict are probably still with ministries or individuals, it has not been possible to consult them. Nevertheless, secondary literature, the press and testimonies have helped reconstruct these views to a certain extent. Above all, documents from other governments who were particularly close to the belligerents proved very useful. Thus, the very rich holdings of UK national archives illuminated the Nigerian position on humanitarian issues during the war. The decisive support provided by the former metropole to the Nigerian federal military government during the conflict explains their closeness as well as the mediating role played by the British between Lagos and relief organisations. Given the French government's support for the secessionists, its archives are possible sources for understanding the point of view of the Biafran authorities (particularly the holdings of the Secretariat for African and Malagasy Affairs at the national archives and, to a lesser extent, those of the Ministry of Foreign Affairs in Nantes and Paris). But it is especially in terms of illuminating the interplay between humanitarianism and politics in the French and British national arenas that these collections were useful. Supplemented by published diplomatic documents from the United States and Switzerland, they also make it possible to examine the relations between non-governmental actors and governments.

The Nigerian, Swiss, French, British and American written and illustrated press were consulted as required. Finally, the reports, accounts, memoirs and analyses published by Nigerians and Westerners who were directly or indirectly involved in the media coverage of the crisis and the responses of relief organisations have provided additional resources for empirically approaching these processes.

Acknowledgement

This book is a translation of *L'humanitaire en guerre civile. La crise du Biafra (1967–1970)*, originally published by the Presses universitaires de Rennes (PUR) in 2018. I would like to thank the PUR for authorising the translation, and the editors of the *Humanitarianism* series, Bertrand Taithe and Rebecca Gill, for accepting this book into their series. I would also like to express my gratitude to Laure Humbert for her support and guidance.

Notes

1 J.-C. Rufin, *Le piège, quand l'aide humanitaire remplace la guerre* (Paris: Lattès, 1986), p. 61.
2 P. Micheletti, *Humanitaire, s'adapter ou renoncer* (Paris: Marabout, 2008), p. 29.
3 P. Ryfman, *La question humanitaire* (Paris: Ellipses, 1999), p. 34.
4 J. Lebas & J. Mamou, "Éditorial", *Humanitaire*, 1 (2000), p. 2.
5 B. Kouchner, *Charité business* (Paris: Le Pré aux Clercs, 1986); B. Kouchner, *Le malheur des autres* (Paris: Éditions la Seine, 1992).
6 A. Destexhe, *L'humanitaire impossible ou deux siècles d'ambiguïtés* (Paris: Armand Colin, 1993), pp. 59–69; É. Thévenin, *Ces famines qui ont bouleversé le monde, du XIXe siècle à nos jours* (Tours: Éditions CLD, 2008), pp. 180–90.
7 R. Brauman, *Penser dans l'urgence: Parcours critique d'un humanitaire. Entretiens avec C. Portevin* (Paris: Seuil, 2006), pp. 87–91; R. Brauman, "Les liaisons dangereuses du témoignage humanitaire et des propagandes politiques", in M. Le Pape, J. Siméant & C. Vidal (eds), *Crises extrêmes. Face aux massacres, aux guerres civiles et aux génocides* (Paris: La Découverte, 2006), pp. 188–204.
8 A. Vallaeys, *Médecins sans frontières: la biographie* (Paris: Fayard, 2004), pp. 54–90.
9 D. Maillard, "1968–2008: le Biafra ou le sens de l'humanitaire", *Humanitaire*, 18 (2008), Article 182; E. Davey, *Idealism Beyond Borders: The French Revolutionary Left and the Rise of Humanitarianism, 1954–1988* (Cambridge: Cambridge University Press, 2015).
10 For example: J. Benthall, *Disasters, Relief and the Media* (London: IB Tauris, 1993), pp. 92–108; A. de Waal, *Famine Crimes: Politics & the Disaster Relief Industry in Africa* (London: International African Institute, 1997), pp. 72–7; J. Okpoko, *The Biafran Nightmare: The Controversial Role of International Relief Agencies in a War of Genocide* (Enugu: Delta, 1986).
11 P. Ryfman, *Une histoire de l'humanitaire* (Paris: La Découverte, 2008), p. 44.
12 J. Paulmann, "Conjunctures in the History of International Humanitarian Aid during the Twentieth Century", *Humanity*, 4:2 (2013), 215–38, at 227.
13 M. Barnett, *Empire of Humanity: A History of Humanitarianism* (Ithaca: Cornell University Press, 2011).

14 K. O'Sullivan, M. Hilton & J. Fiori, "Humanitarianisms in Context", *European Review of History: Revue européenne d'histoire*, 23:1–2 (2016), 1–15.

15 K. O'Sullivan, *The NGO Moment: The Globalisation of Compassion from Biafra to Live Aid* (Cambridge: Cambridge University Press, 2021), pp. 1–33.

16 See also: L. Heerten, "The Dystopia of Postcolonial Catastrophe: Self-determination, the Biafran War of Secession, and the 1970s", in J. Eckel & S. Moyn (eds), *The Breakthrough: Human Rights in the 1970s* (Philadelphia: University of Pennsylvania Press, 2014), pp. 15–35; M. C. Morgan, "The Seventies and the Rebirth of Human Rights", in N. Ferguson, E. Manela, C. S. Maier & D. J. Sargent (eds), *The Shock of the Global: The 1970s in Perspective* (Cambridge: Harvard University Press, 2011), pp. 237–50; Sylvia Salvatici, *A History of Humanitarianism, 1755–1989: In the Name of Others* (Manchester: Manchester University Press, 2019), pp. 9–10.

17 For example: D. Jacobs, *The Brutality of Nations* (New York: Paragon House, 1988); E. Urhobo, *Relief Operations in the Nigerian Civil War* (Ibadan: Daystar Press, 1978); M. Aaronson, "The Nigerian Civil War and 'Humanitarian Intervention'", in B. Everill & J. Kaplan (eds), *The History and Practice of Humanitarian Intervention and Aid in Africa* (Basingstoke: Palgrave Macmillan, 2013). Dan Jacobs (UNICEF), Emmanuel Urhobo (Christian Council of Nigeria) and Michael Aaronson (Save the Children) all participated in some way in the relief operations.

18 J. Stremlau, *The International Politics of the Nigerian Civil War, 1967–1970* (Princeton: Princeton University Press, 1977); Z. Cervenka, *A History of the Nigerian War, 1967–1970* (Ibadan: Onibonoje Press, 1972); J. de Saint Jorre, *The Nigerian Civil War* (London: Hodder and Stoughton, 1972); J.-L. Clergerie, *La crise du Biafra* (Limoges: Presses universitaires, 1994); E. Osaghae, E. Onwudiwe & R. T. Suberu (eds), *The Nigerian Civil War and Its Aftermath* (Ibadan: John Archers, 2002).

19 T. Hentsch, *Face au blocus: histoire de l'intervention du Comité international de la Croix-Rouge dans le conflit du Nigeria, 1967–1970* (Geneva: Droz, 1973); L. S. Wiseberg, "The International Politics of Relief: A Case Study of the Relief Operations Mounted during the Nigerian Civil War (1967–1970)" (PhD dissertation, University of California, 1973).

20 S. F. C. Daly, *A History of the Republic of Biafra: Law, Crime, and the Nigerian Civil War* (Cambridge: Cambridge University Press, 2020); C. Achebe, *There Was a Country: A Personal History of Biafra* (New York: Penguin, 2012); M. Gould, *The Biafran War: The Struggle for Modern Nigeria* (London: IB Tauris, 2012).

21 *Journal of Genocide Research*, 16:2–3 (2014); L. Heerten & D. Moses (eds), *Postcolonial Conflict and the Question of Genocide* (London: Routledge, 2018).

22 L. Heerten, *The Biafran War and Postcolonial Humanitarianism: Spectacles of Suffering* (Cambridge: Cambridge University Press, 2017), p. 8; L. Heerten, "Biafra of the Mind: French Postcolonial Humanitarianism in Global Conceptual History", *The American Historical Review*, 126:4 (2021), 1448–84.

23 A. O. Omaka, *The Biafran Humanitarian Crisis (1967–1970), International Human Rights and Joint Church Aid* (Madison: Fairleigh Dikinson University Press, 2016).

24 Ryfman, *La question humanitaire*, p. 17.
25 I. Herrmann, "From Polemical Topics to Magnetic Concepts: Humanitarianism and Anti-Semitism in Switzerland", *Journal of Political Ideologies*, 15:1 (2010), 55–6.
26 M. Barnett, "Humanitarianism as a Scholarly Vocation", in M. Barnett & T. G. Weiss (eds), *Humanitarianism in Question: Politics, Power, Ethics* (Ithaca: Cornell University Press, 2008), pp. 235–63.
27 P. Dauvin, J. Siméant & C.A.H.I.E.R, *Le travail humanitaire: Les acteurs des ONG du siège au terrain* (Paris: Presses de Sciences Po, 2002), p. 17.
28 S. Farré, *Colis de guerre: Secours alimentaire et organisations humanitaires (1914–1947)* (Rennes: Presses universitaires de Rennes, 2014), pp. 14–15.
29 G. Lachenal & B. Taithe, "Une généalogie missionnaire et coloniale de l'humanitaire: le cas Aujoulat au Cameroun, 1935–1973", *Le Mouvement Social*, 227:2 (2009), 45–63.
30 P.-Y. Saunier, "La secrétaire générale, l'ambassadeur et le docteur. Un conte en trois épisodes pour les historiens du 'monde des causes' à l'époque contemporaine, 1800–2000", *Monde(s)*, 1:1 (2012), 29–46, at 32.
31 Dauvin, Siméant & C.A.H.I.E.R, *Le travail humanitaire*, pp. 22–5.
32 For example: A. Iriye, *Global and Transnational History: Its Past, Present, and Future* (New York: Palgrave Macmillan, 2013); P.-Y. Saunier, "Circulations, connexions et espaces transnationaux", *Genèses*, 57 (2007), 110–26; P. Grosser, "L'histoire mondiale/globale, une jeunesse exubérante mais difficile", *Vingtième Siècle*, 110 (2011), 3–18; A. Caillé & S. Dufoix (eds), *Le tournant global des sciences sociales* (Paris: La Découverte, 2013). More broadly, see A. Iriye, *Global Community: The Role of International Organizations in the Making of the Contemporary World* (Berkeley: University of California Press, 2002).
33 A. Thompson, "Unravelling the Relationships between Humanitarianism, Human Rights, and Decolonization: Time for a Radical Rethink?", in M. Thomas & A. S. Thompson (eds), *The Oxford Handbook of the Ends of Empire* (Oxford: Oxford University Press, 2018), pp. 453–76; Andrew Thompson, "Humanitarian Principles Put to the Test: Challenges to Humanitarian Action during Decolonization", *International Review of the Red Cross*, 97:897/898 (2016), 45–76; O' Sullivan, *The NGO Moment*; Emily Baughan, *Saving the Children: Humanitarianism, Internationalism, and Empire* (Berkeley: University of California Press, 2021); M. Thomas, *The End of Empires and a World Remade: A Global History of Decolonization* (Princeton: Princeton University Press, 2024); Gregory Mann, *From Empires to NGOs in the West African Sahel: The Road to Nongovernmentality* (Cambridge: Cambridge University Press, 2015).
34 For example, "Organisations internationales et ONG: coopération, rivalité, complémentarité de 1919 à nos jours", *Relations internationales*, 151:3 (2012), 152:4 (2012).
35 D. Laqua, "Inside the Humanitarian Cloud: Causes and Motivations to Help Friends and Strangers", *Journal of Modern European History*, 12:2 (2014), 175–85.

36 Cf. P.-Y. Saunier, *Trajectoire de recherche: de l'histoire de Lyon à l'histoire des organisations internationales: un récit à l'envers de l'évidence* (Habilitation à diriger les recherches, EHESS, 2010).

37 The careers and profiles of some individuals reflected particularly well the porosities between these different traditions: É. Morier-Genoud, "Missions and Institutions: Henri-Philippe Junod, Anthropology, Human Rights and Academia between Africa and Switzerland, 1921–1966", *Schweizerische Zeitschrift für Religions und Kulturgeschichte* (2011), 193–219; J. Siméant, "Entrer, rester en humanitaire: des fondateurs de MSF aux membres actuels des ONG médicales françaises", *Revue française de science politique*, 51:1 (2001), 47–72; B. Taithe, "Reinventing (French) Universalism: Religion, Humanitarianism and the 'French Doctors' ", *Modern and Contemporary France*, 12:2 (2004), 147–58.

38 J. F. Hutchinson, *Champions of Charity: War and the Rise of the Red Cross* (Boulder: Westview Press, 1996); P. de Sénarclens, *L'humanitaire en catastrophe* (Paris: Presses de Sciences Po, 1999); S. Farré, *Colis de guerre.*

39 K. O'Sullivan, "A 'Global Nervous System': The Rise and Rise of European Humanitarian NGOs, 1945–1985", in M. Frey, S. Kunkel & C. R. Unger (eds), *International Organisations and Development, 1945 to 1990* (Basingstoke: Palgrave Macmillan, 2014), pp. 196–219.

40 Aaronson, "The Nigerian Civil War and 'Humanitarian Intervention' ".

41 Destexhe, *L'humanitaire impossible.*

42 J. Moore, *Hard Choices: Moral Dilemmas in Humanitarian Intervention* (Oxford: Rowman & Littlefield, 1998); J. L. Holzgrefe & R. O. Keohane (eds), *Humanitarian Intervention: Ethical, Legal, and Political Dilemmas* (Cambridge: Cambridge University Press, 2003).

43 On the ICRC during World War Two, cf. J.-C. Favez, *Une mission impossible? Le CICR, les déportations et les camps de concentration nazis* (Lausanne: Payot, 1988).

44 S. Farré, "Le CICR et les détenus des camps de concentration nationaux-socialistes (1942–1945)", *Revue internationale de la Croix-Rouge*, 94:4 sélection française (2012), 191–219.

45 On "victims", cf. D. Fassin, *La raison humanitaire. Une histoire morale du temps présent* (Paris: Gallimard/Seuil, 2010).

46 Urhobo, *Relief Operations in the Nigerian Civil War*, and A. S. Z. Mohammed, "Relief Services in the Nigerian Civil War", in T. Tamuno & S. C. Ukpabi (eds), *Nigeria Since Independence, Vol. 7: The Civil War Years* (Ibadan: Heinemann, 1989), pp. 234–51.

47 P. Mesnard, *La victime écran. La représentation humanitaire en question* (Paris: Textuel, 2002), p. 24.

48 R. Brauman & R. Backmann, *Les médias et l'humanitaire* (Paris: CFPJ Éditions, 1996), pp. 48–51.

49 Heerten, *The Biafran War and Postcolonial Humanitarianism*, p. 7.

50 On these debates, see L. Heerten & D. Moses, "Introduction", in Heerten & Moses (eds), *Postcolonial Conflict and the Question of Genocide*, pp. 16–31.

Part I

From an African civil war to the making of an international humanitarian crisis

1

The war and the question of genocide

The images of starving children were not the only reason for the emotion that the civil war generated in the West. Added to this were the different arguments employed. On the one hand, as Lasse Heerten has pointed out, the Biafran authorities sought to present their cause as a struggle for the self-determination of the Biafran people, a rhetoric that at the time characterised the struggles of colonised peoples against imperial metropoles.[1] On the other hand, they claimed that the Biafran population was the victim of genocide. Indeed, beginning with 1966 they made the independence of Biafra an imperative for the survival of the people from the Eastern Region of Nigeria and in particular the predominantly Igbo population that lived there.[2] Although it was firmly denied by the federal government during the war and by a team of international observers sent on the ground, this theory persisted among some journalists and humanitarian actors. The diversity of the positions taken and their evolution during and after the conflict raise questions about the violence suffered by the civilian population during this period and about the way in which these stances were used in the belligerents' rhetoric. In this respect, coming up with a war casualty toll still poses a considerable problem. While in the decade following the conflict the number of deaths was put at between one and three million,[3] the recent trend has been to revise these estimates downwards, with some studies suggesting figures of between 100,000 and 200,000 deaths.[4] As for the issue of genocide, it too has been the subject of controversy. Although some authors argue that the Igbo population was the victim of genocide during the war,[5] they remain in a minority. Most research holds that the term was used by secessionist propaganda in order to rally Westerners to the Biafran cause. Ultimately, this analysis says little about the violence suffered by the civilian population and does not explain the prevalence of this thesis among certain observers at the time of the conflict, or among a part of the Igbo population to this day.

In order to examine the use of the term genocide to describe the violence committed against civilians it is first necessary to reflect on the definition of such a concept. Ever since Raphaël Lemkin first used the term, many researchers have looked at it and what it describes. Without going into detail here, there are various divisions within the research conducted on this concept, particularly with regard to its more or less restrictive use and its definition.[6] The Convention on the Prevention and Punishment of the Crime of Genocide of 9 December 1948 defines it as follows:

> In the present Convention, genocide means any of the following acts committed with intent to destroy, in whole or in part, a national, ethnical, racial or religious group, as such: (a) Killing members of the group; (b) Causing serious bodily or mental harm to members of the group; (c) Deliberately inflicting on the group conditions of life calculated to bring about its physical destruction in whole or in part; (d) Imposing measures intended to prevent births within the group; (e) Forcibly transferring children of the group to another group.

This definition was the result of a political compromise between states in order to secure the adoption of a legal text but it does not allow us to grasp genocide in all its complexity. For example, the restrictive nature of the list of categories that can be subjected to genocide considerably limits its scope. The work of Frank Chalk and Kurt Johansson has thus emphasised the need to identify victim groups according to the criteria by which they are defined by their persecutors rather than on the basis of religious, ethnic and other qualifiers.[7] As Eric Weitz notes, however, despite the problems it raises, this definition highlights the two elements of genocide, namely, a material element which consists of a group's destruction, and an intentional element which consists of establishing a policy aimed at destroying that group.[8] However, it is not always easy to identify these, especially in the context of internal conflicts where the term civil war has sometimes been used to mask genocide.[9] In order to understand these concrete and complex situations Jacques Sémelin suggests that we should first return to the study of "the nature of the processes of extreme violence at work in a given historical situation, in order to ultimately determine whether the process of destruction seeks the total eradication of a community". Drawing on a typology of massacres established on the basis of their purpose, he provides an analytical framework for mass violence as a whole and not just genocide. Sémelin distinguishes various categories of massacre, the concept of which he defines as "a form of mostly collective action of destroying non-combatants, men, women, children, or unarmed soldiers".[10] He differentiates between those seeking to subdue a group of people ("destroy to subdue") and those intent on eradicating a community ("destroy to eradicate"). This second category corresponds to genocide, which the author defines as "that particular process of destroying civilians which seeks the complete eradication of a community whose criteria are defined by those who decide to annihilate it".[11]

The method and definition outlined above seem relevant to the Nigeria–Biafra case insofar as, while at the end of the conflict observers agreed that there had been no genocide, earlier there had been reports of genocidal behaviour in relation to various events. These various accusations gave rise to considerable controversy but did not lead to any in-depth studies into the violence that occurred during this conflict. In order to understand how the war progressively became an international humanitarian crisis, this first chapter is structured around the three elements – the 1966 massacres of the people from the Eastern Region of Nigeria, the brutality of the hostilities, and the famine – on which the discourse of a genocide of the Igbo population was based. Distinguishing these elements makes it possible to study the nature of the violence that occurred and better understand their evolution in relation to various issues including, crucially, their use by the Biafran and Nigerian authorities.

Although there is a wealth of sources on the conflict that can be used to deal with these questions, they often seem very contradictory due to the belligerents' use of the humanitarian crisis for propaganda purposes. Thus, while the Biafran authorities were happy to exaggerate its magnitude, the Nigerian government and its British ally had no qualms about minimising it. Furthermore, there were few detailed reports on the situation in Biafra. All observers at the time agreed, for example, on the uncertainty of the estimated number of famine victims and the impossibility of accurately determining the extent of the massacres.[12] As work on the rhetoric of NGOs facing "extreme crises"[13] has shown, the data from humanitarian organisations were also heavily influenced by the context in which they were produced and should therefore be used with caution. Alexander de Waal has pointed out that the mortality predictions made by voluntary agencies often proved to be too alarmist,[14] as the tendency to dramatise a situation helps move people and donor governments to raise funds. Although it is less likely, there is also the possibility that they may have under-reported the reality on the ground in order to demonstrate the effectiveness of their interventions. Thus, the information provided on the massacres, the brutality of the conflict and the famine can only be attempts to get as close as possible to a reality that was particularly difficult to grasp and controversial.

Following Dirk Moses and Lasse Heerten, this chapter does not seek to determine whether genocide took place.[15] However, understanding how this concept was used during the war necessitates proper examination of the violence faced by the Biafran people, especially as the thesis of "no genocide" happened to be that of the victor, the Nigerian government, and its main supporter, the United Kingdom. Looking at the situation during the war further means not neglecting the point of view of the defeated. In this respect, the surveys conducted by Axel Harneit-Sievers, Jones O. Ahazuem and Sydney Emezue are an essential resource which makes it possible to include the impressions left by these events on the Biafran population and to show their importance in the memory of the victims or actors in the conflict.[16]

The 1966 massacres

The genocide thesis has its roots in the events that took place before the conflict. In the autumn of 1966 the future leader of Biafra, Lieutenant-Colonel Ojukwu, then governor of the Eastern Region of Nigeria, spoke of "the genocide of easterners which is the result of the combined action of northern soldiers, police, and civilians, and which has been going on for the last four months in the North and in other parts of the country".[17]

Various studies and accounts have highlighted the turbulent nature of the Nigerian political scene after the country gained its independence in 1960.[18] There were considerable tensions between the three highly disparate regions that made up the Federation of Nigeria: the Northern, the Eastern and the Western (from which a mid-Western region was created in 1963). Although each of these regions had a diverse set of populations, the Hausa-Fulani, the Igbo and the Yoruba were in the majority in the North, the East and the West respectively, where they dominated the regional governments. The political parties competing for federal power broadly reproduced these cleavages.[19] The tensions between the regions were all the more significant since they were reinforced by British colonisation during which the political elites had little incentive to collaborate.[20] As political analyst Rotimi Suberu explains, despite the unification in 1914, direct formal political relations between southerners and northerners were not established until 1946. Moreover, a gap had developed between the North and the country's southern regions, which had a head start in many areas including education, per capita income, urbanisation, employment, trade and industrialisation.[21] In the 1950s, with the prospect of independence, this dichotomy became a source of tension. There were disagreements about the proposed timeframe: the southern regions wanted it to be tight, whereas the North favoured a slower process. As the latter was less well endowed than the former in terms of human resources and business infrastructure, the Northern People's Congress feared that moving too quickly towards decolonisation would put the region at a disadvantage compared to the others who were better prepared.

In order to bridge this gap and fearing that British domination would be replaced by domination by the mainly Christian southern elites – the North being predominantly Muslim – in 1954 northern leaders began implementing a policy of Northernisation. This consisted of promoting local employees in local institutions and was accompanied by policies to limit the influence of people from the south within the region. However, there was a large Igbo community there whose members held positions in the federal civil service as well as in companies and business networks. The atmosphere between this community and the northern elites deteriorated from the 1950s onwards, as evidenced by the riots that broke out in the city of Kano in 1953.[22]

Nigeria gaining independence in 1960 did not ease these tensions; on the contrary. The fear that one or other of the regional groups could dominate the country's federal political system fuelled the competition between the parties. Furthermore, the issue of revenue distribution within the federation exacerbated the competition for power,[23] especially with the discovery and exploitation of large oil deposits in the south-east of the country. Instability and corruption became widespread, leading to initial crises such as during regional elections in the West in 1964 and culminating in a military coup six years after the country had become independent.

In January 1966 a small group of military officers overthrew the federal government which was heavily influenced by the North, seizing and handing power over to General Ironsi. The coup was relatively well received throughout the country and was also tolerated in the North,[24] as it raised hopes that a less corrupt government would be put in place.[25] However, the death of several northern soldiers and politicians during these events, as well as the predominantly Igbo origin of the officers who had taken power, reinforced fears in the North and helped frame the problem in terms of an opposition between the northerners and the Igbo. Moreover, the policy of centralisation developed by General Ironsi in the following months caused great resentment.[26] The northern elites saw in this project the end of the privileges that the Northernisation policy had granted them.[27] It was following a unification decree which was promulgated by the new government on 24 May 1966 that the first series of violence and massacres targeting the Igbo and more generally people from the East took place.

The federal government was overthrown at the end of July 1966 by a new *coup d'état*, this time led mainly by northern officers. During these events the head of state and many Igbo officers were killed. In a climate of particularly high tension, power was handed over to Lieutenant-Colonel Yakubu Gowon, a compromise figure since he was both a Christian and the member of a northern minority.[28] This change in leadership seemed for a while to satisfy the northern elites, who gave up on the secession they had been considering. Nevertheless, tensions remained high and in September 1966 new massacres were perpetrated against easterners.

In an extremely well-documented study Douglas Anthony shows the organised and premeditated nature of the violence committed against the Igbo in 1966, which had been anticipated by the British representatives in Nigeria after the January 1966 coup.[29] The massacres carried out in May, June and not least September were intended to "purge" the North of the Igbo elements still living there.[30] The population as a whole did not take part in these massacres, which were mainly carried out by soldiers and civilians organised into militias. Furthermore, although they were explicitly targeted, the Igbo were not the only victims of these riots. It was what they represented rather than their supposed ethnicity that was the object of the violence, as evidenced by the criteria of language, appearance or place of residence that were used to identify targets.[31] However, the consequences of these massacres on the development of a strong feeling of insecurity among the Igbo population should not be underestimated. Many testimonies attest to the violence of these events, which resulted in several thousand deaths.[32]

As these massacres very quickly became the object of propaganda and counter-propaganda by the authorities in the East and the federal government, it is difficult to assess their precise scale (see Table 1.1). The literature is still divided on this issue and estimates vary from fewer than 5,000 to 80,000 deaths,[33] but the majority of studies agree on approximately 30,000 deaths.[34] In the speech that accompanied Biafra's declaration of independence in May 1967, Lieutenant-Colonel Ojukwu mentioned 30,000 deaths. Later in the conflict he went as far as to speak of 50,000 killed.[35] This figure appears in the findings of a Biafran tribunal of inquiry into the 1966 massacres and victims of the war, which was based on mainly unfounded projections.[36] These assessments therefore appear to be exaggerated, something which a study of the first publications on the crisis produced by the eastern government seems to confirm. Indeed, in the autumn of 1966 and January 1967 there was talk of 3,000 deaths in the May riots and 7,000 in September.[37] These figures raise questions insofar as the eastern authorities had no real reason to minimise them; on the contrary. The ICRC's delegate general for Africa, who reported on these events in late 1966, did not, unfortunately, identify his sources but gave the same estimates.[38]

In the documents produced by the federal government from late 1966 onwards figures are lower. It was in its interest to minimise the number of casualties in order to show that, contrary to Ojukwu's claims, the Igbo were not under threat in Nigeria. Federal pamphlets would later report 5,000 Igbo deaths in September 1966.[39] Thus, to a certain extent they agreed with the eastern authorities' initial estimates. In his study Douglas Anthony cites the British Consulate's tally of the September massacres as between 3,000 and 4,000 deaths, although he describes this figure as conservative.[40] In a recent work on the conflict Michael Gould refers to a summary paper on

Table 1.1 The 1966 massacres in several Biafran and federal sources

Date	Number of deaths (Igbo/East) in 1966 according to Biafran sources	Presentation of the 1966 massacres in federal sources
1966–67	Ojukwu's press conference, January 1967: 10,000 dead (3,000 in May and 7,000 in September 1966)	*Nigeria 1966*, early 1967: no explicit reference to the Igbo massacres
1967	Ojukwu's speech when Biafra declared independence, May 1967: 30,000 dead	*The Struggle for One Nigeria*, October 1967: brief mention of the massacres suffered by the Igbo (no figures given)
1968–69	Ojukwu's speech, Ahiara Declaration, May 1969: 50,000 dead	*The Collapse of Ojukwu's Rebellion and Prospects for Lasting Peace in Nigeria*, 1968: recognition of the massacre of around 5,000 Igbo in September 1966

the events produced by the research department of the British Foreign and Commonwealth Office in which it was stated that, according to calculations done in the North, the September attacks had resulted in 5,000 deaths. Gould adds that during a meeting with the Italian ambassador in Lagos in January 1967 Ojukwu, seeking to exaggerate the number of victims, reportedly claimed that 7,000 deaths had occurred in the spring and autumn of 1966.[41] Whilst it seems difficult to verify this last statement, these estimates, together with those in the first publications produced by the eastern authorities, would put the number of victims at around 10,000 rather than 30,000.

Can these mass killings, aimed at "purifying" the North of its Igbo population, be considered acts of genocide? The introduction to this chapter has highlighted Sémelin's distinction between violence committed against a group in order to subdue it and violence committed in order to eradicate it. Within this second category the author distinguishes between massacres that are intended to "purify and destroy" – which are akin to genocide – and those that are intended to "purify and drive out". He adds that in the second case "the massacres are not an end in itself but a means of spreading terror in order to hasten the flight of the survivors".[42] This analysis seems to apply here. Indeed, Douglas Anthony shows that the violence that broke out in late September 1966 was foreshadowed by rumours and threats encouraging the Igbo to leave the region.[43] Thus, the author points out that if the term ethnic cleansing had existed in the 1960s, the events of 1966 would probably have been described as such. Indeed, the massacres resulted in significant population movements, mainly from the North to the East, the extent of which is also difficult to assess. Several studies agree, however, that we are not talking millions, as the Biafran leadership stated during the conflict, but rather hundreds of thousands of displaced people.[44] According to a report by the League of Red Cross Societies, whose delegate was on the ground, up to 700,000 individuals fled the North.[45] These people arrived in the East in difficult conditions. Their accounts, given on their return or later, bear witness to the trauma left by these events. As Jones O. Ahazuem points out, the massacres persuaded the Igbo population that it was no longer welcome within the Nigerian nation and that only a separate existence could guarantee its safety and future.[46] This sentiment was reinforced by the propaganda of the eastern authorities.

As the political crisis between them and the federal military government gradually escalated in the autumn of 1966, the eastern leaders used the massacres and their consequences to legitimise their move towards secession. They published a series of pamphlets entitled *Nigerian Crisis 1966*, which put forward the eastern view on the events of 1966 by presenting and reproducing speeches, minutes of meetings, press conferences and sometimes photographs. Print runs varied from 10,000 to 40,000 copies.[47]

The main purpose of all these pamphlets was to show that the population of the East could no longer live safely in a state incapable of protecting them. As an example, the front cover of the first booklet published in October 1966 featured a man with a disfigured face, while the back cover showed the photo of four men carrying a wounded person. The documents contained no caption or information but the reference to the massacres was clear.[48] As for the third volume, *Nigerian Pogrom*, it was entirely devoted to this subject. The term genocide appeared in this pamphlet,[49] and was subsequently used regularly during the war in relation to the fate of the Biafrans. After an introduction on the violence suffered by the Igbo and minorities from the East, a series of photographs and testimonies were reproduced. The photographs showed the transport of the wounded in the East, sometimes in particularly violent conditions as with the image of the body of a decapitated man. It is worth noting here the care that the authors of the text took to present all the populations originating from the East as victims of the northerners.[50] Nevertheless, whilst the Igbo were not the only victims of the massacres, according to the British Consulate they were very much the main targets: "During the unrest in May the northerners were careful to spare the Ijaw, Efik, and other minorities in the Niger Delta from the massacres inflicted on the Igbo. They have since tried to reassure the Delta people in the North that they are not considered Igbo".[51] Thus, from the summer of 1966 the northerners sought to show their benevolence towards the non-Igbo eastern minorities and prevent any solidarity from developing between the peoples of the Eastern Region. At the same time the eastern government tried to construct the category of victim around the eastern rather than just Igbo identity. This particular focus on the inclusion or exclusion of minorities is explained by the latter's strategic importance in establishing an independent state along the borders of the Eastern Region. Indeed, such a state would hardly have been viable without their inclusion since they lived particularly in the area that provided access to the sea and where Nigeria's main oil resources were located.

The pamphlets produced by the eastern government were primarily intended to publicise the easterners' plight and history outside Nigeria and to elicit the world's understanding and sympathy for them.[52] However, they were also distributed locally. Like Radio Biafra, they helped to convince the population of the danger of living in Nigeria.[53] In addition to this propaganda, the presence of refugees reminded the inhabitants of the East of the reality of the 1966 massacres,[54] and the commission in charge of their reintegration did not hesitate to refer to these events when boasting about its own work.[55] With the outbreak of the hostilities in July 1967 the reference to the massacres made it possible to place the plight of the Igbo on a continuum.[56] Playing a central part in the genocide rhetoric, the killings were used by the Biafran authorities to show that the Igbo were victims not only of the "collateral damage" caused by the conflict but also of an intentional policy of extermination by the federal government which had begun beforehand.

The presentation of these events in federal-government publications contrasts with the way they were reported in the East. While the head of state's speeches condemned the violence and stressed its tragic nature,[57] official publications were more ambiguous. In January 1967 the federal government published a pamphlet entitled *Nigeria 1966* in response to the eastern series *Nigerian Crisis 1966*. In it, it presented its version of the crisis that Nigeria had experienced since January 1966. Responsibility for the situation was attributed to the Igbo because of their involvement in the first coup, whereas in the Biafran pamphlets it was the northerners – referred to as the Hausa – who got the blame. An examination of the passage about the massacres of May and October 1966 illustrates the widening gap in terms of the narrative of these events. The spring massacres were barely mentioned, while those that had occurred in the autumn were explained in terms of northern resentment towards the Igbo. They were thus presented as acts of retaliation for an attack on northerners living in the East which had been reported by the media.[58]

This tendency to minimise the massacres of the easterners, deny their specificity, and consider them as direct consequences of General Ironsi's *coup d'état* in January 1966 can also be seen in later pamphlets. However, a shift gradually took place and the particular extent of the violence suffered by the Igbo was slowly recognised. Alongside this change, the federal government developed a counter-discourse denying the possibility of genocide and claiming, on the contrary, that the Igbo were welcome within the federation.[59] This timid acknowledgement of the atrocities committed in 1966 can thus be interpreted as a way for the federal government to demonstrate its goodwill to the Igbo population and Western public opinion.

A brutal war

Once war was declared, its brutality fuelled the Biafran argument that the Nigerians sought to massacre or even exterminate the Igbo. Whilst the focus here is on the conduct of the federal army, Biafran troops did not behave in an exemplary manner either. For example, minorities in the southern part of the Eastern Region reported acts of violence committed against them by Biafran fighters.[60] However, the very course of the conflict during which the Biafran territory was gradually surrounded and then reduced by the federal army meant there was less frequent contact between Biafran troops and the population they regarded as hostile, than between federal combatants and Biafran civilians.

The histories of the conflict make it possible to reconstruct the main phases of the war. John de Saint Jorre and Zdenek Cervenka have identified five of them,[61] summarised in Figures 1.1–1.4. The first period, covering the months of July and August 1967, was characterised by what the federal government regarded as "police action". During this time its strategy was to surround and isolate Biafra by means of a blockade and then take the main towns. The strategy did not work and the Biafran forces broke through to the Mid-Western Region in early August 1967, making their way towards Lagos. The federal response then turned into an all-out war intended to put down the rebellion. This second phase, which lasted from August 1967 to October 1968, was characterised by the capture of important towns and cities and a significant reduction of the territory held by the Biafrans. Nsukka and Enugu were brought under federal control in late 1967, while Port Harcourt fell in May 1968. Biafra now consisted only of the area between the cities of Aba and Owerri in the south, Onitsha in the west, Okigwe and Umuahia in the north and the Cross River in the east, which corresponded to the heart of Igbo country. Beginning with October 1968 the secessionists received new arms supplies, allowing them to carry out a counter-offensive to which the federals responded by intensifying their aerial bombardments (third phase). In the spring of 1969 the federal troops regained the initiative but faced significant Biafran resistance (fourth phase),

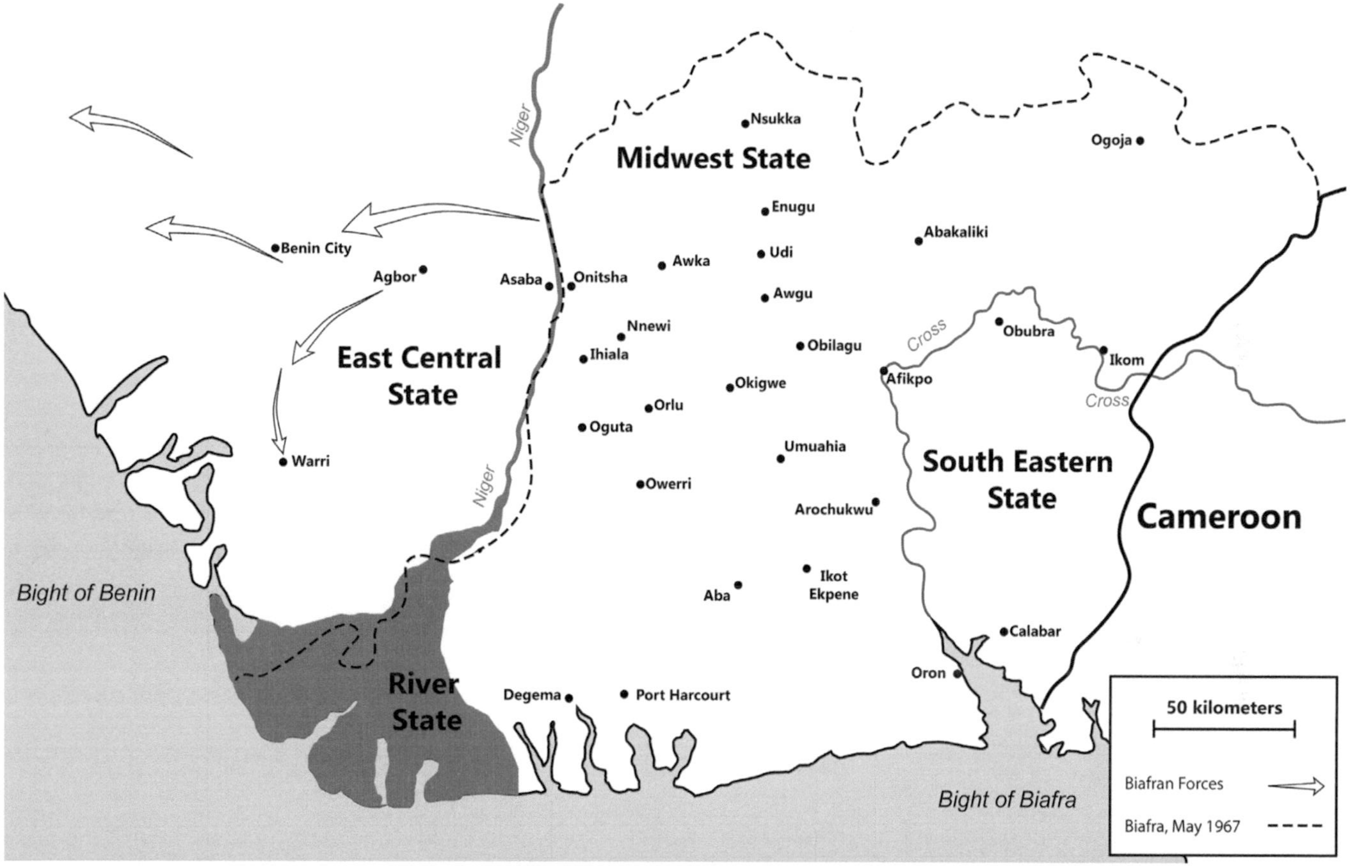

Figure 1.1 Biafra in May 1967 (reworked from John de Saint Jorre, *The Nigerian Civil War*, London, Hodder and Stoughton, 1972; drawn by Pablo Deroulet)

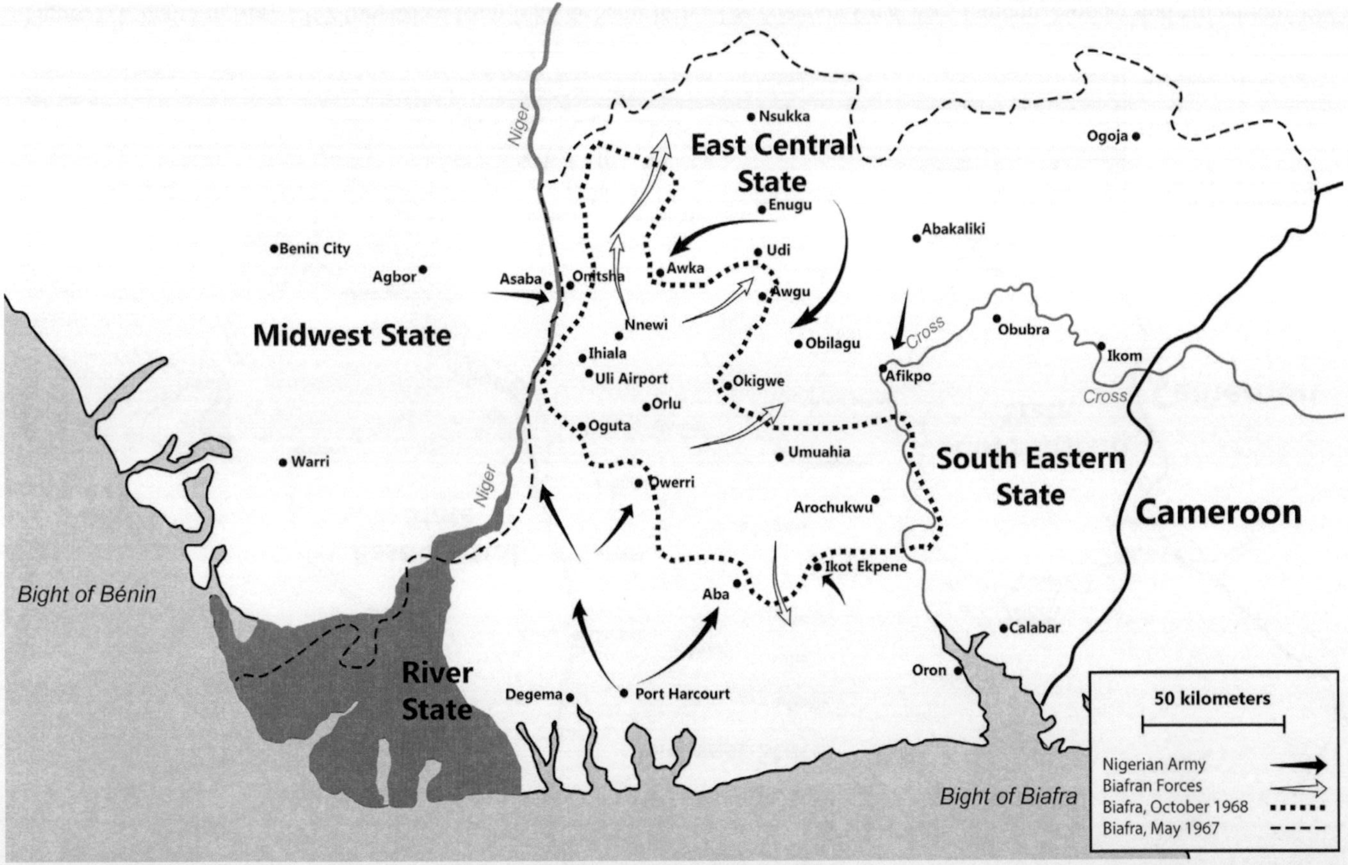

Figure 1.2 Biafra in October 1968 (reworked from John de Saint Jorre, *The Nigerian Civil War*, London, Hodder and Stoughton, 1972; drawn by Pablo Deroulet)

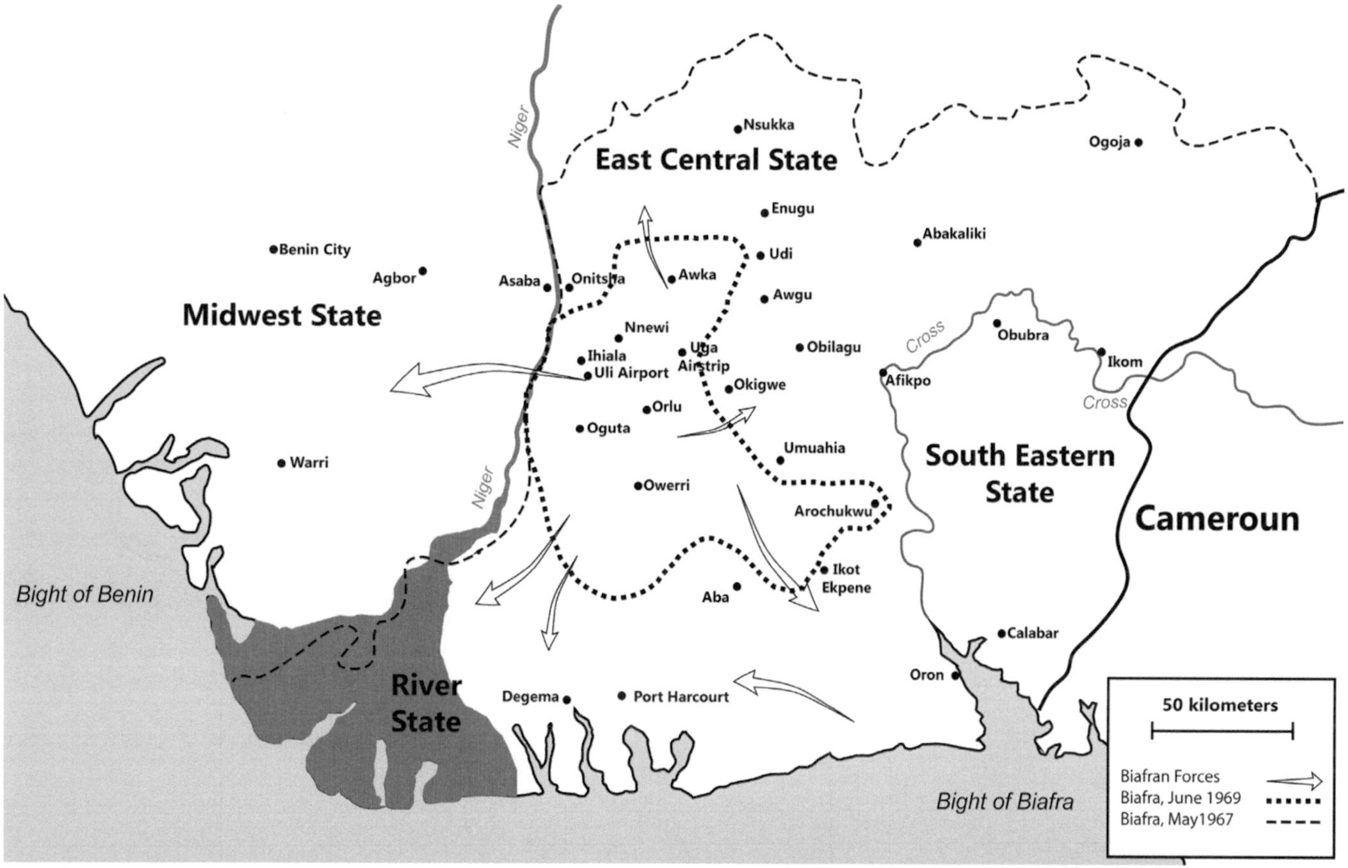

Figure 1.3 Biafra in June 1969 (reworked from John de Saint Jorre, *The Nigerian Civil War*, London, Hodder and Stoughton, 1972; drawn by Pablo Deroulet)

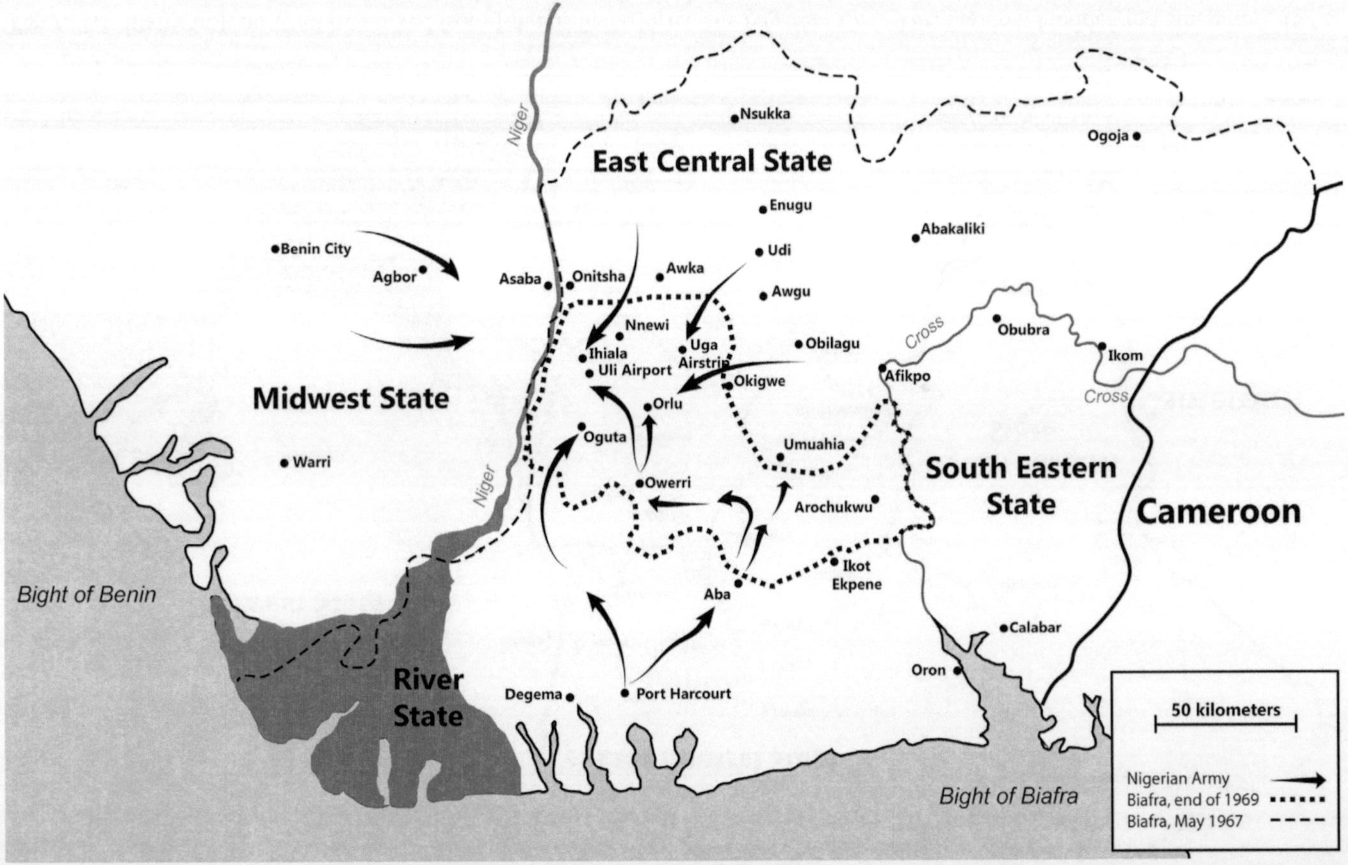

Figure 1.4 Biafra at the end of 1969 (reworked from John de Saint Jorre, *The Nigerian Civil War*, London, Hodder and Stoughton, 1972; drawn by Pablo Deroulet)

and then from November they conducted a final offensive until Biafra's surrender in January 1970 (fifth phase).

In terms of the conduct of the hostilities, even before the war started the belligerents agreed to respect international humanitarian law. The International Committee of the Red Cross, whose job it was to ensure it was observed during armed conflicts, had concerned itself with this issue since May 1967. The ICRC's delegate general for Africa, Georg Hoffmann, travelled to Nigeria to prepare a future ICRC action in response to the looming war. In June he was received by the Nigerian head of state, General Gowon, and the Biafran leader, Lieutenant-Colonel Ojukwu, who both welcomed the idea of sending an ICRC mission in the event of an armed conflict. Even though there was no formal written agreement,[62] they both committed to respecting the Geneva Conventions.[63] The applicability of international humanitarian law despite the internal nature of the conflict was confirmed by the existence of a recognition of belligerence in the form of Nigeria's declaration of war against Biafra on 11 August 1967.[64] Furthermore, the four Geneva Conventions of 1949, signed by Nigeria on 20 June 1961, included a common Article 3 which listed a number of principles to be observed in non-international armed conflict:

> In the case of armed conflict not of an international character occurring in the territory of one of the High Contracting Parties, each Party to the conflict shall be bound to apply, as a minimum, the following provisions:
>
> 1) Persons taking no active part in the hostilities, including members of armed forces who have laid down their arms and those placed "hors de combat" by sickness, wounds, detention, or any other cause, shall in all circumstances be treated humanely, without any adverse distinction founded on race, colour, religion or faith, sex, birth or wealth, or any other similar criteria.
>
> To this end, the following acts are and shall remain prohibited at any time and in any place whatsoever with respect to the above-mentioned persons:
>
> a) violence to life and person, in particular murder of all kinds, mutilation, cruel treatment and torture;
>
> b) taking of hostages;
>
> c) outrages upon personal dignity, in particular humiliating and degrading treatment;
>
> d) the passing of sentences and the carrying out of executions without previous judgment pronounced by a regularly constituted court, affording all the judicial guarantees which are recognized as indispensable by civilized peoples.
>
> 2) The wounded and sick shall be collected and cared for.

> An impartial humanitarian body, such as the International Committee of the Red Cross, may offer its services to the Parties to the conflict.
>
> The Parties to the conflict should further endeavour to bring into force, by means of special agreements, all or part of the other provisions of the present Convention.
>
> The application of the preceding provisions shall not affect the legal status of the Parties to the conflict.

Despite these commitments, by the end of July 1967 the Biafrans spoke of the brutality of the federal offensive and some went as far as to use the term genocide again.[65] This resulted in the flight of part of the population fearing the arrival of federal troops (Figure 1.5). As Reverend Alexander Somerville, a Scottish missionary in Biafra, reported: "When a place is in danger of being invaded, the entire population flees because it rightly fears being exterminated, and our policy is to advise missionaries to do the same because, in the eyes of the Hausa army, the Europeans still present in the region can only be sympathisers of the Biafran cause".[66] The population either took refuge in Biafran territory – this was particularly the case with the Igbo – or remained within a relatively close area but hid wherever they could to avoid contact with the federal army.[67] As early as September 1967 ICRC delegates in Biafra attested and shared the fear caused by the

Figure 1.5 Biafran people fleeing the combat zone, V-P-NG-N-00051-06A (© ICRC / Max Vaterlaus, September 1968)

behaviour of the Nigerian soldiers. Within the United Nations Children's Fund (UNICEF) too there were alarming reports about the plight of the Igbo.[68]

As with the 1966 massacres, it is difficult to assess whether these fears were well-founded or the result of Biafran propaganda fuelling them in order to unite the Biafrans behind the country's independence and to elicit sympathy on the international stage.[69] The authorities used Radio Biafra to convince the population of the danger it faced,[70] so that whoever might come into contact with the outside world would be convinced of the reality of the threat.[71] Two elements, however, qualify the assertion that the population's fears were solely the result of the secessionist propaganda machine. On the one hand, civilians fled massively upon the arrival of the federal army, even though the Biafran authorities had tried to persuade them to stay put and resist. To achieve their end, the latter did not hesitate to, for example, provide false information on the progress of the troops or prevent people from escaping by using roadblocks, which is what happened when Port Harcourt was taken in the spring of 1968.[72] But it did not work. On the other hand, these fears were fuelled by very specific events which then spread by word of mouth and reinforced the feeling of insecurity among the Igbo population. Indeed, it seems that the second phase of the war, which was the federal army's offensive from summer 1967 to autumn 1968, was particularly brutal. Nsukka, Benin, Asaba[73] and Ikot Ekpene were the scenes of the massacre of thousands of people.[74] The Red Cross rules regarding the neutrality of medical centres were not respected either (Figure 1.6), as some of the wounded were killed.[75]

However, at the present stage of research it is not possible to either generalise these behaviours to all federal troops or see these events as an overall policy adopted by the Nigerian government. According to ICRC delegates, the head of state's willingness to observe the Geneva Conventions was above all suspicion, but his influence on the commanders on the ground was weak.[76] The promulgation by the federal authorities of a code of conduct for the troops from the outset of the conflict seems to support this.[77] While not entirely satisfactory in the eyes of the ICRC, it contained important provisions and in some respects followed the spirit of the Geneva Conventions.[78] Furthermore, soldiers who did not comply with its directives were sometimes strongly reprimanded.[79] General Momoh's analysis of the relationship between the army command and the soldiers on the ground also confirmed that the general headquarters had little control over the actual conduct of the hostilities, whether in terms of the military strategy to be followed or the behaviour of the troops towards prisoners of war, the wounded and civilians.[80] This problem seemed to worsen in the second phase of the conflict following the Biafran offensive towards Lagos. After this operation a

Figure 1.6 Abakaliki, hospital, V-P-NG-N-00040-00 (© ICRC / Jérôme Santandréa, April 1968)

virulent discourse developed in the Nigerian press against the Biafrans, who were portrayed as ambitious characters seeking only to establish their domination over the whole of Nigeria.[81] It is likely that this violence was also reflected in the army, for which it was no longer a question of a "police operation" but of an all-out, merciless war.[82]

In the first part of 1968 the scale of the issue led the Nigerian authorities to react. Indeed, the thesis of a genocide spread on the international scene, justifying in the eyes of some heads of state the need to recognise Biafra's independence. Beginning with these events the federal military government sought to persuade the Igbo, on the one hand, and international public opinion, on the other, that its troops were not committing genocide. Thus, it published a series of pamphlets which were intended to demonstrate to the Igbo and the world that the former were safe to return to Nigeria,[83] using, for example, photographs that showed federal soldiers looking after Igbo children.[84] Above all, in September 1968, following a British proposal, the Nigerian government invited international observers to come and witness the good behaviour of its troops.[85] Whilst the reliability of their investigations is questionable, the reports they produced suggest the absence of a policy of extermination. This, in contemporary eyes, was confirmed by the fact that Biafra's surrender was not at all followed by the much feared bloodbath.

Figure 1.7 Bombing, Mary Slessor Hospital, V-P-NG-E-00360 (© ICRC, January 1968)

From September 1967 the Nigerian government was able to support its ground operations with aerial bombardments thanks to its acquisition of military equipment from abroad (Figure 1.7). These bombings quickly raised serious concerns in Biafra and were met with protests from its authorities. On the one hand, civilian infrastructures, such as markets, suffered the consequences of this offensive. On the other hand, buildings and especially hospitals rendered neutral by the Red Cross sign were particularly affected. Whilst the very nature of the war – in which it was sometimes difficult to distinguish between civilian and military targets – and the very high population density in Biafra increased the likelihood of civilian casualties, the frequency of the strikes left no doubt as to their deliberate nature. In May 1968 an internal note from Melchior Borsinger, who dealt with the Nigerian case at the ICRC headquarters, summarised the situation as follows:

> There is no longer any doubt that there have been repeated and systematic attacks on at least twenty or so hospitals in recent months. Several of these

> establishments bore the Red Cross emblem. Many of these incidents were verified a few hours later by our delegate, Mr Jaggi, who himself observed, as did some journalists, indiscriminate attacks on the civilian population. It is also clear that equally systematic attacks have been carried out against churches, schools, cities, towns, and even villages or markets in the bush, far from any military targets.[86]

While in the spring of 1968 the progress made by the federal army had led the latter to envisage a relatively rapid victory, during the summer it failed to break the Biafrans. On the contrary, resistance increased and the secessionists went on the offensive again in the autumn of 1968 thanks to a large influx of arms from outside. These difficulties on the ground prompted the federal government to step up its air operations and, beginning with the late summer of 1968, the bombing of civilian targets and hospitals increased in intensity.[87]

These events revived the Biafran thesis of a genocide. Indeed, while the Nigerian troops were cleared of any suspicion by the international observers' reports, the indiscriminate bombings provided the Biafran authorities with new arguments to show that the federal government was conducting a policy of extermination. As for Biafra's inhabitants, it is certain that from 1968 onwards they were particularly marked by these bombings and that the latter helped spread fear among the population.[88] As the ICRC delegate Karl Heinrich Jaggi put it: "The airstrikes carried out over the past two weeks make no sense whatsoever, they have no 'value' even in terms of demoralising the population. On the contrary, they merely remind everyone that the aggressor is engaged in a genocidal war".[89] The federal government, for its part, denied the reality of the indiscriminate nature of these bombings and maintained that this was merely a propaganda tool employed by the Biafrans who, in any case, deliberately hid soldiers or military equipment in areas close to the civilian population. While secessionist troops did move into civilian buildings,[90] this argument cannot be applied to all bombings and in particular to those involving hospitals which were clearly marked and neutralised.

It is undeniable that the way in which the hostilities were conducted led to civilian massacres. However, unlike the events of 1966, during the conflict the object of the process of violence seems to have been, to use Jacques Sémelin's categories, to "subdue" the secessionist authorities rather than "eradicate" the Biafran civilians. Indeed, the main aim was to put an end to the Biafran secession even if it meant terrorising and massacring part of the population. This does not in any way lessen the reality of the violence which helped develop the fear of genocide among the Biafran population, a fear that was nurtured by the Biafran authorities. Paradoxically, the accusations of genocide against the federal troops, which were relayed in the international media, probably had a relatively positive effect on their behaviour: as far as the Nigerian government was concerned, counteracting the Biafran accusations also meant demonstrating the good conduct of its troops during the hostilities. It is therefore likely that the attention paid to these issues by humanitarians and Biafran communication services led the federal army to improve its behaviour during the conflict. Indeed, apart from the bombings that continued throughout the conflict, it seems that civilian massacres became less and less frequent.

Famine: contesting numbers, questioning responsibility

The famine, which reached its peak in the summer of 1968, was the third element that contributed to Biafra's justification of the use of the term genocide to describe the plight of the Igbo population. Even before the conflict the Eastern Region was not self-sufficient in terms of agricultural production. Indeed, the local cultivation of yams and manioc did not meet the daily protein needs of the population, although fishing in the Niger Delta provided part of the necessary intake.[91] The region still had to import dried fish from abroad and meat or pulses from other parts of Nigeria.[92] In 1966–67 the arrival of Igbo refugees who had previously lived in the north of the country increased the pressure on food supplies in a territory that was already one of the most densely populated in Africa. The authorities in the East responded by providing incentives to encourage arable and animal farming.[93] However, the situation became more complex in May 1967 when a blockade was imposed around the secessionist region, preventing the importation of food. In July 1967 the outbreak of the war compounded the nutritional problem. The population fled from the advancing federal troops, leading to a halt in agricultural production and, more generally, economic activities in the recaptured areas. Those who returned or remained in those areas struggled to feed themselves and depended on food distributed by either federal troops or relief agencies.[94] As for the territory under Biafran control, this shrank considerably between the summer of 1967 and autumn of 1968, and the Biafrans lost their access to the sea as well as part of the most fertile lands. The increase in population on an ever-decreasing area of land exacerbated difficulties. Agricultural production was also hampered by the recruitment of men into the army, which reduced the labour force available. Despite the setting up of a Food and Nutrition Directorate dedicated to developing the Biafra Land Army which specialised in food production, officials were unable to manage the food shortage.

By October 1967 ICRC delegates felt that "the authorities in the Eastern Region no longer seem able to cope with the situation created by the massive influx of refugees arriving on the territory that is still under their control. Some food supplies are starting to run out".[95] Signs of malnutrition and famine began to appear in late 1967. Among children, an increase in kwashiorkor cases was reported by ICRC delegates from February 1968 onwards. Victims of this protein-deficiency disease which leads to death are particularly recognisable by their swollen bellies contrasting with their thin figures. From that point on famine became a concern for the ICRC which until then had sought to, on the one hand, enforce the Geneva Conventions and, on the other hand, provide medical support by supplying equipment and personnel to assist the Nigerian and Biafran Red Cross Societies. In the spring of 1968, however, it seemed increasingly necessary to send food supplies. In April an ICRC delegate on a visit to Lagos stressed the seriousness of the food situation in Biafra due to the lack of proteins.[96] The minutes of the Committee's plenary session of 2 May 1968, which highlighted the dramatic conditions in which the civilian population found itself, attested to this concern: "In Biafra famine has already set in and the infant mortality rate is rising at an alarming rate. On both sides the need for food is even greater than the need for medicines".[97]

The fall of Port Harcourt on 19 May 1968 worsened the situation. The number of refugees increased further, with – again according to ICRC delegates – 350,000 people fleeing within Biafra.[98] Moreover, the taking of this town by the Nigerian army reinforced the isolation of the secessionists in terms of communication routes. The city's airport was no longer usable, which reduced the possibilities of connecting with the outside world and thus bringing in food. The federal victories achieved in the summer of 1968, particularly the capture of Owerri in September, led to a further increase in the number of refugees. The food crisis was probably most acute during the months of June to October 1968, both within Biafra and in the areas that had reverted to Nigerian control. Reverend Somerville revealed in his correspondence a steadily deteriorating situation from the spring of 1968 to the autumn of that year with regard to the refugees, the local population and in particular the children whose deaths "are now so commonplace that they are scarcely mentioned anymore".[99] Described as particularly sincere and objective by its commissioners, a report prepared by two members of the American Friends Service Committee for the US Embassy in London after a visit to Biafra in late August 1968 also emphasised the magnitude of the needs. It described overcrowded hospitals, clinics and refugee camps and a severe shortage of food and medicines.[100]

In the areas taken by the federals there were significant disparities. The north of the former Eastern Region, around the town of Nsukka, did not seem to suffer too much from famine, nor did the South-Eastern State (east and north of Calabar). However, even the latter province, although relief could get to it, was described by a British representative who visited it in late October 1968 in the following way: "What is most striking is the impression of a general lack of readily available food, whether local or imported, of money, doctors, and medicines, both for immediate emergencies and for longer-term rehabilitation activities, so that the work undertaken can continue effectively".[101] The situation around the city of Port Harcourt (Rivers State) was even more delicate. While food and sanitary conditions in the refugee camps appeared to be adequate, thanks in particular to food distributed by the federal army, the British member of the group of international observers, General Alexander, who was usually inclined to play down the seriousness of the situation, painted an alarming picture on his return to Lagos:

> He is convinced there must be widespread suffering in the bush although these people are now emerging in increasing numbers. In his conversation with displaced persons he was told that many old and children are dying in the bush but it is impossible to give any figures.[102]

Alexander's inability to give an accurate picture of living conditions in the area where he was actually an observer shows how difficult it was to assess them. Generally speaking, all those living in or visiting the war zones agreed on the seriousness of the problem at that point.[103]

From late 1968 onwards the situation seemed to stabilise and then gradually improve, whereas several nutrition specialists predicted a major deterioration in early 1969. According to a report by the American agency USAID, this evolution of things was the result of several factors.[104] Thanks to relief organisations supplying protein food (which could be better distributed due to the stabilising military situation) and local production resuming (harvests were sometimes gathered even before they reached maturity) it was possible to partly meet the needs of a population whose weakest members had already perished in large numbers. Despite this improvement between autumn 1968 and summer 1969 the situation was still precarious, as an increase in the food available was often offset by the arrival of new refugees who needed to be fed, at least in some areas.[105] According to a report by the US Central Intelligence Agency (CIA), in March 1969 between two and four million people within the borders of the former Eastern Region were surviving on food supplies from relief operations.[106] This estimate broadly corroborates that made by the ICRC a few months earlier.[107] In June 1969 a study conducted in the federal zone by American doctors on more than 7,000 children from some sixty villages located between the front line and the Atlantic Ocean, in a strip of land stretching from south of Aba to Calabar, concluded that 28 per cent of them suffered from more or less severe malnutrition despite a relative return to normal in these regions and the food supplied from outside.[108]

In June 1969 the halting of ICRC-co-ordinated flights once again led to a deterioration of the situation in Biafra, which continued until the end of the war. In November 1969, upon his return from the country, the humanitarian-aid co-ordinator appointed by the US government, Clarence Clyde Ferguson, told the Foreign Office that the situation had worsened considerably since his last visit in June.[109] This assessment was confirmed by an investigation – probably one of the most serious in the field – conducted by the American doctor Karl Western, who went to the area from 17 to 28 October 1969 to assess the nutritional and sanitary conditions in the enclave. With regard to malnutrition, his conclusions were as follows: more than 60 per cent of the population, which the report estimated at 3.24 million people, required additional food intake to live, of which 11.8 per cent every day and 51.1 per cent three times a week.[110] This deterioration in the second half of 1969 remained engraved in people's memories, as confirmed by the survey conducted by Harneit-Sievers: "When asked to recall the war history today, nearly everybody (except possibly people living on the northern and eastern fringes of the old Eastern Region, i.e. areas captured by Nigerian troops in the early stage of the war) seems to agree that, over time, things got much worse".[111]

Estimating the number of victims is a recurring problem in famine studies,[112] and the Biafran case is no exception.[113] The first reports attempting to count the victims appeared only in the autumn of 1968 and highlighted the great difficulty in providing a reliable picture of the situation. On the one hand, it was complicated to identify people in distress when they were not grouped together in refugee camps, and many fled whichever way they could. On the other hand, the figures given were mostly estimates. They were based on surveys that needed to be treated with caution or on projections. In the latter case the mortality rate was, for example, measured in a refugee camp and then applied to all the camps or the entire population. These projections did not take into account the diversity of the situations and required knowledge of the number of people living within Biafra, a reality which itself did not enjoy consensus. Finally, there was some confusion in the use of the figures produced. The Biafran authorities provided their own data, which they did not hesitate to inflate for propaganda purposes, while the figures provided by US and UK government bodies were equally suspect but for the opposite reason, as they tended to minimise the extent of the crisis.[114] As for the estimates provided by the relief organisations, they could have been exaggerated in order to alert and mobilise the public.

While bearing these caveats in mind, the data provided by these actors do give an idea of the situation (see Table 1.2). In early July 1968 Reverend Edward Johnson, quoting Oxfam Director Leslie Kirkley, who had returned from a two-week trip to Biafra, stated that in the refugee camps that were

Table 1.2 Estimated number of deaths due to famine according to humanitarian sources, July–September 1968 and August 1969–January 1970

Period	**Low estimate**	**High estimate**
July 1968	12,400	12,400
August 1968	155,000	186,000
September 1968	240,000	300,000
August 1969–January 1970	128,800	184,000
Total for both periods (July–September 1968 and August 1969–January 1970)	636,200	782,400

home to 700,000 people 400 were dying every day, while the number of deaths among those who had fled wherever they could was probably double.[115] For the month of August representatives of the aid services of Protestant churches and of Caritas estimated the number of daily deaths at 6,000.[116] In September estimates sent internally to the ICRC headquarters by the delegate Jaggi put the death toll at 5,000 and then 6,000 a day.[117] Other figures given at the end of September and picked up by the press or commented on in various reports as well as by nutritionists put the death toll at 8,000 to 10,000 a day.[118] The mortality rate then seemed to decrease considerably but it was still very difficult to put forward figures for the period from October 1968 to July 1969. New estimates were produced following the deterioration of the situation in mid-1969, in particular by the team of the humanitarian-aid co-ordinator appointed by the US government. In November 1969 a doctor who was interviewed as part of the team's investigations, whilst insisting that it was almost impossible to provide reliable data, estimated that between 700 and 1,000 people a day were dying of starvation.[119] These figures more or less corresponded to those given by a member of Joint Church Aid for August 1969.[120] As conditions did not really improve after November, these can be used to establish an approximate death toll for the months of August 1969 to January 1970.

These few figures show that for the two periods in which estimates were made, the number of deaths was at least 600,000. While these estimates may appear high, they do not include victims of famine in the aftermath of the conflict – conditions did not immediately return to normal – nor those who died between October 1968 and July 1969, nor those who died before July 1968, nor those who did not live in refugee camps. Thus, it is not unlikely that between 600,000 and 1,000,000 people died as a result of the crisis as a whole. Whilst this range remains wide, it is already somewhat narrower than that offered in the secondary literature, which varies from a total of 100,000 to 3,000,000.[121] Nevertheless, regardless of the exact number of victims, it is the trauma left by the famine on the Biafran population that needs to be remembered here. As Sydney Emezue has pointed out: "So much was the suffering caused by food shortages that Biafra to many of our interviewees has become synonymous with human degradation".[122]

From the summer of 1968 onwards the famine was an important propaganda tool which was used in two ways. The first concerned its extent, if not its very existence. The second related to those who were responsible for it and its use for political purposes. For the Biafran authorities media coverage of the famine became a means of attracting world attention, even more so than the presentation of the massacres suffered by the Igbo. In contrast, the Nigerian government tried to play down the severity of the food crisis in order to stem the tide of pro-Biafran sympathy this was stirring around the world.

Paradoxically, until this point both governments had tended to favour opposite policies. As the first signs of malnutrition appeared in 1967, the Biafran propaganda did not particularly seek to make them known; on the contrary. Thus, leaders tried to portray Biafra as a modern, responsible state that cared about the living conditions of its people, unlike Nigeria, which was presented as a state incapable of protecting its own citizens. This way of presenting the situation was part of a strategy to portray the Biafrans as progressive and committed to humanistic values, in contrast with the Nigerians, who were described as barbaric, backward and genocidal.[123] Just like in 1966 when hundreds of thousands of easterners returned to the East, the secessionist authorities strove to demonstrate their ability to manage the basic needs of the population, even under difficult conditions. More generally, since declaring independence, Biafran publications had highlighted the positive contributions the new government had made to the country's economic and social development. Organising vaccination campaigns, making efforts to improve education, and the production of food were given particular emphasis.[124]

On the other hand, from the summer of 1967 the federal press emphasised the nutritional problems in Biafra. In an article entitled "Rebels Badly in Need of Food" published in August 1967, the Nigerian newspaper *Daily Times* highlighted the growing need for certain products such as salt and flour.[125] This national newspaper close to the federal government[126] also reported on a worrying situation in Biafra in the autumn of 1967, to which it devoted a long article entitled "Starvation Is Likely in East Central State", that is, at the heart of Biafra.[127] In October 1967 the newspaper published a report on a refugee camp in Makurdi (in an area retaken by the federal army), showing a photograph of a woman breastfeeding a baby whose swollen belly was reminiscent of kwashiorkor.[128] Paradoxically, this image bears a strong resemblance to those that would make the front pages in the Western media nine months later.

From the moment the famine brought the Biafran conflict into the international press, narratives were turned on their head. The Nigerian authorities played down the severity of the food crisis. On the one hand, the worrying situation in the areas retaken by the federal army was not reported nationally, and on the other hand, the famine in Biafra was presented as a mere secessionist propaganda strategy.[129] As for the Biafran authorities, once the subject of malnutrition caught the world's attention, they were quick to exploit and stage it in order to underline the need for recognising the province's independence.[130] It also became a means of disseminating the genocide thesis: the federal government was allegedly using the famine, by maintaining the blockade and preventing the arrival of aid, in order to exterminate the civilian population. Whilst the Nigerian government denied any such intention, it did confirm the use of famine as a "conventional weapon of war" to subdue the secessionists.[131]

For the proponents of Nigerian unity the responsibility for the famine lay with the Biafran authorities, who persisted in waging a hopeless war that only served their own interests. This argument also gradually spread among the Igbo elite, some of whom changed their minds about secession.[132] The figure of Nnamdi Azikiwe, former president of Nigeria, is for example particularly representative of this trend. Having initially pleaded the Biafran cause,[133] he later tried to persuade Ojukwu to negotiate, and then eventually declared his support for Nigerian unity.[134] A similar evolution of the situation could be seen in some parts of the international public opinion. As both sides procrastinated throughout the conflict whenever it came to finding solutions for bringing food to the province, responsibility for the famine seemed to lie with both the blockade imposed by the Nigerian government and the Biafran authorities' obstinacy in pursuing secession.

Upon analysis of the particularly murderous process of violence to which the Igbo people were especially subjected, it seems difficult to state that this was intended to exterminate them. However, it is important to note that the available historiography on these issues is weak, since little research has been done on them in Nigeria since the end of the conflict. The lack of access to the Nigerian government's archives also makes it difficult to really assess its intentions. In any case, the violence of the 1966 massacres, the fighting that spared few civilians, and the onset of the famine following the blockade help us understand how the Igbo people became convinced that they could no longer safely live in Nigeria. This belief was not only the result of Biafran propaganda but also of the conditions of violence and deprivation to which they were subjected.

Notes

1 Heerten, *The Biafra War and Postcolonial Humanitarianism*.
2 A. Harneit-Sievers, J. O. Ahazuem & S. Emezue, *A Social History of the Nigerian Civil War: Perspectives from Below* (Enugu, Hamburg: Jemezie Associates, Lit Verlag, 1997), pp. 32–44.
3 Clergerie, *La crise du Biafra*, p. 239; Wiseberg, "The International Politics of Relief", p. 461.
4 Gould, *The Struggle for Modern Nigeria*, p. 203; Vallaeys, *Médecins sans frontières*, p. 90.
5 H. Ekwe-Ekwe, *Biafra Revisited* (Dakar: African Renaissance, 2006); F. Ugochukwu, *Biafra, la déchirure: sur les traces de la guerre civile nigériane* (Paris: L'Harmattan, 2009); Jacobs, *The Brutality of Nations*; Achebe, *There Was a Country*, pp. 228–32. The latter uses the figure of two million victims.
6 J.-M. Chaumont, *La concurrence des victimes* (Paris: La Découverte, 1997), pp. 93–201.
7 F. Chalk & K. Johansson, *The History and Sociology of Genocide* (New Haven: Yale University Press, 1990).
8 E. Weitz, *A Century of Genocide: Utopia of Race and Nations* (Princeton: Princeton University Press, 2003), pp. 9–10.
9 H. Fein, "Civil Wars and Genocide: Paths and Circles", *Human Rights Review*, 1:3 (2000), 49–61, at 50; Y. Ternon, *Enquête sur la négation d'un génocide* (Marseille: Éditions Parenthèses, 1989).
10 J. Sémelin, *Purifier et détruire. Usages politiques des massacres et génocides* (Paris: Seuil, 2005), p. 384.
11 Sémelin, *Purifier et détruire*, pp. 389–409.
12 Wiseberg, "The International Politics of Relief", pp. 460–1.
13 Le Pape, Siméant & Vidal (eds), *Crises extrêmes*.
14 De Waal, *Famine Crimes*, p. 144.
15 Heerten & Moses, "Introduction", in Heerten & Moses (eds), *Postcolonial Conflict and the Question of Genocide*, pp. 3–44, at p. 5.
16 Harneit-Sievers, Ahazuem & Emezue, *A Social History of the Nigerian Civil War*.
17 Ministry of Information, Eastern Nigeria, *Nigerian Crisis, Vol. 3: Pogrom: The Organized Massacre of Eastern Nigerians* (Enugu: Government Printer, 1966), p. 3.
18 Osaghae, Onwudiwe & Suberu (eds), *The Nigerian Civil War and Its Aftermath*; Clergerie, *La crise du Biafra*, pp. 27–87. For a point of view from a member of the Nigerian intellectual elite, cf. W. Soyinka, *Il te faut partir à l'aube* (Arles: Actes Sud, 2007).
19 F. Cooper, *L'Afrique depuis 1940* (Paris: Payot, 2008), p. 248.
20 For an analysis of the Nigerian political system, cf. R. L. Sklar, *Nigerian Political Parties: Power in an Emergent African Nation* (Trenton: Africa World Press, 2004 [1963]).
21 R. Suberu, *Federalism and Ethnic Conflict in Nigeria* (Washington, DC: United States Institute of Peace Press, 2001), p. 23.

22 D. Anthony, *Poison and Medicine: Ethnicity, Power and Violence in a Nigerian City, 1966–1984* (Oxford: James Currey, 2002), pp. 43–7.
23 Suberu, *Federalism and Ethnic Conflict in Nigeria*, p. 51.
24 Anthony, *Poison and Medicine*, p. 57.
25 F. O. Egwaikhide & O. O. Alabi, "Economics of the Nigerian Civil War: A Historical Analysis", in Osaghae, Onwudiwe & Suberu (eds), *The Nigerian Civil War and Its Aftermath*, pp. 173–90, at p. 177.
26 Harneit-Sievers, Ahazuem & Emezue, *A Social History of the Nigerian Civil War*, p. 16.
27 Anthony, *Poison and Medicine*, p. 59.
28 Gould, *The Struggle for Modern Nigeria*, pp. 39–48.
29 The National Archives of the UK (hereafter TNA), FO 371/187888, message from Le Quesne to McEntee, 21 January 1966.
30 Anthony, *Poison and Medicine*, pp. 88–118.
31 Anthony, *Poison and Medicine*, pp. 103–6.
32 See the Ministry of Information, Eastern Nigeria, *Nigerian Crisis, Vol. 3*, pp. 13–20. International newspapers also mentioned the massacres: C. Legum, "The Massacre of the Proud Ibos", *The Observer*, 16 October 1966.
33 See respectively Gould, *The Struggle for Modern Nigeria*, pp. 46–7, and Ugochukwu, *Biafra, la déchirure*.
34 Stremlau, *The International Politics of the Nigerian Civil War*, p. 38.
35 Cf. Ahiara declaration, in A. H. M. Kirk-Greene, *Crisis and Conflict in Nigeria: A Documentary Sourcebook, Vol. 2* (London: Oxford University Press, 1971), p. 376.
36 G. C. M. Onyiuke, *Massacre of Ndi-Igbo in 1966: Report of the G. C. M. Onyiuke Tribunal of Inquiry* (Lagos: Tollbrook, [*c.*1968]).
37 Ministry of Information, Eastern Nigeria, *Nigerian Crisis, Vol. 3*.
38 Archives of the International Committee of the Red Cross (hereafter AICRC), plenary session of the Committee, 5 January 1967, report by G. Hoffmann.
39 Federal Ministry of Information, Nigeria, *The Collapse of Ojukwu's Rebellion and Prospects for Lasting Peace in Nigeria* (Lagos: Federal Ministry of Information, May 1968), p. 7.
40 Anthony, *Poison and Medicine*, p. 103.
41 Gould, *The Struggle of Modern Nigeria*, pp. 46–7.
42 Sémelin, *Purifier et détruire*, p. 413.
43 Anthony, *Poison and Medicine*, pp. 93–4.
44 Harneit-Sievers, Ahazuem & Emezue, *A Social History of the Nigerian Civil War*, pp. 89–92; Anthony, *Poison and Medicine*, p. 102.
45 AICRC, B AG 200 147-01, report by G. Hoffmann on his mission: 12 November 1966–1 December 1966.
46 Harneit-Sievers, Ahazuem & Emezue, *A Social History of the Nigerian Civil War*, pp. 18–44.
47 Ministry of Information, Eastern Nigeria, *Nigerian Crisis, Vol. 1* (Enugu: Government Printer, 1966–68), p. 7.
48 Ministry of Information, Eastern Nigeria, *Nigerian Crisis, Vol. 1: Crisis '66* (Enugu: Government Printer, 1966).

49 Ministry of Information, Eastern Nigeria, *Nigerian Crisis, Vol. 3*, p. 3.
50 See also D. Anthony, "'Ours is a war of survival': Biafra, Nigeria and Arguments about Genocide, 1966–70", *Journal of Genocide Research*, 16:2–3 (2014), 205–25, at 213.
51 TNA, DO 186/6, message from Condon to McEntee, 31 August 1966.
52 Ministry of Information, Eastern Nigeria, *Nigerian Crisis, Vol. 1*, p. 9.
53 C. D. Ekwensi, "The Role of Propaganda in Biafran Operations", in H. B. Momoh, *The Nigerian Civil War, 1967–1970: History and Reminiscences* (Ibadan: San Bookman Publishers, 2000), p. 917.
54 Harneit-Sievers, Ahazuem & Emezue, *A Social History of the Nigerian Civil War*, pp. 89–92.
55 National Archives of Nigeria (hereafter NAN), CWC 2/2/4, *Biafra News Bulletins*, n° 256–65.
56 For example: C. O. Ojukwu, *On Aburi We Stand: A Broadcast* (Enugu: Government Printer, 1967); C. O. Ojukwu, *Biafra: Selected Speeches and Random Thoughts of C. Odumegwu Ojukwu* (New York: Harper and Row, 1969).
57 Speech by Y. Gowon, September 1966, reproduced in Kirk-Greene, *Crisis and Conflict in Nigeria, Vol. 1*, pp. 244–55.
58 Federal Ministry of Information, Nigeria, *Nigeria 1966* (Lagos: National Press Ltd, January 1967), pp. 7–10.
59 Cf. the leaflets published by the Federal Ministry of Information, Nigeria, *Nigeria 1966*; *The Struggle for One Nigeria* (Lagos: Federal Ministry of Information, October 1967); *Federal Peace Efforts* (Lagos: Federal Ministry of Information, July 1967); *The Collapse of Ojukwu's Rebellion and Prospects for Lasting Peace in Nigeria* (Lagos: Federal Ministry of Information, May 1968); *Ibos in a United Nigeria* (Lagos: Federal Ministry of Information, 1968); *Voices of Unity* (Lagos: Federal Ministry of Information, 1969).
60 Harneit-Sievers, Ahazuem & Emezue, *A Social History of the Nigerian Civil War*, pp. 46–88.
61 Saint Jorre, *The Nigerian Civil War*; see also Cervenka, *A History of the Nigerian War*, p. 55.
62 AICRC, B AG 202 147-008.12, note from Wilhelm, 14 November 1968.
63 AICRC, B AG 200 147-001.03, report by G. Hoffmann on his mission in Nigeria, 29 June 1967.
64 F. Bugnion, *Le CICR et la protection des victimes de la guerre* (Geneva: Comité international de la Croix-Rouge, 1994), p. 518.
65 Kirk-Greene, *Crisis and Conflict in Nigeria, Vol. 2*, pp. 4–5.
66 National Library of Scotland (hereafter NLS), Papers of Rev. A. G. Somerville, file 5, letter from Somerville, 3 February 1968.
67 Harneit-Sievers, Ahazuem & Emezue, *A Social History of the Nigerian Civil War*, p. 75.
68 See Chapter 8.
69 R. Doron, "Marketing Genocide: Biafran Propaganda Strategies during the Nigerian Civil War, 1967–70", *Journal of Genocide Research*, 16:2–3 (2014), 227–46.

70 Momoh, *The Nigerian Civil War*, pp. 179–90.
71 Stremlau, *The International Politics of the Nigerian Civil War*, p. 112.
72 Harneit-Sievers, Ahazuem & Emezue, *A Social History of the Nigerian Civil War*, p. 98.
73 S. E. Bird & F. Ottanelli, "The Asaba Massacre and the Nigerian Civil War: Reclaiming Hidden History", *Journal of Genocide Research*, 16:2–3 (2014), 379–99. E. Okocha, *Blood on the Niger: The First Black on Black Genocide, The Untold Story of the Asaba Massacre in the Nigerian Civil War* (TriAtlantic Books, 2006).
74 Harneit-Sievers, Ahazuem & Emezue, *A Social History of the Nigerian Civil War*, p. 75.
75 AICRC, B AG 201 147-001, telex from the CICR to Gowon, 21 October 1967; B AG 202 147-001, telex from Pierroz to the ICRC, 30 May 1968.
76 AICRC, B AG 202 147-001, report by G. Hoffmann, 16 October 1967.
77 See the code of conduct, reproduced in Federal Ministry of Information, Nigeria, *Towards One Nigeria, N° 3* (Lagos: Federal Ministry of Information, 1967).
78 AICRC, B AG 202 147-008.12, note by Wilhelm,14 November 1968.
79 AICRC, B AG 202 147-001, telex from J.-R. Pierroz to the ICRC, 30 May 1968.
80 Momoh, *The Nigerian Civil War, 1967–1970*, pp. 144–9.
81 See the *Daily Times* from August 1967.
82 Cervenka, *A History of the Nigerian War*, p. 58.
83 For example: Federal Ministry of Information, Nigeria, *Enough Is Enough: A Challenging Appeal to the Ibos of Nigeria* (Lagos: Federal Ministry of Information, 1968).
84 Federal Ministry of Information, Nigeria, *Ending the Fighting* (Lagos: Federal Ministry of Information, 1968).
85 Organization of African Unity Observers, *No Genocide: Final Report of the First Phase from 5th October to 10th December by the Organization of African Unity Observers in Nigeria, December, 1968* (Lagos: Federal Ministry of Information, 1968); *Observer Team to Nigeria, No Indiscriminate Bombing: Report on Activities of the Representative [sic] of Canada, Poland, Sweden, and the United Kingdom during the period 14th January–6th March, 1969* (Lagos: Nigerian National Press, 1969); Observer Team to Nigeria, *70% Iboland under Federal Control; Report on Activities of the Representatives of Canada, Poland, Sweden, and the United Kingdom during the Period 1st May, 1969–27th June*, 1969 (Lagos: Nigerian National Press, 1969).
86 AICRC, B AG 202 147-008.01, note by Borsinger, 15 May 1968.
87 AICRC, B AG 200 147-003.01, report n° 182, 24 September 1968 and B AG 202 147-008.04, report by Krille n° 6, October 1968.
88 AICRC, B AG 202 147-008.05, report by K. H. Jaggi, 5 February 1968.
89 AICRC, B AG 202 147-008.01, letter from K. H. Jaggi to J. de Heller, 8 February 1968.
90 R. Steiner, *Carré rouge: du Biafra au Soudan, le dernier condottière* (Paris: Robert Laffont, 1976), p. 116.
91 E. B. Ikpe, *Food and Society in Nigeria* (Stuttgart: F. Steiner, 1994), p. 97.

92 C. Aall, "Relief, Nutrition and Health Problems in the Nigerian/Biafran War", *The Journal of Tropical Pediatrics*, 16:2 (1970), 70–90, at 74.
93 Ikpe, *Food and Society in Nigeria*, p. 100.
94 Harneit-Sievers, Ahazuem & Emezue, *A Social History of the Nigerian Civil War*, p. 113.
95 AICRC, Directorate briefing note, 16 October 1967.
96 AICRC, B AG 202 147-008.05, report by K. H. Jaggi, 5 February 1968; B AG 202 147-008.01, telex from J. de Heller, 29 April 1968.
97 AICRC, plenary session of the Committee, 2 May 1968.
98 AICRC, Directorate briefing note, 21 May 1968.
99 NLS, Papers of Rev. A. G. Somerville, letter from Somerville, 13 August 1968.
100 TNA, FCO 38/303, copy of a cable from the US Embassy in London to the State Departement in Washington.
101 TNA, FCO 65/370, report by E. A. Bryant, "Nigeria: Relief: South East State", 26 October 1968.
102 TNA, FCO 65/384, telegram from the British High Commission (hereafter BHC) in Lagos (D. Hunt) to the FCO, 18 October 1968.
103 Nigerian students also report on the situation in the areas taken over by the FMG in a particularly alarming way. Quoted by Ikpe, *Food and Society in Nigeria*, p. 104.
104 USAID, *Emergency Relief in Nigeria and the Biafran Enclave, July 1967 through June 30 1969* (Washington, DC: USAID, 1969).
105 For example, NLS, Papers of Rev. A. G. Somerville, file 5, letter from Somerville, 24 August 1968.
106 TNA, FCO 65/384, CIA report, "Food Crisis", March 1969.
107 AICRC, Directorate briefing note, 29 October 1968. The population in need of food aid is estimated at 4,300,000 people: 3,500,000 in Biafra and 800,000 in Nigeria.
108 L. E. Davis, "Epidemiology of Famine in the Nigerian Crisis: Rapid Evaluation of Malnutrition by Height and Arm Circumference in Large Populations", *The American Journal of Clinical Nutrition*, 24:3 (1971), 358–64.
109 TNA, FCO 65/386, "Record of Mr Foley's meeting with ambassador Ferguson on Friday", 21 November 1969.
110 Harvard Law School Library, Clarence Clyde Ferguson's Papers, 1955–84, Serie 1, Files 4–6, Dr K. Western report on his stay in Biafra in October 1969.
111 Harneit-Sievers, Ahazuem & Emezue, *A Social History of the Nigerian Civil War*, p. 158.
112 S. Devereux, "Famine in the Twentieth Century", *ID Working Paper*, 105, pp. 4–13.
113 Wiseberg, "The International Politics of Relief", pp. 82–9 and pp. 444–62.
114 On the attitude of the Africa bureau of the State Department, cf. J. E. Thompson, *American Policy and African Famine: The Nigeria–Biafra War, 1966–1970* (Westport: Greenwood Press, 1990). On the British attitude, particularly at the end of the conflict, cf. Wiseberg, "The International Politics of Relief", pp. 439–40.

115 Archives of the World Council of Churches (hereafter AWCC), CCIA 1968, letter from Rev. Johnson, 8 July 1968.
116 TNA, FCO 65/384, draft telegram, 7 December 1968.
117 AICRC, Directorate briefing note, 1 October 1968.
118 Wiseberg, "The International Politics of Relief", p. 88.
119 TNA, FCO 65/386, "Record of Mr Foley's meeting with ambassador Ferguson on Friday", 21 November 1969.
120 Wiseberg, "The International Politics of Relief", p. 89.
121 Some go even further; cf. Aall, "Relief, Nutrition and Health Problems in the Nigerian/Biafran War", p. 75.
122 Harneit-Sievers, Ahazuem & Emezue, *A Social History of the Nigerian Civil War*, p. 124.
123 D. Anthony, " 'Resourceful and Progressive Blackmen': Modernity and Race in Biafra, 1967–70", *Journal of African History*, 51:1 (2010), 41–61.
124 NAN, CWC 2/2/3, CWC 2/2/4, "Republic of Biafra News Bulletin", June 1967.
125 "Rebels Badly in Need of Food", *Daily Times*, 17 August 1967, p. 3.
126 A. Olukotun, "The Media and the Nigerian Civil War: An Overview", in Osaghae, Onwudiwe & Suberu (eds), *The Nigerian Civil War and Its Aftermath*, pp. 387–8.
127 "Starvation is Likely in the East Central State", *Daily Times*, 6 November 1967, p. 7.
128 *Daily Times*, 24 October 1967, p. 7.
129 Ikpe, *Food and Society in Nigeria*, pp. 103–4.
130 Kirk-Greene, *Crisis and Conflict in Nigeria, Vol. 2*, p. 247 and p. 279.
131 Ikpe, *Food and Society in Nigeria*, p. 94. H. Fein distinguishes the use of hunger as a weapon of war from genocide by attrition: H. Fein, "Genocide by Attrition 1939–1993: The Warsaw Ghetto, Cambodia and Sudan, Links between Human Rights, Health, Mass Death", *Health and Human Rights*, 2:2 (1997), 10–45, at 13.
132 R. C. Njoku, "An Endless Cycle of Secessionism: Intellectuals and Separatist Movements in Nigeria", in B. Coppieters & M. Huysseune (eds), *Secession, History and the Social Sciences* (Brussels: VUB, 2002), pp. 249–74.
133 Kirk-Greene, *Crisis and Conflict in Nigeria, Vol. 2*, pp. 205–6.
134 The federal government did not hesitate to take advantage of his move by producing a brochure: N. Azikiwe, "I Believe in One Nigeria" – *Zik* (Lagos: Federal Ministry of Information, 1969).

2

A mediatic humanitarian crisis

As Frederick Forsyth, a journalist and fervent supporter of the Biafran cause, explained at the time, media coverage of the Biafran war was not given. African conflicts were not easy topics to "sell" in Western newspapers designed for a white public that quickly grew tired of violence in Africa.[1] Nevertheless, beginning with the summer of 1968 Biafra repeatedly burst into European and American media, so much so that for some authors its resonance opened up a new chapter in the history of humanitarianism.[2]

Based on the number of items (articles, dispatches, advertisements) in which the term Biafra appeared at least once in several European and American dailies, Figure 2.1 sheds light on the main phases of the media coverage that the conflict received in the written press: the summer of 1968, the first months of 1969, the summer of 1969 and the beginning of 1970. The summer of 1968 and January 1970 appear to be the two periods in which Biafra was most noticeable in the press. At these two points in time, in each of the dailies studied, the number of items in which Biafra was mentioned doubled or even tripled compared to the previous month. The extent to which the conflict featured in some of the major illustrated magazines corroborates this trend. On 12 July 1968 the American publication *Life* dedicated its front page to the Biafran famine and on 26 August *Time* devoted a whole issue to it. *Paris Match* also mentioned on its cover "the children of Biafra" and "the horror in Biafra" on 20 July and 10 August 1968. In January 1970 the war was again on the front pages of *Paris Match* (24 January) and *Time* (26 January). A study of the coverage of the conflict in French television programmes reflects the same periodisation. Barbara Jung notes that Biafra became "a major news story" in the summer of 1968 and January 1970.[3] She points to March 1969 as a third moment in the coverage of Biafra on French television, which is also reflected in the graph. Indeed, between the summer of 1968 and January 1970 media coverage of the conflict diminished but did not completely disappear. An initial pickup in interest occurred in early 1969, followed by a second one in the summer of 1969. These variations are more or less pronounced depending on the

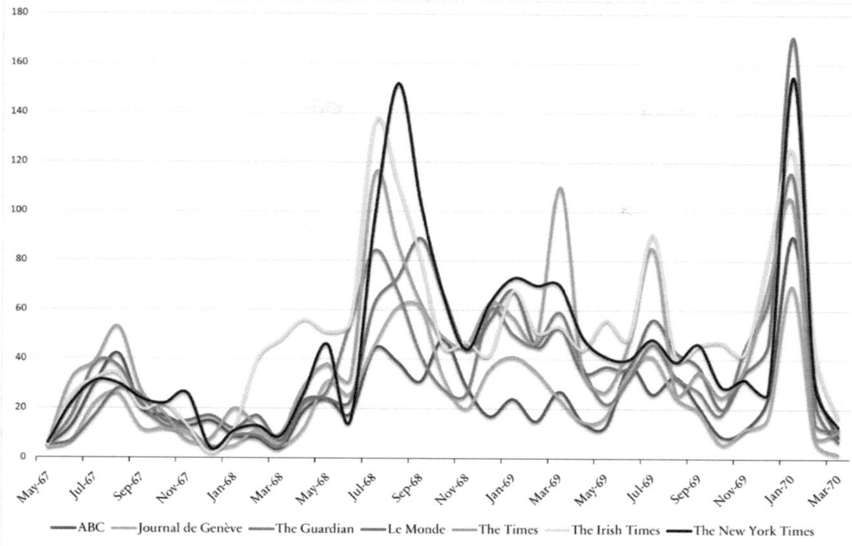

Figure 2.1 Biafra in Western newspapers

newspaper, probably due to divergent national agendas, but are still noticeable in each of the dailies.

Journalists' attention was drawn to various topics during these four moments. As far as the summer of 1968 is concerned, images of the famine played a central role in the media's awakening.[4] In January 1970, in addition to the announcement of Biafra's surrender and the end of the conflict, concerns about the fate of the civilian population, particularly children, and the future of relief operations again dominated the media. The other two moments that the graph highlights are also related to humanitarian issues. Thus, in early 1969 several events rekindled interest in Biafra in the press. First of all, Western aid received renewed attention as airlifts encountered technical, logistical, diplomatic and financial difficulties. The new American administration which took office at this time appointed a co-ordinator for humanitarian operations in Nigeria – Clarence Clyde Ferguson – in order to find a solution to the problem of food delivery. In France a national fundraising campaign for aid to Biafra was held in March 1969. To this were added concerns about the indiscriminate bombing of Biafran territory by the Nigerian air force, which was reported in the press particularly by Westerners who witnessed it. Humanitarians, journalists and politicians on the ground backed up the accusations levelled at the federal government.[5] Similarly, the media's renewed interest in Biafra in the summer of 1969 is explained by the topicality of humanitarian issues. Thus, questions about the delivery of relief supplies resurfaced in the newspapers. These included uncertainties about airlifts coming to an end and the possibility of replacing them. Thus, each time there was an increased focus on Biafra in the press, humanitarian issues were particularly prominent.

Historiography has largely emphasised the role of Biafran propaganda in the media coverage of the conflict.[6] Without minimising its role, putting it in perspective alongside the activities of other actors allows to better understand how Biafra gradually became a humanitarian issue on the international stage. Furthermore, various works have addressed the war's place in the media from specific angles,[7] but few have attempted to grasp this process as a whole. By analysing the role played by non-state actors such as Biafran elites, missionaries and relief organisations, on the one hand, and the British and French governments, on the other, this chapter provides an analysis of the key players and drivers behind the spread of information from Biafra to the rest of the world.

Out of the shadows: the role of missionaries and Biafran networks

Biafra's irruption into the Western media in the summer of 1968 was preceded by the activities of various actors who paved the way for its portrayal through images and words by emphasising the humanitarian issues to the detriment of the political complexity of the conflict. Several authors have highlighted the power of the Biafran propaganda machine, both internally via Radio Biafra and externally by using a Geneva-based public relations agency, Markpress.[8] Before the latter was entrusted with the task of managing Biafra's international communications, other means were used by the secessionist authorities to make their case. Efforts to expose the crisis began as early as 1966 with the publication of the *Nigerian Crisis* pamphlets, mentioned in Chapter 1, which were intended to, among other things, make the plight of easterners known outside Nigeria. Once independence was declared Biafran leaders sought international recognition. To this end, liaison offices were set up in various European cities – notably London, Paris, Lisbon, Vienna, Bonn and Geneva – as well as in the United States and Tanzania.[9] These allowed them to engage in all sorts of activities, from buying weapons and recruiting mercenaries to lobbying governments and international organisations, as well as spreading propaganda. Thus, emissaries sent to African and Western capitals seem to have played a particularly important role in the recognition of the Biafran state by the Ivorian, Tanzanian, Zambian and Gabonese governments in April and May 1968.[10] Furthermore, the Igbo elite, some of whom had forged close ties abroad during their studies or professional trips, were a crucial link in the dissemination of Biafran views throughout the world. A former member of the UN mission in Congo, for example, used his background to obtain a meeting in New York with one of the UN Under-Secretaries-General, Ralph Bunche, in June 1967.[11] In Britain, Ireland and the United States, Biafran students formed associations and conducted campaigns.[12] In the United Kingdom they set up an organisation, the Biafra Union, which lobbied for the Biafran cause.[13]

Former students abroad also mobilised their networks. The case of the Chief Justice of Biafra, Louis Mbanefo, who had studied law in England in the 1930s before being appointed as a judge ad hoc to the International Court of Justice in 1962, is particularly representative in this regard. He contacted his former fellow students and asked them to intervene on his behalf in government circles. Thus, in September 1967 Foreign Office officials reported numerous efforts made by "influential people", particularly in the judiciary, to arrange meetings between Mbanefo and members of the Foreign Office. These ties of friendship with British personalities allowed him to present the secessionist point of view in different circles, in a more or less formal manner, at receptions to which politicians and businessmen were invited.[14] In addition to these connections inherited from his professional career, Mbanefo was also able to use another channel. Being an important figure in Nigeria's Christian churches, he was well integrated in the Protestant networks of the World Council of Churches (WCC), as were other major figures of the Biafran secession,[15] such as Francis Ibiam, who was one of Ojukwu's close advisers.

Francis Ibiam was governor of the Eastern Region before the 1966 coup. Being a prominent figure in the Presbyterian Church of Nigeria, in 1960 he had been elected President of the WCC. Thanks to the ties that these positions enabled him to forge, Ibiam was an important link in encouraging the Christian and more particularly Presbyterian world to take an interest in Biafra. He corresponded personally with the WCC Secretary General, the American Eugene Carson Blake, to whom he did not hesitate to send alarming messages about a situation he described as genocide. His statements, in the context of the early stages of the conflict when it was difficult to obtain accurate information about the fate of the civilian population, caused great concern within the Council. Ibiam further insisted on WCC representatives coming to Biafra to see the situation for themselves and report back to Europe and the USA.[16] Although such a visit did not take place until March 1968, the Secretary for Overseas Missions of the Presbyterian Church in Canada, Ted Johnson, who was close to the WCC secretariat, already went there in January 1968. Although the trip was not made on behalf of the WCC, nevertheless, it was not insignificant since it encouraged the Catholic

Church to send Vatican representatives to the province. Ibiam played a strategic role during Johnson's visit. He ensured that it went smoothly, providing accommodation for the Canadian and facilitating his travels, thus enabling him to convey the secessionist concerns to the Western world.[17] Ibiam was also an important point of contact for missionaries working in Biafra as links with the outside world became increasingly difficult to maintain in a region placed under blockade by the federal government. Scottish missionaries recounted being able to communicate with their church in their home country through him.[18] Finally, in January 1968 Ibiam travelled to Germany and Scandinavia, then to North America and Great Britain.[19] During these trips he did not hesitate to draw a close link between the Biafran cause and the defence of Christianity. Indeed, a propaganda technique was to present the conflict as a religious war pitting Muslim northerners against Christian Igbo in order to convince the predominantly Christian Western nations to support Biafra's independence. Although his views were sometimes deemed too caricatural, causing him to lose credibility among well-informed circles,[20] Ibiam remained one of the great promoters of the Biafran cause in Christian circles.

In the early months of the conflict these lobbying and propaganda activities Biafran personalities engaged in did not translate into significant media success, as Biafra received relatively little attention from the press until the summer of 1968. However, they helped put the Biafran issue on the international agenda. Thus, in February 1968 the official visit from a Vatican delegation put an end to the isolation that the secessionist region had been subjected to since its declaration of independence.[21] The Catholic Church and WCC were then the first to draw attention to the plight of the victims of the conflict by launching, under the leadership of Ted Johnson, a joint world appeal for peace and aid for Nigeria.[22] Beginning with April 1968 there further came the diplomatic successes achieved by the Biafran authorities. In April and May 1968 the heads of state of Tanzania, Côte d'Ivoire, Gabon and Zambia recognised the Republic of Biafra. This helped provide the conflict with international visibility and raise the fear of genocide, which was the main reason the African heads of state gave to justify their stance.[23]

In early 1968 the Biafran authorities improved the international reach of their propaganda by hiring a public relations agency. Based in Geneva and headed by an American – H. William Bernhardt – Markpress was tasked with ensuring that the Biafran issue was reported in the mainstream Western media. Communiqués were transmitted by radio from the breakaway region to the Biafran office in Lisbon, which passed them on to Geneva. Markpress then handled their dissemination to the most important press agencies. These communiqués were also printed and sent to a list of 3,000 individuals, including editors of internationally renowned newspapers and members of the British Parliament.[24] Whilst French secret services were probably involved in bankrolling Markpress,[25] the recipients of the communiqués were also asked to help with the costs of the media coverage by paying money into a Union Bank of Switzerland account, allegedly in order to fund a refugee-aid commission.[26] By supplying the international media with news about Biafra, Markpress helped build interest in its secession in the summer of 1968. Nevertheless, the importance of this agency should not be overestimated, as its results were initially relatively meagre. Moreover, its communiqués gradually lost their value as they were seen by many observers as crude propaganda that could not be used to learn about the situation.[27]

Other sources of information played a crucial role in raising awareness of the Biafran cause among wider sections of Western societies. These were the Protestant and Catholic missionaries present on the ground, who became "mediators" between Biafra and the West. Indeed, Christianity was widespread in the Eastern Region where, in 1963, 77 per cent of the population identified as Christian.[28] Its spread dated back to the mid-nineteenth century when Protestant missionaries had settled in south-eastern Nigeria. Those from the Church of Scotland in particular laid the foundations for the Presbyterian Church of Nigeria. At the turn of the twentieth century they were joined by French Catholic missionaries of the Congregation of the Holy Spirit (the Spiritans), who were gradually replaced by fathers from the Irish branch of the congregation (Holy Ghost Fathers). When hostilities broke out there were apparently around 600 Catholic missionaries in the centre of the Eastern Region, most of whom decided not to leave the area. Historically established mostly on the periphery of the Eastern Region and taken over by the locals at the time of Nigeria's independence, Protestant missions and churches were less numerous in Biafra but remained essential points of contact with the outside world, particularly thanks to the links forged between the Presbyterian Church of Nigeria and its Scottish, Dutch, Canadian and American counterparts.

The correspondence of Reverend Alexander Somerville, the Church of Scotland's representative in Biafra, illustrates the crucial role played by missionaries in raising interest in the conflict in their home countries. The Somervilles had very regular exchanges with friends and family to whom they recounted their daily lives. At the same time Somerville sent weekly reports to Reverend Neil Bernard, head of the Church of Scotland's World Mission Council, providing first-hand information that Bernard could then circulate among the church's governing bodies as well as the faithful. For example, in early 1968 Somerville provided a report on the bombing of the Mary Slessor Hospital by the federal army and explicitly asked that it be publicised.[29] In the eyes of the British government Scotland's growing preoccupation with Biafra was clearly due to the ties that had been forged with the former Eastern Region through its missionaries,[30] while the latter also sought to exert their influence in London. For example, a Reverend Bernard, armed with testimonies from those on the ground, went to the Foreign Office to challenge the British policy of supporting the Nigerian government.[31]

Catholic missionaries played a similar role. They initially worked to raise interest in Biafra in their own communities and regions, as illustrated by the initiative of the Irish Holy Ghost Father Raymond Kennedy, who in the early winter of 1967–68 tried to organise a first gathering and collection for Biafran relief in Ireland.[32] Whilst other reasons such as opposition to the UK's policy of support for Nigeria, or a particular sensitivity to famines given the country's history, can be enlisted to explain the emotion that Biafra's situation raised in Ireland, the Spiritans' activism too played a part.[33] The latter were also active in the Vatican to encourage the Holy See to act on the crisis.[34]

In addition, very early in the conflict missionaries became familiar with the routes in and out of Biafra. The trips they made back and forth between the region and their home countries provided them with an opportunity to share their views on the situation. In Scotland, for example, they were asked to give interviews to journalists and published press articles in which they testified to the brutality of the federal offensive against the Biafran population. They saw it as their duty to make the Biafran point of view known in what was, at that time, "a forgotten African war".[35] This concern was shared by the Catholics, who were even more visible in the media. The Spiritans were an important source of information for journalists, bringing back testimonies, sometimes even visual ones, as they travelled back and forth between Europe or North America and Biafra.[36] This trend became more pronounced as living conditions in the province deteriorated in the spring of 1968 and more and more Spiritans travelled "to offer first hand accounts of the suffering".[37] As Laurie Wiseberg points out, they probably played a greater role in raising Western public awareness than the Markpress agency did.[38]

Missionaries acting as bridges between their home societies and the places where they officiated, passing on information and mobilising humanitarian aid, was not specific to Biafra. Ian Tyrrel has more generally shone a light on the role of cultural middlemen and -women that American missionaries played in mobilising support in the United States for the victims of the disasters they had witnessed.[39] The case of Cardinal Lavigerie during the Algerian famine in the late nineteenth century also illustrates the fundamental part that churchmen played in the media coverage of such events.[40] Indeed, clerics could rely on strong networks to relay information that was then, for example, spread to the faithful during sermons. In the 1960s progress in communication methods accentuated this phenomenon. Besides the fact that missionaries were able to travel more quickly between Africa, Europe and the United States, their information was no longer relayed only through Catholic and Protestant networks and the print media, it was also broadcast on television and radio.

In Biafra the missionaries distinguished themselves by their ability to bring journalists to the region beginning in early 1968, at a time when relatively few journalists travelled to this hard-to-reach area that was not yet of interest to the newsrooms. And the Biafran authorities, who were suspicious of foreigners, did not easily grant requests to enter the country, as evidenced by their refusal at the time to allow French reporters in.[41] In this context it was thanks to the Spiritans' activism that journalists made their first visits. The missionary Raymond Kennedy, who had many contacts in American media circles[42] and did not hesitate to establish links with French and Swiss broadcasters,[43] brought Western journalists to Biafra in January 1968.[44] The latter, during a meeting with a Biafran bishop at the end of their stay, recommended that the secessionist authorities regularly invite fellow journalists and unanimously proposed that Father Kennedy, without whom they themselves would not have come, should organise the trips.[45] Some also wished to be able to stay for longer periods and that their visits be less formal.[46] Not all of these recommendations were immediately followed to the letter, but the Biafran authorities clearly saw the importance of the journalists' visits and encouraged Kennedy to bring to Biafra anyone who might prove useful to the cause of independence.[47] They then took up this practice themselves with the help of Markpress, and from April 1968 the transport of journalists to Biafra became one of the main activities of the agency,[48] which organised their entry into the region by means of clandestine flights from Lisbon.

The missionaries did not stop at bringing reporters to Biafra. They also strove to facilitate their work on the ground thanks to their knowledge of the area, the population and the authorities. In this respect, a Holy Ghost Father's account of the foreign journalists' visit instigated by Kennedy provides an enlightening testimony:

> There I over-heard a very serious discussion and tempers were high – an organized tour had been arranged for the Bonny front. A few [journalists] refused to go and said they wanted to walk around Port-Harcourt. They had deliberately missed the bus: "the officials would not let us walk freely around the town", they said. They accused them of hiding something. I saw the Permanent Secretary, a close friend of mine in the middle of the roar I found myself intervening in what I considered a very embarrassing position for the officials. I suggested that I would take the three journalists ... around Port Harcourt. I was offered an escort but I refused so as to show them how normal life really

> was in the city. My soutane would be my escort. We drove to Kingsway, had a quick look round a cup of coffee, bought a few small things, and proceeded to Chellarams. We then went through the market like a flash and proceeded to the Biafran Tobacco Factory which was in production – still making three of their five brands of cigarettes. The manager was charming and told them everything. We called to Bishop Okoye; he was not there, and then to Barclays Bank where the Manager told them the fantastic story of the recovery of the Nigerian currency notes in the space of five days without any announcement in either paper, radio, or television. They seemed amazed and enjoyed their trip around saying "how far better this was than the officials conducted tours". They had seen life for themselves, and contrary to their expectation nobody stood to gawk at them "they took us for granted". ... After lunch I found myself on the road to Okpala again with Mr. Riley ... and Mr. John Barnes, Newsweek, in the car. We had a long discussion on the situation. I showed them the boys in study in Okpala and proceeded without delay to Olakwo refugee camp. They heard fantastic stories from the refugees who fled across the Niger from Mid-West. They took plenty of photographs and copious notes. I over-heard some of the stories. ... The journalists got sufficient material in Olakwo to convince the world of the dreadful atrocities that have been perpetrated against the unfortunate Ibo tribe.[49]

The missionaries were thus more than mere witnesses who could conveniently be asked questions about the situation. They were mediators between the Western world where they came from and Biafra where they lived. They facilitated relations between journalists and the authorities which could sometimes be difficult. They helped ensure that the reporters' stay on the ground went smoothly, but above all they shaped their perception of the conflict by suggesting meetings and itineraries and by expressing their points of view. In this respect, Ken Waters highlights the central role played by another Holy Ghost Father, Kevin Doheny, in producing the first British television report showing children suffering the effects of the famine in the early summer of 1968.[50] The author mentions, on the one hand, the links forged in Europe with British journalists to raise their interest in Biafra and, on the other hand, the role of missionaries on the ground. They were the ones who took journalists to hospitals to show them the malnourished children at a time when the Biafran authorities were not yet trying to call attention to the shortages.

The revelations about the famine in the summer of 1968 sparked Western public interest in the plight of thousands of malnourished children. As a result, more and more journalists travelled to Biafra to document the food disaster. While various communication strategies had been unsuccessfully tried out by the Biafran leadership to turn Biafra into an international issue, the famine brought the conflict into the spotlight. Once this process started, the authorities no longer hesitated to use it by organising, sometimes with a certain degree of complacency, visits to camps and hospitals to "exhibit" children (Figure 2.2).[51]

Jean Buhler, a freelance journalist from Neuchâtel, wrote an account of a reporters' trip to Biafra in the summer of 1968. He went to the Biafran House in Lisbon in July 1968 and, after a few days' wait, obtained a ticket on one of the planes belonging to Hank Wharton's company which flew clandestinely to Biafra. Other journalists – Swedish, Belgian, British, German and American – also took part in the trip. On arrival, they were met by members of the press service who then planned their stay from Aba where they were based:

> We had no difficulty in outlining our plans for interviews in Biafra since we wished to see precisely what the young men and women of the Overseas Press Service wanted to show us: on the one hand, the extreme poverty of the refugees, the suffering of the peasant families deprived of their lands, the agony of the children and the elderly, the poor, the weak, the sick; on the other hand, the efforts of a 50-to-60,000-strong army against an aggressor twice as numerous, twenty times better equipped, and abundantly supplied primarily by Great Britain as well as by the Soviet Union and others.[52]

Buhler was then assigned a guide whose job was to show him around refugee camps, hospitals, and to take him to see combatants, both ordinary soldiers and army leaders. Based in Aba, Buhler spent around ten days touring

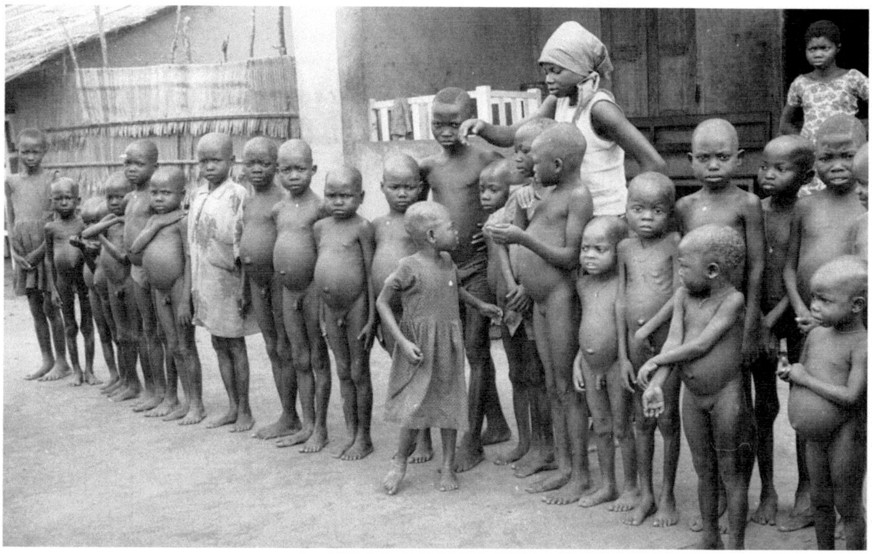

Figure 2.2 Nto-Edino, camp, V-P-NG-N-00061-18
(© ICRC / Max Vaterlaus, September 1968)

around the breakaway province. In his account the journalist recalled the propaganda scenes he witnessed when army recruitment was staged to show the enthusiasm of young recruits; or when, after a visit to a refugee camp, "the most serious cases of kwashiorkor" were gathered by officials so that they could be photographed by journalists. Although Buhler seemed to be aware of and sometimes uncomfortable with such practices, he was nonetheless deeply affected by his stay in Biafra:

> I returned to Europe overwhelmed by what I had seen, heard, and experienced. Convinced that my life had changed and that from then on it would be devoted to searching for the truth with a small "t" which fleetingly crowns the efforts of an itinerant investigator, convinced that it was not worth speaking out if one remained indifferent to injustice and misfortune. I believe that I sought to inform myself in good faith and that my conviction was not essentially shaped by the emotional shocks felt on one side of the barricade. This conviction could only be strengthened by contact with suffering that was unjustly and hypocritically imposed from outside.[53]

Most of the journalists who went there felt the same emotion and wished to share it. Besides the articles or pictures they brought back which appeared in the media, like Buhler, several of them chose to recount what they had seen in a book, sometimes illustrated with photographs. Generally published in late 1968 or during 1969, these testimonies often took the form of pleas in favour of Biafra, in which some did not hesitate to mention the thesis of genocide.[54] Without exaggerating the importance of such works, they did help give Biafra a certain visibility in Western societies.

In Buhler's book the discreet presence of the missionaries was still perceptible, although the Biafran press services were now well in charge of handling the journalists. For example, Buhler recounted how on the plane to Biafra the reporters began a conversation with an Irish missionary who gave them a first glimpse of the region they were about to visit. It is interesting to note that the information he provided was less subject to the journalist's critical spirit, that it appeared more credible than that received from the Biafran services. The meeting, later in the account, with a Dutch missionary doctor, Dr Middelkoop, would reinforce the closeness that developed between the visiting reporters and the expatriates that lived there. The Dutchman too gave a very pro-Biafran view of the conflict, without being challenged by the journalist. The encounter with Middelkoop – one of the few characters to be named in Buhler's book – was all the more important since it contrasted with the absence of other humanitarians.[55] Recalling his trip with Gilles Caron to Biafra in the summer of 1968, Raymond Depardon also remembered being welcomed by the Irish Catholic fathers in the villages they visited.[56] Indeed, the expatriates present in Biafra at that time were still mainly missionaries; they were later joined by humanitarians who quickly caught the attention of journalists.

Maintaining the interest: Western humanitarians and journalists

Once the conflict became a subject of media concern in the summer of 1968, it then continued to attract attention to varying degrees at different times, in different countries. The interdependencies between media and humanitarian organisations played a not insignificant role in maintaining interest. Indeed, by helping to raise awareness of a critical situation, the media facilitated the activities of humanitarians who then had the support of an informed public opinion. Conversely, journalists could also take advantage of the deployment of relief operations to carry out their work. They sometimes used humanitarian logistics to get to and around the area, and approached volunteers for first-hand information on the situation.[57] However, this relationship was not self-evident, as shown by the important debates had on the issue of the testimony of people working on the ground, particularly beginning with the Biafran conflict. These are discussed more specifically in Chapter 8 but are part of a more general discussion on the links between the setting up of relief operations and the media coverage of the crisis.

From the winter of 1967–68 the humanitarian organisations split into two groups. A first group made up of faith-based non-governmental organisations came together in the autumn of 1968 under the name Joint Church Aid (JCA).[58] The activities of this group were mainly structured around the missionaries whose role in the media-coverage process has already been highlighted. Other agencies ready to assist the ICRC formed a second group around this entity, including several National Red Cross Societies, UNICEF, Oxfam and the International Union for Child Welfare (IUCW). These organisations also participated in raising awareness of the conflict.

Despite its tradition of discretion and neutrality, the ICRC launched its first world appeal, called "SOS Biafra", on 24 May 1968. Although it provoked the anger of the federal government, which saw it as an endorsement of the secessionists, its statements were initially given very little coverage in the international media.[59] Oxfam also tried to draw the public's attention to the seriousness of the humanitarian problem in the war-affected areas in May 1968, but without much success.[60] The arrival of journalists in Biafra, who discovered the famine, led to greater media coverage of humanitarian views. In July 1968 remarks made by Oxfam's director were this time reported in the international press. The ICRC delegate in Biafra, Karl Heinrich Jaggi, was quoted in several *New York Times* articles. The head of UNICEF and the UN Secretary-General also spoke to the media in July and August 1968.

By the end of the summer air bridges set up by the ICRC, Joint Church Aid and the French Red Cross provided further means to get to Biafra as links with the enclave remained limited. Following the example of the missionaries, the churches did not hesitate to send journalists.[61] The ICRC would also occasionally allow reporters to use its air bridge to go to the area, provided that they had received prior accreditation from Markpress.[62] In addition, humanitarian operations led to an increase in the number of expatriates witnessing what was happening in Biafra. Indeed, the ICRC and religious organisations called on many volunteers to work in the region who would then bring back their impressions. Like the missionaries, they acted as points of contact between Biafra and in their home countries since they could provide journalists with information. However, for the teams operating under the aegis of the ICRC this was not a given. Indeed, despite paying some attention to communication, the organisation sought to maintain control over its image and what was said about its activities. Thus, volunteers working under its auspices were bound by a duty of confidentiality and undertook not to publish anything about the ICRC's work without its agreement.[63] Despite this rule, those who helped run its operations would sometimes speak out, including, most famously, some of the future founders of Médecins Sans Frontières. They were not the only ones who wished to share their experiences: overall, the volunteers were part of a broad movement started by the missionaries to spread information about Biafra, which helped keep the conflict in the media, primarily as a humanitarian crisis.

The difficulties faced by relief operations and what would happen to them progressively became subjects in their own right for journalists. Indeed, the situation of dying children and Western efforts to save them were more interesting for a Western audience than the vagaries of a civil war in an African country. Relief organisations themselves were involved in this process. In order to continue the operations they had set up in the summer of 1968 they had to find funds, which they obtained from private donations or governments. They also needed to mobilise volunteers willing to go to the region. To this end, it was important to publicise their actions and the need to continue them. They thus resorted to press releases and conferences and tried to polish up their institutional communication. They further produced newsletters or activity reports usually illustrated with striking photographs, which were sent to donors or more widely distributed to members of these organisations. This helped raise awareness of the situation in Biafra among civil society.

Although its communication policy was not very developed, the ICRC is a good example of this. As it struggled to expand its humanitarian-aid operation in the summer of 1968, it realised that highlighting what it had already achieved since the beginning of the conflict would help it respond to criticisms about its inaction and impotence and improve its financial situation. Indeed, governments that might provide it with funding were sensitive to how its activities were reflected in the newspapers. The ICRC then took a series of measures which, while primarily aimed at restoring its image with partners and governments, also contributed to the media coverage of the humanitarian crisis. Thus, the frequency of its briefings with associates and journalists increased considerably from the late summer of 1968 onwards. There was an increasing number of press conferences and trips abroad by Committee members to raise the profile of the ICRC's activities and seek funds. The Swiss organisation commissioned an "audiovisual information specialist", Marko Flaks, to undertake a mission to Biafra in September 1968. The latter conducted a series of radio interviews with participants in humanitarian operations.[64] Two filmmakers who had previously worked with the ICRC's information service, Jérôme Santandréa and Adrien Porchet, were also sent to Biafra and Nigeria, where they shot the films *Rescue* and *War and Starvation*.[65] In the spring of 1969 the person in charge of the ICRC's action in Nigeria–Biafra, August Lindt, recommended that a documentary be made about the organisation's activities on federal territory and indicated the main topics to be covered. The focus was to be on the logistics of delivering relief supplies while showing the populations in need and the "medical work in the bush", not forgetting the activities in support of prisoners of war and the work of those in charge of the operation.[66] On this basis, in May 1969 the ICRC sent a team led by Santandréa to Nigeria to make a new film entitled *Nigeria Two Years After*. Furthermore, the photojournalist Max Vaterlaus made several trips to Biafra to document the relief effort. Indeed, since the 1950s it had not been uncommon for the ICRC to call on renowned photographers and news agencies to cover the conflicts in which it intervened in order to raise funds and highlight its work.[67] These film or photographic documents were then used at briefings or sent to organisations that supported its activities and to interested media outlets.[68] More generally, reports on operations and the people involved in them were broadcast on television, thus gaining a large audience. Finally, the ICRC sought to work more closely with journalists. For example, in the autumn of 1969 it included a *Neue Zürcher Zeitung* reporter in its delegation which went on a mission to negotiate the resumption of the airlifts. However, it found that the result of this experiment had not been sufficiently positive and decided not to repeat it.[69]

Since it dealt with aid in both Biafra and the federal area, in its communication the ICRC was particularly careful to focus on the needs of both sides of the front line and the efforts deployed to meet them. In keeping with its principle of neutrality, it avoided making any judgements about who was responsible for the humanitarian situation. Interestingly, this attitude was gradually replicated by all the organisations that were more or less involved in relief operations. Grouped under the umbrella of Joint Church Aid, the churches were not subject to the same principles as the ICRC and could take a more political stance in support of Biafra. Nevertheless, in their communications they stressed the seriousness of the humanitarian situation and the efforts they were making to improve it.[70] Indeed, whilst missionaries relayed the Biafran views in the West and at the beginning of the conflict they were partly persuasive about the danger faced by the civilian population, the complex evolution of the war subsequently led religious organisations to be more cautious.[71] Despite the fact that they worked for peace, they did not wish to be seen as supporting the Biafran cause. Indeed, too close an association between the Christian religion and the fight for the province's independence could have been awkward for the many Christians who were in favour of keeping Nigeria united. Furthermore, it would have jeopardised their activities, indeed security, on the other side of the front line, especially in the territories recaptured by the federal army where the Christian Council of Nigeria (Conseil chrétien du Nigeria / CCN) and the Catholic Secretariat of Nigeria were involved in relief work among the civilian population.

This concern was reflected in the way religious organisations and missionaries communicated. In late 1967 Raymond Kennedy's superior in Ireland prevented him from involving the Spiritan order in a press conference he wanted to organise on the subject of Biafra.[72] The dismissal of an Irish television crew due to visit the province, following the intervention of a missionary who worked for religious humanitarian operations and wished to preserve his relationship with Lagos, is another enlightening example of these ambiguities.[73] Similar concerns existed within the World Council of Churches. Constant care was taken in press releases and public statements not to appear too pro-Biafran so as not to alienate Nigeria's Protestants. The JCA also focused primarily on needs and the activities undertaken by the churches to meet those needs. In doing so it sought to present the conflict as a humanitarian crisis, relegating to a certain extent the political aspects of the problem to the background.

The relief organisations, whether through communication efforts at management level or through the testimonies of their volunteers working on the ground, helped to keep Biafra in the media after the initial wave of interest generated by the famine in the summer of 1968. As with the missionaries in the previous period, the information and testimonies reported by the humanitarians were perceived by observers as reliable. As Yves Lavoinne explains with regard to the French doctors – but it is possible to apply this analysis to the staff of all relief organisations – their word carried particular weight since they were considered experts capable of assessing the situation.[74] Because they were seen as having no interest other than saving lives, the information they provided to the media appeared to be more "objective" than what was reported in the press releases circulated particularly by Markpress.

Shaping opposite discourses: the French and British governments

Highlighting the role of non-governmental actors, whether missionaries or humanitarians, in the dissemination of information about Biafra should not, however, obscure the attempts made by governments to shape this process. Two particular examples help illustrate the role of state services in the way the crisis occupied national media spaces. The British and French cases are especially interesting, as these two states pursued opposite goals in the conflict. Indeed, as a former colonial power with important interests in Nigeria, the British government under Harold Wilson supported the federal government in its desire to keep the country united. It therefore made many efforts to nuance media coverage of the conflict, which was seen as too favourable to the secessionists. French interests were at odds with this. Although the Élysée never officially recognised Biafra's independence, the President's Secretariat for African and Malagasy Affairs was involved in providing assistance to the secessionists.[75] This included, among other things, mobilising French public opinion in support of the Biafran cause, which could then justify a greater commitment in this direction.

The role of the French authorities in the media coverage given to the Biafran issue was apparent in several respects. For example, scholarship and testimonies from members of the French secret services claim that the latter instigated the use of the term genocide in reference to the conflict.[76] However, the importance of this should not be overestimated since, on the one hand, the eastern authorities tried to spread its use as early as 1966 and, on the other hand, the term was in the end rarely used on television.[77]

More generally, the French government worked to improve media coverage of Biafra in France. In this respect, Jacques Foccart reports that General de Gaulle was concerned there were too few journalists on the ground before the summer of 1968 and wanted to see their numbers increase. There were plans to send Jean-François Chauvel, a well-known *Le Figaro* reporter close to the French special services, who indeed went there in the summer of 1968.[78] Subsequently, the Secretariat for African and Malagasy Affairs sought to ease journalists' access to Biafra through the French embassy in Libreville, Gabon.[79] It further facilitated relations between humanitarian organisations and the media, seeking to use the information received from

French medical personnel working in Biafra in the press. For its part, the embassy in Libreville provided, for example, photographic material on the famine to relief organisations based in Europe so they could use it in their campaigns raising awareness about the situation.[80]

In addition to relaying the news reported by humanitarian workers, the secretariat played a crucial role in launching public appeals to the French population in order to raise funds for the relief operations organised via the French Red Cross. The media's contribution was fundamental to raising public awareness and the government did not hesitate to use its influence to make use of the various means of communication. Thus, through the Office de la Radiodiffusion-Télévision Française (ORTF), which had particularly close links with the Gaullist government,[81] the presenter Pierre Sabbagh launched a first appeal for donations on 2 August 1968. A second appeal was then made on 27 December 1968. In November 1968, as the funds initially raised ran out, representatives of the Ministry of Foreign Affairs and the Secretariat for African and Malagasy Affairs considered launching a second collection to keep Biafra in the media spotlight. Reluctance on the part of the ORTF, which had its own agenda, led to the campaign being moved to the end of December 1968.

As this second mobilisation did not bring the expected results, a third collection was scheduled for March 1969. The minutes of inter-ministerial preparatory meetings reflect the government's desire to use the media as much as possible in order to make the French people aware of the plight of Biafran civilians. To this end, there were plans to work at different levels. Firstly, there would be increased coverage of Biafra on radio and television programmes in order to reach a particularly wide and varied audience:

> The "Contact" programme will explain the subject to young people. ... A daily rhythm will be strictly maintained by moving on air from one programme to the next so that no one can escape the programmes. On the radio there will be interventions in J. Baudrier's talk show and witnesses such as Jean Chauvel, Jean Wolf, Todd, and Lallande will describe what they saw on the ground. Here too there will be regular adverts. "Madame Inter" will provide information on the sale of leaflets, focusing particularly on women. France-Inter will also broadcast information in the morning and Inter-jeunes in the evening.[82]

The content was designed to reach the French population as much as possible. From this point of view, the suffering of children appeared to be a particularly mobilising tool:

> We could imagine a nameless Biafran child being shown on television. ... Another option would be to sell vouchers of a given value representing the amount needed to survive one day in Biafra, or to get Biafran children to draw pictures that could be used to produce leaflets or be sold.[83]

The use of images was just as crucial. For television, for example, one had to choose "the best film on Biafra to show the most striking scenes".[84] The frequency and scheduling of broadcasts were also looked at in order to "condition the audience":

> After reflection, one method could be adopted: launch very brief appeals at very short intervals in order to make affluent listeners feel guilty; these very brief appeals could be accompanied by many images with a low sound which will be showed at meal times.[85]

In addition to enlisting the help of the ORTF, private radio stations were also strongly encouraged to participate in the fundraising efforts. At the time of the first campaign in the summer of 1968, at a meeting between representatives from the Ministry of Foreign Affairs and the French Red Cross, there were already plans to invite "Europe 1 to make itself available to us to help raise funds".[86] This approach was also considered in the March 1969 appeal: "Peripheral stations, Luxembourg, Europe, Monte Carlo, Andorra will be approached at the highest level, insisting that the campaign that is being undertaken has been decided by the government".[87]

By making up the bulk of the conflict's presence in the media, the Biafran relief appeals helped depoliticise the Biafran crisis. As with missionaries, the presentation of humanitarian problems disconnected from politics and the focus on the suffering of children left the public with no choice but to mobilise in order to save lives or feel guilty about the deaths of innocent victims. Thus, while the French government played a crucial role in fostering a discourse of victimhood, the British government stepped up its efforts to counteract this trend on its domestic scene.

The media focus on the famine in Biafra, and more generally on the abuses committed against the civilian population, put the British government in a difficult position because of its support for the Nigerian federal military government.[88] Indeed, some journalists did not hesitate to hold it largely responsible for the suffering endured by the Biafran people.[89] However, convinced of the soundness of its choices, the British government sought to counteract the growing pro-Biafran feelings of sympathy in the United Kingdom for two reasons. On the one hand, on the domestic scene it allowed it to avoid criticisms and find itself less often in a difficult position in parliamentary debates. On the other hand, and to a lesser extent, it was also essential in order to spare the sensitivities of Nigerian leaders who felt that the British media gave too much prominence to Biafran views. These reasons then led the British government to take certain measures to improve Nigeria's image in the eyes of the public and to counterbalance Biafra's portrayal as the victim. These could take different forms, from sending international observers to stop accusations of genocide, to improving Nigerian propaganda, which was considered particularly poor.[90]

In this regard, the media played an essential role in painting Nigeria in a better light, showing that its government was not pursuing a genocidal policy. Thus, Foreign Office officials contacted important figures in the press, such as the editor of *The Times*, to convince them of the soundness of the British policy of supporting the federal government. Journalists working for *The Evening Standard*, *The Mirror*, *The Observer* or *The Guardian* who covered the conflict or travelled to Biafra were also received at the Foreign Office. During these meetings the ministry tried to defend the Nigerian policy while at the same time encouraging and helping reporters to go to Nigeria and not only to Biafra so they could then give more visibility to the federal viewpoint.[91]

The British government also sought to influence the British Broadcasting Corporation (BBC), not least because the Nigerian government had made it known that it was particularly unhappy with the BBC's reporting of the conflict. However, unlike the ORTF in France, the links between the BBC and the British government were looser.[92] It was therefore less easy to influence the content of the programmes as any attempt to exert pressure was met with strong reactions from within the organisation. Nevertheless, there was regular less formal contact with Charles Curran, the Director General, in an attempt to improve relations between the BBC and the Nigerians. Overall, British efforts to make Nigerian views more visible in the media seem to have been successful, although they could also be counterproductive. Indeed, there was a tendency among some in the Foreign Office to dismiss any article or programme that did not portray the Nigerian government in a favourable light as Biafran propaganda. However, these criticisms, when unfounded, helped show London's biased approach to the war and its susceptibility to federal views.[93]

As part of their efforts to restore Lagos's image, British officials also emphasised the secessionists' responsibility for the humanitarian crisis. To this end, they underlined the difficulties caused by the Biafran authorities during negotiations on the delivery of relief supplies and promoted the idea that if they gave up on secession, the blockade would be lifted, humanitarian aid would be distributed and the food situation would return to normal. British officials argued that any support for the secessionists helped to prolong the war and therefore the humanitarian crisis. In this context, they also indirectly criticised the relief organisations and sought to cast doubt on the consequences of their operations on the pursuit of the war, as evidenced by their comments in relation to an article on this subject written by Kennedy Lindsay and published in *The Observer* newspaper:

> We have ourselves been promoting some unattributable publicity in Africa about the connection between relief funds for the Biafrans and the foreign

> exchange for arms purchases, in the hope that this would be picked up in Europe, although the *Observer* article itself was not promoted by us. There is difficulty here, as we do not want to seem openly to cast doubts on the propriety of the charitable organisations' activities or on whether the people are right to contribute to them. Nevertheless, we think the article may have served a useful purpose in drawing attention to what the relief organizations themselves have realized all along, that counterpart funds can be used by the Biafrans for arms purchases. It may also have helped to open the eyes of people who contribute to Biafran fund raising appeals which are paid into Biafran accounts in Europe.[94]

The British government thus sought to draw attention to the political issues inherent in a situation which the West saw primarily in humanitarian terms. It tried to get the media to counterbalance the image of Biafra as a victim by raising the question of the responsibility of the secessionists, and even indirectly of the humanitarians, in the suffering endured by the population. However, the British government remained cautious in this approach as it could not afford to completely discredit the humanitarian operations which had the support of public opinion.

Apart from the media, governmental and non-governmental actors were also involved in the process of giving media coverage to the Nigeria–Biafra war. The room for manoeuvre that missionaries and humanitarians particularly had at their disposal made them especially important conveyors of information. These "mediators" between Western societies and Biafra seem to have been crucial in keeping the media focused on the crisis unfolding in this part of Africa. The specific role they played in conveying information and in the West's growing interest in the conflict helps us better understand why the situation was seen above all as a humanitarian crisis. Governments too played an important role in this process, as shown by the French government which, with the help of the ORTF, helped paint a picture of Biafra as a victim. For their part, British officials tried to get the media to present the situation in a more nuanced way so that the public would ask questions about who was responsible for the humanitarian crisis. This strategy seems to have been partially successful, since it allowed it to continue its support for the Nigerian government. Nevertheless, its policy remained highly contested during the conflict, not least because of the emotion stirred by the media coverage of the humanitarian crisis.

Notes

1 F. Forsyth, *The Biafra Story* (Harmondsworth: Penguin, 1969), p. 222.
2 Barnett, *Empire of Humanity*, pp. 132–47.

3 B. Jung, "L'image télévisuelle comme arme de guerre", *Bulletin de l'Institut Pierre Renouvin*, 26 (2007), 49–63, at 54.
4 For example, V. Gorin, "La couverture médiatique de la guerre civile du Biafra au regard des enjeux humanitaires dans les médias français, suisses et américains (1967–1970)", *Le Temps des médias*, 21:2 (2013), 176–95.
5 See, for example, the ICRC press release, 7 January 1969, and C. Goodell, "Reports on Bombings in Biafra", *The New York Times*, 15 February 1969.
6 Stremlau, *The International Politics of the Nigerian Civil War*, pp. 109–41.
7 A. A. Akinyemi, *The British Press and the Nigerian Civil War: The Godfather Complex* (Oxford: Oxford University Press, 1979); H. Schabowska & U. Himmelstrand, *Africa Report on the Nigerian Crisis: News, Attitudes and Background Information: A Study of Press Performance, Government Attitude to Biafra and Ethno-political Integration* (Uppsala: Scandinavian Institute of African Studies, 1978); F. Ugochukwu, "La guerre du Biafra à la radio, situation militaire et livraisons d'armes en 1968–1969", *Peuples Noirs Peuples Africains*, 80 (1991), pp. 60–76; A. Bamisaiye, "The Nigerian Civil War in the International Press", *Transition*, 44 (1974), pp. 30–5.
8 Momoh, *The Nigerian Civil War*, pp. 179–90; Stremlau, *The International Politics of the Nigerian Civil War*, pp. 110–17.
9 P. Anwunah, *The Nigeria–Biafra War: My Memoirs* (Ibadan: Spectrum Books Limited, 2007), p. 201.
10 Stremlau, *The International Politics of the Nigerian Civil War*, pp. 131–9.
11 Archives of the United Nations (hereafter AUN), S-0884-0013-18, R. Bunch, note, 22 June 1967.
12 Wiseberg, "The International Politics of Relief", p. 200.
13 TNA, FCO 65/250, "The Biafra Lobby", June 1969.
14 TNA, FCO 38/203.
15 Stremlau, *The International Politics of the Nigerian Civil War*, p. 123.
16 AWCC, General Secretariat, 42.3.007, letter from Ibiam, 20 November 1967.
17 AWCC, CCIA 1968, letter from E. J. Johnson, 19 January 1968.
18 NLS, Papers of Rev. A. G. Somerville, file 5, letter from Somerville, 1 December 1967.
19 AWCC, General Secretariat, 42.3.007, memorandum by E. C. Blake, 31 January 1968.
20 AWCC, General Secretariat, 42.3.007, memorandum by K. Grubb, 15 December 1967.
21 Stremlau, *The International Politics of the Nigerian Civil War*, pp. 117–23.
22 L. S. Wiseberg, "Christian Churches and the Nigerian Civil War", *Journal of African Studies*, 22 (1975), 297–331, at 315.
23 Stremlau, *The International Politics of the Nigerian Civil War*, pp. 127–41; E. M'Bokolo, *Médiations africaines: Omar Bongo et les défis diplomatiques d'un continent* (Paris: Archipel, 2009), pp. 92–102.
24 TNA, FCO 65/445, memorandum by A. D. Brighty, 20 May 1969.
25 Cf. J. Calmettes, *Histoires secrètes du Biafra. Foccart s'en va-t-en guerre* (France 3, 2001), 54'.

26 French National Archives (hereafter FNA), 5 AG FPU/686, from V. Balési to J. Foccart, 12 and 15 September 1969.
27 TNA, FCO 65/447, message from Peck to D. Hunt, 26 February 1969.
28 Wiseberg, "The International Politics of Relief", pp. 102–5.
29 NLS, Papers of Rev. A. G. Somerville, file 5, letter, 3 February 1968.
30 TNA, FCO 38/307, telegram from the CO to the BHC in Lagos, 14 July 1968.
31 TNA, FCO 65/186.
32 Archives of the Congrégation du Saint-Esprit, Chevilly-Larue (hereafter ACSE), 11I1.12b1.1, letter from R. Kennedy to Dinan, 14 December 1967.
33 Wiseberg, "The International Politics of Relief", pp. 181–98.
34 ACSE, 11I1.12a3.2, letter from D. Byrne to D. O'Sullivan, 19 February 1968.
35 NLS, Papers of Rev. A. G. Somerville, file 5, letter, 16 February 1968.
36 K. Waters, "Influencing the Message: The Role of Catholic Missionaries in Media Coverage of the Nigerian Civil War", *The Catholic Historical Review*, 90:4 (2004), 697–718, at 702–5.
37 Stremlau, *The International Politics of the Nigerian Civil War*, p. 119.
38 Wiseberg, "The International Politics of Relief", p. 578.
39 I. Tyrrell, *Reforming the World: The Creation of America's Moral Empire* (Princeton: Princeton University Press, 2010).
40 B. Taithe, "La famine de 1866–1868: Anatomie d'une catastrophe et construction médiatique d'un événement", *Revue d'histoire du XIXe siècle*, 41:2 (2010), 113–27. For another example: G. Mailer, "The Origins of Humanitarian Intervention in Sudan: Anglo-American Missionaries after 1899", in B. Simms & D. J. B. Trim (eds), *Humanitarian Intervention: A History* (Cambridge: Cambridge University Press, 2011), pp. 283–99.
41 FNA, 5 AG FPU/346, telegram from the French Embassy in Lagos (Barbey) to the Ministry of Foreign Affairs (hereafter MAE), 18 April 1968.
42 ACSE, 11I1.12b1.1, letter from Kennedy to D. O'Sullivan, 14 December 1967.
43 Waters, "Influencing the Message", p. 702.
44 ACSE, 11I1.12b1.1, note about the journalists' visit organised by R. Kennedy, 30 January 1968.
45 ACSE, 11I1.12a4.1, Spiritan's account of the visit by Western journalists initiated by R. Kennedy in January 1968.
46 ACSE, 11I1.12b1.1, note about the journalists' visit organised by R. Kennedy, 30 January 1968.
47 ACSE, 11I1.12b1.1, letter from M. T. Mbu to R. Kennedy, 31 January 1968.
48 Waters, "Influencing the Message", p. 703.
49 ACSE, 11I1.12a4.1, Spiritan's account of the visit by Western journalists initiated by R. Kennedy in January 1968.
50 Waters, "Influencing the Message", pp. 701–4.
51 See M. Récamier, "Le Biafra sous les bombes", in Centre d'études et de documentation sur l'Afrique et l'outre-mer, *Nigeria: le problème du Biafra* (Paris: La Documentation française, 1970), p. 37; and O. Weber, *French Doctors: les 25 ans d'épopée des hommes et des femmes qui ont inventé la médecine humanitaire* (Paris: R. Laffont, 1995), pp. 37–8.

52 J. Buhler, *Tuez-les tous! Guerre de sécession au Biafra* (Paris: Flammarion, 1968), p. 41.
53 Buhler, *Tuez-les tous!*, p. 222.
54 For other examples: F. de Bonneville & G. Caron, *La mort du Biafra* (Paris: Éditions Solar, 1968); F. Debré, *Biafra, an II* (Paris: Julliard, 1968); Forsyth, *The Biafra Story*.
55 Buhler, *Tuez-les tous!*, p. 80.
56 R. Depardon, "Photographie sinon ils ne vont pas nous croire! …", *Le Monde diplomatique*, 1 November 1998.
57 Brauman & Backmann, *Les médias et l'humanitaire*, pp. 89–92.
58 More precisely on their activities: Omaka, *The Biafran Humanitarian Crisis, 1967–1970*, pp. 91–121.
59 Hentsch, *Face au blocus*, pp. 82–90.
60 Wiseberg, "The International Politics of Relief", p. 203.
61 Wiseberg, "The International Politics of Relief", p. 157.
62 AICRC, B AG 202.147-008.01, telex from K. H. Jaggi, 19 September 1968.
63 AICRC, 2000.038.0003, "Contrat d'engagement, personnel bénévole".
64 AICRC, B RH 1991.000.258, Convention between the CICR and Marko Flaks, 6 September 1968.
65 AICRC, B AG 062-129.02.
66 AICRC, B AG 62-133, note pour l'équipe cinéma, 1 April 1969,
67 V. Gorin, "150 ans de regard sur l'humanitaire: les archives photographiques du CICR", *Revue internationale de la Croix-Rouge*, 94:4, sélection française (2012), 159–89.
68 AICRC, B AG 062.129.01-03, Directorate briefing note, 9 April 1969.
69 AICRC, plenary session of the Committee, 6 November 1969.
70 JCA press release 1, 2, 3, 4.
71 N. I. Omenka, "Blaming the Gods: Christian Religious Propaganda in the Nigeria–Biafra War", *The Journal of African History*, 51:3 (2010), 367–89.
72 ACSE, 11I1.12b1.1, letter from R. Kennedy to Fr Dinan, 14 December 1967.
73 Omenka, "Blaming the Gods".
74 Y. Lavoinne, "Médecins en guerre: du témoignage au "tapage médiatique" (1968–1970)", *Le Temps des Médias*, 4:1 (2005), 114–26.
75 See Chapter 7.
76 R. Faligot & J. Guisnel, *Histoire secrète de la cinquième république* (Paris: La Découverte, 2006); M. Robert & A. Renault, *Maurice Robert "Ministre" de l'Afrique* (Paris: Seuil, 2004), pp. 178–87.
77 Jung, "L'image télévisuelle comme arme de guerre", p. 56.
78 J. Foccart, *Journal de l'Elysée, t. 2: 1968–1969: le Général en mai* (Paris: Fayard, 1998), p. 314.
79 FNA, 5 AG FPU/689, telegram from the MAE to the French Embassy of Libreville, 28 February 1969 and 4 March 1969.
80 Archives of the French Minister of Foreign Affairs (hereafter AMAE), Nantes, Papers of the French Embassy in Libreville, box 100, letter from Terre des Hommes to the French Embassy in Libreville, 7 November 1968.

81 J.-N. Jeanneney, *Une histoire des médias, des origines à nos jours* (Paris: Seuil, 1996), pp. 283–7.
82 FNA, 5 AG FPU/689, note from V. Balési to J. Foccart, 4 March 1969.
83 FNA, 5 AG FPU/689, note for J. Foccart, 6 February 1969.
84 FNA, 5 AG FPU/689, note from V. Balési to J. Foccart, 4 March 1969.
85 FNA, 5 AG FPU/689, note for J. Foccart, 6 February 1969.
86 Archives of the French Red Cross (hereafter AFRC), INT 23 Biafra 01/16, memento for the General Glain, "Biafra" VI, Summer 1968.
87 FNA, 5 AG FPU/689, note for J. Foccart, 12 February 1969.
88 On British policy: R. Lewis, "Britain and Biafra", *The Round Table*, 60:239 (1970), 241–8; D. Hunt, "Diplomatic Aspects of the Nigerian Civil War", *Diplomacy and Statecraft*, 3:1 (1992), 5–22; K. E. Smith, "The UK and "Genocide" in Biafra", *Journal of Genocide Research*, 16:2–3 (2014), 247–62; S. Cronjé, *The World and Nigeria: The Diplomatic History of the Biafran War 1967–1970* (London: Sidgwick and Jackson, 1972); Stremlau, *The International Politics of the Nigerian Civil War*; Gould, *The Struggle for Modern Nigeria*; Heerten, *The Biafran War and Postcolonial Humanitarianism*.
89 A. Waugh & S. Cronjé, *Biafra: Britain's Shame* (London: Michael Joseph, 1969).
90 TNA, FCO, 38/313, note by Anderson, 8 March 1968. See also Chapter 3.
91 TNA, FCO 65/446.
92 Jeanneney, *Une histoire des médias*, pp. 277–81.
93 TNA, FCO 65/447.
94 TNA, PREM 13/2827, letter from the FCO to the10 Downing Street (A. M. Palliser), 24 February 1969.

3

Mobilising emotions

Media coverage of the Biafran conflict generated strong emotions in Western societies. This phenomenon of "collective and international emotional reaction"[1] is not specific to this period and comes in various guises. In the case of "humanitarian" crises or when "atrocities" are committed the prevailing emotions are those of compassion sometimes mixed with indignation.[2] For example, in the nineteenth century the Greek War of Independence and the massacres that occurred in the Ottoman Empire, and then in the twentieth century the 1921 famine in Russia gave rise to collective waves of emotion and led to the mobilisation of civil society and even governments which, depending on their different interests, could decide to intervene diplomatically, militarily or by setting up relief operations for populations in danger.

These processes raise questions about the role played by emotions in collective mobilisations,[3] in politics and in international relations. In the history of these emotions the Biafran case and more generally the late 1960s represent an interesting moment for several reasons. According to Robert Frank the representations of the Biafran and Vietnam wars meant that "for the first time in the West compassion for the 'other' ... is an act of identification not with a 'close other' but with an 'other' outside the Western sphere, indeed with an 'other' on the other side, radically other, a universal and already globalised 'other' ".[4] Furthermore, the media played a particularly important role in generating emotions. From the late nineteenth century onwards the development of the written press together with the first photographs taken on the ground were vehicles for the events that gave rise to collective emotions. The success of photojournalism and the advent of television, which broadcast often shocking images to a large section of the population, amplified the phenomenon in the 1960s at a time when the public had not yet had been saturated with these types of images and the latter were not met with indifference.

Having shown in Chapters 1 and 2 what the humanitarian issues were on the ground and then examined the actors involved in their dissemination in the Western media, the aim of this chapter is to understand the emotions generated among the public. I first look at the various representations of the conflict in order to grasp how the "other" became an object of compassion. Then I examine the different manifestations of a wave of emotion that went beyond the civil-society groups traditionally active in such crises. Finally, I focus on the effects of this mobilisation on government policies. By looking at the British and American cases I shed light on the way in which leaders understood these emotion and took it into account when formulating their policies.

Affective representations of the past

The more or less explicit parallel drawn between the plight of the Biafran population and the genocide of the European Jews is one of the keys to understanding the construction of a pro-Biafran public opinion in Western societies. This parallel was made by both the Biafrans and the Westerners, who used this comparison to render what they saw and experienced on the ground more intelligible. Several elements were enlisted to present the Igbo as the "Jews of Africa". The first point of comparison was the alleged Jewish ancestry of the Igbo population. This idea was part of the myth of the lost tribes of Israel which were said to lie at the origin of certain African population groups.[5] The story of the Jewish origins of the Igbo goes back to the late eighteenth century and is believed to have been developed around the figure of a freed slave, Olaudah Equiano. Similarities between the Jewish and Igbo cultures were also said to be observed by Western missionaries, leading to this hypothesis. Without subscribing to this thesis, the historian Adiele Afigbo points out that this belief became particularly widespread among the Igbo elite during the colonial period thanks to missionary education and the dissemination of the Hamitic theory.[6] This topic can still be found in certain Igbo nationalist discourses to this day.

In the late 1960s this striking origin theory was coupled with other elements of comparison with the Jewish population. These were particularly based on cultural and social stereotypes, as shown for example by this article published in the *Le Nouvel Observateur* magazine, entitled "Les Juifs de l'Afrique" (The Jews of Africa):

> Already during British rule the Ibos, who like to call themselves "the Jews of Africa", were far more advanced than the Hausa or the Yoruba. This intelligent, active people had the best craftsmen and most skilled traders in the country, and the British administration employed many Ibos in its services.[7]

The parallel with the Jewish population allows us to introduce a fundamental component of Biafran propaganda and the way in which the conflict was perceived in Europe: the issue of modernity. As Douglas Anthony has shown, modernity was a recurrent element of the Biafran rhetoric which emphasised the high degree of "civilisation" of the population compared to northern Nigeria, whose inhabitants were described as "barbarians".[8] This narrative was further reinforced by the use of the term genocide which implied the barbarity of those who perpetrated it. Observers on the ground echoed this rhetoric about the modernity of the Biafran people. They repeatedly pointed to what they perceived to be a particularly high level of organisation, development and education of the Igbo, who were seen by some as the most "Western" of the African populations. This process is fundamental to understanding the emotions stirred by the suffering of the Biafran people in the West. As Luc Boltanski explains, a certain degree of closeness needs to be established between the viewer and the victim so that the former may feel concerned by the plight of the latter, without which

> happy and unhappy people can live on the same earth without the former seeing the latter either because of a sort of physical blindness … or because of a moral blindness, the difference in conditions creating a gap that prevents the class of "those who do not suffer" from developing a representation of the suffering of those who are unhappy.[9]

The emphasis on the "modernity" and "civilised character" of the Biafrans helped reduce this "difference in conditions" and establish a certain degree of closeness to the plight of the Igbo. In this respect, stereotypes naturally played an important role in creating this closeness:

> It is true that the Ibos willingly crossed the Niger to settle by their thousands in the West and North where, thanks to their undeniable intelligence and highly developed sense of commerce which make them Africa's Jews, they took up key positions in the federal administration, commerce, education, and the army. But this superiority, this willingness to work would make them aggressive, even dominant. They would end up being hated and persecuted. Just like the Jews, once again …[10]

The third element of comparison between the Jews and the Igbo was their victim status. In an article published in September 1967 an anonymous author explicitly compared the situation of the Jews, victims first of Hitler and then of Muslims in the Middle East, with the plight of the Biafrans in Nigeria.[11] This parallel could also be seen in the vocabulary employed. The brutal events of 1966 were described as pogroms, a term which, before it was used to refer to massacres of minorities, explicitly referred to the acts of violence committed against Jewish populations. The word genocide, although used in the 1960s to describe different situations,[12] ultimately referred to the plight of these populations during the Second World War. Ojukwu himself did not hesitate to make direct use of this comparison.[13]

Figure 3.1 Badge sent to the WCC by the International Witnesses Against Genocide Association, 1968 (Archives of the WCC)

The reference could also be visual as in the case of a Harvard University student association which drew parallels between the Armenian, Jewish and Biafran genocides, and in the summer of 1968 suggested that a badge reminiscent of the yellow star should be worn and distributed to draw attention to the plight of the Igbo (Figure 3.1).[14]

This comparison resonated particularly in the West, where some explicitly referred to the Jewish genocide to justify their involvement in providing aid to Biafra. Bernard Kouchner, for example, explained the importance of the memory of the Shoah in his engagement. The American Jewish Committee, an American Jewish relief organisation which was for the first time involved in aiding non-Jewish populations by helping to fund humanitarian operations in Biafra, also referred to the Shoah to justify its action. In Israel there were strong reactions especially because of the way the Biafrans were portrayed as victims, the status of "absolute victim" having until then been reserved for the Jewish people.[15]

Furthermore, the Biafran conflict came at a time when the memory of the Jewish genocide was changing. The 1960s marked the beginning of a turning point that began with the Eichmann trial.[16] There was a gradual shift from a stance of "guilty of not having fought" to one of victimhood[17] in which "there is no shame, either collective or individual, in having been a victim of the Holocaust".[18] These two images co-existed when the comparison with the Biafrans began to be made. The figure of the victim was the most frequently enlisted but some also recalled the criticism of the Jewish population for not having put up organised resistance to their persecutors under the Third Reich. President Julius Nyerere, for example, alluded to this in the speech he gave to justify the Biafrans' struggle and Tanzania's recognition of their independence.[19]

Finally, the perceived similarities between Biafrans and Jews invited a more general comparison with the atrocities committed during the Second World War. Journalists who went there and reported their impressions used language that explicitly evoked them. For example, on his return from a trip to Biafra, François Debré wrote:

> This summer public opinion, alerted by a vast press campaign, discovered with horror sights that had been forgotten since the Nazi concentration camps. … Here the term "death camps" regains its meaning, everywhere around the towns still held by the Biafran troops, around the villages that have not been abandoned, in churches, hospitals, and missions where tens, hundreds of thousands of refugees who have been wandering in the bush, fleeing the advance of the Hausa soldiers, are gathered.[20]

Photographs in particular seemed to give rise to this parallel. As Lasse Herten has shown, some of the images from Biafra were reminiscent of the Allied liberation of the camps in 1945.[21] These more universal references made it possible to move away from the exclusive comparison between Jews and Biafrans and extend it to the victims of Nazism in general. They were able to reach a wider range of audience as shown by this appeal launched in August 1968 by a section of the Union Nationale des Déportés, Internés et Victimes de Guerre (National Union of Deportees, Internees and War Victims):

> The atrocity in the pictures shown on television on Friday 2 August, reporting the ravages of hunger in Biafra, reminded us so much of the memories experienced in the Nazi extermination camps 24 years ago that today we take the liberty to implore our fellow citizens to respond to the French Red Cross appeal.[22]

The Jewish genocide was not the only historical event with which connections were made. On the Irish national scene the Biafran crisis was reminiscent of the Irish famine experienced in the mid-nineteenth century.[23] The conflict caused a great deal of mobilisation in the country due to the presence of many Irish missionaries who did not hesitate to establish a direct link between the plight of the Biafrans and that of the Irish a century earlier. The summoning of the popular memory of the famine managed to persuade the Irish population to provide aid.[24] The parallel was made all the more effective by the fact that in both cases the designated culprit was Great Britain, which, after having allowed the Irish to die, was once again responsible for the plight of the Biafrans because of its support for the Nigerian government.

Generally speaking, the presentation of the conflict from the perspective of the famine was particularly effective since it called for a response that did not require any political or ideological affinity with the Biafran cause, but rather relied on the feeling of compassion that representations of hunger victims gave rise to in the richest societies. This reaction was the result of a long evolution of the way in which they were perceived. For James Vernon, from the mid-nineteenth century onwards malnutrition and famines were no longer seen as the responsibility of those who experienced them. Whilst it had long been believed that the wealthier sections of societies were required to provide relief to the poorer ones when food was scarce,[25] during this period this scourge acquired the status of a collective social problem and thus became relevant to the health, wealth and security of societies as a whole. In this process of "humanising hunger" the victims aroused compassion and gradually appeared worthy of the attention of, at first, national governments and then of international bodies which were created in the twentieth century to deal collectively with the problem of hunger.[26]

The representation of conflict-induced famine during the Biafran crisis is therefore an essential element in understanding the primarily humanitarian responses to it. Although in most cases famines have political causes,[27] these are usually not very intelligible. The phenomenon can then be treated as a natural disaster, which further accentuates the innocence of the victims. In the iconography of the conflict the place occupied by children, the figures most likely to arouse pity in a distant spectator, reinforced this tendency and further encouraged the rush to provide relief to Biafra (Figure 3.2).

In the summer of 1968 a qualitative change accompanied the quantitative change in Biafra's visibility in Western media. Children now occupied a prominent place in representations of the conflict. This development could be seen, for example, in the work of the photographer Gilles Caron, whose images of the conflict were widely circulated by the Gamma agency, one of the most important photographic agencies of the time. Gilles Caron made three trips to Biafra from which he brought back several reports that were published in various magazines – notably *Paris Match* and *Jeune Afrique* – as well as in a small book entitled *La mort du Biafra* (The death of Biafra).[28] He made his first trip from 6 to 22 April 1968 together with his colleague Floris de Bonneville. Their aim was to repatriate the body of their colleague Marc Auerbach, who had died in Biafra a few months earlier. Caron was also joined by the British photographer Don McCullin, who worked for *The*

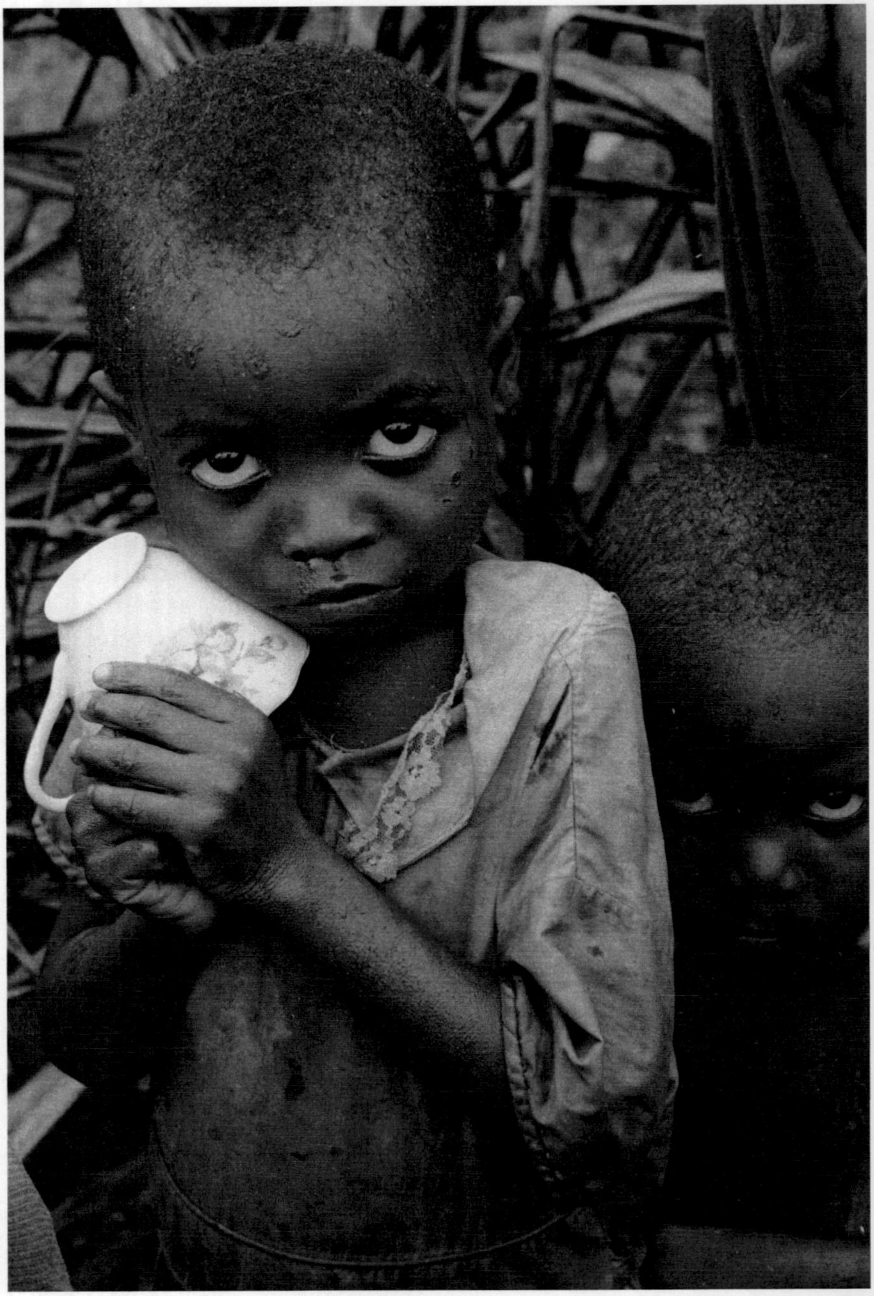

Figure 3.2 Nto-Edino, sick-bay, V-P-NG-N-00030-31 (© ICRC / H. D. Finck, September 1968)

Sunday Times Magazine. During this first visit Gilles Caron shot thirty-three rolls, and some of the pictures were reproduced in *Paris Match* in early May 1968.[29] The subjects of the photographs were particularly varied and, on the whole, reflected life in the province at war. The military aspects were central, with many of the shots focusing on soldiers training. Civilians were also photographed and images of children, some of whom were already showing signs of malnutrition, could be found on Caron's contact sheets.[30] These pictures were not those chosen for publication in *Paris Match* on 4 May 1968, as the focus was still on the fighting spirit and determination of the Biafran people rather than their suffering. These photographs, which were among the first shots of Biafra to be shown in France, received relatively little attention. The dramatic events of May 1968 explain this lack of interest but the way in which the conflict was presented in this first report may also have had something to do with it. Between May and July 1968 there was a shift in topics which could be seen in the *Paris Match* issues covering Biafra. Thus, in its 20 July and 10 August 1968 issues the magazine published fewer photographs of combatants and this time chose images of children.[31]

This shift also occurred in Caron's work as attested by the pictures he brought back from his second trip to Biafra from 18 July to 1 August 1968. Gilles Caron was accompanied by Raymond Depardon, who shot films for the Gamma agency. Images of soldiers or the head of state still figured prominently in the thirty-seven rolls Caron shot, but those of small coffins, which suggested the death of children, were increasingly frequent, being followed by burial scenes. Small, emaciated bodies also featured to a considerable extent. Alongside their prominent place, particular attention was paid to how they were presented, emphasising their tragic character. A photograph on Caron's contact sheets which comes before a shot of Depardon filming an emaciated child provides an enlightening example.[32] It shows that, at first, the child filmed by Depardon was not alone but close to a woman (Figure 3.3). The woman then seems to have been moved away from the child so that Depardon could focus on the child's small and emaciated body, alone, on the ground (Figure 3.4).

More generally, children were both singled out and photographed in large numbers, evoking both specific and universal suffering. As Luc Boltanski explains, "for each of the unfortunate ones summoned there is a pressing crowd of substitutes. The sufferings made manifest and touching by the accumulation of details also need to be able to merge into a unified representation. Though singular, they are no less exemplary".[33] This analysis is particularly relevant to pictures of Biafrans, in which the focus was often on the face or body of a single child, but also showed that several children shared the same distress (Figure 3.5).

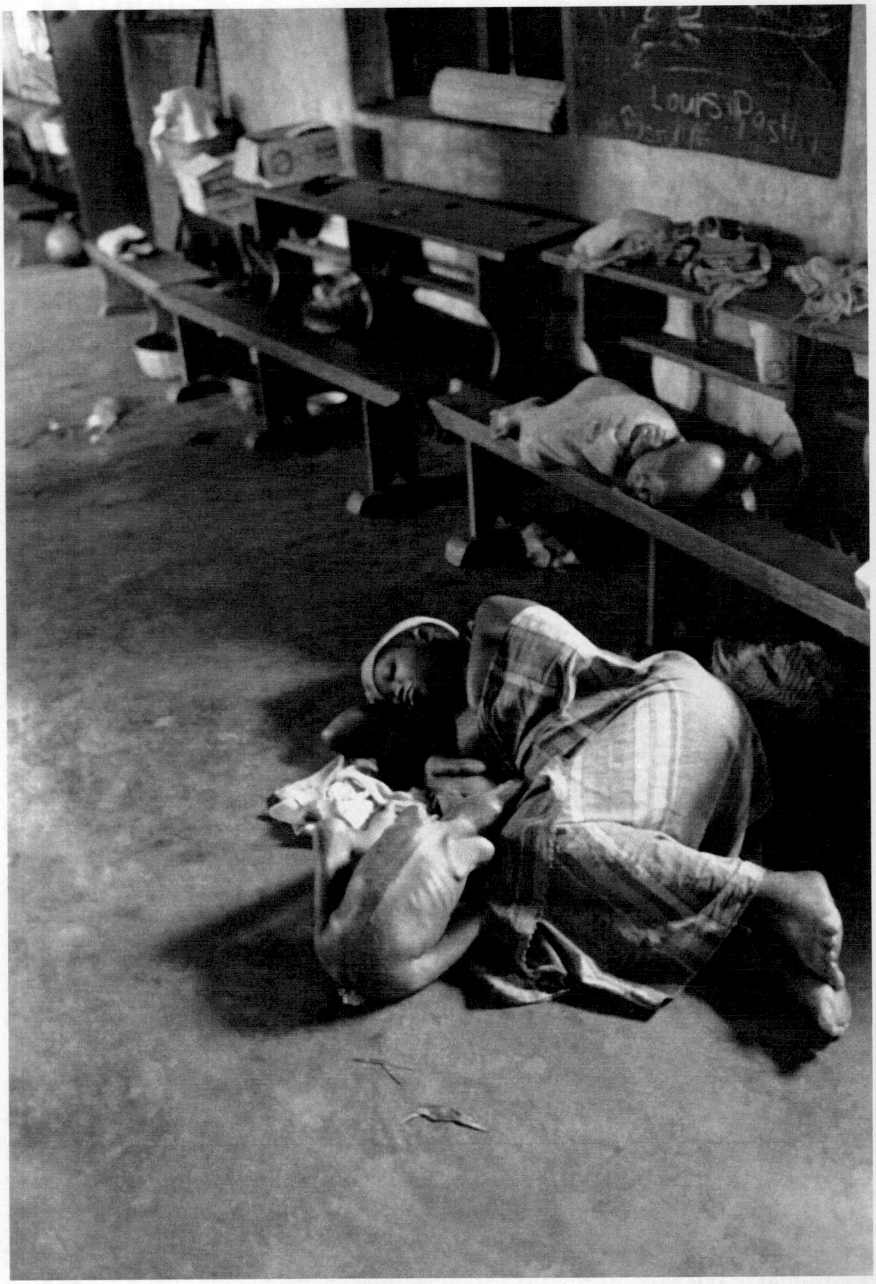

Figure 3.3 Biafra, 1968: hungry woman and children lying in a room (© Donation Gilles Caron, Ministère de la Culture (France), Médiathèque du patrimoine et de la photographie)

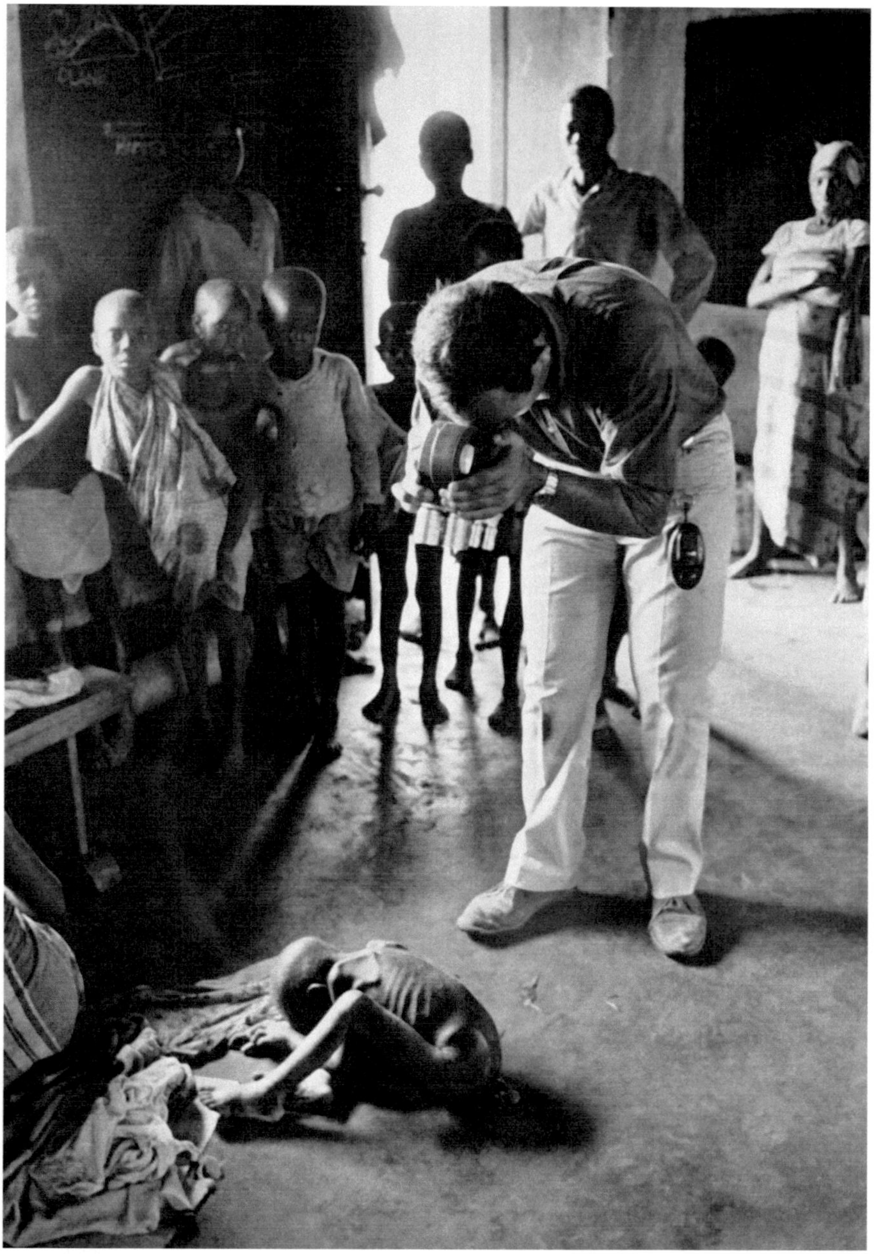

Figure 3.4 Biafra, 1968: Raymond Depardon filming an extremely weak child (© Donation Gilles Caron, Ministère de la Culture (France), Médiathèque du patrimoine et de la photographie)

Figure 3.5 Feeding centre, Umuosu, V-P-NG-N-00023-32 (© ICRC / H. D. Finck, September–October 1968)

Humanitarian organisations helped disseminate such images by using them to raise funds. Thus, an article published in *France Dimanche* in mid-July 1968, entitled "Dans deux heures cette petite fille sera morte" (In two hours this little girl will be dead) and showing the photograph of an extremely thin girl, sitting alone on the floor under a hospital bed, was followed by an insert asking for donations to the French Red Cross.[34] Similar images were used by humanitarian agencies in their own newsletters. They documented the relief operations carried out in Nigeria–Biafra and highlighted the need for support to continue them. The tight framing and sometimes the absence of a background or the sole presence of the ground accentuated the children's identity as victims (Figure 3.6).[35]

The use of children in campaigns by humanitarian organisations is not specific to Biafra and is part of a tradition that goes back to the First World War when the first relief organisations specifically dedicated to helping children were created, including the International Save the Children Union and Save the Children (SCF). Children are portrayed both as victims who are singled out in order to elicit compassion and as the objects of humanitarian organisations' attention. More generally, the aim is to "show the humanitarian gesture", which remains one of the key elements of NGO communication.[36]

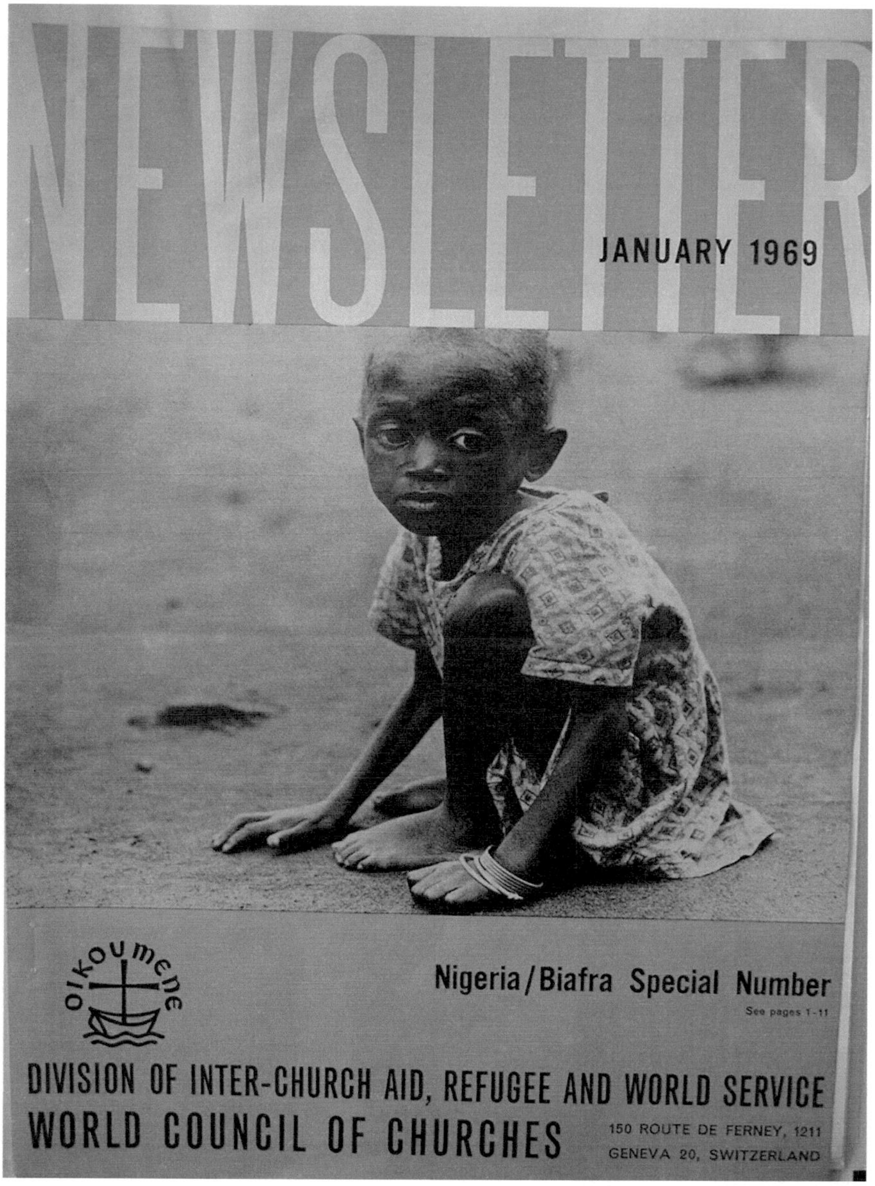

Figure 3.6 Newsletter of DICARWS (Division of Inter-Church Aid, Refugee, and World Service) (© WCC, January 1969)

In Biafra, in the summer of 1968 white humanitarians began to frequently appear alongside children in filmed and photographed images of the war. For example, in the reports on Biafra broadcast by Télévision Suisse Romande the concerns and testimonies of Western volunteers occupied a central place. The same was true of French television, where the representation of the conflict was inseparable from the relief effort.[37] Their presence took on a particular meaning because of the postcolonial context in which the operations unfolded and was reminiscent of the way in which Africa had been represented during the colonial period. The continent and territories under European rule in general had been depicted as the terrain of the white man's "civilising mission". As Catherine Coquery-Vidrovitch writes: "Health, educational, or moral and religious actions were the pillars of this comprehensive work which was widely exalted in all the publications dealing with the colonies, missionary magazines, postcards, and school textbooks".[38] In them, Westerners had generally been portrayed as indispensable in bringing "civilisation" to these regions. These representations had not been limited to the French case but had also had an impact on the collective imagination in the United Kingdom,[39] as well as in states that did not directly have colonial territories.[40] Some of the pictures taken during the Biafran conflict in which white humanitarians were at the centre of organising the distribution of food, medicines and medical activities were reminiscent of this type of representation. This was, for example, the case with the photograph in Figure 3.7, which was used for the cover of the French Red Cross magazine in October 1968.[41]

These images bear similarities to colonial representations, particularly with regard to Westerners' protective, and possibly paternalistic, attitude towards "little Africans". They testify to the fact that the humanitarian movement was part of the tradition of colonial and missionary medicine on the African continent. At the time of the Biafran crisis the link with the activities of the missionaries was all the more visible since the latter played a central role in setting up relief operations. Having been present in Biafra when journalists first began sending their reports, they were the first Westerners to appear in the pictures taken. Despite their attire, their identity as religious men was relegated to the background and they were seen as those who "brought civilisation" or, in the case of Biafra, "helped" and "enabled the survival" of a population in distress, especially children, which was reminiscent of the missionary propaganda of the colonial period. In an analysis of the White Fathers in the first half of the twentieth century, Anne Hugon underlines the importance of the figure of the child in photographs that illustrated the activities of congregations. She also shows how the Christianisation of the local populations was synonymous with the "civilising mission", which made it possible to rally the consensus of the entire

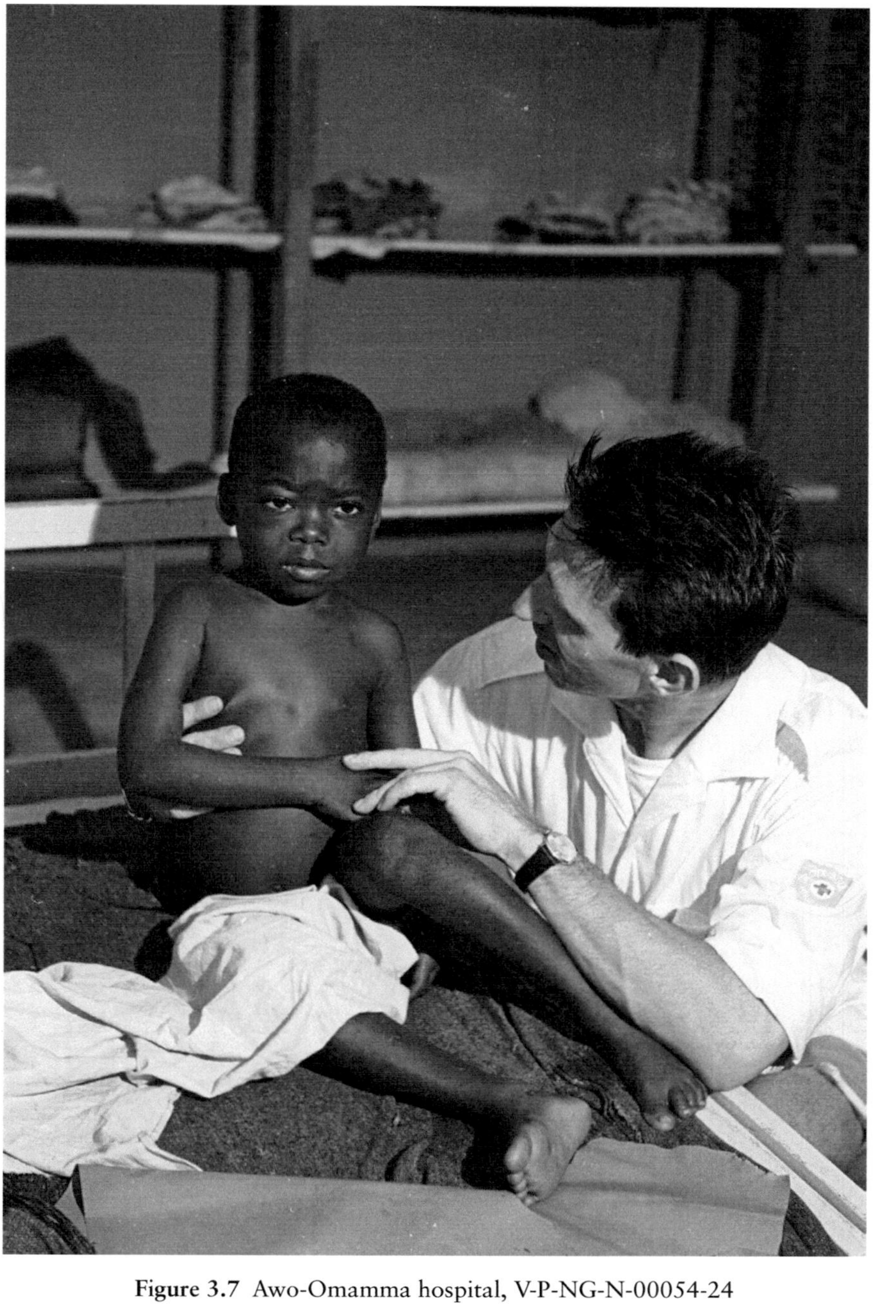

Figure 3.7 Awo-Omamma hospital, V-P-NG-N-00054-24 (© ICRC / Max Vaterlaus)

civil society, even the most anticlerical sections, to the missionary work.[42] In Biafra things were fundamentally no different, and the proselytising that some missionaries might engage in when running their relief operations was barely challenged.

While the presence of Westerners evoked continuities with the colonial period, these were all the more remarkable since they were juxtaposed with representations of the African continent that had actually changed with the wave of independence. As Gilles Manceron and Jean-Barthélemi Debost note:

> While representations of the colonies had long conveyed the image of a peaceful, idealised Africa where poverty and war did not seem to exist, beginning with the mid-1950s and the decolonisation movements Europe started to focus on much more frightening representations in which the peaceful and serene aspect was replaced by images of unrest and war.[43]

This evolution could also be seen in the different media used to depict the continent. In the case of colonial propaganda posters, for example, the choice of images, often drawn in bright colours, was not insignificant and served to highlight the Western action.[44] The drawings then gradually disappeared to be replaced by photographs, which probably helped disseminate a more frightening type of images of Africa. Those of Biafra confirm this shift since, in the photographs taken of children in particular, the tight framing of their faces or small bodies, a background that was difficult to distinguish, or the use of black and white helped provide a miserabilist representation of the continent.

Overall, the reconfiguration taking place between the representation of the colonial "civilising mission" and the postcolonial humanitarian mission mobilised stereotypes about "Africans" that persisted in the nineteenth and twentieth centuries:

> The Africans' apparently obvious inferiority, their technological backwardness, and the burden of nature that seemed to weigh on their minds gave rise to the seemingly self-evident belief that civilisation belonged to the Western white man, while the Africans lived "in the heart of darkness" materially, religiously, and mentally. It was therefore necessary to save them, civilise them, in other words colonise them in order to fulfil the "colonial duty", the "white man's burden", bringing light to the dark continent … Decolonisation clearly did not fundamentally transform this vision of a continent populated by inferiorised human beings. The primitive savage who had to be rescued from his deplorable condition was in fact "euphemised". There still remained the underdeveloped, those that the West must help to escape famines, wars, and genocides of all sorts, and at the very least support so that they would not slip into an atechnical, "developing" economy, that is, one that was not yet developed. The Western superiority complex was still very much present, the Africans

being first and foremost objects of humanitarianism, of interference turned into duty to save the African man from his own demons.[45]

By mixing images of emaciated children with warriors ready to fight, within the context of a symbolic frame of reference developed during the colonial period, the representations of the Biafran conflict portrayed the Western presence as necessary to save a continent in the grip of war and famine by means of humanitarian intervention.

An impactful but short-lived sentiment

For Robert Frank the internationalised emotion aroused by the Bulgarian crisis in the late nineteenth century can also be explained by the response of the press which was starting to become a mass medium. Subsequently the development of photography and more specifically press photography in the 1930s took the audience directly to the heart of the fighting.[46] Then, from the 1950s–1960s onwards television took over, ensuring a wide dissemination of conflicts as, by the end of the 1960s, it was present in 62 per cent of French households and 98 per cent of American households. These vectors help explain the emotion aroused by Biafra, which was presented as the first "televised famine", images of which were shown particularly during news and current-affairs programmes. Illustrated magazines with a circulation of millions published the photographs taken by photojournalists and played an equally crucial role. Indeed, the dissemination of still images, perhaps more memorable than moving images,[47] continued to have an important impact on the public. Thus, with the development of mass media the contemplation of suffering from a distance took on a new dimension which had the potential to deeply move wider sections of society.

In 1968 images of the Biafran crisis touched a large part of the population and not just members of humanitarian organisations, missionary communities or individuals with a special interest in the region. The thousand or so letters kept in the archives of the French Red Cross, for example, testify to the diversity of the people affected. Their authors came from different socio-professional backgrounds, all age groups were represented, and both men and women were involved. These letters usually came with cash donations, ranging from the small savings of a pensioner or a child to collections run by works councils, schools or associations. There were also many offers to volunteer in Biafra. Furthermore, the diversity and spontaneity of the donations and offers received were highlighted by Red Cross leaders in order to encourage the population to react further to its appeals.[48] The mobilisation of the Catholic and Protestant churches also helped spread concern for Biafra to large sections of society through religious services or Christian youth organisations such as chaplaincies where, for example, fundraising activities (collections, windscreen washing etc.) were organised.

The wide dissemination of images of the Biafran famine helped construct a collective imagination that closely associated Africa with famine. This association was reinforced in the following decades by representations of food crises in the Sahel and Horn of Africa for which mobilisation was even more significant and visible, as shown by the Live Aid concert organised to raise funds for the Ethiopian famine in 1985. Before it was gradually replaced by the Sahel, Ethiopia and then Somalia in the 1990s, Biafra became established in the collective memory as the symbol of hunger in Africa. In France, for example, several films referred to it at different times in order to briefly evoke a place where food was scarce. In the United States, Jello Biafra is the pseudonym of a 1990s punk rock singer who associated the Jell-O brand of gelatine with the famine in Biafra. In France, food-related phrases became widespread and jokes were made about "skinny Biafrans". Many parents reminded their youngest children of the plight of the Biafrans to encourage them to finish their plates. As Alain Destexhe sums it up:

> Biafra made a lasting impression on Western public opinion and became a symbol of famine and emaciated children. Thousands of French children who refused to eat their soup would be told: "Think of the little Biafrans". Perhaps they wanted to get their own back when they came up with many jokes of dubious taste … "What does a Biafran do when he finds a grain of rice? He opens a supermarket". Or, "What is a watch used as? A belt for a fat Biafran". It wasn't until the 1985 famine in Ethiopia that similar emotions re-emerged and the exact same jokes resurfaced in secondary schools.[49]

An exhaustive analysis of the reactions generated by the media coverage of the Biafran crisis would be beyond the scope of this chapter.[50] However, using a few examples of mobilisation in Europe and the United States, the aim is to try to understand how the responses to a "humanitarian crisis" in a country of the South were shaped, something which has in fact occasionally resurfaced on the Western media scene since the 1960s.

Correspondence kept in the archives of the French Red Cross confirms the importance of images in mobilising those ready to give their time or money to humanitarian operations in Biafra. People who decided to respond to Red Cross appeals usually did so after a radio or television programme was broadcast, or a particularly striking photograph appeared in a newspaper. Indeed, the letters often referred to reports seen on TV news programmes and to photographs that accompanied appeals run by humanitarian organisations in the written press or illustrated magazines such as *Paris Match*.[51]

A similar process could also be observed at the ICRC. Some delegates said they wanted to go to Biafra because of what they had seen in the media. While media coverage did lead to many individuals becoming involved in providing relief to Biafra, it did not seem to generate sufficient public support for its independence. Is it then possible to establish a correlation between the way in which the conflict was presented in the media and the type of reaction it generated among audiences? For Boltanski different ways of showing suffering lead to different types of engagement among audiences. It is thus possible to distinguish between political engagement in support of victims which does not hesitate to denounce the culprits, and engagement in aid of victims by means of relief activities. The choice of one or the other would depend particularly on how victims are portrayed. Explicit or implicit references to "oppressors" seem more likely to encourage audiences to denounce them and support the cause of the victims; whereas more apolitical representations of the conflict focusing mainly on the "sufferers" and their "benefactors" seem to lead audiences to support the activities of the latter out of a desire to alleviate the suffering of the victims, without really taking an interest in those responsible for the situation.[52]

Although this theory has been criticised, it does offer keys to understanding the mobilisation of Western public opinion. The latter oscillated between simple support for relief operations and engagement in support of the Biafran cause. In France associations set up during the crisis and identified as such by the government fell into two distinct categories: on the one hand, political groups campaigning for Biafran independence, and on the other hand, relief organisations.[53] While the desire to help the civilian population seems to have been very widely shared, mobilisation in support of the secession of the province was less widespread[54] and decreased in Europe in the second half of the war. Indeed, the Nigerian government's rhetoric on the non-existence of genocide, as well as Biafran stubbornness in seeking to break away despite the famine weakened support for this political cause.[55] However, these two types of engagement were not mutually exclusive, since a political settlement to the conflict or at least the cessation of hostilities could be seen as a sine qua non for providing adequate aid and preventing genocide.

Mobilisation in support of the relief effort was particularly evident in the volunteers who applied to humanitarian organisations to go to Biafra, as well as in the donations received. The French and American examples seem significant in this respect. In France, during the major fundraising efforts undertaken for the benefit of Biafra, donations were made in the form of relatively small but numerous amounts of money.[56] The three national collections run in August 1968, January 1969 and March 1969 managed to raise 20,645,000 francs from the French people.[57] This money was the main source of funding for the relief operations carried out by the French Red Cross for the benefit of the Biafran population. By comparison, in the period from June 1968 to the end of July 1969 the official state contribution amounted to only 2,225,000 francs. In the United States private donations to the Biafran relief effort were also significant. According to a report by the United States Agency for International Development (USAID), between the summer of 1968 and June 1969 the sum of 11,757,631 dollars was provided by voluntary organisations and private groups, including contributions from individuals.[58] By contrast to the French example, US government aid remained much higher than private donations (65,996,300 dollars in June 1969). Thus, humanitarian aid remained a state affair despite the important role played by money raised from civil society. In the US case in particular, support for relief operations was seen by the administration as a way of responding to public pressure over Biafra, without taking a political stance in the conflict.

The characteristics of the representations of war mentioned above may be seen as factors favouring this type of engagement. Thus, the journalist Jean-Claude Guillebaud establishes a link between what was shown of Biafra and the type of response elicited among the population:

> We journalists had become, unwillingly, a kind of merchants of horrors and our articles were expected to be affecting, rarely to explain. Biafra waited for us to take an interest in its cause and we cautiously dealt only with its suffering. It led to its death.[59]

The lack of political engagement in the media coverage of the conflict was mainly reflected in responses centred around the issue of aid, but there were also other forms of mobilisation. In 1968 several associations were set up in support of Biafra in France, the United States, Great Britain and Switzerland. While some promoted Biafran independence, they all called on governments and the international community to help provide relief to Biafra. They thus frequently called for a cessation of hostilities and criticised Britain's support for the Nigerian government.[60] They often took the lead in building up international concern for Biafra,[61] being made up mainly of individuals who had more or less close ties with eastern Nigeria or the Igbo diaspora. For example, the retired Oxford University Professor Harold G. Hanbury, a prominent member of the Britain Biafra Association, had been the Dean of the Law Faculty of the University of Nigeria in Nsukka during the 1960s.[62] In France the president of the Comité d'action pour le Biafra (Biafra Action Committee), "which with its high-level parliamentary patronage and the most prominent intellectual circles intends to take rigorous political action",[63] was a member of parliament and former diplomat in Nigeria in 1960. Another example is the Comité international de lutte contre le génocide au Biafra (International Committee for the Fight against Genocide in Biafra), which was formed by Bernard Kouchner on his return from the region.

These associations sought to raise awareness of the Biafran cause by means of open letters, petitions and public events (concerts, demonstrations etc.). The resonance of these initiatives in the public arena reached more than just those with a specific interest in Nigeria. In the United States activists, congressmen and senators, both Democrats and Republicans, challenged the American government's policy on the crisis.[64] The presidential candidate Richard Nixon even used the term genocide. In August 1968 2,500 people marched outside the UN headquarters in New York to protest against the passivity of the international community. Several demonstrations took place in London and several Swiss cities in support of Biafran relief.[65] This emotion was also reflected in the positions taken by certain politicians and intellectuals. In Germany[66] and France[67] figures from both the left and the right expressed their concern in public statements. In Britain the government's policy attracted a lot of criticism, both from the Conservative and Labour ranks. Famous figures also expressed their disapproval, including John Lennon, who had been awarded the Order of the British Empire in 1965 but returned it in 1969 in protest against the government's involvement in Nigeria–Biafra and its support for the Americans in Vietnam.

These criticisms extended far beyond the borders of the United Kingdom. In the summer of 1968 British diplomats posted to major European capitals noticed a growing climate of hostility towards their government's policy. Switzerland is a particularly good example of this. In June 1968 the British consulate in Zurich was confronted with a demonstration of around 1,000 secondary-school pupils who came to voice their grievances against British policy. Although the event had been instigated by Aktion pro-Biafra, an organisation with branches in various Swiss cities which sought to promote the Biafran cause and raise donations, British diplomats stressed its spontaneous and determined nature. They saw it as being representative of a broad public opinion which was not limited exclusively to circles close to the Biafrans and was deeply moved by the situation in the breakaway province. This demonstration was soon followed by larger ones in Basel and Bern. Furthermore, diplomats reported being inundated with letters and phone calls protesting against their government's policy. This discontent was also reflected in very concrete actions. Swiss politicians and church delegations travelled to Britain in an attempt to change the British stance in support of Nigeria and, above all, to express Swiss concern about the need to deliver relief supplies to the region. In the late summer of 1968, in the face of increasingly unfavourable opinion, the British were forced to cancel a "British Shopping Week" event which had been due to take place in Basel to promote British products in Switzerland. Indeed, the Swiss organiser of this event resigned in protest and an opposition campaign was started, portraying Britain as being mainly responsible for the situation in Biafra (Figure 3.8).[68]

Figure 3.8 Leaflet opposing British Week (TNA, FCO 38/254)

These demonstrations were, to a lesser extent, reminiscent of the Third World mobilisations denouncing US imperialism in Vietnam and stirring up university and secondary-school circles in the US and Europe in the 1960s. This political engagement criticising British interference remained minor and marginal compared to the scale of mobilisation against the Vietnam War. Nevertheless, it reflected an emotion shared by the population. In a Gallup survey conducted in Europe in the autumn of 1968, 42 per cent of the respondents said they were primarily concerned about Biafra, compared with 17 per cent about Vietnam.[69] This result may seem surprising but it confirms the impact of images of the conflict.

While in the late 1960s political activism was one of the prevalent forms of engagement, as evidenced by the events of May 1968, by avoiding the East–West divide Biafra offered a "humanitarian" mobilisation that did not require belonging to a specific political camp or subscribing to a clearly defined partisan line. Media representations of the conflict, in which the emphasis was placed on the suffering and innocence of the victims while the complexity of the situation was glossed over, encouraged this type of response from civil society. Indeed, many authors note that in the 1970s and 1980s human-rights and humanitarian activism gradually became a real alternative to traditional political engagement, which was in decline[70] after the last illusions about the reality of communist regimes had been shattered: "Identified with ideology and sectarianism, and suspected of being potentially totalitarian, politics was discredited in favour of ethics".[71]

Containing compassion: US and UK governmental responses

While emotions were palpable in the public arena, what were their effects on the policies of the governments most mobilised behind the Nigerian federal military government (FMG) seeking to restore the unity of the country? The British, who openly showed their support for Lagos, were especially affected by the contradiction between public opinion and government policy. The Americans, who had taken the decision to abstain militarily and politically, while delegating to the British the responsibility of preserving Western interests in the region, also had to face a public opinion that wanted them to show more active support for Biafra.

Defining public opinion, understanding how it is constructed and measuring its effects on politics remain a delicate and controversial exercise.[72] As far as humanitarian crises are concerned, the early 1990s saw these issues become more acute and there was much debate about the role of the media in the major powers' decisions to intervene or not in countries torn by conflict.[73] Having looked in Chapter 2 at the ways in which the French and

British governments tried to influence public opinion, this section shows how "public opinion" as perceived by British and American leaders influenced the latter's decisions.

In British government documents relating to the conflict, beginning with the summer of 1968 there were frequent references to public opinion and the pressure it exerted on the executive. It is difficult to know exactly what was meant by this term. It probably included opinions expressed in Parliament, in the media and in civil society where groups opposed to British policy were formed, working for peace or in aid of the victims of the conflict. They could take the form of statements, opinion pieces, books or even demonstrations. In Parliament, opposition to, or at least questioning of, government policy was expressed both by ruling-party and opposition members.[74]

The rise of pro-Biafran opinion in Great Britain began to attract particular attention from the leadership in late June 1968. The extent of this sympathy, which the Cabinet attributed solely to Biafran propaganda, led it to reconsider its policy.[75] From then on, public opinion became a recurring issue in government discussions of the Nigeria–Biafra war, exerting pressure on its decisions. In late August 1968 major demonstrations outside 10 Downing Street accompanied a particularly heated debate on the UK's policy of supporting the FMG:[76] "as the Secretary of State told Chief Enahoro, the scenes in the House of Commons in the closing stages of the debate were quite unprecedented in his whole Parliamentary experience, including Suez".[77] In late 1968 the emotion aroused by the Nigerian problem was still extremely strong, and the executive felt that it was shared by the whole country. It did not rule out the possibility that it could lead to a major political and parliamentary crisis in which the government could either be overthrown or have to change its policy, which would have had significant political but also economic consequences for the UK.[78]

Although the British government felt this pressure strongly, it did not change its attitude to the conflict in any significant way. It did, however, undertake a series of initiatives, ranging from attempts at peace talks to better communication on the soundness of supporting the FMG. This included demonstrating that the aim of this support was not to exterminate the Igbo population but only to maintain the borders of the Nigerian Federation. As highlighted in Chapter 2, the UK government sought to directly influence the way in which the media dealt with the conflict, insisting that journalists present the Nigerian perspective. More generally, it decided to improve the image of British politics and that of the FMG, particularly with regard to humanitarian issues to which the public seemed particularly sensitive. To this end, initiatives were undertaken in the two main areas that contributed to the portrayal of Biafra as a victim on the international stage, namely the famine and the conduct of hostilities by the Nigerian troops.

As early as June 1968, in order to show its concern for the situation, the British government decided to increase its contribution to Nigerian relief operations by allocating £250,000 for humanitarian aid to the war-torn areas. This decision was accompanied by the appointment of a co-ordinator who was to travel to Nigeria and Biafra and advise the government on how to best use the money.[79] The choice of the person responsible for the mission depended on their ability to carry it out but also on the impact that their appointment would have on the public. In other words, London wanted to appoint someone who was both popular and credible. Lord John Hunt was thus chosen because of his links with voluntary organisations, but also because he was somewhat famous for having led a successful expedition on Mount Everest a few years earlier. This appointment was intended to show the public that the FMG was not solely responsible for the difficulties encountered during negotiations with humanitarian organisations, pointing to the negative attitude of the secessionists:

> When I was with you in Lagos you expressed concern about the attitude of the British press, radio and television on matters affecting the rebellion in your country and I made it clear that this concern was something I shared with you. I am glad to say that there are already distinct signs of change in the attitude of the press here which is beginning to contrast your own forthcoming attitude towards the shipment of relief supplies and that of Ojukwu who is seen as using the Hardships of the Ibo people for political purposes. I know you will agree this shift of opinion should continue and be encouraged. I believe that the announcement of Lord Hunt's mission of enquiry will help us both to make progress with the relief of suffering but to place responsibility for any hold up where it properly lies, namely with Ojukwu.[80]

Whilst these decisions did have an impact on the ground, not least by allowing the ICRC to strengthen its operations, London did not hesitate to make suggestions aimed solely at blaming the Biafran camp for the famine. For example, in July 1968 the British government suggested that the Royal Air Force drop relief supplies over the secessionist-controlled area. This statement was in fact a communications exercise, since the British were well aware that such a suggestion would be completely unacceptable to Ojukwu.[81]

Persuading public opinion that adequate action was being taken on humanitarian aid also meant demonstrating Nigeria's goodwill in this respect, something which the Foreign Office did by emphasising the FMG's co-operative attitude towards relief agencies during parliamentary debates for example.[82] The British also put pressure on the Nigerian government to be accommodating towards ICRC proposals. To this end, London pointed out to its Nigerian counterparts that British public opinion could lead the executive to review its policy on supplying arms. These factors probably help explain the tolerance shown by the federal government towards the Red Cross air bridge between 1968 and 1969. However, in the early summer of 1969 the situation became too conflictual and London's influence was no longer enough to maintain the airlifts. The British once again insisted that the Nigerian government be co-operative and let the Biafrans break off the negotiations in order to show that it was not solely responsible for the impasse.

The second area in which London sought to improve the image of the federal government was related to the conduct of hostilities and the accusations of genocide levelled at Lagos. Indeed, while it was difficult to support leaders who did not come to the aid of a starving population, it was even more difficult to supply arms to a government accused of committing genocide. The British tried, on the one hand, to convince the FMG to better control the conduct of hostilities and, on the other hand, to persuade the world that it did not seek to exterminate the Igbo population. Thus London suggested that the Nigerians ask for a team of international observers to be set up and attest to the good behaviour of their troops.

> Following the discussion on relief, Lord Shepherd reminded Enahoro of what he (Lord Shepherd) had said yesterday about Biafran propaganda and the Federal Military Government's position in the event of the Nigerian issue being raised in the Security Council. He said that pressures of public opinion on FMG and other sympathetic countries were bound to build up not only if relief supplies could not get through to the distressed areas but also if heavy civilian casualties should follow in the wake of present fighting around heavily populated areas like Aba ... Lord Shepherd suggested to Enahoro that the only effective way of countering the flood of propaganda from Biafran sources which must be expected to accompany federal military operations, was for the Federal Government to invite impartial outside observers to the fighting zone, and he urged Enahoro to persuade his government to invite ICRC teams both to observe treatment of civilians during the fighting and to help with relief.[83]

As Karen Smith has shown, this idea was not entirely new, having already been considered in 1967 when there was talk of sending Commonwealth troops to guarantee the security of the Igbo population, should a peace agreement be reached.[84] In late August 1968, when public opinion was particularly moved by what was being reported in the media and expressed its opposition to the British policy of supporting Nigeria, this proposal was of crucial importance. It was therefore accepted by the FMG, who invited a team of international observers to visit the area in order to prove that, contrary to the secessionists' assertions, it was not carrying out an intentional or planned policy of systematically destroying the civilian population and its possessions.[85] However, the FMG refused to allow observers to be provided by the ICRC whom it deemed too susceptible to Biafran rhetoric.[86] It preferred enlisting states that it considered either sympathetic to its cause or relatively neutral. The United Kingdom, Sweden, Poland and Canada were thus invited to send military personnel of a sufficiently high rank to observe the army. The Organisation of African Unity (OAU), which had been involved in attempts at reaching a settlement since the beginning of the conflict and had always been in favour of keeping Nigeria united, was also invited. Finally, in order to enhance the scope and credibility of this operation, the UK government insisted that the missions take place within an international framework.[87] As the possibility of ICRC involvement was quickly ruled out, the FMG approached the UN.

In the British case the choice of observer proved to be a particularly delicate one. As with the appointment of the relief co-ordinator, the government was looking for someone who had a degree of authority and a solid reputation but was not too obviously close to the executive, so as not to invite accusations of bias. It was indeed important to avoid the perception that London was directly involved in setting up the observation missions. Furthermore, it was better not to select a serving officer so as not to be seen as a military advisor sent by the United Kingdom. Finally, the FMG also had a say in the choice of this observer. These various criteria, together with the availability of potential candidates, led the British to nominate a retired British army general, General Alexander, who had been Chief of Staff in Ghana in the early 1960s and had commanded the Ghanaian contingent taking part in the UN force in Congo.[88] Moreover, Alexander enjoyed some fame thanks to a book he had published on his Ghanaian experience.[89] The choice of the observer was therefore well thought through so that his statements and reports would carry maximum weight and credibility with public opinion. This need diminished over time and Alexander was subsequently replaced by less well-known figures.[90]

While the investigators' reports were primarily intended for the media,[91] they were also specifically sent to those civil-society groups most mobilised and concerned by the situation in Biafra, that is religious and missionary circles.[92] The statements of the British observer were also widely disseminated and closely scrutinised as he acted as a tool to demonstrate the good faith of the FMG. For example, on his returns from Nigeria the British representative was given strict instructions about the content of the statements he was to make to the media:

> We would like to discuss with Fergusson on Monday main points he should bring out in his press conference. This ought to concentrate on what he has seen as an Observer and skirt round any comment on political questions. Points we would suggest are: (1) Integrity, experience and strength of team, which make ridiculous suggestions that team only saw what FMG wished it to see and was taken in by efforts to conceal massacres; (2) no evidence

> of genocide despite careful investigations, e.g. at Urua Inyang; (3) generally responsible and helpful behaviour of Federal troops towards civilians and evidence of return of confidence among civilians; (4) discipline of Federal troops and observance of code of conduct; (5) evidence of Ibo oppression of minority people as on Fergusson's letter of 21 November to Wilson; (6) present state of relief operations on federal side, needs of displaced person and prisoners of war, competency of relief organization; (7) measures taken by FMG to facilitate re-integration of Ibos and normalization of life e.g. protection of Ibo property.[93]

The British strategy worked in Western countries, where the observers' reports and the way in which they were presented gradually discredited the secessionists' accusations of genocide. However, their effect was not immediate and they failed to fully neutralise public opinion for several reasons. First of all, the conditions in which the observers were present on the ground detracted from the quality of their investigations. They were based in the capital of the Nigerian Federation, Lagos, which was located several hundred kilometres away from the front line, and made only brief visits to the conflict area. During the first four months of observations from 15 September 1968 to 17 January 1969 they only spent twenty days in eastern Nigeria. Nevertheless, their reports concluded that there was no genocide.[94] On the ground, their trips were organised by the federal government and military authorities. They could only access the areas where hostilities were taking place once the situation had stabilised, which meant that it was difficult to observe how the troops behaved towards the civilian population. Whilst the ability to enter the areas taken over by the federal army was overall deemed satisfactory by the observers, this was also sometimes restricted by some commanders who did not wish to be burdened with their presence. Thus, some areas remained inaccessible to investigators and humanitarian aid for a long time.

Moreover, as the representative of the UN Secretary-General explained, they almost always travelled in groups together with many journalists and under Nigerian military escort. This modus operandi did not facilitate the collection of testimonies from the local population who sometimes feared reprisals.[95] Finally, their autonomy was problematic. On the ground, they were heavily dependent on the government and the federal army for their transport, but also when they had to make contact with the population. Indeed, while on the whole they appeared to be able to talk to civilians without the presence of the military, the latter were an indispensable intermediary for communicating with the non-English-speaking population. These limitations, which the UN observer was aware of, led to much criticism of the reliability of the investigations.[96] In order to overcome these pitfalls the US government considered the possibility of setting up other observation missions, this time led by civilians[97] and based close to the front lines for long periods in order to build trust with the population.[98] But nothing came of it.

The reservations expressed about the reliability of the observers' reports during and at the end of the conflict partly explain why accusations of genocide persisted. Another reason can be found in the fresh upsurge of bombings by Nigerian air force against Biafran civilian or neutralised targets such as hospitals, which were witnessed by Westerners and in particular British journalists in early 1969.[99] The observers were unable to put an end to the controversy, since they operated only on federal territory, despite a British proposal to also send them to the breakaway province which was rejected by both the Biafran authorities and the FMG. Thus, the bombing of Biafran civilians remained of concern to Parliament and the general public, forcing the British government to reconsider its policy towards Nigeria.[100]

In the spring of 1969 the British Prime Minister went to Nigeria to try to negotiate and defuse growing criticism of Great Britain. London also tried to persuade the FMG to better control its pilots and give them stricter orders about the distinction between civilian and military targets. The results of this attempt were mixed, as the pressure it put on the Nigerian government was not enough to bring about real change. Indeed, the measures taken by London were primarily intended to restore Nigeria's image and an actual improvement in the conduct of hostilities on the ground was not the main goal. Indeed, the British government remained convinced that the accusations against the Nigerian army were primarily the product of opposing propaganda and in no way reflected reality. Public pressure was therefore not enough to produce a real shift in the support for the FMG, interests at stake proving too important for the British.

The American scene was another case where public pressure opposed the general policy of the Johnson and Nixon administrations towards the conflict.[101] In 1967, following the Biafran secession, the Johnson administration adopted a position of non-engagement in a crisis that did not represent a major issue, at a time when the Vietnam War very much required the attention of the American executive. It left it to its British allies to counter the influence that the Soviets were trying to gain in the region by supporting the Nigerian government in its war effort. This policy came mainly from the State Department, which relied on its ambassador in Lagos, who was in favour of maintaining Nigeria's unity.

However, beginning with the summer of 1968 media coverage of the humanitarian crisis and the emotion it aroused put pressure on the American government, several politicians urging it to "take action" and "do more than make empty gestures".[102] It was thus no longer possible to ignore the Biafran question, which became a topic in the election campaign. The statements made by the presidential candidate Richard Nixon, who did not hesitate to speak of genocide, gave hope to some members of Congress and pro-Biafran groups when he arrived at the White House in January 1969. However, the new president never introduced any radical change in attitude towards the conflict. His policy, which was ultimately in line with the previous administration, was to distinguish between political and humanitarian issues and to intervene only on the latter. Various measures were taken which were intended to help set up relief operations but above all served to satisfy public opinion. Thus, in late 1968 the American government decided to make eight planes available for the transport of food supplies organised by the churches and ICRC. This inexpensive solution made it possible to show the public that the leaders were engaging in Biafran relief and were doing it in a more dramatic way than discreetly putting pressure on Lagos to allow aid to pass. However, the effectiveness of such a decision on the ground needs to be put into perspective, since the planes were in a dilapidated state and were not really operational.

A second step was taken by President Nixon shortly after taking office. In order to affirm the commitment of the United States to Biafran relief, a US humanitarian-aid co-ordinator was appointed in the person of Clarence Clyde Ferguson. In February 1969 access to the secessionist enclave remained the main issue for the relief operations. Because of their cost and danger, airlifts were seen as a stopgap measure until a river or land route could be negotiated between the belligerents. Ferguson's task was therefore to find a compromise with the Nigerian and Biafran authorities so that such a solution could be implemented. However, he was unsuccessful and the issue of delivering relief supplies by means other than air bridges was never resolved. This outcome was relatively unimportant to the US government since, although Ferguson's mission in Nigeria in the spring of 1969 had failed, it did satisfy public opinion in the United States and helped reduce the pressure exerted by Congress and lobbies on the executive.[103] At the end of the conflict, in January 1970 when the secessionists capitulated and Nigeria expelled most of the relief agencies that had been operating in Biafra until then, the Nixon administration further announced that it would provide substantial resources for civilians. Once again, this statement was enough to appease Western public opinion, even though their deployment on the ground proved to be very complex and the US administration gradually lost interest.

Media coverage of the humanitarian crisis in Nigeria–Biafra, the result of both an active policy on the part of the Biafran authorities and the media's enthusiasm for the issue, generated a widely shared emotion in the Western public sphere. The parallels drawn with the Jewish genocide perpetrated during the Second World War, as well as the extensive use of the figure of the child, the victim par excellence, helped obscure the political issues involved in the conflict. Its portrayal as an essentially humanitarian crisis generated a form of mobilisation among a wider audience that did not necessarily require belonging to or opposing a particular political camp. This engagement differed from a certain partisan activism and was structured around helping a "victim", as shown by the diversity of the political backgrounds of those who became mobilised in support of Biafra. Nevertheless, the emotion aroused by the crisis as a result of the depoliticisation of the conflict did have political implications. Indeed, the pressure it exerted on leaders was particularly felt by those who wanted to preserve Nigeria's unity. On the other hand, while it helped put humanitarian issues on their agendas, this only lasted the relatively short time the emotion did. Thus, the measures taken by governments were primarily intended to calm public opinion, while their effects on the suffering populations were ultimately of little importance.

Notes

1 R. Frank, "Émotions mondiales, internationales et transnationales, 1822–1932", *Monde(s)*, 1:1 (2012), 47–70.
2 On emotions in politics, P. Braud, *Petit traité des émotions, sentiments et passions politiques* (Paris: Armand Colin, 2007).
3 C. Traïni (ed.), *Émotions ... Mobilisation!* (Paris: Presses Sciences Po, 2009).
4 Frank, "Émotions mondiales", p. 68.
5 T. Parfitt, *Black Jews in Africa and the Americas* (Cambridge, MA: Harvard University Press, 2013).
6 A. E. Afigbo, "Tradition of Igbo Origins", *History in Africa*, 10 (1983), 1–11, at 2–3.
7 "Les Juifs de l'Afrique", *Le Nouvel Observateur*, 14 February 1968.
8 Anthony, "Resourceful and Progressive Blackmen".
9 L. Boltanski, *La souffrance à distance* (Paris: Métailié, 1993), p. 18.
10 Bonneville & Caron, *La mort du Biafra*, p. 72.
11 Kirk-Greene, *Crisis and Conflict in Nigeria, Vol. 2*, p. 172.
12 Some use the term genocide to describe the situation in Algeria, and the Russell Tribunal also used the term during the Vietnam War; L. Cesari, "Les droits de l'homme à l'époque de la guerre du Viêt Nam", *Relations internationales*, 132:4 (2007), 5–21, at 17.
13 Anthony, "Resourceful and Progressive Blackmen", p. 44.
14 AWCC, General Secretariat, 42.3.007, letter from the International Witnesses Against Genocide Association to the WCC, 2 August 1968.
15 M. Givoni, "Des victimes pas comme les autres", in W. Ossipow (ed.), *Israël et l'autre* (Geneva: Labor et Fides, 2005), pp. 195–242. On Israel during the conflict, Z. Levey, "Israel, Nigeria and the Biafra Civil War, 1967–70", *Journal of Genocide Research*, 16:2–3 (2014), 263–80.

16 A. Wieviorka, *L'ère du témoin* (Paris: Hachette, 2002), p. 134.

17 According to H. Rousso, the period that began with the 1960s marked the era of the victim more than the era of the witness; H. Rousso, "Vers une mondialisation de la mémoire", *Vingtième Siècle. Revue d'histoire*, 94:2 (2007), 3–10.

18 Wieviorka, *L'ère du témoin*, pp. 134–5.

19 "Tanzania Recognizes Biafra", in Kirk-Greene, *Crisis and Conflict in Nigeria, Vol. 2*, pp. 210–11.

20 Debré, *Biafra an II*, pp. 17–23.

21 L. Heerten, " 'A' as in Auschwitz, 'B' as in Biafra: The Nigerian Civil War, Visual Narratives of Genocide, and the Fragmented Universalization of the Holocaust", in H. Fehrenbach & D. Rodogno (eds), *Humanitarian Photography: A History* (New York: Cambridge University Press, 2015), pp. 249–74.

22 AFRC, INT 23 Biafra, 14/16, "Famine au Biafra: d'anciens déportés lancent un appel angoissé", *Courrier de l'Ouest*, 6 August 1968.

23 C. O'Grada, *A Short History of Famine* (Princeton: Princeton University Press, 2009), p. 196.

24 K. O'Sullivan, *Ireland, Africa and the End of Empire: Small State Identity in the Cold War 1955–1975* (Manchester: Manchester University Press, 2013), p. 114.

25 O'Grada, *A Short History of Famine*, pp. 195–202.

26 J. Vernon, *Hunger, A Modern History* (Cambridge, MA: Harvard University Press, 2007), pp. 17–40.

27 S. Devereux, "Famine in the Twentieth Century", IDS Working Paper 105, Brighton, 2000.

28 The pictures from the third stay, which took place from 7 to 15 November 1968, were mainly devoted to mercenaries in Biafra. This report was published by the magazine *Jeune Afrique*.

29 The pictures were published in *Paris Match*, n° 995, 4 May 1968, pp. 62–7.

30 Archives of the Fondation Gilles Caron, Geneva.

31 *Paris Match*, n° 1002, 20 July 1968; *Paris Match*, n° 1005, 10 August 1968.

32 M. Poivert, *Gilles Caron, Le conflit intérieur* (Arles: Éditions photosynthèse, 2013), pp. 392–5.

33 Boltanski, *La souffrance à distance*, p. 28.

34 "Dans deux heures cette petite fille sera morte", *France Dimanche*, 9 July 1968, p. 17. Similar articles appeared in other newspapers: for example, " 'Terre des hommes' évacue des enfants du Biafra", *Journal de Genève*, 7 September 1968.

35 Bulletin of the Division of Inter-Church Aid, Refugee and World Services of the WCC, 1969. For another example, see Oxfam's activity report, 1968–69, where a very skinny black child is shown alone and without a background on the cover.

36 P. Juhem, "Parler ici des malheurs lointains. La nécessité des énoncés humanitaires et leurs effets sur la constitution des angles journalistiques", in P. Dauvin & J. Siméant (eds), *ONG et humanitaire* (Paris: L'Harmattan, 2004), pp. 213–53.

37 Jung, "L'image télévisuelle comme arme de guerre", p. 63.

38 C. Coquery-Vidrovitch, "Apogée et crise coloniale", in P. Blanchard & A. Chatelier (eds), *Images et colonies: nature, discours et influence de l'iconographie coloniale liée à la propagande coloniale et à la représentation des Africains et de l'Afrique en France, de 1920 aux indépendances. Actes du colloque organisé par l'ACHAC du 20 au 22 janvier 1993 à la Bibliothèque nationale* (Paris: Syros, 1993), p. 54.
39 R. F. Betts, "Les images anglaises de l'Afrique noire dans les années 20 et 30", in P. Blanchard & A. Chatelier (eds), *Images et colonies*, p. 126.
40 P. Minder, *La Suisse coloniale: les représentations de l'Afrique et des Africains en Suisse au temps des colonies (1880–1939)* (Bern: Peter Lang, 2011).
41 Croix-Rouge française, *Vie et bonté, Revue officielle de la Croix-Rouge française*, n° 186, October 1968.
42 A. Hugon, "La propagande missionnaire", in P. Blanchard & A. Chatelier (eds), *Images et colonies*, p. 82.
43 G. Manceron & J.-B. Debost, "Conclusion", in P. Blanchard & A. Chatelier (eds), *Images et colonies*, p. 144.
44 P. Blanchard, "La représentation de l'indigène dans les affiches coloniales: Entre concept républicain, fiction phobique et discours racialisant", *Hermès*, 30:1 (2001), 149–67.
45 P. Boilley, "Les visions françaises de l'Afrique et des africains", in A. Ba Konaré (ed.), *Petit précis de remise à niveau sur l'histoire de l'Afrique à l'usage du président Sarkozy* (Paris: La Découverte, 2009), p. 115.
46 R. Frank, "Émotions mondiales, internationales et transnationales, 1822–1932".
47 S. Sontag, *Sur la photographie* (Paris: C. Bourgeois, 2008), p. 35.
48 Croix-Rouge française, *Vie et bonté*, pp. 6–7.
49 Destexhe, *L'humanitaire impossible ou deux siècles d'ambiguïtés*, p. 68.
50 On the development of humanitarian preoccupations in Ireland, the UK, the US and Canada, see Wiseberg, "The International Politics of Relief", pp. 180–2.
51 AFRC, INT 23 Biafra 01-07/16 1968–1970, "Biafra Personnel: proposition d'engagement août décembre 1968", 06/16, "Biafra, courrier reçu suite à l'article de France Dimanche du 9 juillet 1968", 13/16.
52 Boltanski, *La souffrance à distance*, pp. 91–141.
53 AMAE Nantes, French Embassy in London, box 1456, note by Pierret, 10 March 1969.
54 Jung, "L'image télévisuelle", p. 62.
55 Heerten, "The Dystopia of Postcolonial Catastrophe".
56 AFRC, INT 23 Biafra 10-13/16 and INT 23 Biafra 14-16/16.
57 FNA, 5 AG FPU/689, Co-ordination meeting, 29 July 1969 (August 1968 collection: 13,245,000 francs; December 1968 collection: 1,400,000 francs; *semaine nationale* in March 1969: 6,000,000 francs). These figures do not include all private donations in France at the time of Biafra, as some organisations organised parallel collections, but they do give an idea of the main funds raised.
58 USAID, *Emergency Relief in Nigeria.*
59 Quoted in Brauman, Backmann, *Les médias et l'humanitaire*, p. 71.

60 See the publications from the *Britain Biafra Association*: A. Waugh, *Britain and Biafra: The Case of Genocide* (London: Britain-Biafra Association, 1969); H. G. Hanbury, *Biafra: A Challenge to the Conscience of Britain* (London: Britain-Biafra Association, 1968); G. Knapp, *Aspects of the Biafran Affair: A Study of British Attitudes and Policy towards the Nigerian-Biafran Conflict* (London: Britain-Biafra Association, 1968).
61 Wiseberg, "The International Politics of Relief", pp. 199–222.
62 TNA, FCO 65/250.
63 AMAE Nantes, French Embassy in London, box 1456, note by Pierret division Afrique Levant, 10 March 1969.
64 B. McNeil, " 'And Starvation is the Grim Reaper': The American Committee to Keep Biafra Alive and the Genocide Question during the Nigerian Civil War, 1968–70", *Journal of Genocide Research*, 16:2–3 (2014), 317–36.
65 On the mobilisation in Switzerland, S. Page, *Le Nigeria et la Suisse, des affaires d'indépendance: commerce, diplomatie et coopération 1930–1980* (Bern: Peter Lang, 2016), pp. 197–236.
66 Heerten, "The Dystopia of Postcolonial Catastrophe".
67 "Une trentaine de médecins, pilotes et journalistes dénoncent 'le génocide au Biafra' ", *Le Monde*, 12 February 1969.
68 TNA, FCO 38/254.
69 Kirk-Greene, *Crisis and Conflict in Nigeria,* Vol. 2, p. 84.
70 Fassin, *La raison humanitaire*, pp. 286–7.
71 J.-P. Le Goff, *Mai 1968, l'héritage impossible* (Paris: La Découverte, 1998), pp. 452–8.
72 B. Gaïti, "L'opinion publique dans l'histoire politique, impasses et bifurcations", *Le Mouvement Social*, 221:4 (2007), 95–104.
73 L. Minear, C. Scott & T. G. Weiss, *The News Media, Civil War, and Humanitarian Action* (Boulder: L. Rienner, 1996); I. Smillie & L. Minear, *The Charity of Nations: Humanitarian Action in A Calculating World* (Bloomfield: Kumarian Press, 2004), pp. 163–82.
74 L. Heerten, "The Biafran War in Britain: An Odd Alliance of the late 1960s Humanitarian Activists", *Journal of the Oxford University History Society* (2009), 1–18, at 3.
75 TNA, Cabinet papers, conclusions, 20 June (CAB/128/43/31) and 4 July 1968 (CAB/128/43/34).
76 K. E. Smith, *Genocide and the Europeans* (Cambridge: Cambridge University Press, 2010), p. 73.
77 TNA, FCO 38/225, note from D. C. Tebbit, CO, 28 August 1968.
78 TNA, Cabinet papers, memorandum, 9 December 1968 (CAB/129/139/26), and conclusions, 10 December 1968 (CAB/128/43/50).
79 TNA, FCO 38/300, telegram from the FO to the consulate in Geneva, 4 July 1968.
80 TNA, FCO 38/306, telegram from the CO to the BHC in Lagos, 1 July 1968.
81 TNA, FCO 38/307, preliminary version of a CO telegram to the BHC in Lagos, 5 July 1968.

82 TNA, FCO 38/300, telegram from the CO to the consulate in Geneva, 13 June 1968.
83 TNA, FCO 38/225, telegram from the CO to the BHC in Lagos, 20 August 1968.
84 Smith, *Genocide and the Europeans*, p. 74.
85 TNA, FCO 38/225, letter from the Nigerian Ministry of Foreign Affairs to British High Commissioner in Lagos, 6 September 1968.
86 TNA, FCO 38/225, telegram from the BHC in Lagos to the CO, 21 August 1968.
87 TNA, FCO 38/302, meeting between Lord Hunt, Lord Shepherd, Chief Enahoro and Brigadier Ogundipe, 20 August 1968.
88 TNA, FCO 38/225.
89 H. T. Alexander, *African Tightrope: My Two Years as Nkrumah's Chief of Staff* (London: Pall Mall Press, 1965).
90 TNA, FCO 65/169, "Observer Team – Nigeria", 21 January 1969.
91 TNA, FCO 38/226, telex from the CO to the BHC in Lagos, 15 October 1968.
92 TNA, FCO 65/166, letters from the FCO accompgnying the second report of the Observers Team, 23 October 1968.
93 TNA, FCO 65/168, telegram from the FCO to the BHC in Lagos, 6 December 1968. Bernard Fergusson took over from General Alexander as British observer in Nigeria.
94 AUN, S-0884-0014-11, fourth intermediate reports of the Special Representative of the Secretary-General for humanitarian affairs in Nigeria (9.10.1968; 30.10.1968; 21.11.1968; 17.01.1969).
95 AUN, S-0884-0014-11, second intermediate report of the Special Representative of the Secretary-General for humanitarian affairs in Nigeria, 30 October 1968.
96 For example, AICRC, B AG 202 147-001, note from Basset to Bignami and Martin, 16 October 1969.
97 Apart from the observer sent by the UN, the other observers were all military personnel.
98 AICRC, B AG 200 147-003.02, note from P. Tacier to A. Lindt, Spring 1969.
99 See for example the articles published by W. S. Churchill in *The Times* on his return from Biafra.
100 TNA, Cabinet papers, conclusions, 6 and 12 March 1969 (CAB/128/44/11 and CAB/128/44/12).
101 Thompson, *American Policy and African Famine*; G. A. Obiozor, *The United States and the Nigerian Civil War: An American Dilemma in Africa* (Lagos: Nigerian Institute of International Affairs, 1993); R. B. Shepard, *Nigeria, Africa and the United States from Kennedy to Reagan* (Bloomington: Indiana University Press, 1991), pp. 34–48.
102 *Foreign Relations of the United States, 1964–1968, Vol. XXIV, Africa*, ed. by N. Davis Howland (Washington, DC: Government Printing Office, 1999), document 398.
103 *Foreign Relations of the United States, 1969–1976, Vol. E-5, Part 1, Documents on Sub-Saharan Africa, 1969–1972*, ed. by J. Hilts & D. C. Humphrey (Washington, DC: Government Printing Office, 2005), document 54.

Part II

Responding to a humanitarian crisis

4

Breaking the blockade: the rise of non-governmental actors

The presence on the international agenda of the last two decades of the twentieth century of humanitarian crises to which states and international organisations have tried to respond, the debates around the notion of *ingérence* these have given rise to,[1] and then, in 2005, the adoption by the UN General Assembly of a resolution on the "responsibility to protect", all these have brought (back) to the forefront the notion of humanitarian intervention which Cold War issues had helped relegate to the background.[2] This has led to a large body of literature in the fields of political science and international relations that has explored this notion.[3] It generally deals with the usually military intervention by a state, or a group of states, who, for example, are part of an international organisation, in the internal affairs of another state for humanitarian reasons, that is particularly in order to protect populations whose survival is under threat. Studies by historians have helped put these debates into perspective by showing that the humanitarian interventions of the last few decades ultimately bore strong similarities to what in the nineteenth century European powers claimed to be *interventions d'humanité*.[4] The campaigns conducted in the Ottoman Empire throughout the nineteenth century are telling examples in this respect.[5]

Although Bernard Kouchner described the Biafran war as the decisive moment in his thinking on the duty to interfere, a notion he went on to develop with Mario Bettati in the late 1980s,[6] studies on humanitarian interventions, which mostly deal with those carried out by states or groups of states, rarely mention this conflict. Indeed, while the crisis was described as particularly deadly because of the massacres that were taking place and the famine, at no point did the international community seriously consider the possibility of a humanitarian intervention in the classic sense of the term.

Nevertheless, the idea was not totally absent from the debates. In September 1968, for example, a group of lawyers from Yale University argued for UN intervention on humanitarian grounds.[7] Furthermore, relief operations were set up, most of which were run without the formal approval of the Nigerian government. Thus, although they were conducted by non-governmental actors, these actions were akin to humanitarian interventions in the sense defined by Brendan Simms and David Trim, who use this terminology to describe interventions by foreign – not necessarily state – actors in the internal affairs of a state in order to protect the lives of populations, without that state's explicit consent.[8] The creation of Médecins Sans Frontières in the aftermath of the conflict is also seen in this way since this NGO symbolised a new humanitarianism characterised by witnessing but also by *sans-frontiérisme* ("without-border-ism"), that is "the willingness to act where needed and the refusal to be constrained by the absolutisation of state sovereignty".[9]

Focusing on the period from secession in June 1967 to the churches and ICRC setting up regular airlifts to Biafra in September 1968, this chapter examines the process that led to the decision by these non-governmental actors to intervene without the formal agreement of the Nigerian government. Their links with the area in which they operated, their relationships with each other and with states, as well as their sensitivity to public pressure are crucial to understanding how they decided to impose themselves on the territory of a sovereign state. Their stance was more generally consistent with the rise of NGOs on the international scene. For Alex de Waal the relief operation in Nigeria–Biafra was thus an example of the crucial role these actors played in emergency aid.[10] This evolution was not specific to the humanitarian field, since during the same period they also asserted themselves in the areas of development and human rights. Moreover, this process did not take place without the involvement of states and inter-state organisations which provided them with resources and let them operate in a space that they themselves did not wish to occupy directly.[11]

A wide range of humanitarian actors

In his book on humanitarian action Philippe Ryfman identifies the main protagonists in the humanitarian operations of the late twentieth century: states, international intergovernmental organisations and NGOs.[12] In the case of Nigeria–Biafra these three types of actors were involved to varying degrees and did not respond in the same way to the emotion aroused by the humanitarian crisis. As subjects of international law, states and international organisations should in theory observe the principle of non-intervention in the internal affairs of a state, as set out in the UN Charter. Indeed, the Nigerian government did not hesitate to remind them of this as soon as the secession of Biafra was proclaimed. On 30 May 1967 General Gowon sent a message to the Secretary-General of the United Nations (UN) and the Secretary General of the Organisation of African Unity (OAU) stating that "any attempt to recognise the so-called Republic of Biafra as a sovereign state will amount to interference in the internal affairs of my country and will be regarded as an unfriendly act. I would be grateful if you could have this message circulated to all member states of the organisation".[13] Secession was an internal Nigerian issue, and any move that might lend credibility to Biafran independence had to be avoided.

However, in the summer of 1967 various governments tried to mediate between the two sides on an ad hoc basis or within the OAU.[14] Despite the reluctance of the FMG,[15] in 1967 this regional intergovernmental organisation created a special consultative committee of African heads of state in order to deal with the Nigerian question.[16] Throughout the conflict there were various talks within the OAU to find a negotiated solution; its members, who feared that a possible Biafran independence would mean calling into question the existing African borders, were mostly in favour of the Nigerian point of view. Four states departed from this stance as Tanzania, Côte d'Ivoire, Gabon and Zambia recognised Biafra in the spring of 1968. Only Haiti joined them, in 1969, while the French, Portuguese and South African governments gave unofficial support to the secessionists, without ever formally recognising them.[17] Overall, most states remained cautious. The United States refused to take a position in favour of either side, and even the Nigerian government's requests for arms support from the former British metropole were initially met with a lukewarm response. As far as the supply of heavy military equipment was concerned, the FMG found initial support from the Soviet Union,[18] which was seeking to increase its influence in Africa.[19] Frightened by the spectre of communism, the British adopted a more favourable policy towards their former colony. They became closely associated with the Nigerian cause in order to protect Western interests in general and their own in particular, many of which pertained to the economic and oil sectors. In doing so, they prevented the conflict from degenerating into an East–West confrontation, with the Americans relying on their British allies to counter the communist influence in Nigeria. Indeed, keeping Nigeria's unity was especially important, as the country had everything to become a leading African power. Above all, it had many oil resources which were particularly exploited by British and American companies. The latter were based in the secessionist region but also in the areas that were rapidly recaptured by the federal army.

In the first months of war other organisations such as the Commonwealth also tried to mediate but without much success. As for the United Nations, it did not take any position, since its member states did not wish to see it interfere in what the majority considered to be a domestic political matter. The issue therefore was not discussed in the Security Council or General Assembly. For his part, the Secretary-General did not particularly insist on involving the UN in resolving the crisis, whether in relation to political or humanitarian issues.[20] The organisation was just coming out of its tricky experience in Congo, where it had been severely tested. This was helped by the fact that the OAU was seized of the matter which, under the principle of subsidiarity, could be used to justify the lack of UN involvement in attempts to resolve the conflict. Indeed, Gowon did not hesitate to point this out to U Thant, who in early 1968 had suggested making a public statement: "I consider the issue you raise to be extremely sensitive and my first reaction is that a public statement by you would be a departure from the course of action we have agreed on, which is that you would not take any initiative not least because the OAU is seized of the matter".[21]

The same restrictions that applied to the United Nations also applied to the specialised UN agencies or funds, such as the Office of the UN High Commissioner for Refugees (UNHCR), the World Food Programme and the United Nations Children's Fund (UNICEF), whose resources were otherwise likely to be used in humanitarian crises. In order to intervene, these bodies had to be in theory approached by the government of the state concerned, in this case the Nigerian government, as the Republic of Biafra was not recognised. Thus, with the exception of UNICEF which found a way to get involved in the relief efforts very early on, they did not play a key role.[22] In the autumn of 1967 the UNHCR indicated that it was not competent to intervene in Nigeria–Biafra,[23] and it was not until late 1968 that, following strong encouragement from the UN Secretary-General, the FMG accepted that the World Food Programme should provide it with resources.[24] Thus, during the first year of the conflict two categories of potential humanitarian actors – states and international organisations – only played a minimal role in the relief efforts which were still in their infancy. It was therefore the non-governmental actors, some of whom had been specialising in emergency aid for several decades, who took centre stage.

The International Red Cross Movement, which had developed from the second half of the nineteenth century onwards, was one of the main players on the humanitarian scene in the 1960s. Made up of the International Committee of the Red Cross, which was founded in Geneva in 1863, and the first National Red Cross Societies, it gradually grew in size as more and more National Societies were formed and came together to form a new organisation in 1919, the League of Red Cross Societies (now the International Federation of Red Cross and Red Crescent). The existence of these different organisations within the Movement was not without tensions, particularly with regard to defining the areas of competence of the League and the ICRC. In the late 1960s, by virtue of an agreement reached in 1951, the League was responsible for co-ordinating international relief efforts in peacetime, such as in the event of a natural disaster, whereas the

ICRC was responsible for co-ordinating emergency aid operations in the event of an armed conflict. The latter therefore became a key player in the relief operations conducted during the Nigeria–Biafra war. Whilst it was not strictly speaking an intergovernmental organisation, to the extent that it was not made up of states and its status was governed by Swiss private law, it was not an NGO either, with legislation assigning it a special role on the international scene.[25] As guarantor of the Geneva Conventions of 1949 it conducted its activities in accordance with international law, whilst also having the right to "take any humanitarian initiative which comes within its role as a specifically neutral and independent institution and intermediary, and may consider any question requiring examination by such an institution".[26] Its activities, like those of other members of the Movement, were guided by the seven fundamental principles of the Red Cross – humanity, impartiality, neutrality, independence, voluntary service, unity and universality – which were proclaimed at the 20th International Conference of the Red Cross in Vienna in 1965.[27] Based in Geneva, it was funded primarily by contributions from governments, particularly the Swiss government, and National Red Cross Societies. Despite the crisis it underwent at the end of the Second World War when its failure to act in support of victims of Nazi racial and political persecutions as well as prisoners on the Eastern Front earned it much criticism,[28] thanks to its long experience it was seen by governments and other organisations as a key player in humanitarian aid during armed conflicts.

Numerous non-governmental organisations dedicated to humanitarian activities emerged alongside the International Red Cross Movement, particularly during the two world wars. Thus, the end of the First World War saw the creation of Save the Children and the International Save the Children Union, which in 1946 became the International Union for Child Welfare. Oxfam was set up to help the victims of the Greek famine in 1942 during the Second World War, while the Cooperative for American Remittances to Europe (CARE) was established in 1945 to provide emergency aid to people who found themselves in war-torn areas. Their activities gradually became more permanent and, with the process of decolonisation, were directed towards developing countries. This period corresponds to a third phase which saw the creation of NGOs that were more specifically geared towards these regions, as illustrated by the organisation Terre des Hommes, which was founded by Edmond Kaiser in 1960. In the late 1960s these various organisations, some of which vacillated between emergency aid and development aid, were among the most important actors in the region that found itself in the grip of civil war.

Of these, faith-based organisations occupied a particularly important place.[29] Beginning with the late nineteenth century, "Catholic relief" organisations, also known under the name Caritas, were gradually formed in many countries. Whilst these associations were active in their respective home countries, where they were primarily concerned with improving the lot of the poorest, from 1945 onwards they began developing their activities internationally, particularly in the decolonised regions. In order to co-ordinate and carry out joint relief actions they worked together as part of Caritas Internationalis, which had been established in the Vatican in 1951.

Protestant churches, too, had their own humanitarian agencies. Examples include the Church World Service in the United States, which had emerged from the Second World War, Christian Aid in Great Britain, and the relief organisations of Protestant churches in northern European countries such as DanChurchAid, Das Diakonisches Werk in Germany and Cimade in France. There was no equivalent Caritas Internationalis in the Protestant world, but the World Council of Churches, which brought together Protestant churches from around the world, had an Inter-Church Aid Division that ran and co-ordinated development projects.

These organisations pursued their goal of taking part in relief operations but the nature of the Nigeria–Biafra conflict complicated matters. Their involvement was not straightforward because of the blockade imposed around the breakaway region. That said, they took a relatively early interest in the situation for a variety of reasons and began, depending on their means and not always in a concerted manner, to provide some assistance. However, they did not all play the same role in operations, with some providing mainly financial resources to others who intervened directly on the ground. The rest of this chapter analyses the different dynamics of co-operation and competition that led these non-governmental actors to challenge the sovereignty of the Nigerian government by mounting a humanitarian intervention.

Timid first steps

As Johanna Siméant explains, "each NGO has a formal and informal decision-making system which gives a greater or lesser role to the actors that make up the structure – whether they are associates or employees, and whether or not they have specific expertise (medical, managerial, logistical) – and come together within that organisation".[30] Despite entities having their own specific features, the author identifies three scenarios that can help us understand how they become interested in launching a mission. The first one is that of "networks that have already been established", that is when, thanks to their contacts or experiences in a country, NGO members become "intervention intermediaries" by drawing the attention of their organisation to a particular situation. In the second scenario the availability of funds is the decisive factor in understanding the choice to set up a mission. The third scenario relates to situations where, particularly in high-profile crises, there is real pressure on humanitarian actors who then decide to intervene because they "cannot not be there".[31] Although developed on the basis of late twentieth-century NGO practices, these models, particularly the first and the third, apply particularly well to the decisions taken by relief organisations during the Nigeria–Biafra war, even though they were less institutionalised and fewer in number than in the 1990s. Indeed, the links that religious organisations had with local actors through missionaries, as well as the competition that existed between humanitarian agencies, structured the deployment of relief operations.

In the spring of 1967, even before the civil war in Nigeria began, the ICRC contacted the federal government and Biafran authorities to demand that international humanitarian law be applied, despite the non-international nature of the conflict, and to offer its services. Both parties agreed to this in principle and as soon as hostilities began in July 1967 the ICRC intended to send a delegate to each side of the front line to check on the prisoners of war and visit the places where they were being held. It would also assess the needs of local Red Cross societies in terms of personnel and medical equipment in order to shore up their capacities. Whilst on the federal side these early stages went relatively smoothly, the situation in Biafra was much more difficult because of the conditions there and the distrust of the Biafran authorities. In particular, the organisation experienced difficulties in designating a delegate and transporting medical personnel and equipment due to the blockade imposed by the Nigerian government around the region.[32]

Despite the initial problems it came up against and the limited means at its disposal, in December 1967 the ICRC decided to embark on a much larger operation and extend its activities to the civilian population.[33] The arrival of other actors on the scene seems fundamental to understanding this decision. In late 1967 various voices raised concerns about the situation of the civilians on the ground. UNICEF was one of the first organisations to put forward a real proposal to work with the ICRC on this issue. Having initially been set up as an emergency aid fund to manage child relief immediately after the war, little by little UNICEF expanded its activities to countries outside Europe. Following in the footsteps of the UN, for whom development would be its priority throughout the 1960s, it gradually moved away from emergency aid operations in order to focus on long-term prevention operations. As it was relatively well established on the ground through its local representatives who ran programmes not least in Nigeria,[34] UNICEF quickly became concerned about the problems caused by the conflict. Its managers, who were informed by their correspondents in Lagos of the alarming situation the civilian population found itself in, contacted the ICRC to offer the Fund's assistance in setting up an operation to help the children.[35] There were two reasons for UNICEF's appeal to the ICRC. Firstly, as a UN organisation, it was difficult for it to engage directly in an intervention without a request from the Nigerian government. In order to get around this problem the UNICEF Deputy Director suggested that the operation be negotiated and led by the ICRC as a neutral organisation, using funds and food supplies provided by UNICEF. Secondly, the UN agency was ill-prepared to carry out relief work in the field in the context of a civil war.

At the same time the ICRC received other partnership proposals. In November 1967 Caritas Internationalis donated $25,000 to the ICRC for its first relief shipments. The World Council of Churches also offered support in providing aid to the civilian population.[36] This body had a particular interest in the conflict because of the links between it and some members of Biafran Protestant churches. Moreover, the WCC's Inter-Church Aid Division had no experience in emergency aid. On the other hand, it could provide medical teams and launch appeals in the Protestant community for funds to support the activities of the ICRC, which it saw as an experienced, neutral organisation able to operate both in the breakaway province and in the areas recaptured by the federal army.

There was a third element in addition to these collaboration proposals. ICRC delegates in Nigeria reported in Geneva that the League of Red Cross Societies was in the process of setting up a programme together with the Nigerian Red Cross to assist the civilian population in the areas retaken by the federal army. Under the 1951 agreement governing the division of responsibilities between these two organisations, the League was authorised to intervene in peacetime, whereas in wartime this responsibility fell to the ICRC. During the winter of 1967–68, however, the ICRC found that the relief activities undertaken by the Nigerian Red Cross with the support of the League bypassed it completely.[37] This realisation caused great concern to the ICRC which, since the League's creation in 1919, had regularly felt threatened by this competitor within the Movement.[38] In 1967 the League's continued activities in Nigeria could set a precedent that would call into question the ICRC's pre-eminent role in conflict situations, in a context where the League seemed better prepared to act,[39] since, in its capacity as trainer of National Societies, it already had many contacts on the ground with the Nigerian Red Cross. The ICRC therefore urgently needed to take control of the situation if it was to mount a relief operation for civilians on both sides of the front line.

These various factors played a crucial role in the ICRC's decision to set up its own operations. On the one hand, it was keen to continue to be seen as the leading humanitarian-aid actor in the context of an internal conflict, and on the other hand, working with other organisations provided it with the necessary means to set up a relief operation for the civilian population. An agreement was therefore reached on 28 December 1967 between the Nigerian government, the Nigerian Red Cross and the ICRC whereby a relief programme would be deployed under the responsibility of the latter throughout the war-affected area.[40] As far as the delivery of relief supplies to Biafra was concerned, a storage base was to be established on the island of Fernando Poo. From there, once their cargo had been inspected by FMG officials and their flight route made known to Lagos, the ICRC planes could proceed to the breakaway province.[41] However, the implementation of this agreement was fraught with difficulties and did not lead to the delivery of relief supplies. No sooner had it been negotiated than it was challenged by the Biafran authorities followed by the Nigerian government, and it was not until April 1968 that the situation was temporarily unblocked.

The difficulties encountered by the ICRC between January and April 1968 led some of the organisations that had offered it help to explore independent avenues. Caritas Internationalis was the first to take its own initiatives, not least because of the presence in Biafra of many Irish Catholic missionaries from the Congregation of the Holy Spirit.[42] In December 1967, alarmed by the various reports on the situation since the beginning of the conflict, Pope Paul VI sent two representatives to Nigeria–Biafra – George Rochau and Dominic Conway – on a mission to negotiate a Christmas truce between belligerents and assess the extent to which Caritas Internationalis could look after the needs of those affected by the war. Once in Nigeria, the two met with Gowon but were unable to travel to Biafra as all communication routes had been cut off. The failure of this initiative caused great discontent in the breakaway region, and the eight eastern bishops (three of whom were Irish) decided to send an Irish Spiritan missionary, Anthony Byrne, to Rome to persuade the Pope to make another attempt. Byrne's mission was a success, not least because in the meantime a Protestant missionary close to the World Council of Churches, Ted Johnson, had managed to get to Biafra. Indeed, in the context of the rivalry between Protestants and Catholics, this achievement, which the bishops did not hesitate to point out in their appeal to the Pope, played a decisive role.[43] Thus, in early February the Vatican sent its emissaries to Biafra and dispatched the Secretary General of Caritas Internationalis, Carlo Bayer, to Nigeria to inform the government of the mission and discuss relief efforts on the federal side.[44] The Vatican's representatives travelled to the breakaway province via Lisbon, one of the places from where planes flew to Biafra.[45] Their trip was organised by Byrne, who chartered a plane from Henry (Hank) Wharton, a German-American who transported arms for the Biafran authorities and acted as a liaison between Biafra and the outside world.[46] They brought a first load of Caritas relief supplies with them, which showed that Catholics were distancing themselves from the ICRC and paved the way for more regular shipments directly to Biafra in the spring of 1968. Indeed, on the return of its representatives who confirmed the extent of the needs on the ground, the Vatican tasked Carlo Bayer and Jean Rodhain (President of Caritas Internationalis) with developing a programme to help victims on both sides of the front line. These programmes were co-ordinated and implemented in the field by two Irish Spiritan missionaries who shared the same surname but were not related: Desmond Byrne in Nigeria and Anthony Byrne in Biafra. The former was at the time the head of the social-affairs department of the Catholic Secretariat in Lagos, while the latter was the director of the Catholic social centre and social services in Onitsha.[47]

During his stay in Rome, Anthony Byrne made contacts and sounded out organisations that could help with the relief programme.[48] Building on the links he had established with Wharton, he then arranged for the first two loads to be transported to Biafra. The first shipment of 50 tonnes was sent in March 1968. Some of it was flown by Wharton's planes directly from Lisbon, but the bulk of the cargo was transported by ship from Lisbon to the Portuguese colony of São Tomé in the Gulf of Guinea as the sea route was significantly cheaper than the air route.[49] This allowed food supplies to be brought closer to Biafra without the need to increase the number of intermediate stages and customs problems since they did not leave the Portuguese empire. Furthermore, should military developments prevent their arrival at their destination, this system offered the advantage of facilitating their repatriation to Europe, again via Lisbon.[50] In this city, as in São Tomé, Byrne could count on the presence of other Spiritans or Catholic missions to help him establish the transit route for relief supplies.[51] Once arrived in São Tomé, the cargo was then flown by Wharton's planes to Port Harcourt, the last airport in Biafran hands in the spring of 1968. Caritas's regular partnership with Wharton for sending shipments from São Tomé to Biafra began on 27 March 1968. Such an arrangement was possible because, although the American was primarily in charge of delivering arms to the secessionists, the latter did not always manage to fill his planes with military equipment. Wharton was therefore free to offer his air transport services to relief organisations.[52] Once this first shipment had reached its destination, Byrne, who had travelled to Biafra in early April 1968 to organise the distribution on the ground, prepared the transport of a second load. He negotiated with Wharton to make six flights but be paid only for five.[53] Thus, between 27 March and 1 August 1968 Wharton made thirty-eight flights for Caritas using his own planes. The source of the relief supplies brought to Biafra varied at the beginning of the operations. Shipments included goods provided directly by European organisations, as well as food and medicines bought in the Portuguese empire with funds raised in Europe. For example, the first cargo of 50 tonnes was made up of medicines, flour, salt, rice, tins of sardines and meat, and dried fish purchased in Lisbon and São Tomé with money from Caritas Internationalis and War on Want, as well as 35 tonnes of milk powder donated by Caritas Switzerland, which also paid for the transport.[54]

These initiatives did not leave the Protestant world indifferent. Tired of seeing the ICRC's negotiations fail and relief supplies and medical personnel remain in Europe, those in charge of the WCC's Inter-Church Aid Division decided to use Wharton's services as well. In order to organise the flights, one of them, Helmut Reuschle, went to Lisbon to meet with Wharton and see to what extent the WCC could charter a plane. On the ground he was able to count on the support of one of the Spiritan missionaries, Dermot Doran, who provided him with contacts to obtain the necessary authorisations for the passage of the relief supplies.[55] On 22 March two WCC representatives flew from Lisbon in one of Wharton's planes with a load of several tonnes of aid. Between March 1968 and June 1968 nine flights to the breakaway province were subsequently funded by the WCC. Organising these airlifts was not without its problems, since little by little the number of initiatives increased without being particularly well co-ordinated. Thus, during a trip to Lisbon in April 1968 Reuschle discovered that a German pastor connected to the German Protestant aid organisation Das Diakonisches Werk was organising shipments to Biafra on his own without going through the WCC. This situation created tensions and confusion, particularly in relation to negotiations with the Biafran and Portuguese authorities and the airline.[56] The impatience of this organisation, and of Protestant circles more generally, is explained by the increasing needs of the civilian population, but also by the initiatives of Catholic agencies in a region where the rivalry between Protestant and Catholic churches persisted. The faith-based organisations' distancing from the ICRC marked the beginning of a dual shipping system to Biafra which was confirmed in the summer of 1968.

For its part, the ICRC was still trying to find common ground between belligerents with regard to sending aid. While some within the Committee wanted to take the same route as the religious organisations and use Wharton's airline to bring some food supplies to Biafra, others were strongly opposed, being of the opinion that "it is not possible for the ICRC to have its relief supplies transported among weapons".[57] This position, however, changed during the months of February and March. Indeed, a second failure to send a plane to Port Harcourt in mid-February led the institution to turn to Wharton.[58] Aid initially transited through Lisbon and then, in late March 1968, it was decided to use the clandestine route more regularly to transport the food supplies that the ICRC had stored on the island of Fernando Poo.[59]

There were probably many factors involved in this decision. First of all, the organisation justified its approach by invoking the principle of impartiality. It argued that it could not afford to provide relief only to the Nigerian side and that it also had a duty to assist the Biafran population. The insistence of its delegate in Biafra who stressed the urgency of the region's needs reinforced this point. Finally, the decision of faith-based organisations to undertake their own operations also pushed it in this direction.[60]

Whilst the ICRC was becoming more proactive, this did not stop it from continuing to seek Lagos's approval for its flights. It failed, however, to persuade it and had to turn to the Swiss and British governments to help with negotiations. Thus, on 20 March 1968 the Swiss ambassador to Nigeria lobbied the FMG not to formally oppose the ICRC setting up flights to Biafra. The support of the Swiss government, although in many respects fundamental for the Geneva-based institution, was probably not a decisive factor in the ICRC's subsequently being authorised to fly since, in any case, the FMG did not really distinguish between the humanitarian organisation and the Swiss Confederation.[61]

British help, on the other hand, was of considerable importance because of London's crucial support for the Nigerian war effort. Relief shipments to Biafra proved useful to Britain as British citizens who were still there could be repatriated on the return flights, and they could also help improve Lagos's image.[62] The Commonwealth Office therefore put pressure on the FMG to allow these flights, especially since many planes were already flying clandestinely to and from Biafra without the FMG really being able to prevent them.[63] Its efforts were successful and in early April the federal government informed the ICRC that it would tolerate its air shipments to the breakaway province "at its own risk". On this basis, on 8 April the ICRC delegate to Biafra, Karl Heinrich Jaggi, signed an agreement with Wharton which made it possible to bring to Biafra some of the supplies that had been stored on Fernando Poo for several months. In the period from March to June 1968 the ICRC sent 179 tonnes of aid to Biafra, while Caritas and the WCC sent 315 tonnes (Figure 4.1).[64]

However, the events of late May 1968 in Biafra quickly showed the precariousness and inadequacy of the air route that had been set up. The advance of Nigerian troops, who took the city of Port Harcourt around 19 May, led to a large influx of refugees into the breakaway region, where people's needs increased considerably. The refugees lacked everything and starvation became widespread. The ICRC brought the urgency of the situation to the attention of the international world by launching an appeal called "SOS Biafra".[65] Whilst it marked the beginning of more substantial responses from Red Cross societies and governments, nevertheless the appeal did not generate the expected donations, as the cost of the airlifts

Figure 4.1 Geneva, departure for Santa Isabel of a DC 4 transporting 6.5 tonnes of medicines and vitamins to Biafra, V-P-NG-E-00233 (© ICRC / Vaslav Markevitch, May 1968)

remained particularly prohibitive. According to the arrangement negotiated with Wharton the cost of transporting 50 tonnes of aid from the Gulf of Guinea islands to Biafra, which required six round trips, was $19,000.

Beginning with June 1968, donations began to flow in and to some extent helped solve the financial difficulties, but the air route as it stood proved to be inadequate for the situation on the ground. Fulfilling requirements – estimated at around 200 tonnes per day at the beginning of July – would require constant flights back and forth to Biafra, which Wharton was unable to provide. While his services were hired by the churches, ICRC and Biafran authorities, the airline only had three planes. Moreover, following the fall of Port Harcourt, the Biafrans demanded that the transport of weapons be given priority over aid. Whilst these circumstances affected the effectiveness of the operations run by both the churches and the ICRC, the latter also faced specific problems. Unlike the religious organisations which were based in São Tomé, where arms deliveries also passed through, the ICRC operated from the island of Fernando Poo. This situation raised difficulties with regard to timetables since Santa Isabel airport was closed at night, which was exactly when flights to Biafra took place. Wharton's planes therefore had to fly from São Tomé to Fernando Poo, where the food cargo was loaded, and then fly back to São Tomé, where they waited until nightfall before taking off. Finally, as the routes became more and more dangerous, pilots sometimes refused to fly.[66] These hazards led the various humanitarian actors to rethink their operations so they could better meet the magnitude of the needs involved.

Acting in the midst of controversies

In order to find other solutions, it was necessary to resume negotiations with the belligerents. To this end, and prompted by the emotion stirred by the alarmist reports that followed the fall of Port Harcourt, the ICRC sent its delegate general for Africa to Kampala, where talks were being held between belligerents to secure a ceasefire, in order to ask for a partial lifting of the blockade.[67] This solution was rejected by Lagos, who instead proposed setting up a land corridor under ICRC control to deliver aid to Biafra. This idea aroused the interest of the Geneva-based organisation, who saw it as a less expensive way of transporting food supplies.[68] Nevertheless, there were significant political and practical difficulties that prevented the rapid implementation of this solution. First of all it was rejected by the Biafran authorities. From a military point of view, it was not in their interest to see the end of the clandestine flights which took place at night and provided cover for the transport of weapons. Politically, they could not admit that the aid meant for them was transiting Lagos since it would have meant that Biafra's survival depended on the very state from which it was seeking to free itself. Finally, they also refused to let food supplies pass through Nigeria, on the pretext that it could be poisoned there. Whilst the latter argument was the easiest to counter, for example by proposing that the ICRC inspect the supplies,[69] there were other obstacles. Indeed, the state of the communication routes from Lagos to Biafra in the summer of 1968 would slow down the setting up of a land corridor and give rise to a series of practical difficulties which, according to the ICRC delegate on the federal side, could not be underestimated.[70] Whether it was Biafran resistance or practical problems, implementing this solution would probably be a long and arduous process. Thus, although it was favoured by the FMG and to some extent by the ICRC, it was not enough given the urgency of the needs on the ground. Thus, the ICRC continued at the same time to seek agreement on airlifts until the land solution could be implemented.

From a Nigerian perspective, however, the evolving military situation meant that the previously tolerated air route was proving increasingly unacceptable. As all that was left of Biafra was the heart of Igbo country, makeshift airports became real targets for the Nigerian army since the resistance of the secessionists depended on these airstrips where weapons were being delivered. According to the British the FMG had the following military options open to it: if a negotiated solution to the conflict was not found, it could either continue the war in the heart of Igbo country, or wait until the blockade and its adversary's inability to acquire arms "brought the Igbo back to reality".[71] The British wished to discourage it from the first solution, probably because a direct attack in what remained of Biafra would have had disastrous consequences for the FMG's image. Troops were expected to face strong resistance, which would have meant heavy fighting at a time when the FMG was already regularly accused of genocide. However, in order for the Nigerians to accept the second solution they had to be able to act effectively to stop the flow of arms into Biafra, something that the ICRC's demands prevented them from doing. In the end this strategy of subduing by means of blockade and starvation seemed to be favoured by the FMG,[72] who reinforced its anti-aircraft assets and intensified its attacks on the airports within Biafra. In these circumstances, whilst the FMG still tolerated some relief shipments, it was not prepared to guarantee their safety.[73]

Looking to find a compromise, the ICRC suggested setting up a neutralised airstrip within the breakaway province, for its own exclusive use. At first the Nigerian leadership did not seem to object to such a possibility, provided that observers checked that it was used only for aid.[74] However, the solution was very quickly subject to military and political considerations on both sides, making an agreement on its implementation virtually impossible. An initial question arose about which airstrip should be used as options in what was left of Biafra were limited. A second problem pertained to flight timetables (day or night). Once the Biafrans also agreed in principle to the setting up of a neutralised airport,[75] negotiations stumbled over these two points in particular. Initially there were plans to use the Uli airstrip, which was in the best condition but also received most of the weapons. Nevertheless, the secessionists suggested that the airstrip be neutralised and used by humanitarian workers during the day, whilst reserving its use at night to continue receiving military equipment.[76] This solution proved unacceptable to the ICRC – which could not officially accept shipping aid to an airstrip used for the delivery of weapons – as well as to Lagos. There were then plans to set up an alternative landing site controlled by the ICRC and specifically intended to receive its cargo.[77] The Biafran authorities and the Geneva-based organisation agreed on the Obilago airstrip (Figure 4.2), which was located near Uturu in the east of what remained of Biafra.

Once this agreement had been reached, the ICRC informed the federal government that the site had been neutralised and flights had begun. The FMG, which considered itself presented with a fait accompli, rejected this solution, arguing that the ICRC had negotiated only with the secessionists and that the neutralisation of the Obilago airstrip was unacceptable for

Figure 4.2 Building Uturu/Obilago airstrip, V-P-NG-N-00033-07
(© ICRC / H. D. Finck, September–October 1968)

military reasons. Indeed, the federal army was conducting an offensive in the region and feared that the airstrip's new status could be used to hinder its advance.[78] Moreover, at the time it did not want flights to take place during daylight hours either as this might make the transport of military equipment a little easier. Indeed, Gowon was concerned that it would be easier for arms-carrying planes to fly alongside ICRC aircraft by day than by night.[79] Furthermore, it would demoralise his soldiers, who would see relief planes destined for the enemy flying over their heads.[80] Instead, the FMG again suggested that the Uli airstrip be neutralised for the purpose of night flights,[81] something which the Biafrans could not accept for the reasons mentioned above. Although the air corridor and the neutralised airstrip were at the heart of the discussions led by Haile Selassie at the OAU Summit in Addis Ababa in August 1968,[82] no solution was found.

Whilst up until June 1968 it was mainly non-governmental actors who advocated providing aid to Nigeria–Biafra, the emotions stirred by the media coverage of the humanitarian crisis led some members of the international community, who had remained silent until then, to become more proactive. British leaders were the first to be pressured into taking action. In the United Kingdom charities were strongly mobilised and did not hesitate to make statements about the extent of the needs involved, indicating their willingness to break the blockade. This put the British government in a difficult position vis-à-vis its Nigerian counterpart,[83] leading it to seek to channel their various initiatives by encouraging them to join the efforts of the ICRC whom the FMG recognised as an interlocutor. When in July 1968 the British humanitarian-aid co-ordinator, Lord Hunt, went on a trip to Nigeria together with a representative of the British Red Cross and Save the Children, he reinforced London's view that the best way to show concern for the humanitarian situation without totally alienating the FMG was to send relief through an international body.[84] The ICRC, which claimed to be neutral and impartial, seemed to be the best potential partner and should therefore be supported in its efforts and provided with resources.[85] This second point represented a change in the attitude of the UK leadership, which had previously not always welcomed the ICRC's requests. Thus, in late May the Geneva-based organisation had asked it for a plane to make it easier to travel within Nigeria but the response had been negative.[86] A few weeks later London no longer hesitated about offering the ICRC the support of its air force in order to bring the relief supplies arriving in Lagos closer to Biafra's borders.[87]

In terms of negotiations, this course of action helped avoid the responsibility of a possible failure in the eyes of public opinion. For example, in early July the UK government relayed to the FMG requests made by Oxfam and the British Red Cross, who wished to fly relief supplies to Biafra quickly.[88]

The refusal of the Nigerian authorities to accede to these requests was made public in the press, putting London in an awkward position at a time when a debate was due to take place in Parliament on its policy towards Nigeria. Whilst the government justified its military support for the FMG on the grounds that it provided it with influence in Lagos, this episode was more indicative of its inability to soften the FMG's position. In order to avoid criticism, the line adopted by the UK leadership was to take shelter behind the ICRC, indicating that the latter was solely responsible for the negotiations.[89]

Nevertheless, the British did try to smooth the often tense relations between the Geneva-based organisation and the FMG. Behind the scenes they urged the ICRC to respect the sovereignty of the Nigerian government as much as possible, which inevitably led to tensions as the Committee also faced pressure from the public, who wanted it to be more proactive. At the same time they asked the Nigerian leadership to make as many concessions as possible. Thus, when relations became particularly strained between the FMG and the ICRC over the issue of the neutralised airport in Biafra, the British government insisted that the FMG take the initiative and reach an agreement on airlifts. It argued that its own position would become untenable if a solution was not found as the federal offensive intensified.[90] American diplomats did the same, explaining that the pressure of public opinion was becoming too great and that the FMG's refusal to accept the solution proposed by the ICRC put it in a very uncomfortable situation.[91]

The British and American governments were not the only ones to show support for the ICRC in its efforts. In the summer of 1968 the Scandinavian governments offered it material support, including by buying planes for the air bridge.[92] It was the Swiss Confederation, however, that was most concerned about the success of its humanitarian operations in the summer of 1968.[93] The links between the ICRC and the Swiss government are known to be particularly close,[94] with Switzerland also benefiting "in terms of its good reputation from the ICRC's unique work in the world".[95] The resulting close "community of interest" had a clear impact both financially – the Swiss government's support enabled the ICRC to start its action in Nigeria–Biafra in 1967 – but also with regard to personnel. The country was all the more attuned to ICRC's needs since the difficulties encountered by the organisation in its operations were seen as having an impact on Switzerland's image. As the Swiss ambassador to Lagos, Fritz Real, wrote in June 1968:

> There may be an opportunity for you to help the ICRC find the right people for its action in Nigeria. At the end of the day, the reputation of our country is indirectly at stake insofar as the whole action is to be run by Swiss nationals. It would indeed be unfortunate should donor states and other organisations helping to fund the operation feel that the Swiss are not up to the task they have been entrusted with.[96]

Indeed, the growing number of initiatives in the summer of 1968 raised fears that the ICRC would be deprived of its role as co-ordinator of relief operations in Nigeria and Biafra. Thus, when in mid-July 1968 the ICRC, stuck in negotiations that were going nowhere and facing complex logistical problems, decided to entrust the operation to someone who could take it in hand, its request was favourably received by the Swiss government.[97] The Confederation offered the services of the Swiss ambassador to Moscow, August Lindt, who had served as UN High Commissioner for Refugees in the late 1950s. Thus, in mid-July 1968 Lindt became the general commissioner for the action in Nigeria–Biafra, for which he had full responsibility.[98] The appointment of this high-profile figure was intended to enable the ICRC to get out of the quagmire of negotiations and improve the co-ordination of its action on federal territory.

In the summer of 1968 the ICRC received further support from the UN in its dealings with the belligerents. Although the latter organisation's line of political non-engagement was clearly established, the humanitarian situation and its visibility in the press and on television led the Secretary-General to speak out on the subject. U Thant broke his silence in mid-July to call on the warring parties to allow the passage of aid to areas affected by the blockade, advocating the land-corridor solution. He further stated that the UN did not wish to become directly involved, but supported the ICRC.

These few steps were made particularly necessary by the pressure exerted by some UN agencies wishing to become more actively involved in the provision of humanitarian aid to Biafra. Given the considerable extent of the needs on the ground, since June 1968 UNICEF had increased the number of its initiatives in order to develop activities in support of children. Consultants were recruited to strengthen the team dealing with the situation, and the organisation's involvement in the breakaway province was formalised with the Nigerian leadership.[99] UNICEF also secured a contribution of several thousand tonnes of aid from the US government, thus seeking to send a strong signal about the magnitude of the needs involved.[100] In July 1968 its Executive Director, Henri Labouisse, travelled to Lagos to assess the situation on the ground and support the ICRC in its negotiations. He was encouraged in this by the UN Secretary-General, who was looking for ways to offer the assistance of UN humanitarian agencies to Nigeria.[101] Although he did not directly associate himself with the trip, he did use it as an opportunity to suggest to the FMG to allow a UN representative for humanitarian issues to be sent to Lagos, to which Gowon agreed.[102] Thus, in late July 1968 U Thant appointed Nils-Göran Gussing – a senior official with the Office of the High Commissioner for Refugees who had already carried out missions on behalf of the Secretary-General in Cambodia, Thailand and the Middle East – as the UN's representative for humanitarian issues to Nigeria.

Based in Lagos, Gussing's task was to facilitate negotiations on aid delivery between the Nigerian government and humanitarian agencies, in particular the ICRC. Having very little power, it seems that his purpose was merely to provide the General Secretariat with information about the situation in Nigeria and not to play any decisive role on the ground. It was indeed necessary to meet the requirements of the federal government, which did not want the appointment to be in any way political. It was equally important to avoid the ICRC feeling threatened in its role as co-ordinator.[103] For the UN this decision was a way of showing support for humanitarian operations while leaving the responsibility to the ICRC. However, the lack of concrete results achieved by the latter showed the limitations of this strategy.

Whilst, in general, governments and international organisations decided to show their support for the ICRC's endeavours, the months of June, July and August 1968 also saw other initiatives flourish. The case of Oxfam and the British Red Cross mentioned earlier is an enlightening example as these organisations considered buying their own plane in order to be able to deliver food supplies directly to Biafra.[104] In the United States the major Catholic and Protestant relief agencies – Catholic Relief Services and Church World Service – joined by the American Jewish Committee had so far been forced to follow the US government policy of providing aid through the ICRC. However, in the summer of 1968 they decided to change tack and join the religious relief operations carried out without Nigerian agreement.[105]

Indeed, the churches were running more and more illegal flights. From June 1968 onwards they benefited from the mobilisation of German organisations who were particularly moved by the parallel drawn with the Jewish genocide.[106] Caritas Germany, Das Diakonisches Werk and Misereor provided substantial funds,[107] and on the initiative of the former two, a fleet of five planes were bought from the Sudflug airline, which helped improve the capacity of the air bridge between São Tomé and Biafra. They entrusted Wharton's men with flying these planes and thus increased the number of their flights in early July.

At the large Protestant gathering in Uppsala, Sweden, in July 1968, where the WCC's Fourth Assembly was held, the Biafran question was on the agenda. As talks were attempted between the Biafran and Nigerian Christian delegations, the assembly recognised the need to increase aid to Biafra by working together with Catholic organisations and especially the ICRC. However, the agencies of northern European Protestant churches thought that the Geneva-based institution was too slow in carrying out operations and decided to follow the example of the German Protestants from Das Diakonisches Werk. A first plane was chartered in July from a different airline to Wharton's,[108] but it could not fly immediately to Biafra because it did not have the landing codes which the American had a monopoly on.

A few days later, when Wharton's pilots refused to fly because Nigeria had reinforced its anti-aircraft defence, the ICRC and the churches joined forces to obtain the codes and unblock the situation.[109] They broke the blockade after convincing Count von Rosen, a Swedish pilot who had distinguished himself in the Italo-Ethiopian War and the Second World War, to attempt the passage. On 12 August 1968 he was able to trick the Nigerian air defence system by flying low at nightfall and managed to get to Biafra from São Tomé. He was then recruited for a short period by the relief agencies of the Protestant churches in Denmark, Norway, Sweden and Finland which came together under the umbrella of Nordchurchaid, an ad hoc organisation designed to improve the air transport of relief supplies to Biafra.[110] Joining the air bridges already set up by Caritas Internationalis and German organisations, Nordchurchaid considerably helped increase the frequency of flights organised by church relief agencies, which was noticeable from September onwards. Whilst during the five months from late March to late August 1968 ninety-four flights were made between São Tomé and Biafra on behalf of religious organisations, in September alone 189 flights were made.[111]

Meanwhile, the ICRC remained bogged down in negotiations. Given the urgency of the situation which was making the headlines, the few humanitarian flights it had managed to organise from Fernando Poo paled into insignificance. The figures for the tonnage shipped to Biafra further underline the lead taken by the churches. From late March to late August 1968 they brought in more than twice as much aid (940 tonnes compared to 398 tonnes in the case of the ICRC).[112] And journalists did not hesitate to deplore the ICRC's lack of initiative.[113] For example, Jean Buhler highlighted the effectiveness of Dr Middelkoop, a Dutch missionary who organised the distribution of relief supplies sent by Protestants to Biafra, contrasting it with the absence of the Red Cross: "We have vainly been looking for the delegate of the International Committee of the Red Cross who is probably in Fernando Poo or Geneva. There is an imposing red cross on his office door. The door is closed. Across the street, people are dying".[114] The ICRC itself was well aware that it had to act, its members pointing out in early August that it would be "increasingly difficult to justify to public opinion the indefinite storage of hundreds of tonnes of semi-perishable foodstuffs in Santa Isabel, while in Biafra people are dying of hunger every day".[115]

This situation also led the partners of the ICRC to question the wisdom of leaving the latter the responsibility of finding a solution. They did not hesitate to express their discontent, as reported by Lord Hunt to the British government on his return from Geneva,[116] where he had attended a very tense meeting between volunteer agencies. Indeed, whilst religious organisations were the first to disassociate themselves from the ICRC, their decision also raised questions among other ICRC partners. For example, deeply annoyed by the ICRC's inability to find a solution in response to the urgency of the situation, the UNICEF team in charge of operations in Nigeria–Biafra chose to entrust the churches rather than the ICRC with the food supplies it had obtained from the US government.[117] The Fund also recruited six former US Peace Corps members and seconded them to Nordchurchaid in São Tomé to help run the churches' air bridge.[118] These decisions were telling as UNICEF was in this way supporting an operation that was considered illegal by the Nigerian government and contravened UN and US policies. They were all the more significant since the Fund was one of the driving forces behind the ICRC's initial operations in Nigeria–Biafra.

Finally, the members of the Red Cross Movement, in particular the National Societies of northern European countries, also put increasing pressure on the ICRC. They became all the more impatient since some of them had provided resources for its action. Thus, the exasperation of its partners, public criticism and the demonstration by the churches that it was possible to act without the agreement of the Nigerian government played a crucial role in the ICRC's decision on 29 August 1968 to launch its own airlifts (known as Operation INALWA / International Airlift to West Africa) in the conditions envisaged in mid-August, that is flying to the neutralised Obilago airstrip first by night and then, theoretically, by day.[119]

> These same National Societies are, through Mr Beer, urging the ICRC to get the INALWA plan going without delay, now that the necessary staff and equipment are in place. Indeed, they believe that if action is not taken as soon as possible the Red Cross will dismally fail in the eyes of public opinion, the consequences of which it will have to bear for years to come. Noting, on the one hand, that given the enormous needs of the Biafran civilian population it is urgent to rapidly increase the volume of aid to Biafra and, on the other hand, that everything is ready for a large-scale operation to begin, the president and management believe that it is no longer possible to postpone the INALWA operation again and propose that it starts as soon as possible, unless Mr. Lindt, who will be returning to Geneva this evening, brings back in his briefcase a clear last-minute agreement.[120]

As this was a particularly risky manoeuvre that could anger the Nigerian leadership, the ICRC called on the governments with the most influence in Lagos and the UN to support its decision by lobbying the FMG to avoid at all costs shooting down one of its planes. Whilst some responded positively, the decision caused panic among representatives of the British government, the UN and even the ICRC in Lagos, where it was feared that it could lead to disastrous consequences. Whilst warning the FMG against attacking any Red Cross plane, the British, but also the UN representative, urged Lindt to go to Lagos to attempt one last negotiation with the FMG, which he did in early September. After several twists and turns and the intervention of the Swiss and British ambassadors, a meeting finally took place between Lindt and General Gowon on 3 September.[121] It resulted in a renewable agreement between the ICRC and the FMG which allowed daytime flights from Fernando Poo to the airport in Uli for one week, while waiting for a land corridor to be set up.[122] This time it was the Biafran authorities who rejected the agreement. They feared that the Nigerian government would take advantage of the daytime flights to attack Uli, which would no longer be protected by the Biafran air defence system as it would have to let the relief planes through. The pilots of the aircraft chartered by the ICRC also refused to fly by day.[123] This time the ICRC could no longer wait and, thanks to the planes and crews provided by the Red Cross organisations from northern Europe, decided to intensify the night flights it had so far timidly run between Fernando Poo and Biafra using the Uli and Obilago airstrips. It thus followed the path opened by the churches.

Paradoxically for the ICRC, which was known for its commitment to humanitarian law, this decision did not have a solid legal basis. In Thierry Hentsch's view it could even be described as unjustifiable in terms of positive international law, that is there was no satisfactory legal explanation for this behaviour.[124] Article 23 of the Fourth Geneva Convention, which provided that in the case of a blockade it was incumbent on the blockading power to allow the passage of humanitarian aid to civilians under conditions set by it, could not be applied directly since it had been designed for use in international conflicts. Whilst in the case of an internal conflict the ICRC tended to apply it by analogy,[125] it had to be adapted to these particular circumstances.[126] During the negotiation phase in which it sought the agreement of Nigeria and Biafra on flight conditions, this article was relatively little invoked. When the FMG tried to use it in order to justify its procrastination over the conditions for the passage of food supplies, the ICRC replied that, having accepted the application of the conventions in the conflict, it simply had to facilitate relief activities.[127] In fact, it was not until August 1969 that the President of the ICRC asked the legal department to draw up a legal opinion on "the interpretation of the control clauses and the obligation of free passage of aid as contained in Article 23 of the Fourth Convention".[128] Unlike its attitude a year later, in September 1968 the ICRC was driven by an imperative to act that stemmed above all from the situation on the ground and the pressure from its partners and public opinion, which at the time took precedence over looking for a legal basis or respecting Nigerian sovereignty. This decision seemed particularly significant for an organisation generally known for its legalism. One wonders whether the memory of the criticism of its activities at the end of the Second World War, the use of the term genocide by the Biafrans, and the sometimes explicit comparison of the current situation with Germany in the Second World War particularly resonated within the ICRC. It is difficult to say, and the evidence for this is not easy to find in the organisation's archives. Nevertheless, these elements, whilst never really spelled out in the Committee's decision-making meetings, were perhaps not unconnected with the idea prevailing in the Committee in the late summer of 1968 that it was not possible not to act.

The study of the way in which in the late summer of 1968 humanitarian organisations took the decision to break the blockade, despite opposition from the FMG, which did not hesitate to describe it as an act of air invasion, makes it possible to identify the different forces that pushed for a humanitarian intervention led by non-governmental actors in a country that found itself in the grip of civil war and famine. Cross-referencing sources from different organisations offers the possibility of reconstructing this process and highlighting the extent to which the positions taken by the various actors echoed each other. The early initiatives by the churches are explained by their very strong links with the Biafran people, their strong presence on the ground and their ability to mobilise various resources on the international stage, whether in terms of obtaining support from the Vatican or appealing to the generosity of Christians around the world. Their initiatives very quickly brought to light the difficulties faced by the ICRC, even though the latter had been identified by other potential actors as the leading aid agency in the event of an armed conflict. Whilst the emergence of the humanitarian crisis in the media led the latter to distance itself from it, nevertheless the Geneva-based organisation did not lose its pre-eminent position in the eyes of state actors. Thus, for some states and international organisations, supporting it became the best way to show their concern for the situation without getting too involved. States were therefore partly responsible for the rise of non-governmental actors who were an excellent alternative in terms of satisfying public opinion, without being seen by Nigeria as intervening directly in the crisis.

Notes

1 N. Herlemont-Zoritchak, "'Droit d'ingérence' et droit humanitaire: les faux amis", *Humanitaire, enjeux, pratiques, débats*, 23 (December 2009); M. Bettati, *Le droit d'ingérence. Mutation de l'ordre international* (Paris: Odile Jacob, 1996).

2 D. Rodogno, *Against Massacre: Humanitarian Interventions in the Ottoman Empire, 1815–1914* (Princeton: Princeton University Press, 2012), pp. 250–1.

3 For example, Weiss, *Humanitarian Intervention*; Holzgrefe & Keohane (eds), *Humanitarian Intervention*.

4 D. Rodogno, "Réflexions liminaires à propos des interventions humanitaires des Puissances européennes au XIXe siècle", *Relations internationales*, 131:3 (2007), 9–25.

5 Rodogno, *Against Massacre*.
6 M. Bettati & B. Kouchner, *Le devoir d'ingérence: Peut-on les laisser mourir?* (Paris: Denoël, 1987). For clarification on these notions and their development in the French humanitarian community, see E. Davey, "The Language of *Ingérence* in France: Interventionist Debates in France, 1970s–1990s", in N. Frei, D. Stahl & A. Weinke (eds), *Human Rights and Humanitarian Intervention: Legitimizing the Use of Force since the 1970s* (Göttingen: Wallstein Verlag, 2017), pp. 46–63.
7 AUN, S-0098-0002-03, memorandum by Michael Reisman, research associate at the Yale Law School, September 1968. Others argued for the UN to take over the settlement of the conflict; see, for example, C. Zorgbibe, "L'ONU peut-elle et doit-elle intervenir dans l'affaire du Nigeria", *Le Monde*, 16 October 1969.
8 Simms & Trim (eds), *Humanitarian Intervention*, pp. 2–7.
9 Ryfman, *Une histoire de l'humanitaire*, p. 52.
10 De Waal, *Famine Crimes*, pp. 72–9.
11 O'Sullivan, "A 'Global Nervous System'".
12 Ryfman, *La question humanitaire*, pp. 68–126.
13 United Nations Press Services, NV/81, 1 June 1967, quoted in Clergerie, *La crise du Biafra*, p. 322.
14 Stremlau, *The International Politics of the Nigerian Civil War*, p. 86.
15 Thompson, *American Policy and African Famine*, p. 39.
16 Kirk-Greene, *Crisis and Conflict in Nigeria, Vol. 2*, pp. 172–3.
17 A. F. Guardião, "Between the 'Colonial' and the Post-Colonial': Portugal and Humanitarian Engagements During the Nigeria–Biafra War (1967–1970)", *The International History Review* 46:6 (2024), 785–803.
18 Stremlau, *The International Politics of the Nigerian Civil War*, pp. 79–80.
19 O. J. B. Ojo, "The Soviet Union and Nigeria: The Quest for Influence 1967–1983", *Africa Spectrum*, 20:2 (1985), 167–89.
20 Clergerie, *La crise du Biafra*, pp. 258–66.
21 AUN, S-0370-0036-04, letter from the chargé d'affaires of the permanent mission of Nigeria to the UN to U Thant, 6 February 1968.
22 Wiseberg, "The International Politics of Relief", pp. 346–63.
23 Barnett, *Empire of Humanity*, p. 142.
24 AUN, S-0303-0005-04, cable from Rolz-Bennett to N.-G. Gussing, 25 October 1968 and 11 November 1968; see also the file S-0291-0011-11, press release form the UN Secretariat (SG/1719; WPF/173), 14 November 1968.
25 F. Bugnion, "Le Comité international de la Croix-Rouge et les Nations unies: oppositions, complémentarité, partenariats", *Relations internationales*, 152:4 (2012), 3–16, at 4.
26 Bugnion, *Le CICR et la protection des victimes de la guerre*, pp. 401–12.
27 Bugnion, *Le CICR et la protection des victimes de la guerre*, pp. 427–32.
28 C. Rey-Schyrr, *De Yalta à Dien Bien Phu: histoire du Comité international de la Croix-Rouge, 1945–1955* (Geneva: CICR, Georg, 2007); F. Perret & F. Bugnion, *De Budapest à Saigon: histoire du Comité international de la Croix-Rouge, 1956–1965* (Geneva: CICR, Georg, 2009).
29 On faith-based NGOs, see B. Duriez, P. Mabille & K. Rousselet, *Les ONG confessionnelles. Religion et action internationale* (Paris: L'Harmattan, 2007).

30 Dauvin, Siméant & C.A.H.I.E.R, *Le travail humanitaire*, p. 207.
31 Dauvin, Siméant & C.A.H.I.E.R, *Le travail humanitaire*, pp. 210–16.
32 AICRC, Presidential Council meeting, 17 August 1967. On the ICRC first steps in the conflict, see Hentsch, *Face au blocus*, pp. 26–38.
33 On the protection of civilians, cf. F. Bugnion, *Le CICR et la protection des victimes de la guerre*, pp. 935–81.
34 Black, *Children First*, p. 197.
35 AICRC, Directorate briefing note, minutes of a meeting with C. Egger, 6 December 1967.
36 AWCC, CCIA 428.6.25, memorandum from Carr to Aburnoth, 20 September 1968.
37 AICRC, Directorate briefing note, 15 December 1967.
38 I. Herrmann, "Décrypter la concurrence humanitaire: le conflit entre Croix-Rouge(s) après 1918", *Relations internationales*, 151:3 (2012), 91–102.
39 AICRC, plenary session of the Committee, 5 January 1967.
40 AICRC, Directorate briefing note, 28 December 1967, minutes of a meeting between representatives of the Nigerian government, the Nigerian Red Cross and the ICRC delegate in Lagos.
41 Agreement of 28 December 1967, T. Hentsch, *Face au blocus*, p. 264.
42 On their first initiatives, see O'Sullivan, *Ireland, Africa and the End of Empire*, p. 113.
43 Wiseberg, "The International Politics of Relief", p. 117.
44 ACSE, Nigerian Civil War: 1967–70, Box 2 SD-E1.2/111537, Caritas internationalis, "The Nigerian Relief programme".
45 Byrne, *An Airlift to Biafra*, p. 74.
46 On the role of Hank Wharton in the arms shipments to Biafra, cf. M. I. Draper, *Shadows: Airlift and Airwar in Biafra and Nigeria, 1967–1970* (Aldershot: Hikoki Publications, 1999), pp. 9–70.
47 Draper, *Shadows*, p. 78. See also ACSE, 11I1.12a4.2, file n° 0483/71.
48 ACSE, 11I1.12a4.2, file n° 0483/71, letter from Anthony Byrne to O'Sullivan, 15 January 1968.
49 On the humanitarian operations in São Tomé, see A. F. Guardião, "Idealism and Pragmatism: The Christian Churches' Humanitarian Aid to Biafra in and from Colonial São Tomé", *Revista de História da Sociedade e da Cultura*, 24:2 (2024), 109–32.
50 ACSE, 11I1.12a5.1, file n° 0484/71, "Caritas internationalis relief programmme to Biafra, Proposal for a second consignment".
51 Wiseberg, "The International Politics of Relief", p. 118. A. Byrne explained that he uses Latin to communicate with the fathers of the Catholic mission in São Tomé.
52 AWCC, General Secretariat, 42.003.07, memorandum by H. Reuschle, 11 March 1968.
53 ACSE, 11I1.12a5.1, file n° 0484/71, "Caritas internationalis Biafra Refugee relief programme: progress report on the 2nd Consignment".
54 ACSE, 11I1.12a5.1, file n° 0484/71, "Third progress report, Caritas internationalis Biafran refugees programme", April 1968.

55 AWCC, General Secretariat, 42.003.07, memorandum by H. Reuschle, 11 March 1968.
56 AWCC, General Secretariat, 42.003.07, memorandum by H. Reuschle, 11 and 26 April 1968.
57 AICRC, plenary session of the Committee, 1 February 1968.
58 AICRC, Directorate briefing notes, 20, 26 and 28 February 1968.
59 AICRC, Presidential Council meetings, 22 February and 21 March 1968.
60 Hentsch, *Face au blocus*, pp. 64–5; AICRC, Directorate briefing note, 15 March 1968.
61 TNA, FCO 38/300, telegram from the CO to the BHC in Lagos, 1 April 1968.
62 TNA, FCO 38/300, telegram from the FO to the consulate in Geneva, 21 March 1968.
63 TNA, FCO 38/300, telegram from the CO to the BHC in Lagos, 1 April 1968.
64 Hentsch, *Face au blocus*, pp. 52–79.
65 Hentsch, *Face au blocus*, pp. 85–91.
66 Draper, *Shadows*, pp. 116–18.
67 On Kampala's peace talks, cf. Stremlau, *The International Politics of the Nigerian Civil War*, pp. 166–74.
68 AICRC, plenary session of the Committee, 4 July 1968.
69 TNA, FCO 38/300, telegram from the CO to the BHC in Lagos, 19 June 1968.
70 TNA, FCO 38/300, telegram from the BHC in Lagos (E. G. Willan) to the CO, 27 May 1968.
71 TNA, FCO 38/300, telegram from the BHC in Lagos (D. Hunt) to the CO, 31 May 1968.
72 TNA, FCO 38 307, telegram from the BHC in Lagos (D. Hunt) to the CO, 4 July 1968.
73 TNA, FCO 38/300, telegram from the consulate in Geneva (Miss Polak) to the FO, 20 June 1968.
74 TNA, FCO 38/306, telegram from the BHC in Lagos (D. Hunt) to the CO, 28 June 1968.
75 TNA, FCO 38/307, telegram from the CO to the BHC in Lagos, 26 July 1968.
76 AICRC, Presidential Council meeting, 18 July 1968.
77 TNA, FCO 38/301, telegram from the consulate in Geneva to the FO, 22 July 1968.
78 TNA, FCO 38/302, telegram from the BHC in Lagos (D. Hunt) to the CO, 15 August 1968.
79 AICRC, AVM 2005003-14/77, note by F. Pictet, 7 December 2008.
80 Hentsch, *Face au blocus*, p. 112.
81 TNA, FCO 38/302, telegram from Washington (Dean) to the FO, 19 August 1968.
82 On Addis-Abeba's conference, cf. J. Stremlau, *The International Politics of the Nigerian Civil War*, pp. 181–214.
83 TNA, FCO 38/306, telegram from the BHC in Lagos (D. Hunt) to the CO, 1 July 1968.
84 TNA, FCO 38/298, meeting between Lord Hunt and the Prime Minister, 4 July 1968.

85 TNA, FCO 38/302, Lord Hunt and M. Hodgson's visit to Lord Shepherd, 19 August 1968.
86 TNA, FCO 38/306, telegram from the BHC in Lagos (William) to the CO, 29 May 1968.
87 TNA, FCO 38/307, telegram from the CO to the BHC in Lagos, 5 July 1968.
88 TNA, FCO 38/306, telegram from the CO to the BHC in Lagos, 28 June 1968.
89 TNA, FCO 38/306, telegram from the BHC in Lagos (D. Hunt) to the CO, 1 July 1968.
90 TNA, FCO 38/302, telegram from the CO to the BHC in Lagos, 19 August 1968.
91 TNA, FCO 38/302, telegram from Washington (Dean) to the FO, 19 August 1968.
92 AICRC, Presidential Council meeting, 18 July 1968.
93 Page, *Le Nigeria et la Suisse*, pp. 251–66.
94 Much has been written about the proximity of the CICR to the Swiss Confederation, not least because of the policy the CICR followed during the Second World War: I. Vonèche-Cardia, *Neutralité et engagement, les relations entre le Comité international de la Croix-Rouge (CICR) et le gouvernement suisse, 1938–1945* (Lausanne: Société d'histoire de la Suisse romande, 2012).
95 *Documents diplomatiques suisses* (hereafter DDS), file "Avances du CICR (1967–71)", circular to the Swiss missions, from E. Thalmann, 20 February 1968 (dodis.ch/32835).
96 DDS, "Actions d'entraide au Nigéria (1967–69)", letter from the Swiss Embassador in Nigeria to the Head of the International Organisations' Division, 14 June 1968 (dodis.ch/33772).
97 DDS, "Actions d'entraide au Nigéria – Biafra – Handakten de M. l'Ambassadeur Thalmann (1967–1969)", Aktennotiz from the Head of the International Organisations' Division, 17 July 1968 (dodis.ch/33790).
98 On his experiences as commissioner-general at the time of the action in Nigeria–Biafra, see August R. Lindt, *General Hungern Nie, Geschichte einer Hilfsaktion in Africa* (Bern: Zytglogge Verlag, 1983).
99 Wiseberg, "The International Politics of Relief", pp. 350–9.
100 Interview with G. Orick, UNICEF's consultant for the Nigeria–Biafra emergency, by D. Jacobs, 29 July 1983, p. 5.
101 AUN, S-0303-0005-04, cables from U Thant to H. Labouisse, 13 and 18 July 1968, and from H. Labouisse to U Thant, 12, 13 and 17 July 1968.
102 AUN, S-0303-0005-04, cable from U Thant to Sadruddin Agha Khan, 29 July 1968.
103 AUN, S-0303-0005-04, cable from Rolz-Bennett (New York) to Winspeare (Geneva), 31 July 1968.
104 TNA, FCO 38/306, telegram from the CO to the BHC in Lagos, 28 June 1968.
105 Thompson, *American Policy and African Famine*, pp. 47–83.
106 On the German context, see F. Hannig, "West German Sympathy for Biafra, 1967–1970: Actors, perceptions, motives", in Heerten & Moses (eds), *Postcolonial Conflict and the Question of Genocide*, pp. 218–38; Heerten, *The Biafran War and Postocolonial Humanitarianism*, pp. 218–35.

107 Between March 1968 and March 1969, funds from German organisations represented 45 per cent of the amounts received by Caritas Internationalis for the Nigeria–Biafra relief operations. ACSE, Nigerian Civil War: 1967–70, Box 2 SD-E1.2/111537, Caritas internationalis, VIII AG 69 – SS – 8, "Nigeria Biafra Relief Programme 1968", financial report; VIII AG 69 – SS – 9. "Nigeria – Biafra Relief Programme", January, February, March 1969, financial report.
108 Wiseberg, "The International Politics of Relief", pp. 138–42.
109 Draper, *Shadows*, pp. 121–2.
110 H. G. Lloyd, M. L. Mollerup & C. A. Bratved, *The Nordchurchaid Airlift to Biafra 1968–1970: An Operations Report* (Copenhagen: Folkekirkens Nodhjaelp, 1972).
111 ACSE, 1111.12a5.1, file n° 0484/71. Rev. Fr Anthony Byrne's Diary, São Tomé, July, August, September 1968.
112 Hentsch, *Face au blocus*, p. 278.
113 Hentsch, *Face au blocus*, pp. 109–14.
114 Buhler, *Tuez-les tous!*, p. 80.
115 AICRC, plenary session of the Committee, 8 August 1968.
116 TNA, FCO 38/302, minutes of the visit of Lord Hunt and M. Hodgson to Lord Shepherd, 19 August 1968.
117 Within UNICEF, the memory of the collaboration with the ICRC was not particularly positive; interview of Strahinja Bacic by Dan Jacobs, 29 July 1983. See also the book by Dan Jacobs, who worked as a consultant for UNICEF from the summer of 1968 to the end of 1969, D. Jacobs, The *Brutality of Nations* (New York: Paragon House, 1988), p. 113.
118 D. L. Koren, *Far Away in the Sky: A Memoir of the Biafran Airlift* (San Bernardino, 2011).
119 Hentsch, *Face au blocus*, p. 122.
120 AICRC, extraordinary plenary session of the Committee, 29 August 1968.
121 TNA, FCO 38/303, correspondence between the BHC in Lagos and the CO, 1, 2 and 3 September 1968.
122 Hentsch, *Face au blocus*, p. 124.
123 AICRC, B AG 280 147-002, Directorate meeting, 18 September 1968.
124 Hentsch, *Face au blocus*, p. 129.
125 AICRC, plenary session of the Committee, 11 January 1968.
126 AICRC, B AG 12-044, "Interprétation de l'article 23 de la IVe convention de Genève en regard de l'action du CICR au Nigeria", note by J. Pictet, Summer 1969.
127 TNA, FCO 38/303, telegram from the Consulate in Geneva to the FO, 1 September 1968.
128 AICRC, Presidential Council meeting, 14 August 1969.

5

On the ground: the missionary, colonial and military genealogies of humanitarian aid

As Guillaume Lachenal and Bertrand Taithe have noted, grasping the history of humanitarianism in terms of rupture and renewal raises several difficulties. Rooted in institutional histories, this approach "disregards ideological and individual continuities, the trajectories of important actors, and the role played by older charities".[1] In the case of the Nigeria–Biafra conflict this portrayal only shows the emergence of a certain type of humanitarianism – above all Western, secular and the product of civil society – whose activities were directed towards the newly independent countries and which made efficiency and operationality on foreign soil (presented as hostile) one of its main characteristics.[2] It was symbolised by the figure of the "French doctor", a modern-day hero who did not hesitate to put their life in danger to go and save "victims" throughout the world. Although it claimed to be different, it was marked by older traditions of humanitarian aid. Lachenal and Taithe have highlighted the similarities between the figure of the French doctor and missionary doctors. Johanna Siméant has shown the importance among volunteers working for large secular French NGOs of their relationship with religion, whether positive or negative.[3] She has also stressed that the humanitarianism that developed in the late 1960s retained a particular relationship to violence and a heroic dimension that borrowed from military culture.[4]

Examining relief operations through their deployment on the ground sheds light on the relationship between this new humanitarianism and older traditions, namely those stemming from the movement for humanising war and providing aid to its victims, and those that resulted from the social work of missionaries. Such an approach also reveals the variety and diversity of humanitarian actors who by the late 1960s had already developed their capacity to act in the field. The concrete problems encountered by these organisations on Nigerian and Biafran soil, and the means, knowledge and individuals mobilised to solve them, all provide clues for understanding the often ambiguous relationship between emergency aid and the religious and military spheres. Examining their effectiveness also helps illuminate the dynamics of co-operation and competition that run through the humanitarian world. The field is in fact the privileged place where institutional identities are expressed, but also where they are put to the test.[5] The complexity of the situations on the ground sometimes requires coming up with joint responses in which volunteers from different organisations have to live and work together despite coming from very different cultures and backgrounds. They therefore have to make compromises. By focusing on what happens on the ground we are better able to understand the tensions between two trends that characterise humanitarianism, namely the emergence of an international space where actors recognise each other and share a vocabulary and common codes,[6] but also where singular and well-defined identities endure. Whilst studies of international NGOs have in recent years greatly stressed the similarities and convergences between major non-governmental organisations in the humanitarian world (MSF, Oxfam, CARE), these entities also remain particularly marked by their distinct national origins and cultures.[7]

These different dynamics came to the fore in Nigeria and Biafra at the peak of the humanitarian operations, that is between the summer of 1968 when regular airlifts began and the second half of 1969 when the various actors involved stopped their shipments (in the summer in the case of the ICRC, and then at the end of the war in the case of the churches). To understand them, this chapter focuses on the different facets of the materiality of humanitarian aid. The first section is dedicated to the air operations. The use of air transport, which was particularly expensive and complex, reflected both the resources available to NGOs and the importance of logistical, technical and financial issues in humanitarian operations. As they emerged, these challenges became central to the concerns of non-governmental organisations and shaped their response to the crisis in the same way that legal or political issues did. The second section examines the humanitarian activities deployed in the territory under Biafran control by multiple actors. It questions the implications of their diversity for the effectiveness of the action and, more generally, reflects on the elements that make up a "humanitarian" identity. The third section looks at the less well-known international operations co-ordinated by the ICRC on the Nigerian territory. Both the problems encountered and the solutions found illustrate the difficulties of implementing humanitarian aid on the ground, whether it be logistical issues or tensions between the various actors who nevertheless had to work together.

Four airlifts

The delivery of supplies to Biafra via air operations is probably the best-known aspect of the response to the humanitarian crisis. During the

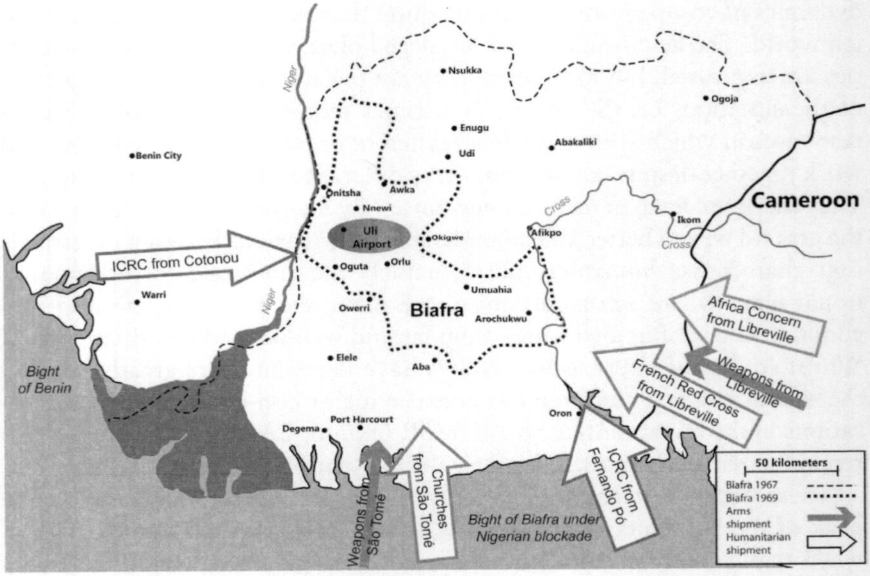

Figure 5.1 Airlifts to Biafra, March 1969 (drawn by Pablo Deroulet)

period 1968–69 various airlifts brought aid and weapons (Figure 5.1) to Uli Airport. The latter, although primarily intended for military activities, also remained the main arrival point for aid. There were sporadic moments when there were also other airstrips within Biafra. This was the case of the Obilago airstrip – mentioned in Chapter 4 – which was situated on the road between Afikpo and Ogikwe and was only operational in September 1968; or the Uga airstrip, located halfway between Awka and Orlu, which was used between March 1969 and January 1970.[8]

During the war shipments were divided between the various airlifts as follows. Those from the churches, grouped under the umbrella of Joint Church Aid (JCA), and the ICRC were the most important, followed by the French Red Cross (FRC) and the Irish organisation Africa Concern (see Table 5.1). September 1968 to June 1969 was the period when humanitarian air activity in support of Biafra was at its most substantial.

The Red Cross airlifts (shown in Figure 5.1), which were overseen by the ICRC, began in September from the island of Fernando Poo. This Spanish colony gained its independence on 12 October 1968 and by the end of that year started to question the ICRC's activities on its territory. There followed a dispute between the new state of Equatorial Guinea and the Geneva-based institution, leading the latter to set up a second base for its airlifts in Cotonou, Dahomey (now Benin), from January 1969.

Table 5.1 Summary of airlifts to Biafra

Organisation	Place of departure	Period	Tonnes of aid shipped	Number of flights
JCA	São Tomé	Late March–August 1968	940	94
		September 1968–January 1970	60,000	5,220
ICRC	Fernando Poo	April–August 1968	398	47
	Fernando Poo and Cotonou	September 1968–June 1969	20,610	2,000
	Cotonou	August 1969–January 1970	20	2
FRC	Libreville	3 September 1968–13 January 1970	2,861	475
Africa Concern	Libreville	April 1968–January 1970	3,203	306

More than twenty planes were used in this air bridge for periods ranging from several months to one week. They were chartered by the ICRC and the Swiss, Swedish, Danish, German and Canadian Red Cross societies from different companies, or they were made available by certain governments.[9] This made it possible to ship around 21,000 tonnes of relief supplies between September 1968 and June 1969. For example, in November 1968 the main imported goods were milk powder, dried fish, salt, rice and medicines. They made up 90 per cent of all shipments, with the remaining 10 per cent consisting of equipment and food for employees and fuel for vehicles making deliveries on the ground (Figure 5.2).[10] In order to work, these airlifts required the employment of dozens of people. In December 1968, when the Cotonou base did not yet exist, fifty-three people provided by the Danish, Finnish, Norwegian, Swedish and Swiss Red Cross societies were working in Fernando Poo.[11] These personnel, plus the pilots, were responsible for the daily loading and unloading of the planes, their maintenance and the radio links. The ICRC was in charge of the overall co-ordination.

As mentioned in Chapter 4, throughout the summer of 1968 the churches developed their own air activities. The creation of the Nordchurchaid structure in August marked a first step in co-ordinating northern European agencies which worked together to charter planes from different companies and then share the transport costs. By September 1968 the other relief agencies also felt the need to better co-ordinate their activities. They first formed a Committee of International Church Relief Organizations which initially brought together the American Catholic Relief Services, the Protestant Church World Service, Nordchurchaid, the German Protestant (Das Diakonisches Werk) and Catholic (Caritas Germany) groups, as well as Caritas Internationalis.[12] In October 1968 it was renamed Joint Church Aid (JCA). These organisations formed the core of the air bridge set up by the churches, to which must be added some twenty other Catholic, Protestant and non-religious organisations that did not always directly take part in the airlifts but helped fund them. For example, Oxfam and UNICEF worked alongside national Catholic relief agencies and the aid agencies of Reformed churches. The JCA's plenary sessions (in November 1968 and January, June and December 1969), which were also attended by representatives of organisations that were not involved in its activities but were interested in the unfolding situation – such as the ICRC, the UNHCR and USAID – were places where the Biafran problem was internationalised and the responses to it were discussed. The latter were then put into practice from the island of São Tomé, a veritable air base where representatives of these various agencies, the volunteers they sent, pilots, mechanics, but also journalists, mercenaries etc. lived together as best they could.[13]

This collaboration seemed to work as a real division of labour was established between the main members of the JCA.[14] The German Protestant organisation Das Diakonisches Werk, working together with Caritas, was in charge of transporting relief supplies from Europe to São Tomé, maintaining reserves and managing stocks on the island. Caritas also dealt with the issue of who could or could not board the churches' planes. In addition, Catholic Relief Services representatives in Geneva were in charge of communications in partnership with the Markpress agency, flooding Europe and the United States with press releases about the JCA's action. Several organisations specifically worked on organising the flights between Biafra and São Tomé. This was the case of Nordchurchaid, which was later joined by Canairelief, a structure created in November 1968 by Oxfam Canada and the Presbyterian Church in Canada, which had been particularly active since the beginning of the conflict. Whilst planes were usually chartered from existing airlines, there were also companies set up for the occasion. For example, when Joint Church Aid received the four planes from the US government in late 1968, a Joint Church Aid–USA company was set up to operate them. Canairelief did the same by creating CanRelief Ltd in order to be able to buy and use an aircraft for the air bridge. Finally, in April 1969 Nordchurchaid, which since its inception had chartered planes from five different companies, set up a non-profit airline with the Lutheran Church of Iceland under the name Flughjalp (Aid by Air). It acquired six aircraft,

Figure 5.2 Santa Isabel, loading of a Hercules plane chartered by the Swedish Red Cross, V-P-NG-N-00042-02A (© ICRC / Max Vaterlaus, 1968)

thus reducing the costs previously incurred from hiring them from various companies and making it easier to manage the crews.[15] These arrangements allowed the churches to ship around 57,000 tonnes of aid by making 5,314 flights to Biafra in the period from September 1968 to January 1970. In total, over forty planes were used for these airlifts. On their way back, the planes would sometimes bring children deemed to require special medical care. They would be looked after and treated in São Tomé through a programme set up by the Portuguese governor of the island, Caritas Internationalis and Das Diakonisches Werk.[16]

The ICRC and JCA operations were the largest in terms of tonnes of aid shipped, planes and personnel. Two other organisations operated their own flights from Gabon's capital, Libreville. For reasons inherent to the French government's policy during the conflict, the French Red Cross set up a system for providing aid to Biafra which was independent of the ICRC's and was mainly funded by the French government and population. This air bridge began in September 1968 and lasted until the end of the conflict in January 1970. It used Air Fret planes and Air France pilots. During that period five aircraft were mobilised by the French Red Cross, carrying around 2,861 tonnes of aid between 3 September 1968 and 13 January 1970, the date of the last of the 475 flights carried out by this organisation. On the way back, 4,311 Biafran children were taken to Gabon to be treated at the French military hospital and then looked after in various Gabonese centres run by Caritas Germany, Caritas Internationalis, the Order of Malta and Terre des Hommes. Further reception centres were opened in Côte d'Ivoire.

Also operating from Libreville, the Africa Concern organisation, which had been created in March 1968 in Dublin on the initiative of the Holy Ghost Fathers, chartered a plane from a Belgian airline to transport the relief supplies it sent by boat from Ireland.[17] While the previous airlifts were truly international ventures, those from Libreville were national in character since they were meant to be an expression of French and Irish mobilisation in support of Biafra.

Although set up under very varied conditions, on a day-to-day basis the airlifts faced similar difficulties. These firstly lay in the management of the air fleet. Enough planes had to be acquired in order to be able to deal with the hazards of an air bridge that operated in tricky conditions. The aircraft could be either chartered from private companies or obtained from various states. Once acquired, they needed rigorous maintenance which sometimes required repatriating them to Europe. They were occasionally grounded due to a lack of spare parts not readily available. In the summer of 1969, for example, when the ICRC was forced to cease its airlifts, the Nigerian government exceptionally allowed it to send three planes loaded with aid to Biafra. However, one of these planes had to remain grounded because maintenance had not been properly carried out and a technical problem was discovered too late, thus preventing the ICRC from taking full advantage of the opportunity offered by the FMG.[18]

Generally speaking, managing the air bridge required humanitarian organisations to acquire specialised knowledge of all aeronautical issues, from flying the aircraft to maintaining it. The pilots' task was particularly perilous, as passengers' accounts testify. In order not to be detected by the Nigerian air defence system and fighters, the planes had to fly with all their lights off and could not signal their presence over Biafra until just before landing. The same applied to the runway markings, which were only switched on at the last moment so as not to attract the attention of Nigerian bombers. The high frequency of arrivals and departures, which occurred only at night and often in difficult weather conditions, further complicated the crews' task. Twenty-five people died in accidents or attacks when arriving near Uli.[19]

The pilots, who were mainly European and American and made up the aircrews for periods ranging from a few days to several months, were generally supplied together with the planes by the airlines from which they were chartered. Many of them had had experience in the air forces of their respective countries. Emmanuel d'Herbès, a pilot with Air France when he agreed to take part in the French Red Cross airlifts, had gained experience in the French air force during the Indochina and Algerian wars.[20] According to Michael Draper's study, which provides many other examples, the motivations of the pilots who agreed to take these risks varied.[21] Some were moved by the Biafran cause or simply wanted to take part in the Biafran adventure and fly planes they would not have had the opportunity to try out elsewhere.[22] Others flew out of a religious conviction but the great risks they faced would sometimes weaken their resolve. Finally, the lure of financial gain was not insignificant since pilots were paid about $500 per round trip, making it one of the most lucrative jobs in aviation in the late 1960s.[23] The variety of motivations and commitment on the part of the pilots was sometimes a source of conflict with the airlift organisers. The French Red Cross, for example, complained about the casual attitude of some of them.[24] The ICRC and the churches had to deal with their fears but also their demands on several occasions, with some of them refusing to fly without a pay rise.[25] Furthermore, the use of airlines that also carried arms to Biafra and the profiles of some of the pilots helped blur the lines between humanitarian and military operations.

However, the resources used were still those of civil organisations which only received support from governments in terms of financing operations. As Laurie Wiseberg notes, the air bridge to Biafra paled in comparison to the one set up during the Berlin blockade by the American and British air forces.[26] Certainly, there were different issues at stake, and providing relief to an African population caught up in a civil war did not inspire the same mobilisation in the West as the threat of losing Berlin in the late 1940s when the areas of influence between the two blocs in Europe were crystallising. Nevertheless, the bridge to Biafra showed that it was possible for civilian organisations to use the air route without necessarily having to involve states and their armies, but such an undertaking required particular skills. Subsequently this means of transport became a major component of humanitarian operations as evidenced by the creation, a decade later, by former pilots involved in the Biafran airlifts, among others, of an NGO specialising in air travel for humanitarian operations: Aviation Sans Frontières (Aviation Without Borders).[27] Active to this day, it offers its services to other relief organisations that operate in the field, who thus do not need to acquire their own planes.

Red Cross and missionaries networks in competition

Although the literature has placed much emphasis on the airlifts because of their spectacular and controversial nature, they were only one facet of the humanitarian operation in Biafra. Once delivered, the aid was then distributed on the ground by the churches and Red Cross. It was used for the various activities developed by these organisations which included caring for the wounded or sick – wounded soldiers were more specifically referred to Red Cross teams – as well as distributing food to starving civilians. To avoid the spread of epidemics in a context where the population was already weakened by malnutrition, vaccination campaigns against tuberculosis, smallpox and measles were also conducted. Whilst the primary focus was on responding to the emergency situation, longer-term activities such as agricultural development programmes were also implemented. The ICRC had a further specific mandate regarding prisoners of war whom it recorded and whose conditions of detention it verified. In addition, it ran a special operation, called Medicairlift, for the severely war-wounded who found themselves in the breakaway province and could not be treated there due to the severity of their condition. They were evacuated on Red Cross planes and taken to places where they could receive adequate care.[28]

Relief efforts were deployed based on three distinct and relatively independent networks. The first one was a Catholic network, known as Caritas, which relied on the presence of missionaries in the province. The composition of this network at the beginning of 1969 is shown in Table 5.2, based on the Caritas lists.[29] It began to be established with the first Caritas Internationalis shipments in the spring of 1968. By the end of 1968 this network claimed to be distributing food rations in over 800 feeding centres that were located in refugee camps run by missions, in churches and in schools. Relief came via the JCA air bridge, with shipments alternating between Catholics one night and Protestants the next. The Catholic network also received cargo from flights chartered by Africa Concern.

Table 5.2 Composition of Catholic (Caritas) operations in Biafra, early 1969

Nationality	Order and position
108 Irish nationals	1 bishop 75 Holy Spirit Fathers 3 Patrician Brothers 1 Vincentian Father 2 Marist Brothers 19 Sisters of Our Lady of the Holy Rosary 2 Sisters of St John of God 3 Assumption Sisters 2 Sisters of the Presentation of Mary
326 Biafrans	1 archbishop 2 bishops 88 priests 7 priests belonging to the Congregation of the Holy Spirit 50 Marist Brothers 15 St Joseph Brothers 147 Sisters of the Immaculate Heart of Mary 15 Sisters of Misericorde 1 Sister of the Holy Rosary

Among Irish missionaries, a particular feature of Caritas operations was the prominence of Spiritans among men and of Sisters of the Holy Rosary among women. This is explained by their presence in the heart of Igbo country, the part of the region that put up the longest resistance to the advance of federal troops, as well as by their decision to follow their flock further into Biafra.[30] At the beginning of the war the other missionaries present in large numbers – such as the Kiltegan Fathers of the St Patrick's Missionary Society or the Medical Missionary Sisters of Mary – tended to be found on the periphery of the Eastern Region where the minorities who did not flee from the advancing Nigerian troops lived. They remained with their flock on land that quickly reverted to Nigeria and were thus less involved in humanitarian operations within Biafra, but played their part in the federal area. As a result, the Catholic network was the most homogeneous group among relief systems. Expatriates were mostly Irish, belonged to the same orders, and seemed to be particularly well established among the Biafran population and authorities. In terms of food distribution, they also benefited from the structures set up as early as the nineteenth century during missionary work.[31]

The situation of the Protestant operations was slightly different because of the gradual Nigerianisation policy followed by the Reformed churches since Nigeria's independence. Thus, the European or American missionaries and officials of these churches were less present in the country, with consequences for the Protestant network, which was more heterogeneous and not directly linked to religious orders. It was co-ordinated by Dr Hermann Middelkoop, a Dutch doctor based at Queen Elizabeth Hospital in Umuahia. In the second half of 1969 he was succeeded in this task by Reverend Alexander Somerville, a Church of Scotland missionary. Table 5.3 shows the composition of Protestant operations in the autumn of 1968.[32]

This network was known as the "World Council of Churches" and more specifically by its acronym "WCC". In reality, however, it did not come under the control of the WCC, which preferred as far as possible to take part in ICRC operations. Indeed, Burgess Carr, a representative of the WCC's Inter-Church Aid, Refugee and World Service Division, was particularly surprised when he went to Biafra in late 1968 and discovered that Protestant activities had taken on the name "WCC".[33] He seemed put out by its use as it did not reflect the reality of the involvement of the WCC, which was more concerned with helping to fund the ICRC's activities in order to be seen to be as neutral as possible and thus preserve its relations with the Protestants on the other side of the front line.[34] The Secretary General, Eugene Blake, wrote to the head of Protestant operations in Biafra, Dr Middelkoop, asking him to distinguish between the activities of the Reformed churches and those of the WCC.[35] However, the latter was also aware of the benefits of this exposure, which turned out to be a good way to make it better known and help its reputation in the region. This second point seems to have finally prevailed, since the WCC did not try too hard to prevent the Protestant

Table 5.3 So-called "World Council of Churches" operations, December 1968

Individuals provided (Total = 44)	**Nationality**	**Position (mostly missionaries)**
Church of Scotland (12)	Scottish	Doctor, nurse, pharmacist, agronomist, engineer, administrator, accountant etc.
Church Missionary Society (10)	British, Irish	
Methodist Missionary Society (5)	Irish, New Zealand	
Dienst Over Grenzen (4)	Dutch	
Queen Elizabeth Hospital (2)	Dutch	
Various (11)	American, British, Canadian, Norwegian	

network from continuing to use its acronym. Indeed, in order to combine their activities and give them a distinct identity, Protestants needed to share a name that could serve as a counterpart to the Caritas brand of Catholic operations or to the Red Cross.

Those involved in this network were spread across ten or so different provinces within Biafra. In each of them a "WCC" representative, usually an expatriate, had the task of receiving the relief supplies which arrived several times a week from the central warehouse located near Uli airport. They were also in charge of allocating and distributing food and relief supplies to the various refugee camps – which were run by the Biafran authorities but supplied by different organisations – to clinics and to feeding centres. Their duties also included managing large sums of money used to buy local food or deal with any emergency situation. In addition to working with refugee-camp administrators and members of other relief operations, "WCC" managers in each province co-ordinated the work of Biafran volunteers. Several hundred pastors, teachers and congregants of Biafran Christian churches took part in these so-called "WCC" operations. Indeed, this network was based on the structure of the Christian Council of Biafra which brought together the Protestant churches in the region and took its name following the province's secession. These churches had previously belonged to the Christian Council of Nigeria which operated in the federal area under the aegis of the ICRC. Just as with the Catholic network, the fact of having been established before the conflict meant that Protestant relief efforts could start relatively early, although it was not until the air bridges were set up that adequate supplies were available.[36]

The ICRC, on the other hand, did not have a network already established on the ground which it could draw on to develop its activities. Certainly, the head of its delegation, Karl Heinrich Jaggi, was well known among Biafran circles as he had been living in Eastern Nigeria for several years when the war broke out. Furthermore, the ICRC could rely on the Biafran Red Cross to run relief operations (Figure 5.3). This organisation stemmed from the Nigerian Red Cross which, after being founded in the early 1960s, had been structured into several branches, one in each of the regions of the Nigerian Federation. Thus, when Biafra declared independence the Eastern branch became the Biafran Red Cross, in which Biafran women were particularly engaged as social workers or nurses.[37] Although its work and organisation were particularly praised by the ICRC delegate,[38] this embryonic National Society was never recognised as such by the Red Cross Movement. Indeed, the ICRC made it clear from the start of the conflict that its collaboration with this entity did not in any way mean that Biafra's existence was recognised on the international scene.[39]

Figure 5.3 Umuosu, feeding-centre, V-P-NG-N-00012-22A (© ICRC / H. D. Finck, September–October 1968)

The ICRC could therefore rely almost only on it until the summer of 1968, but from the moment the emergency led to the regular dispatch of large quantities of food supplies this situation became problematic. It was necessary to ensure that the food reached only civilians and not Biafran soldiers. Furthermore, in the interests of impartiality, the ICRC had to be able to show the Biafran authorities and the general public that it operated not only in Nigeria but also in Biafra by deploying personnel there. However, before the end of the summer of 1968, apart from its delegate and two medical teams which had gone to Biafra one after the other during 1967, the ICRC had not succeeded in recruiting volunteers ready to go into the field. At the beginning of August 1968 it only had three people in the region. Media coverage of the crisis as well as its various appeals to Red Cross societies enabled it to recruit personnel from September 1968 onwards and to reach a total of 140 expatriates in the field by October (see Table 5.4). For security and budgetary reasons, in December the number of personnel was reduced to sixty-five and never increased thereafter. The personnel was divided into four medical teams working in four hospitals and sixteen medico-social teams stationed mainly in the regions of Uli, Owerri, and Umuahia. They treated the wounded as well as distributed food, working together with the Biafrans (Figures 5.4–5.5).[40]

Table 5.4 ICRC personnel in Biafra, October–December 1968

Number of people	Provided by	Nationality	Profile
70	Swedish Red Cross	Swedish	Military, former peacekeepers in Congo, Cyprus and Korea
15	French Red Cross	French, Guatemalan, Yugoslav	Medical personnel
15	ICRC, Swiss Red Cross	Swiss	Medical personnel
40	Danish, Finnish, Norwegian and Yugoslav Red Cross, Oxfam, SCF, IUCW, Seventh-Day Adventist etc.	Danish, Finnish, Norwegian, Yugoslav, British, Italian, German, Israeli, Belgian, Australian, American	Medical personnel, nutritionists, social workers, drivers
600	Biafran aid organisations	Biafran (Nigerian)	Medical personnel, social workers, drivers

Individuals involved in Red Cross operations came from particularly diverse backgrounds, and a common culture was struggling to develop. There were members of different churches, NGOs from outside the Red Cross world, as well as volunteers from various National Societies. Tasks were allocated between teams based on organisations' areas of expertise or personnel provided. In April 1969 Jaggi reported on the situation as follows:

> At present our action comprises eleven different activities: food aid, medical aid, surgical aid, vaccination campaign, clothing aid, soap production, agricultural aid (seeds, tools), help with organising the local Red Cross, temporary orphanages, blood bank, and traditional activities (prisoners, family news, and searches). Each Red Cross Society and each charity specialises in one of the above activities; for example, the IUCW specialises in nutrition, CARE in agricultural aid, the American Red Cross in blood banking, and the Swedish Red Cross in food distribution.[41]

This allocation of tasks among organisations helped to some extent counterbalance existing tensions between personnel in the field. Thierry Germond, a volunteer sent by the IUCW, recalled that most of the young French doctors did not get on well with the Swedish Red Cross teams, who

Figure 5.4 N'Nobi refugee camp, dry fish distribution, V-P-NG-N-00051-29A (© ICRC / Max Vaterlaus)

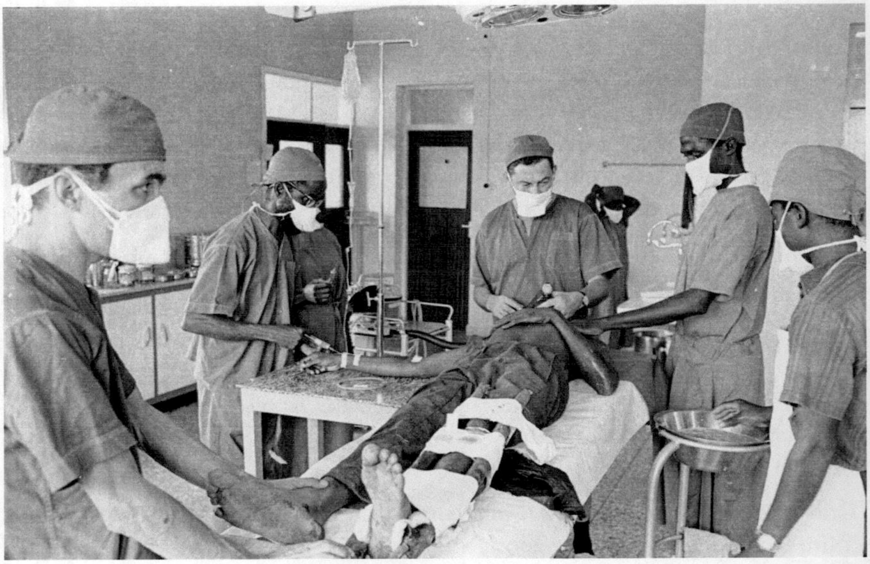

Figure 5.5 Okigwi, Red Cross hospital, V-P-NG-N-00048-31 (© ICRC / Max Vaterlaus)

operated in an almost martial way.[42] In the late 1960s National Societies and the ICRC were still very much imbued with a certain military culture. The latter set up "staff headquarters" to manage and analyse its action in Nigeria–Biafra, and would sometimes recruit its delegates from the ranks of the Swiss army. August Lindt himself praised the "very military organisation" in the field thanks to the personnel provided by the Swedish Red Cross.[43] This culture was also evident in some NGOs. Thus, beginning with the 1950s Save the Children employed former members of the military who dealt with humanitarian aid in the manner of military manoeuvres. According to Matthew Hilton the Second World War played an important role in this process, which led to an increased focus on efficiency, logistics and urgency at the expense of other dimensions of humanitarian work.[44] Nevertheless, in the late 1960s relief organisations also saw the arrival of a new generation of volunteers who were the product of the events of May 1968 and whose relationship with order and authority was not always compatible with this way of operating. Indeed, authors who nowadays analyse military-humanitarian operations underline the differences between the military and humanitarians: "the military's quasi-obsession with order, clarity, preservation, and discipline itself does not sit at all well with the more ambiguous, chaotic, abstract, democratic, and tolerant environment of NGOs".[45]

The diversity of profiles is expressed within the organisations but also among the professions represented. A general practitioner, Louis Schittly, recounted for example that there were significant rivalries between the medico-social team in Santana and that of surgeons in Awo-Omamma, even though both had been provided by the French Red Cross: "In Biafra as in France surgeons and doctors did not lead the same life and did not practise the same profession; mutual esteem was rare, though this was obviously only discreetly admitted: brotherhood among colleagues was the norm".[46] These differences were made worse by the particularly tricky conditions in which volunteers worked in the field. Tensions were exacerbated by the stress caused by recurrent bombings by the federal government and the killing of four aid workers by Nigerian soldiers in October 1968. Conversely, this exceptional situation could also sometimes smooth out difficulties. This particularly shattering shared experience could also help develop solidarity between volunteers, which could then lead to other collective experiences. The most emblematic case is that of the French Red Cross medical personnel who in 1971 helped create Médecins Sans Frontières (MSF), where they continued to be known as the "Biafrans".[47] When MSF and Médecins du Monde split in 1980, this distinction still played a fundamental role.[48]

This climate of conflict was not specific to the teams within the Red Cross network. The case of a reception centre for severely malnourished children brought from Biafra to Libreville was typical of the tensions that also existed in Catholic circles. This centre, funded by Secours Catholique Français, was run by French missionaries. In 1969 Irish missionaries came to support the staff, who were too few in number and sometimes lacked the language skills to communicate with the English-speaking Biafran children and nurses. Their arrival caused a major crisis which crystallised around educational methods to be used. The differences around national origins and distinct missionary orders did not help solve the problems, with everyone accusing each other of mutual misunderstanding.[49]

These difficulties multiplied in Biafra since not only people from different backgrounds had to come together within the same relief system, but also different networks had to work together while they sought to assert their own identity. Nevertheless, organisations tried to minimise the competition between them so as not to be accused of advancing personal interests under the guise of humanitarian aid. Indeed, in their public statements they were keen to show that they were working together without any problems and that they were only interested in helping people in need.[50] The accidental publication of notes referring to rivalries between the organisations present in Biafra therefore caused a minor diplomatic incident between the WCC and ICRC.[51]

Despite this desire to do everything possible to ensure that relations between relief agencies remained as cordial as possible, the proximity in the field posed specific problems which are hinted at in the archives. The competition between Protestant and Catholic churches in Biafra was evident during relief operations as some engaged in proselytising.[52] Members of the Protestant network reported, for example, that some Catholic priests distributed food only after having attended Sunday mass, while others only fed people who declared themselves Catholic or ready to convert.[53] These accusations were brought to the attention of and angered Caritas operations managers, who argued that even if such practices existed “they should be kept quiet”.[54] Meanwhile, some Catholics reported that Protestants fed soldiers or engaged in anti-Catholic propaganda with the Biafran authorities.[55] Nevertheless, concrete proposals were made on the ground to ensure that the distribution of aid was not discriminatory. Thus, a “WCC” representative wrote to his Catholic counterpart suggesting that an observer be sent to the “WCC” feeding centres whenever aid was given out. According to him the complaints from both sides were due to a climate of suspicion rather than real facts and the presence of a representative from the other religion could help make them go away.[56] These dynamics did not pertain only to the churches. Some ICRC teams were also criticised by religious organisations. During a visit to Biafra the representative of the WCC’s Inter-Church Aid Division, Burgess Carr, learned for example that after the arrival of the

Swedish team, co-operation between the ICRC and "WCC", which had been working well together up until then, was no longer possible.[57]

Overall, those in charge of relief operations did their best to solve these problems and everyone seemed to live and work together well enough. Thus, during the last months of the conflict, when the ICRC no longer had the resources to supply its teams, some of its volunteers joined the "WCC" operations, which went to show the porosity of these different networks.[58] Furthermore, organisations themselves could often see that they complemented each other in the field. In the summer of 1969, for example, Reverend Somerville, who ran the Protestant operations, lamented the announced departure of the ICRC. He recognised the problems its withdrawal posed, particularly with regard to the care of wounded soldiers which was primarily the responsibility of the Red Cross.[59] They would now have to be looked after by the Catholic or Protestant networks, which did not have the mandate to do so. Conversely, the ICRC repeatedly acknowledged the complementary role played by the churches, especially when it had to suspend its airlifts in early 1969 and could no longer supply its teams. While some Committee members made the point that the problems the organisation was facing benefited the churches which were able to increase their flights, August Lindt replied that seeing them as rivals was out of the question and that "without them it would have been a disaster".[60] However, their competition was keenly felt in the final phase of the humanitarian operations when the JCA refused to stop its night flights as the ICRC sought to put pressure on Ojukwu to accept the conditions for daytime flights.[61]

Despite the positive rhetoric coming from Caritas, the "WCC" and the ICRC about their relations, the organisation of relief distribution within Biafra revealed certain limitations. At night food supplies were airlifted to Uli. They were then stored in the main warehouses of each of the organisations present in the area. In the morning trucks carried them to secondary warehouses located in the ten provinces that made up what was left of Biafra. Finally, they were shared out among the distribution points that dotted the whole region. In late 1968 each network claimed to be supplying food to approximately 1,000 feeding centres. In addition, supplies were sent to refugee camps, but also to clinics and hospitals to which medicines were also shipped. While some depended exclusively on Catholic, Protestant or Red Cross organisations, others were supplied by all three networks.

This way of working had a direct impact on the efficiency of operations within the province. Dr Karl Western, who had been sent by the US government to assess the situation in late 1969, noted that it had led to aberrations. As humanitarian agencies repeatedly faced shortages of fuel and had to import petrol in order to be able to distribute aid within Biafra, a proper allocation of places to be supplied would have been a first response to the problem.[62] Attempts at co-ordination between these organisations were explored but met with limited success. For example, there were plans for the ICRC to supply the refugee camps while the churches would focus on feeding centres and health clinics, but this allocation seems to have remained theoretical.[63]

These difficulties were explained by the organisations' desire to demonstrate their responsiveness as much as possible. Thus, the churches sought to show that they were not abandoning their members, as well as win over new ones. For the Red Cross it was an opportunity to gradually establish itself in regions where its activities had previously been almost non-existent and where it was relatively unknown. Each organisation wished to be present in as many places as possible and recognised by as many people as possible. This need on the ground was coupled with the imperative of ensuring the representativeness of the actions carried out in the world. The pressure that volunteer agencies felt from public opinion and Western media led them to report significant figures so as to demonstrate their commitment. As soon as the ICRC operation in Biafra was up and running Karl Jaggi employed a person tasked solely with compiling statistics since, in his words, "it is clear that the public who donate money would like to know exactly what is being done with it".[64] In the breakaway province in December 1968, for example, the ICRC fed 850,000 women and children a day, and by May 1969 it announced it had reached one and a half million people. But these figures often masked a more complex reality. There was widespread confusion between the number of people fed and of rations distributed. Rations did not make up a full meal but rather supplemented food that was provided by the government or other organisations.[65] In any event, these figures were used by humanitarian agencies in their press releases and progress reports, highlighting the tonnes of aid airlifted in, the number of feeding centres supplied and the number of people reached by the action.

Co-ordinating relief in the federal occupied territories

Less well known than the operations within the breakaway province, the deployment of humanitarian aid in the federal area is a good place to examine the collaboration between the different protagonists. Whilst the analysis conducted in the previous pages has shown that Biafra was the place where humanitarian actors asserted their distinct identities, Nigeria illustrates that their multiplicity was sometimes necessary in devising ways to respond. This raised the question of co-ordination which made it possible to bring together actors from different backgrounds and cultures under the same banner.

The ICRC's involvement in relief operations in support of the civilian population began with the agreement it signed with the federal government and the Nigerian Red Cross in late 1967. This provided for the deployment of a relief programme throughout the war-affected territory under the responsibility of the ICRC and Nigerian Red Cross. While on the Biafran side this agreement resulted in the impossibility of finding a compromise on modes of shipment, on the federal side, in early 1968 the ICRC set up a delegation in Lagos that had the task of implementing humanitarian operations in the areas recaptured by the army. Before the summer of 1968 its action remained modest and consisted of sending a few medical teams as the ICRC did not have the financial, human or material resources necessary to conduct large-scale operations.[66] Other actors were also involved in supporting local relief structures. Thus, as early as February 1968 Caritas Internationalis funded a programme in the federal area through the Catholic Secretariat of Nigeria, while Oxfam assisted the Nigerian Red Cross by providing vehicles. With the help of the WCC, the Christian Council of Nigeria sought to set up four mobile socio-medical teams recruited through the Nigerian churches.[67] These initiatives were the result of the independent policies of various organisations which, just like in Biafra, relied on the social-work activities especially developed by the missions and churches. Given their relatively modest scale, they initially co-existed without any difficulty.

Later, as relief agencies ready to engage in Nigeria were increasingly mobilised, it became necessary to appoint a co-ordinator. However, in the history of humanitarian aid, co-ordinating efforts has always been a difficult problem to solve as it involves assigning a specific role to one organisation rather than others. Within the Red Cross Movement, in the event of an armed conflict the ICRC was responsible for organising members' relief efforts. On this basis it acquired a central position in the Nigerian operations and in April 1968 the FMG entrusted it with the task of co-ordinating all foreign aid together with the Nigerian Red Cross.

At first this decision seemed to be relatively well received by the actors who did not belong to the Red Cross world and wished to take part in the humanitarian work. They saw the ICRC as an experienced organisation with a mandate to operate in times of conflict. The Christian Council of Nigeria, for example, considered placing its teams and resources under the aegis of the Red Cross as early as February 1968, in the hope that this would facilitate their deployment in the field and simplify relations with the Nigerian army, who may have been more inclined to allow them to operate in the areas it had retaken.[68] However, by the summer of 1968 the ICRC's management of the relief operation in the federal area began to show its limitations.

In the summer of 1968 the emotion provoked in the West by the situation in Nigeria–Biafra resulted in a haphazard influx of equipment and personnel into the Nigerian capital, from where it was still thought possible to send aid to the Nigerian- and Biafran-controlled areas via a land corridor. In July food supplies were piling up in the port of Lagos because the ICRC lacked the resources to then ship them to the east of the country. This lack of resources resulted in major difficulties in managing stocks and in transporting and distributing aid. These tasks required the recruitment of medical teams and people in charge of distributing food, but also staff able to plan, co-ordinate and carry out an operation on a whole new scale, involving various actors. However, the ICRC, which did not have a reserve of delegates and medical teams, struggled to mobilise personnel before the summer of 1968.

In this respect, some discontent was expressed in Lagos as early as June 1968. The Swiss ambassador reported that the ICRC delegation did not seem able to handle the magnitude of the task. Undelivered food spoiled in the port of Lagos and the behaviour of some of its staff was criticised.[69] The ICRC tried to redress the situation by entrusting the co-ordination of the operation to Robert Hitz, the Swiss director of an international transport company who was chosen for his knowledge of "African problems" and management skills. This measure, which was accompanied by the dispatch of a Dutch medical team, relief supplies and vehicles, was intended to restore the ICRC's image in the Nigerian capital.[70] Unfortunately, the initiative did not live up to the expectations it had raised, and criticism of the way in which the operation was managed increased.[71]

In early August the aid that arrived in Lagos still struggled to find its way to those in need. The problem of transporting volunteers and aid proved particularly difficult for the ICRC as the routes to the regions bordering what remained of Biafra were not yet fully open. Several possibilities existed but they were costly and neither air, nor sea nor land routes appeared to be ideal solutions. As far as air routes were concerned there was the question of where planes would land since airports in the former Eastern Region, particularly Enugu and Port Harcourt, had suffered extensive damage since the beginning of the war. They therefore had to first be repaired. The ICRC also needed to obtain permission from the federal authorities to run these flights and this was not a matter of course since in August 1968, for example, they removed this possibility.[72] Moreover, the Nigerian army also needed to use the air route to supply its troops on the ground, which led to conflicts of priorities between aid workers and the military.

Once the south-eastern part of the former Eastern Region was well under the control of the federal army, the sea route became a much cheaper alternative (Figure 5.6). A warehouse was set up in the city of Calabar but, once the food was stored there, it still had to be moved closer to the areas near the front lines. The use of waterways, in particular the Cross River, to bring relief supplies inland again led to conflicts of priorities with the army, who also used this method to transport its equipment and men to the war zones. The ICRC therefore had to acquire or charter its own boats as it could not use the Nigerian infrastructures which had been requisitioned by the army.[73]

The only remaining option for transporting aid into the area bordering northern Biafra was by land which, although also proposed by the FMG for delivering food supplies within Biafra, was not straightforward in practice. The state of the railways and roads made it difficult to organise transport. The only railway from Lagos to the east was the one connecting Lagos to Kano. Shortly after Kaduna another railway descended towards Port Harcourt but stopped at Otukpo and did not reach Enugu. Despite negotiations with the Nigerian railway company this route was not very practical since goods had to make a long detour and stopped relatively far from the affected areas. It did, however, allow setting up

Figure 5.6 Apapa, the *Pia Vesta* chartered by the ICRC, V-P-NG-N-00076-04A (© ICRC / R. Farquharson, June 1969)

a warehouse north of Biafra from which aid could then be more easily brought to Enugu. The other way of getting food supplies to the area west and north of Biafra was via the main road that ran east from Lagos through Benin City. Indeed, there were plans for a warehouse to be set up in Agbor (west of Onitsha). However, the roads were not in good condition and journeys took a long time (Figure 5.7). Furthermore, making arrangements with local companies to hire trucks required a lot of work. In order to improve its efficiency the ICRC had to once again acquire or charter its own vehicles.[74]

All these difficulties meant that in early August 1968, when the emergency was at its height and the media were covering the issue, relief was still far from reaching people in need (Figure 5.8). Thus, 600 tonnes of food were on standby in Lagos, 500 tonnes were in transit via the routes mentioned above, but the secondary warehouses in Agbor and Enugu were still empty and only 30 tonnes were available in Calabar. The ICRC's task was further complicated by the instability in the areas retaken by the federal army. As long as the front line had not stabilised it was impossible to get relief supplies to these areas and it would therefore take at best one or two months before the local population could be reached. Moreover, in these areas the organisation of a distribution system was hampered by the disappearance of the civil administration and therefore relied mainly on the relief teams and on the army, whom the population distrusted;[75] this was unlike

Figure 5.7 Medical mission of the Lutheran Church of Missouri, V-P-NG-E-00211 (© Lutheran Church–Missouri Synod)

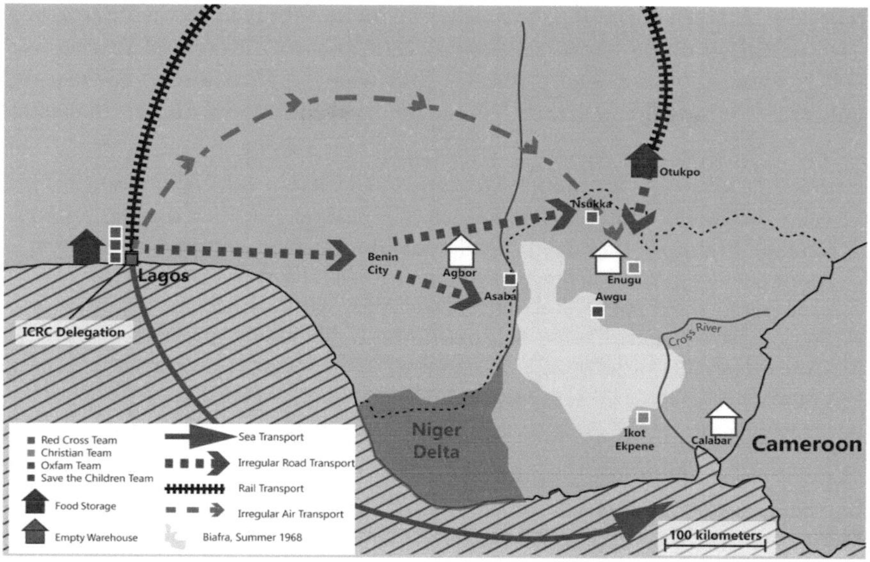

Figure 5.8 Humanitarian operations in federal territory, August 1968 (drawn by Pablo Derloulet)

the situation inside Biafra, where it could also rely on the structures set up by the authorities.

In the summer of 1968 the ICRC had only five teams in the affected areas. Provided by Save the Children and Lutheran Church–Missouri Synod, among others, they were located in Nsukka, Enugu, Awgu, Asaba and Ikot Ekpene. This poor coverage of the territory was all the more obvious as there were available personnel in Lagos where there was a large ICRC delegation and teams from other organisations were waiting to be able to go into the field. This situation was quickly noticed and criticised by the international media. The BBC described the expatriates as idle, wandering the streets of Lagos as they waited to find ways to get into the field.[76] Relief organisations involved in ICRC operations also highlighted this problem. For instance, three other teams funded or supported by Oxfam (but provided by the Salvation Army), Save the Children and the Nigerian Red Cross waited in Lagos until 10 August, when they finally set off for Calabar. They pointed out that although the Geneva-based organisation was in charge of the operations, it was not thanks to it that they had managed to reach their mission sites but rather to the representatives of the Nigerian Christian Council and Oxfam.[77] Similar criticisms were made by Nigerians working with the Red Cross. Overall, there were palpable tensions between the ICRC and other agencies involved in the operations. The British thought these problems were due to differences in the way things were done between an ICRC that was too slow and cautious, and volunteers who were portrayed as particularly motivated and enthusiastic:

> The ICRC's general effort has been handicapped by the lack of organization and resources and they have taken longer to get into their stride than many people wished. Their insistence, for example, on not sending teams into the field until they are properly equipped and on not sending forward supplies until proper arrangements exist to handle them has seemed over cautious to some critics and enthusiastic relief workers keen to get on with the job have resented being held back. No doubt past experience has convinced them that orderly organization pays in the long run even at the cost of initial delays.[78]

These comments by the British diplomats recall the opposition between "maverick" individuals and unresponsive, overcautious institutions which has been established as one of the main characteristics of the new humanitarianism that emerged in Biafra.[79] However, in this particular case these remarks were not based on the dissatisfaction of French doctors but on the experiences of volunteers from organisations working on the federal side, such as Save the Children, Oxfam or the Quakers. They testify to the widespread dissatisfaction with the ICRC at that time.

American diplomats posted to Lagos came to similar conclusions. According to them, these difficult beginnings were due to unpreparedness on the part of ICRC, which initially lacked heads of mission able to manage relations with the FMG, bureaucratic problems and the inclusion of volunteer agencies. The latter saw the Geneva-based organisation as a closed institution which did not take their suggestions into account and did not include them in the decision-making process. Moreover, they felt that their contribution to ICRC operations was not sufficiently valued or promoted. This last dimension was particularly problematic for organisations that were planning to stay in Nigeria for the long term and therefore wished that they rather than the ICRC receive credit and recognition for their achievements.[80]

Despite these difficulties, in the eyes of the governments with the most influence over Lagos – British and American – the ICRC remained the actor best able to carry out the humanitarian task. Indeed, the British doubted that "anyone else could do better".[81] It was therefore preferable to provide it with aid and to encourage it in its work rather than seek to replace it. British officials therefore supplied it with vehicles from army stocks and used their influence in Lagos to sort out its problems with the Nigerian authorities over the issue of sea and air transport.

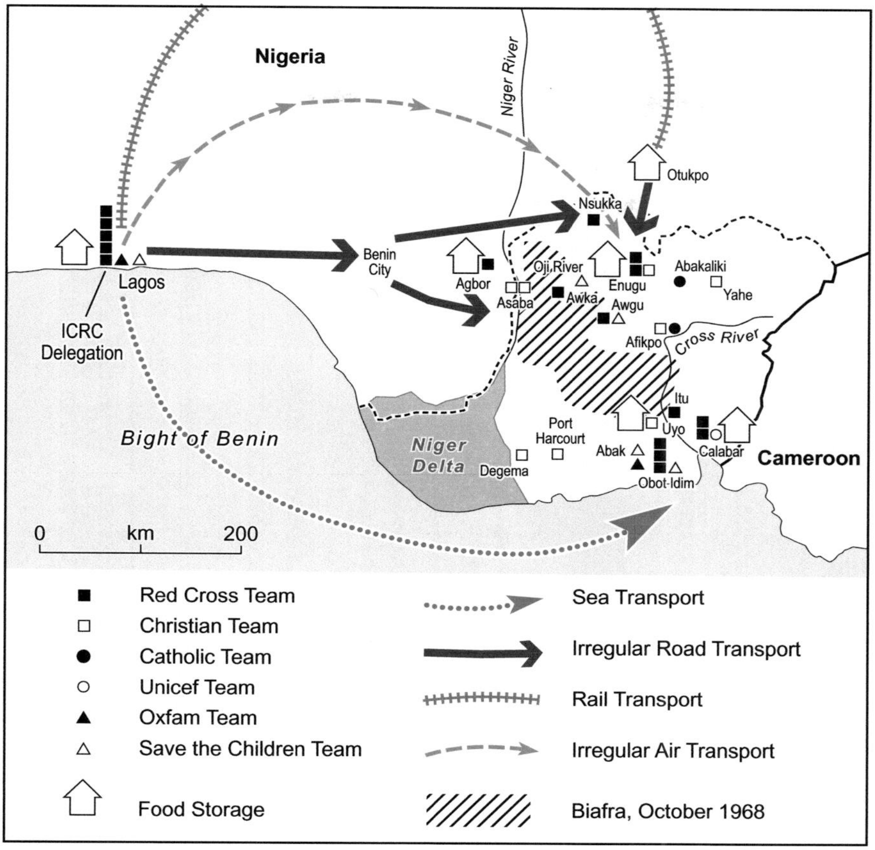

Figure 5.9 Humanitarian operations in federal territory, October 1968 (drawn by Pablo Deroulet)
Map based on TNA, FCO 38/305, "Contact n° 3, Liaison Bulletin for ICRC personnel in Nigeria".

More generally, due to the media coverage of the war and famine, the month of July saw an influx of aid pledges to the ICRC from governments, National Red Cross Societies, and other humanitarian actors, which enabled the organisation to acquire means of transport, build up stocks, and set up teams throughout the area. There was a clear shift from August (Figure 5.8) to October 1968 (Figure 5.9), when ICRC-co-ordinated operations began in earnest in the federal area. Teams were much larger and better spread out, and it was possible to deliver aid close to the disaster areas thanks to several vehicles that had been acquired or made available. By the end of 1968 the

Figure 5.10 Air transport, V-P-NG-N-00085-13A (© ICRC Archives / ARR)

ICRC operation was using over 300 trucks and cars, three ships, two planes and three helicopters. The latter, for example, were provided by UNICEF to facilitate the movement of food that arrived by boat in Calabar to the affected areas (Figure 5.10).

These resources helped improve the situation, and beginning with late October 9,404 tonnes of aid were distributed around what was left of Biafra (see Table 5.5).[82] At that point teams distributed almost 300 tonnes of food supplies every week. The operation continued to grow and, by way of comparison, in March 1969 stocks reached around 40,000 tonnes (Figures 5.11–5.12). In the case of the warehouse in Calabar alone where 7,000 tonnes were being stored, 700 tonnes were being distributed each week.[83]

These improvements were not simply due to the influx of resources but were also the result of a better overall organisation of the relief operation. August Lindt's appointment as head of the ICRC's action, which was

Table 5.5 Change in stock levels in the federal area, August–October 1968

Site	Stocks early August 1968 (tonnes)	Stocks October 1968 (tonnes)
Lagos	600	5,097
Enugu	0	1,296
Otukpo	500	402
Agbor	0	626
Calabar	30	854
Uyo	0	411
In transit between Lagos and Enugu	500	718

Figure 5.11 Apapa, ICRC inflatable warehouse, V-P-NG-N-00079-10 (© ICRC / R. Farquharson, June 1969)

Figure 5.12 Enugu, ICRC warehouse, V-P-NG-N-00039-05 (© ICRC / R. Burgy)

motivated by the need to reach an agreement with the belligerents on aid to Biafra, was also intended to improve the management of the operation in the federal area. He managed to restore order in the Lagos delegation, where Robert Hitz was replaced by Gerhart Schürch, a member of the Grand Council and the City Council of Bern, who had carried out missions for Le Don Suisse in 1947 and 1949. His arrival in Lagos in mid-August 1968 seemed to help improve relations with the volunteer agencies.[84] In Geneva steps were taken to better integrate the various partners: from August 1968 the ICRC set up weekly meetings with interested organisations "in order to manage the exchange of information on operations in Nigeria and Biafra".[85] In addition, by mentioning them in its press releases[86] and by regularly producing a bulletin on activities in the federal area beginning with 1969,[87] it also made its collaborations with other organisations more visible and thus associated them a little more with its action. This recognition seemed all the more necessary as these various entities made a decisive contribution to the ICRC. Indeed, their help enabled it to resolve the thorny issue of available personnel, whom it found so difficult to recruit in the first year of the conflict. Table 5.6 illustrates the diversity of backgrounds and funding of the teams working under its responsibility on Nigerian territory on 10 October 1968.

While on the Biafran side the month of October 1968 saw the highest number of expatriates involved in ICRC operations, on the Nigerian side their numbers continued to grow. For example, in December 1968 257 of

Table 5.6 Composition of the relief operation in the federal area, October 1968

Site	Name and composition of team	Working for
Lagos	Delegation: 12 people	ICRC
	Relief action: 29 people of whom 2 provided by the American RC, 1 by the CCN and 1 by the Nigerian RC	ICRC
	Danish technical team: 6 people	ICRC
	Yugoslav Red Cross medical team (Yaba Military Hospital): 4 people	ICRC
	Waiting to go to the East: 14 people of whom 8 provided by the ICRC, 1 by Oxfam, 4 by the SCF and 1 by the CCN	
North sector		
Enugu	Logistical team: 6 people including 2 provided by the SCF	ICRC
	ICRC transport team: 12 people	ICRC
	CCN team 4: 8 people	CCN
Yahe	1 person provided by the Lutheran Church–Missouri Synod (LCMS)	
Nsukka	Logistical team: 3 people	ICRC
Awgu	SCF team 1: 5 people	SCF
Going to Awgu	Swiss RC team: 7 people	Swiss Red Cross
Oji River (Udi)	SCF team 4: 7 people	SCF
Going to Awka	ICRC team: 8 people	ICRC
Abakaliki	Drogheda team 1: 5 people	Catholic missions
Afikpo	Drogheda team 2: 4 people Catholic Relief Services: 1 person	Catholic missions
Going to Afikpo	Saint Albans team: 5 people	Seventh-Day Adventists
South sector		
Calabar	Swedish RC team: 5 people	ICRC
	Logistical team: 4 people	ICRC
	Helicopters team: 9 people	UNICEF

(*continued*)

Table 5.6 (Cont.)

Site	Name and composition of team	Working for
Uyo	CCN team 3: 6 people provided by Dienste in Übersee (Germany), Lutherska Väldsförbundet (Sweden), Christian Aid (UK), United Church of Canada and Presbyterian Church of Canada	CCN
Obot Idim	German RC teams 1, 2 and 3: 27 people	German Red Cross
	SCF transport team: 2 people	SCF
Abak	SCF team 3: 5 people including 1 provided by the Quakers	SCF
	Salvation Army team: 6 people	Oxfam
Itu	German RC: 1 person Irish RC: 2 people	
Rivers sector		
Port Harcourt	Saint Louis team 1: 7 people including 2 provided by the CCN	LCMS
Degema	Saint Louis team 2: 4 people including 1 provided by the ICRC	LCMS
West sector		
Agbor	2 people including 1 provided by the Swedish Red Cross but funded by the ICRC	ICRC
Asaba	CCN team 1: 6 people provided by the Church of Denmark's aid organisation	CCN
	CCN team 2: 6 people provided by the Church of Norway's aid organisation	CCN
18 sites	**229 people provided by 23 different organisations and divided into 28 teams**	**Working for 10 different organisations**

them were working in the operation co-ordinated by the ICRC,[88] reaching over 300 by May 1969. To these must be added the Nigerian personnel, amounting to around 200 in November 1968,[89] whose proportion gradually increased with the process of "Nigerianisation". The breakdown presented here changed over the course of the operation as expatriates often only spent approximately three months in the field.

Just like on the Biafran side, teams were funded by various entities and their members sometimes came from different agencies. Of the twenty-three organisations involved, only seven were part of the Red Cross Movement (ICRC; German, Danish, Irish, Swedish, Swiss and Yugoslav Red Cross). The involvement of these various organisations, whether by providing personnel or funding teams, allowed for better coverage of the Nigerian territory as by October they were better spread out in the region around Biafra. This evolution also demonstrates the importance of mobilising private actors – NGOs and churches – which nevertheless received public subsidies. For example, Save the Children teams were funded by a part of the £250,000 released by the British government in the summer of 1968.

However, this system also had its drawbacks. It resulted in a rather random process of volunteer engagement which was mostly dependent on each individual organisation. The ICRC even complained about the quality of some of them, although its own recruitment process was not much better. Moreover, the relatively short duration of the volunteers' missions – 3 months – led to constant staff rotation which posed problems in terms of continuity and control. The ICRC tried to solve them by sending financial and management inspectors to ensure that food supplies did go to the people for whom they were intended.[90] As on the Biafran side, relief operations were affected by a desire for autonomy on the part of the institutions co-ordinated by the ICRC, who sought to assert their own identity in the field. This problem was particularly well understood by G. Schürch:

> There is a certain spirit of competition among volunteer agencies and a tendency, clearly visible in some missions, to favour their followers. They prefer to continue what they have done so far rather than become involved in the ICRC's general action. I do not wish to exaggerate this difficulty but it needs to be taken into consideration. Each volunteer agency wants to maintain its identity and even goes as far as to ask us where the packet of rice donated by American X went, which child ate it![91]

Despite the frustrations among some of the participants, it seems that from October 1968 onwards the operation in the federal area worked relatively well. It continued in this form until the summer of 1969 when the Nigerian government decided to withdraw the ICRC's mandate as co-ordinator.

After a chaotic start, during the period from 1968 to 1969 humanitarian organisations seemed to be able to solve the thorny issue of co-ordination among themselves. This, however, was not a matter of course due to the heterogeneous composition of relief operations in Nigeria–Biafra, which included organisations from many different traditions and backgrounds. These were a reflection of the fact that humanitarian aid was rooted in missionary, colonial and military traditions, as well as national ones. These diverse influences help us understand the ambiguous relationship that the

NGOs that emerged during and after the conflict had with these different dimensions. As Johanna Siméant explains, MSF proposed "a renewed humanitarianism, less military in its composition and hierarchical functioning than the Red Cross, but nevertheless retaining this dimension of virile fraternity and 'adventure' ".[92] A parallel can be drawn with the relationship between Africa Concern – created by Catholic missionaries – and religious orders. Beginning with the early 1970s this very strong link with the clergy became problematic within the organisation where a majority argued in favour of its secularisation.[93] This evolution was not unlike that which took place in the 1960s in the Catholic circles of other countries, namely the passage from mobilisation in support of missionary works to engagement in the development of and co-operation with the Third World through organisations that were still Catholic but less clerical, such as the Comité catholique contre la faim et pour le développement (Catholic Committee against Hunger and for Development).[94]

During the Nigeria–Biafra conflict, whilst relief agencies managed to co-ordinate themselves and operate under the same banner in the federal area, the existence of three separate distribution networks within Biafra was particularly revealing of the competition that also characterised their relationship. In order to improve their visibility, relief actors focused more on the quantitative rather than qualitative aspects of their action. The emphasis on logistics, evident in both the airlifts and operations conducted in the Biafran and Nigerian areas, reinforced this trend. In the case of the ICRC, the enthusiasm generated in the spring of 1969 by its action running smoothly from this point of view helped relegate to the background the political problems raised by the deployment of an operation of this scale in an independent state.

Notes

1 Lachenal & Taithe, "Une généalogie missionnaire et coloniale de l'humanitaire", p. 45.

2 A. Yala, "Les paradigmes coloniaux de l'action humanitaire", in N. Bancel & P. Blanchard (eds), *Cultures post-coloniales, 1961–2006* (Paris: Éditions Autrement, 2005), pp. 203–14, at p. 205.

3 J. Siméant, "Socialisation catholique et biens de salut dans quatre ONG humanitaires françaises", *Le Mouvement Social*, 227:2 (2009), 101–22.

4 Siméant, "Entrer, rester en humanitaire", pp. 54–5.

5 Siméant, "Entrer, rester en humanitaire", pp. 338–9.

6 On the concept of 'humanitarian field', Ryfman, *La question humanitaire*, pp. 142–9.

7 S. S. Stroup, *Borders Among Activists: International NGOs in the United States, Britain, and France* (Ithaca: Cornell University Press, 2012).

8 Draper, *Shadows*, p. 207.
9 Draper, *Shadows*, pp. 144–8, pp. 161–7 and pp. 268–9.
10 AICRC, plenary session of the Committee, 23 October 1968, report by K. H. Jaggi.
11 CICR, *Rapport d'activité du CICR pour l'année 1968* (Geneva: CICR, 1969), p. 19.
12 Joint Church Aid press release, 24 October 1968.
13 See, for example, Koren, *Far Away in the Sky*.
14 Lloyd, Mollerup & Bratved, *The Nordchurchaid Airlift to Biafra*, p. 103.
15 Draper, *Shadows*, p. 158, p. 168 and pp. 266–7.
16 Guardião, "Between the 'colonial' and the 'postcolonial'", p. 798; G. Seibert, "São Tomé and the Biafran War (1967–1970)", *The International Journal of African Historical Studies*, 51:2 (2018), 263–92.
17 T. Farmar, *Believing in Action: Concern the First Thirty Years 1968–98* (Dublin: A. & A. Farmar, 2002), pp. 9–28; O'Sullivan, *Ireland, Africa and the End of Empire*, pp. 107–30.
18 AICRC, Directorate briefing note, 25 August 1969.
19 Draper, *Shadows*, p. 275.
20 Interview of Emmanuel d'Herbès, 30 October 2009.
21 Draper, *Shadows*, p. 153.
22 Interview of André Gréard, 25 July 2009.
23 Koren, *Far Away in the Sky*, p. 84.
24 FNA, 5 AG FPU/687, telegram from the French Embassy in Libreville (Delauney) to the MAE, 6 March 1969.
25 AICRC, plenary session of the Committee, 28 August 1969.
26 Wiseberg, "Humanitarian Intervention", p. 75.
27 B. Chauvreau, *Pilotes sans frontières: trentes ans de vols humanitaires* (Paris: France Empire, 1999), pp. 33–61. Interview with André Gréard, 25 July 2009.
28 These two aspects of ICRC operations are studied in details here, as they were relatively marginal in relation to the total relief work carried out by the ICRC.
29 ACSE, Nigerian Civil War: 1967–70, Box 3, SD-E1.2/111537, International Fides Service, 26 March 1969 – n° 2176 – NE 157.
30 Wiseberg, "The International Politics of Relief", pp. 105–10.
31 C. Prudhomme, "Mission religieuse et action humanitaire: quelle continuité?", *Annales de Bretagne et des Pays de l'Ouest*, 112:2 (2005), 11–29.
32 Table drawn up on the basis of the list of expatriate "WCC" operations personnel. AWCC, DICARWS, 425.4.048, Divisional Committee, 4–6 December 1968, "Personnel in Biafra".
33 AWCC, DICARWS, 425.4.048, Divisional Committee, December 1968, B. Carr, "Visit to Biafra, November 9–14, A diary".
34 AWCC, DICARWS, 425.04.057, "Commentary on Diary".
35 AWCC, General Secretariat, 42.3.008, letter from Blake to Middelkoop, 19 December 1968.
36 NLS, Papers of Rev. A. G. Somerville, files 5 and 6.

37 G. Chuku, "Women and the Nigeria–Biafra War", in Moses & Heerten (eds), *Postcolonial Conflict and the Question of Genocide*, p. 345.
38 AICRC, plenary session of the Committee, 5 June 1968.
39 AICRC, B AG 200 147-003.01, report by G. Hoffmann, 29 June 1967.
40 CICR, *Rapport d'activités*, 1968, Geneva, CICR, 1969, p. 18–19; AICRC, plenary session of the Committee, 23 October 1968, report by K. H. Jaggi.
41 AICRC, plenary session of the Committee, 3 April 1969, report by K. H. Jaggi.
42 Interview with T. Germond, 24 February 2011. See also O. Weber, *French Doctors*, p. 43.
43 AICRC, plenary session of the Committee, 7 November 1968, report by A. Lindt.
44 M. Hilton, "Ken Loach and the Save the Children Film: Humanitarianism, Imperialism and the Changing Role of Charity in Postwar Britain", *The Journal of Modern History*, 87:2 (2015), pp. 357–94.
45 T. Cross, "Interactions entre militaires et ONG", in K. M. Cahill (ed.), *Le secours humanitaire* (Paris: NIL Éditions, 2006), p. 188.
46 L. Schittly, *L'homme qui voulait voir la guerre de près* (Paris: Arthaud, 2011), pp. 79–85.
47 Siméant, "Entrer, rester en humanitaire", p. 55.
48 Vallaeys, *Médecins sans frontières*, pp. 243–306. The author presents the tensions that led to the creation of Médecins du Monde in terms of an opposition between "Biafrans" and "*soixante-huitards*".
49 ACSE, 11I1.12a6.1, file n° 0486/71, file on the Sainte-Marie at Libreville.
50 AICRC, Presidential Council meeting, 12 September 1968.
51 AWCC, General Secretariat, 42.3.008, memorandum from B. Carr to E. Blake, 24 June 1969.
52 AWCC, General Secretariat, 42.3.008, "Random notes".
53 AWCC, DICARWS, 425.4.048, Divisonal Committee, December 1968, B. Carr, "Visit to Biafra, November 9–14, A diary".
54 AWCC, General Secretariat, 42.3.009, letter from the Anglican bishop of Owerri, G. Cockin, to E. Blake, 16 January 1969.
55 ACSE, 11I1.12a4.1, Iheoma relief activities; ACSE, 11I1.12a3.1, letter from D. O'Sulllivan to D. Byrne, 3 July 1969.
56 ACSE, 11I1.12a3.2, letter from the representative of the committee of the "WCC" at Umuahia to Father Ryan, 21 February 1969.
57 AWCC, DICARWS, 425.4.048, Divisional Committee, December 1968, B. Carr, "Visit to Biafra, November 9–14, A diary".
58 Interview with T. Germond, 24 February 2011.
59 NLS, Papers of Rev. A. G. Somerville, file 8. In fact, the CICR kept its medical teams in Biafra despite the end of the air bridge; CICR, *Rapport d'activité, 1970* (Geneva: CICR, 1971).
60 AICRC, plenary session of the Committee, 6 February 1969.
61 AICRC, B AG 12-044, critical note by P. Basset, 12 November 1970. On these events, see Chapter 6.

62 Harvard Law School Library, Clarence Clyde Ferguson's Papers, 1955–84, Series 1, Files 4–6, report by Dr K. Western on his visit to Biafra in October 1969.
63 AWCC, DICARWS, 425.4.048, Divisional Committee, December 1968, B. Carr, "Visit to Biafra, November 9–14, A diary".
64 AICRC, plenary session of the Committee, 23 October 1968, report by K. H. Jaggi.
65 AICRC, plenary session of the Committee, 23 October 1968, report by K. H. Jaggi.
66 Hentsch, *Face au blocus*, pp. 82–94.
67 AWCC, DICARWS, 425.04.057, Christian Council of Nigeria, "Relief programme", February 1968.
68 AWCC, DICARWS, 425.04.057, Christian Council of Nigeria, "Relief programme", February 1968.
69 DDS, file "Actions d'entraide au Nigéria (1967–69)", letter from the Swiss ambassador to Nigeria to the head of the International Organisations' Division, 14 June 1968 (dodis.ch/33772).
70 AICRC, Directorate briefing note, 25 June 1968.
71 TNA, FCO 38/301, letter from the BHC to Lagos (E. G. Willan) to the CO, 10 August 1968.
72 AICRC, plenary session of the Committee, 8 August 1968, report by A. Lindt; TNA, FCO 38/302, telegram from the CO to the BHC in Lagos, 22 August 1968.
73 AICRC, Directorate briefing note, 21 August 1968, report by R. Hitz, 12 August 1968.
74 AICRC, Directorate briefing note, 21 August 1968, report by R. Hitz, 12 August 1968.
75 AICRC, plenary session of the Committee, 7 November 1968, report by A. Lindt.
76 TNA, FCO 38/301, telegram from the BHC in Lagos (D. Hunt) to the CO, 31 July 1968.
77 TNA, FCO 38/301, report by E. A. Bryant, Lagos, 10 August 1968.
78 TNA, FCO 38/301, telegram from the BHC in Lagos (D. Hunt) to the CO, 12 August 1968.
79 Taithe, "Reinventing (French) Universalism", p. 149.
80 TNA, FCO 38/304, copy of a telegram from the US Embassy in Lagos (Matthew) to the Department of State, 20 September 1968.
81 TNA FCO 38/301, telegram from the BHC in Lagos (D. Hunt) to the CO, 31 July 1968.
82 On the situation in August cf. AICRC, Directorate briefing note, 21 August 1968, report by R. Hitz, 12 August 1968; on the one in October, cf. TNA, FCO 38/305, "Contact n° 3", October 1968.
83 TNA, FCO 61/497, report from Lord Hunt, "The relief operations in Nigeria", 1 April 1969.
84 TNA, FCO 38/304, copy of a telegram from the US Embassy in Lagos (Matthew) to the Department of State, 20 September 1968.

85 AICRC, B AG 280 147-002, Directorate meeting, 9 August 1968.
86 AICRC, Presidential Council meeting, 12 September 1968.
87 AICRC, Directorate briefing note, 9 April 1969.
88 CICR, *Rapport d'activité du CICR, 1968*, p. 18.
89 AICRC, Directorate briefing note, 26 November 1968.
90 AICRC, B AG 280 147-004, fourth meeting of the Commission consultative, 7 May 1969, report by H. Egli. On the volunteers, see also TNA, FCO 65/391.
91 AICRC, plenary session of the Committee, 9 January 1969, report by G. Schürch.
92 Siméant, "Entrer, rester en humanitaire", p. 55.
93 Farmar, *Believing in Action*, p. 37.
94 C. Prudhomme, "De l'aide aux missions à l'action pour le tiers monde: quelle continuité?", *Le Mouvement Social*, 177:4 (1996), pp. 9–28.

6

Contesting the legitimacy of humanitarian aid

The large-scale operations undertaken in Nigeria–Biafra in 1968 raise the question of the relationship between Western organisations and the places where they operate. For the anthropologist Didier Fassin humanitarian aid is essentially a "policy of compassion" aimed at "poorer, more unfortunate, more fragile individuals",[1] which leads to a relationship of domination between those who receive it and those who provide it. This unequal nature of aid was exacerbated by the postcolonial context in which most relief operations took place from the 1960s. Research in other disciplines, particularly anthropology and sociology, has highlighted how humanitarian actors are to this day marked by frameworks of thought inherited from colonisation, even though they claim to want to move away from them. According to Amina Yala this continuity can be seen in the sometimes caricatural view that some volunteers have of the regions in which they work. Because of the fascination it holds for some of them, the African continent is particularly susceptible to clichés: "it is seen as the poorest and therefore in most need of help; a place where living conditions are the most rudimentary, which will require them to make a real effort to adapt and be tested. It is also the most mythical and exciting continent, of which they have 'images in their heads' ".[2] According to this author two main ways of seeing local populations have emerged from their experiences, which are reminiscent of the ideal of the civilising mission and the myth of the good savage. Thus, the culture of the "Other" may be perceived as unadaptable, incompatible with the Western model of development, and therefore in need of change, giving rise to a feeling of superiority among Westerners. Conversely, it can be magnified, idealised, and the host society is then seen as "a kind of lost paradise".

Surveys conducted among beneficiaries, staff and local authorities explored the way in which aid was perceived in the societies in which it was deployed.[3] Carried out in the 2000s, at a time when there were recurrent humanitarian operations in the countries surveyed, they highlighted the fact that many of the recipients were unfamiliar with the characteristics and principles of NGOs. Whatever their specific features, the latter were above all seen as Western organisations who imposed their agendas and practices without always taking into account the complexity of the contexts they were dealing with.

These different perceptions, summarised all too briefly here, allow us to grasp the unequal nature of the relationship between beneficiaries (victims) and humanitarian-aid distributors (benefactors).[4] It is thus necessary to analyse its repercussions on the conduct of relief operations and on the relationships, often more complex than they seem, between these different categories of actors. Johanna Siméant highlights the tensions in the relationships between international NGOs, who have significant material resources at their disposal, and the authorities of the states in which they operate.[5] The role of local organisations and staff, who are both dependent on and necessary go-betweens for Western agencies,[6] also illustrates the room for manoeuvre these actors have in order to take part in, and even reappropriate, actions that are decided and implemented by others. From a historiographical point of view these questions often remain a blind spot in research. Still heavily influenced by institutional histories, the history of humanitarian aid has thus reduced "target populations" to passive recipients and has shown relatively little interest in how aid was perceived by the societies in which it was deployed.[7] This omission can also be explained by the difficulty of accessing sources, which means that it is not always possible to reconstruct these points of view.

The humanitarian operations in the Nigeria–Biafra war are no exception. In the course of doing research for this book, the impossibility of consulting Nigerian government archives and conducting extensive fieldwork meant that other solutions had to be found. Thus, the FMG's position could be grasped thanks to documents drawn up by British representatives in Lagos who were especially knowledgeable about the situation in Nigeria. As for the position of Nigerian relief organisations, this could be reconstructed by means of published sources. These different documents made it possible to examine the relationship between foreign humanitarian actors and Nigerian authorities and organisations. Thus, the crisis that erupted between the ICRC and the federal government in June 1969, which led to the latter taking over the relief operations, illustrates how the perceptions that these various actors had of each other influenced the situation on the ground. Whilst the FMG's decision to dismiss the ICRC is usually presented as the sole result of the FMG's annoyance with a humanitarian action that allowed the Biafran regime to persist, consideration of these factors shows that strategic issues were not the only ones that led to it. Finally, the growing role played by local relief organisations, which acted as interfaces between international agencies and the Nigerian government, attests to the ambivalence of the latter with regard to the deployment of humanitarian aid on its territory and raises questions about what happens to relief actions once the conflict and international mobilisation are over.

The ICRC and its African interlocutors: a growing misunderstanding

Although the crisis between the ICRC and Nigerian government did not erupt until June 1969, the tensions arising from the ICRC's presence and behaviour in Nigeria were palpable from the start of the conflict. These crystallised particularly around two issues: the negotiations on the delivery of food supplies to Biafra and the handling of the relief operation in the federal area. The way in which the ICRC conducted the discussions that were to lead to an agreement on the delivery of relief supplies was very quickly described by the FMG and its British allies as revealing a certain contempt for its African interlocutors. Thierry Hentsch has stressed that the casual way in which the Geneva-based organisation handled its first negotiations with Lagos affected their interactions from the start. Indeed, it did not really take the time to establish a relationship of trust with the Nigerian government and, as a result, by late 1967 doubt had taken root in the minds of its interlocutors about the meaning and credibility of its humanitarian undertaking.[8] The way in which the ICRC then tried to set up an air bridge to Biafra helped raise tensions which crystallised around three events in particular.

The deterioration of the situation in the Biafran province in May 1968 led the ICRC to alert the public by means of several appeals which did not go down well with the Nigerian government since they gave rise to a wave of negative opinion against it.[9] One of them, launched at the same time as peace talks were taking place in Kampala, particularly displeased the FMG. Called "SOS Biafra",[10] it urged belligerents to spare the civilian population, implicitly referring to the violence used by the federal army, and also to lift the blockade. As far as the British were concerned this appeal, although directed at both warring sides, was quite poorly worded since, by asking that relief supplies be allowed to be sent to Biafra, the ICRC was implying that the FMG was the main obstacle to such operations.[11] Because of its timing and wording it was seen as endorsing the Biafran point of view and not following the procedure established for the negotiations, and Lagos was quick to criticise the Geneva-based organisation for this.[12]

In the summer of 1968 a second episode contributed to the perception among Nigerians that they were neither taken seriously nor respected by the ICRC, and even led some to say that the latter was "the agent of certain colonialists and neocolonialists".[13] It involved a statement put out by the organisation in mid-August 1968 announcing that an agreement had been reached with the Biafran authorities on the neutralisation of the Obilago airstrip. According to the British, this incensed the FMG:

> Not unreasonably, FMG had expected ICRC to consult them about the outcome of their discussions with rebel authorities before definite arrangements for airstrip were put in hand and to give them opportunity to consider proposals. Fact that the ICRC, having negotiated and signed a formal agreement with rebel authorities without consulting them, only told the federal government about it five hours before making it public must have been a severe shock.[14]

Finally, tensions rose again in early September when August Lindt decided that Red Cross planes would try to break the blockade. Once again, the manner in which the ICRC acted on this occasion was particularly criticised by the British, who felt that the method employed by Lindt, namely telegraphing an ultimatum to Gowon, "without either taking up the Federal suggestion of a meeting with Enahoro or (still more serious) going to Lagos personally is to handle the Federal government in the manner most calculated to infuriate them and evoke a negative, obstinate and perhaps violent reaction".[15] Lindt's initial refusal to come to Lagos to discuss this issue was taken as evidence of his prejudices against the Nigerian government. It was only at the last minute that a meeting finally took place between Lindt and Gowon. It helped avoid a breakdown in relations and reach an agreement, as the FMG had made it clear that any unauthorised ICRC flights over Nigerian territory could lead to serious incidents.[16]

But the calm was short-lived. The ICRC's failure to observe the terms of this agreement, as well as the fact that it was considering the possibility of dropping food supplies directly into Biafra, led to a new crisis in late September 1968. On this occasion the Nigerians were already thinking of putting an end to all ICRC activities in the country.[17] Once again, difficulties lay mainly in the way the Swiss organisation dealt with its interlocutors, putting pressure on them to accept the measures it determined. The Nigerians were all the more sensitive since the FMG believed that it would never dare behave in this way with European governments. Another problem was the ICRC's failure to acknowledge the efforts made by the FMG, which felt that it had been accommodating to the relief effort up until then.[18] This behaviour provoked strong resentment among Nigerians, who did not hesitate to speak of a certain racism among humanitarian organisations: "It will help if the Organizations drop their racist overtones of the 'whiteman's burden in Nigeria' and quietly and more effectively supplement our local efforts where they can".[19] Following British advice and seeking to restore the ICRC's standing with Nigeria, the ICRC Director, Roger Gallopin, made a trip to Lagos in October 1968. His visit improved relations with the FMG for a while, especially as Gallopin met the country's leaders without August Lindt, who seemed to be the focus of their discontent.[20]

The crisis that unfolded with the young government of Equatorial Guinea in the winter of 1968–69 was another indication of the difficulties the ICRC had with its African interlocutors following decolonisation. In the summer of 1968 it set up its air bridge on the island of Fernando Poo in Equatorial Guinea when the latter was still a Spanish colony. As soon as Equatorial Guinea gained independence on 12 October 1968 difficulties arose between the ICRC and the new government. They culminated one evening in December 1968 when, following the discovery of petrol on the planes bound for Biafra, the local authorities refused to allow the convoys to leave. The local ICRC head of mission was imprisoned and airlifts were suspended for several weeks. The Geneva-based organisation was therefore forced to find another starting point. Several options were considered before Cotonou, in Dahomey, presented itself as the most suitable solution. At the same time, negotiations and the intervention of various actors with the Equatorial Guinean authorities finally made it possible to restore regular flights from Fernando Poo starting from mid-March. It was indeed thanks to the intercession of US diplomats and the UN that the ICRC was able to continue flying from the island. Under the cover of establishing diplomatic relations with the newly independent state, the Americans and the UN each sent an emissary to the capital of Equatorial Guinea. Their interventions, coupled with promises of development aid from the US government, helped move the negotiations forward.

There were multiple reasons behind this crisis between the ICRC and the Equatorial Guinean authorities. It was triggered by the ICRC's so-called failure to declare barrels of petrol on its planes – an established practice endorsed by the organisation since the beginning of the airlifts since fuel was necessary for the smooth running of its operations in Biafra. However, there seemed to be deeper reasons for the Equatorial Guinean regime's decision. The presence of the air bridge on its territory seemed particularly troubling to this young state. It worsened relations with its powerful Nigerian neighbour, who may have had a hand in the authorities' decision to no longer allow flights. Furthermore, the presence on the island of many Westerners and an Igbo diaspora working at the airbase fuelled the concerns of the new state's leadership. The latter feared that these might lend their support to dissidents seeking to overthrow it. Finally, the way in which the ICRC dealt with the government and handled the crisis added to the problem.

The importance of one or other of these factors varies considerably depending on the source. According to August Lindt, Nigerian pressure on Equatorial Guinea's leaders was the main reason for the difficulties encountered.[21] On the other hand, according to David Hunt, the British High

Commissioner in Lagos, who was influenced by Nigerian denials, the FMG bore little responsibility for a crisis that was primarily the result of the ICRC's behaviour on the island.[22] The UN Secretary-General also reported that the Equatorial Guineans were complaining about the attitude of the Red Cross towards them.[23] The idea, instilled by OAU Secretary General Diallo Telli, that the ICRC was a neocolonial agent was widespread.[24] Moreover, the organisation's blunders about the payments for the airlifts did not help its cause. Indeed, before the crisis that erupted in December 1968, Equatorial Guinea derived virtually no benefit from the presence of the air bridge on its territory. The airport was still managed by the Spaniards, and the financial windfall that resulted from the air bridge being set up on the island did not go into the coffers of Equatorial Guinea, but into those of the former coloniser.[25] Finally, August Lindt's supposed lack of tact was repeatedly decried by the British:

> It is Lindt who has stopped all flights. This is a further example of his belief that the best way to treat with African governments is by bullying and blackmail, using the threat of invoking world opinion against them.[26]

The British questioned his ability, and that of the ICRC in general, to deal with "African interlocutors": "You could explain to the Americans in confidence that we have some doubts about Lindt's tact and flexibility as a negotiator and, in general, in the capacity of the ICRC officials in Lagos and Fernando Poo to handle their relations with touchy Africans with the necessary patience and delicacy".[27] This remark may illustrate both a certain racism towards "the Africans", with whom one should deal in a specific manner, but also the ICRC's almost cavalier way of dealing with its interlocutors precisely because they were African. Given the precautions that the Geneva-based organisation generally took in its dealings with governments in order to avoid offending them, this hypothesis does not seem wholly improbable.

The ICRC's handling of the crisis also affected its relationship with Nigeria. Holding the FMG responsible for the situation, it sought to put pressure on it by threatening to stop its activities in the federal area. This idea provoked the ire of both the government and press in Nigeria.

> Impatience with the ICRC is the product of a long series of encounters in which they, and particularly Lindt, have shown scant regard for sensitivities or interests of FMG. Although some federal leaders may realise it would damage FMG's position, expulsion of ICRC would unfortunately be a popular move locally. Thus Morning Post leader of 13 January warmly welcomed decision to expel ICRC from Fernando Po and criticised FMG for its tolerance of their flights to rebel areas: ICRC should now be asked to channel all aid through FMG or cease operating in Nigeria. Gallopin's reported threat to consider

> stopping relief supplies to Federal territory if Equatorial Guinea action prevent ICRC from flying relief to rebel areas will merely reinforce conviction here that they are indifferent to suffering in Federal areas and that their primary interest is in helping the rebels. In this situation I am at a loss to suggest what action can usefully be taken, other than to urge government of Equatorial Guinea not to act precipitately and ICRC to mend its fence.[28]

Before Equatorial Guinea finally agreed to the resumption of flights, Lindt sought to find an alternative base for the air bridge. He approached various parties, notably Cameroon, which turned him down. Lindt then seriously considered moving it to Gabon, which would have been an affront to and cause the final rift with the FMG given that country's declared support for Biafra and the arms transport activities taking place there. The Committee's intervention prevented him from going through with this plan and led him to favour the Dahomey solution.[29] Despite this decision, which avoided a major crisis with the FMG, the blunders continued. In a meeting with the US Secretary of State, the Nigerian ambassador to the United States criticised the ICRC for not having taken the trouble to properly inform his government of its new air base being established in Cotonou. According to him, this way of doing things which was typical of the organisation helped explain why it had constant difficulties with African leaders.[30] This remark by the FMG representative attested to the Nigerian authorities' propensity to explain all the tensions in their relations with the ICRC as the result of the latter's disrespectful behaviour towards them. While its attitude was certainly not exemplary, accusing it of neocolonialism was also particularly convenient. The FMG thus absolved itself of all responsibility for the deadlocks which it was not always in its interest to see resolved.

The issue of the interactions between the ICRC and its Nigerian interlocutors also arose when the former began its work as relief co-ordinator on Nigerian territory. The Nigerian Red Cross (NRC), founded in 1960 when the country gained its independence, was a fledgling organisation at the time of the war but was seen as one of the most developed Red Cross societies in Africa (Figure 6.1). Since its creation it had been supported by the expertise of northern European Red Cross societies which developed various training programmes through the League of Red Cross societies. However, when the war broke out the means and skills of this National Society remained limited. The League therefore continued to provide it with support so it could cope with the situation, especially since the ICRC was slow in setting up its own activities. Indeed, whilst, on paper, it seemed clear from late 1967 that the action in Nigeria was the responsibility of the ICRC,[31] on the ground, the presence of the League's representative at the NRC until May 1968 blurred things and doubts persisted as to whether the ICRC or the League would co-ordinate the relief activities. In April 1968 the NRC, in agreement

Figure 6.1 Red Cross volunteers, V-P-NG-N-00005-43 (© Swedish Red Cross, July 1967)

with the League, launched an appeal to the National Red Cross Societies to raise funds, without consulting the ICRC. This appeal, which was specifically intended for victims in the federal area and referred to the forthcoming occupation of Biafra by the Nigerian army, was not well received by the ICRC, which did not approve of its wording.[32] The latter then launched its own appeal to all National Societies on 18 April 1968. In the eyes of the Nigerian Red Cross it was only beginning with this episode that the ICRC really assumed the role of co-ordinator.[33]

Although the situation had been clarified, this did not make the relationship between the Geneva-based organisation and the NRC any easier. While the latter had so far been at the centre of the League's and Nordic Red Cross societies' initiatives fostering its development, the ICRC's taking over operations meant that it was relegated to the background. The ICRC's being in charge of the humanitarian action was all the more difficult to accept since it was "seen here as purely European, whereas the League gives the impression of being a truly international body in which Africa, thanks to its National Red Cross Societies, has a voice".[34] In June 1968 the delegate general for Africa, Georg Hoffmann, drew the Committee's attention to the need to involve this National Society in its activities as much as possible and to work on its development.[35] Although the ICRC tried to provide it with increased material assistance, this was not enough. Thus, in early August the Secretary General of the Nigerian Red Cross, Timothy Udondek, launched a violent diatribe in the press against the Geneva-based organisation. At the same time, a controversy arose with the port authorities in Lagos, who accused it of criticising them and giving them a bad image abroad. They therefore decided to no longer facilitate the reception of its goods. The situation was such that in late August the president of the Nigerian Red Cross, Chief Ojo, was forced to speak publicly to restore the ICRC's image, insist that it was acting appropriately and affirm that the collaboration was going smoothly. Despite his positive statements, criticism of the ICRC did not go away.[36]

The main problem was a failure to integrate local staff into the relief effort. This was particularly highlighted in a report produced by observers from the Organisation of African Unity in late 1968. The document was met with a categorical denial by the ICRC, which believed it was making numerous efforts in this regard, and in particular argued that the relief centre in Lagos was headed by the president of the Nigerian Red Cross and employed many local volunteers.[37] Nevertheless, these observations were indicative of the way in which the ICRC was perceived by some in Nigeria and explained, in the eyes of those who made them, the unpopularity of the organisation whose activities could be "interpreted as an attack on national sovereignty and dignity".[38] To this was added the fact that, at first, the ICRC did not really use local companies for transport, storage and procurement, preferring most of the time to rely on a Swiss company already present in Nigeria, the Union Trading Company.[39] These various elements led the Quaker representative, for example, to say that this situation was akin to "a foreign invasion by means of relief; there is not 'one black person involved' ".[40]

This white presence was all the more keenly felt as it was not a guarantee of efficiency. Indeed, at first the Nigerians saw the arrival on the ground of some Swiss men who knew little about humanitarian work, let alone Nigeria, but whose nationality was supposed to give them the necessary skills for humanitarian work. This policy was criticised and helped discredit the ICRC's operations to a certain extent. As Emmanuel Urhobo, who was in charge of humanitarian aid for the Christian Council of Nigeria, pointed out: "The ICRC was more particular about recruiting Swiss nationals than recruiting experienced, sensitive and culturally adaptable people".[41] Urhobo also criticised it for its lack of flexibility and adaptability on the ground, particularly with regard to the distribution of relief supplies to those in need. Finally, Nigerian organisations made the same criticism as Western agencies involved in the relief operations: the ICRC did not acknowledge their involvement enough. Indeed, their efforts were diluted within the more general framework of "ICRC operations", whereas, according to Urhobo, the Nigerian Catholic and Protestant churches were conducting four fifths of the relief work. These different elements, to which must be added the way in which the ICRC handled negotiations with the government, explain the resentment that gradually developed towards the Geneva-based organisation and became particularly apparent during the events of June 1969, despite several attempts to improve its situation.

Probably because of its lack of experience on the newly independent African continent and its prejudices about black populations, during the first year of the war the ICRC was relatively unconcerned about the way in which its behaviour was perceived by Nigerian organisations. Nevertheless, the criticisms against it and the tensions that arose in the summer of 1968 led it to take steps to improve its position in the country. It was encouraged in this respect by the British government who, as a former colonial power, was more mindful of what the ICRC described as Nigerian "touchiness" in relation to relief efforts.[42] The British were indeed careful not to be too intrusive in this area. They refrained, for example, from offering the help of British experts to rebuild airports so as not to appear too paternalistic, since the country had its own specialists.[43]

The Geneva-based organisation then tried to improve its relationship with the NRC by including it more in important discussions with the Nigerian government. Thus, when the ICRC director visited Lagos in October 1968, a meeting with the Nigerian head of state was postponed because the president of the National Red Cross was not available. Furthermore, the ICRC began implementing a policy of "Africanising" its operations in order to include more local staff. By late November 1968 there was a ratio of "ten Africans to one white" in Biafra and "one African to one white" in Santa Isabel. Paradoxically, although this integration was eagerly awaited by the Nigerian Red Cross, it was on the federal side that it was least well applied: "three whites to two Africans".[44] Nevertheless, progress was made and mixed teams became an increasingly frequent occurrence. However, on the ground, key positions remained in Western hands despite some efforts by the ICRC in this respect. Indeed, it was not until June 1969 that three of the four regional directors of the operation run in the federal area were from the Nigerian Red Cross.[45] Within the Geneva-based organisation these measures were not self-evident and gave rise to a certain degree of reticence, some Committee members fearing that the inclusion of African staff would lead the action to lose its neutrality. They were nevertheless implemented since many believed that "the only chance for the ICRC to pursue its work in Africa is to involve the Africans themselves".[46]

Greater inclusion of the Nigerians had other benefits too. It helped improve relations with the military, which considered that there were too many foreign volunteers in the areas close to the fighting.[47] The presence of the latter, who did not always speak English and therefore could not communicate with the authorities, helped fuel the army's suspicions of the humanitarians. The ICRC noted of Nigerian teams that "their knowledge of the language and mentality of their compatriots makes them more effective than non-African teams".[48] Having mixed teams also made it possible to go into areas where access might be denied, as the ICRC's head of operations in the federal area explained:

> You probably know that Colonel Adekunlé has forbidden us to do anything whatsoever in the Port Harcourt area. But thanks to the policy followed, and in agreement with the Nigerians, we were able to get mixed teams to work there, meaning that out of twenty or so Nigerians, ten or so Europeans or Americans could be admitted as work teams in the region.[49]

Finally, the gradual implementation of this Nigerianisation policy allowed the ICRC to solve its recruitment problems and reduce its costs. Indeed, by the autumn of 1968 some Committee members were of the opinion that it was too involved in the relief effort, which cost a lot of money and could be carried out by other bodies, especially the Nigerian Red Cross. They would have preferred to see the organisation focus on what they saw as its traditional tasks, namely negotiations, dissemination and enforcement of humanitarian law, and visits to prisoners of war. Thus, at the end of the summer of 1968, when the ICRC had just managed to set up the relief operations, some of its members were already thinking of freeing it of this responsibility. As early as September the organisation was preparing to hand over the distribution of food to the Nigerian Red Cross and was thus considering hiring more Nigerian staff, including for managerial roles.[50] This was never really put into practice and the ICRC retained responsibility for the action until June 1969 when the Nigerian government decided to withdraw it. Nevertheless, this possibility was raised on several occasions and contributed to the ICRC's conviction that the organisation was providing a real service to Nigeria, which explains its incomprehension at the time of the events in June 1969.

Tensions between the ICRC, relief organisations and the FMG reached their climax during several events that unfolded in June 1969. August Lindt, the ICRC's commissioner general for the operations in Nigeria–Biafra, was arrested and detained on his arrival in Lagos on 28 May 1969, and then declared persona non grata by the FMG, which demanded his replacement. In these circumstances, Lindt submitted his letter of resignation to the ICRC on 19 June 1969. At the same time, the FMG's tolerance of night-time airlifts to Biafra was being called into question. Since September 1968 the FMG had regularly asked the ICRC to change its mode of action and send relief supplies either by day or by land, since night flights facilitated the delivery of weapons to the province. It had only accepted them thus far because it had been more or less forced into it by the British, who did not hesitate to use their military support to induce it to be very careful, and also because it did not always have the means to prevent them. However, by March 1969 there were reports in Lagos that "the Nigerian air force had achieved total control of Nigerian airspace, both by day and by night".[51] In May the Nigerian air force began bombing the Uli airstrip during the day. At the end of May there were reshuffles at the head of the army which led to tougher military operations. On the night of 2–3 June a JCA plane was targeted by Nigerian fighters but managed to escape and land in the breakaway province. Three days later, on the night of 5–6 June 1969, a Swedish Red Cross plane flying on behalf of the ICRC was targeted by the Nigerian air force. Hit by fire from a fighter, probably because it had left Fernando Poo a little too early, the Red Cross aircraft crashed near Eket and the entire crew perished in the accident.[52] As a result, the ICRC stopped its airlifts on 11 June 1969.

The ICRC's initial reaction to these events showed the rift that had opened up between the organisation and its Nigerian interlocutors. Indeed, in Nigeria relief operations were increasingly seen as Western interference which enabled the survival of Biafra and which the FMG was forced to tolerate in order to satisfy the demands of the international community. The ICRC, on the other hand, took a very different view. The members of the Committee, which was put under a lot of pressure by the situation in Nigeria–Biafra, felt that the Nigerian authorities should instead be indebted to it, especially for the food it brought to the areas retaken by the federal army. Moreover, any tensions that might emerge with its Nigerian interlocutors were usually seen by the ICRC as the result of the inability of "the Africans" to understand the principle of neutrality and of the absence of charity in African societies.[53] This paternalistic and racist stance did not encourage the organisation to question itself, especially since it relied on reports from its delegates and commissioner general which, in the spring, were particularly positive given the large amounts of aid delivered. Thus, in May 1969 the ICRC had no idea of the extent of the crisis in the making. When Lindt was arrested it even thought it still had some room for manoeuvre with the Nigerian government and considered keeping the Swiss diplomat in charge of the relief effort.[54]

The Geneva-based organisation saw Lindt's repudiation mainly as a manifestation of the FMG's discontent over international humanitarian aid as embodied by the commissioner general: "And to this suspicion was added a growing jealousy of a man who, in the eyes of world public opinion, embodied a humanitarian action that hampered the development of military action and thus became a third force that had to be destroyed".[55] In May 1969 this discontent was exacerbated by Nigerian military setbacks. Although the FMG had been announcing the end of the war for several months, it had still not managed to put an end to the secession. Moreover, from May 1969 onwards it suffered attacks from the Biafran air force which had been built by Count von Rosen. By setting up a small air fleet, the Swedish pilot had enabled the secessionists to regain ground in the south of the region and threaten the oil infrastructure. The fact that the he had previously been involved in relief operations reinforced the Nigerians' anger towards humanitarians.

The enthusiasm that the June events aroused in the country reflected the frustration with the attitude of the relief organisations that had built up in various parts of society over many months. The Nigerian media did not hesitate to describe ICRC staff as spies in the pay of Biafra and to ask the government to ban August Lindt from Nigeria,[56] forcing the Geneva-based organisation to deny the accusations levelled against it in a press release.[57] University professors and students also called for a tougher policy towards the ICRC and humanitarian organisations in general.[58] These stances, as reported in the press, led the British to say:

> The campaign against the ICRC has not been waged only by and within the Government and that the pressures on the Government to take drastic action against the ICRC have been real and strong. Nigerians at all levels have felt humiliated at the way outside bodies appear to have been allowed to ride roughshod over their Government, and while there has been much misunderstanding of the role and motives of the international relief organizations, there is little doubt that the Government's apparent decision to put its foot down over night flights has been very widely welcomed.[59]

In these circumstances, the ICRC had little room for manoeuvre to restart its air operations which had been halted on 11 June. This suspension was intended to be temporary, to allow it to assess the situation and find other ways of delivering relief supplies to Biafra. However, despite continuous negotiations since the summer of 1968, no agreement was reached between belligerents on setting up a corridor using land and water routes.[60] The ICRC therefore resigned itself to negotiating the resumption of its airlifts in the form of daytime flights. In order to avoid becoming trapped again in endless discussions on the practicalities of these flights, the ICRC's acting president, Jacques Freymond, proposed to be firm with the belligerents. When dealing with Biafra, the idea was to suspend night flights, if possible in agreement with the churches, in order to deprive the province of relief and force the secessionists to accept daytime flights in reasonable conditions. As for Nigeria, the pressure tactic envisaged was for the ICRC to withdraw from the operation it was co-ordinating in the federal area (food and medicine supplies would no longer be sent and teams would not be replaced). In this way, Freymond hoped to "make Lagos understand that the ICRC is not only a distribution body, it is also making a major and decisive contribution to the supply of food and medicines and to funding the operation".[61]

While the ICRC failed to secure the churches' support for the first measure, the FMG did not give it time to threaten it with the second. At a meeting held with humanitarian organisations on 30 June 1969, Minister Enahoro announced a new relief policy. He reminded them that humanitarian aid was first and foremost a national matter and announced, without having given any prior warning to the ICRC, that the latter would no longer co-ordinate the relief operation. This decision came as a complete surprise to the Geneva-based organisation, which had thus shown its lack of understanding of the Nigerian context by thinking it could use the threat of its withdrawal to get the FMG to compromise. Following this announcement, tempers flared in Geneva, with some considering resuming night flights in defiance of the Nigerian government.[62] Once again, intervention by British diplomats prevented a definitive break between Geneva and Lagos. The FMG invited an ICRC delegation to the federal capital to discuss daytime flight conditions and the Nigerian Rehabilitation Commission's taking over relief operations.

The ambivalences of Nigerian sovereignty

The way in which the FMG's new policy was implemented attested to the ambivalence of the various actors involved, whether it was the ICRC who had grown somewhat weary of the situation but found it difficult to officially throw in the towel, or the FMG who did draw some benefits from the contribution of foreign actors on its territory, despite its rhetoric to the contrary. In July an ICRC delegation led by its newly appointed president, Marcel Naville, went to Lagos to try to get the Red Cross air bridge reopened. The positions of the belligerents could be summarised as follows: the FMG wanted the flights to take place during the day and stop over in Lagos so that their cargo could be inspected by the Nigerian authorities. For its part, Biafra agreed to daytime flights on condition that the security of the Uli airstrip be internationally guaranteed. The ICRC's objective on this trip was to get the Nigerians to compromise on the location where the planes would be inspected, which could be Cotonou or Fernando Poo but not Lagos since Biafra would not agree to it. Once an agreement had been reached on this point, the ICRC president was planning to travel to Biafra to get Ojukwu's approval, reminding him if necessary that, should he refuse, he would have to take responsibility for the famine.[63]

The Committee was fairly enthusiastic about the plan and approved it, although some had reservations about its chances of success. Those who were most familiar with the situation were less optimistic. Indeed, Jacques Freymond pointed out that the FMG was likely to be intractable on the subject of inspecting the aircraft in Lagos, and that Biafra would not be easily persuaded to agree to daytime flights given that other humanitarian actors were continuing to supply it at night, with the French Red Cross even increasing the frequency of its flights.[64] Subsequent events proved him right. Having arrived in Lagos on 9 July 1969, the delegation failed to get the FMG to compromise and instead acceded to its demands, declaring in a joint statement that "the ICRC will not enter Nigerian airspace without the consent of the federal government".[65] Moreover, Naville failed to convince the FMG to give up on inspecting the flights in Lagos. As this clause remained unacceptable to the Biafran side, the ICRC president gave up the idea of going directly to Biafra to present this proposal. Thus, the delegation returned to Switzerland without having obtained any concessions from the FMG and having agreed not to resume shipments without its explicit authorisation.

As the ICRC had never really succeeded in obtaining the parties' agreement on flights, this new failure did not come as a surprise. On the other hand, the discrepancy between the hopes raised in Geneva by this trip and its results was indicative of the gap that had opened up between the Geneva-based organisation and its Nigerian interlocutors. When dealing with the latter, the ICRC had no real means of pressure but relied on its prestige and the respect that the presence of its president should inspire, which showed the gulf that existed between the ICRC's idea of itself and the way it was perceived in Lagos. Indeed, once it arrived in the Nigerian capital, the delegation was surprised by the virulence of the press attacks against it, making it realise that the situation was even worse than it had appeared in Geneva.[66]

For Thierry Hentsch, the hostility that reigned in the country against the Red Cross probably destabilised the newly appointed president, who had only followed the Nigerian affair as a member of the Committee and of the Presidential Council. Certainly, he surrounded himself with people who were familiar with the situation. He was accompanied by Georg Hoffmann, the delegate general for Africa, who had offered the ICRC's services to the belligerents at the beginning of the conflict. A former head of the ICRC delegation in Lagos, Hans Egli, the deputy head of the relief operations, Bernard Frey, and the delegate in charge of medical affairs, Jean-Maurice Rubli, also came on the trip. Finally, a special adviser to the ICRC president on Nigerian affairs, Enrico Bignami, was enlisted for his negotiating skills following August Lindt's resignation. Bignami was not a Red Cross man, having spent his entire career at Nestlé, which he helped to establish in Nigeria, and was its vice-president when he took up the ICRC position.[67] After the delegation's trip he was tasked with continuing discussions with the Nigerians. Apart from him and the president, they had all been on ICRC missions to Nigeria during the conflict, but the way some of them perceived their African interlocutors was indicative of the mindset with which they approached the negotiations. Thus, before taking part in this mission, one of them sent a report to Jacques Freymond in which he analysed the crisis experienced by the organisation in Nigeria. According to him, this crisis should not be taken seriously due to the "African character":

> Africans react in ways that are irrational and therefore unexpected to those who do not know them; they still live in a world where magic and taboos play a role outside of any reality or acquired knowledge ... Thankfully, these reactions – which to us are "hysterical" – never last long; African apathy or other local events make them quickly forget the object of their anger or resentment, especially when they know they need those they have attacked.[68]

Although this quote does not suggest that all members of the delegation thought in the same way, it is indicative of the racism and condescension of some humanitarians. Such preconceptions probably did not help discussions and helped fuel the feeling of superiority of the Westerners, who did not come well prepared to the negotiations as some of them thought they were indispensable and did not take their interlocutors seriously.

During the last months of the conflict discussions continued, unsuccessfully. Although some journalists at the time saw the statement made by President Naville during his trip as "the death warrant for the last chance the Red Cross had to deliver supplies to Biafra on terms that General Ojukwu could accept",[69] nevertheless, the ICRC did not throw in the towel. On 1 August it put forward a plan for introducing daytime flights, whereby the cargo would be checked by a team made up of both international observers and representatives of the two warring parties.[70] While these proposals seemed to satisfy the Biafran authorities, who agreed to them in principle on 14 August, the FMG was unhappy to see that the terms discussed in Lagos in July had been changed and was slow to respond. The ICRC then gave itself until the end of August to reach a compromise on daytime flights. A further deterioration of the situation in the breakaway province and pressure from delegates working there led it to consider giving its undelivered stocks sitting in Cotonou and Fernando Poo to the JCA and French Red Cross, in the event that a solution was not found.[71]

Its stubbornness in negotiations that seemed unlikely to succeed could be explained by the differences of opinion that existed within the Committee.

Indeed, its members fell into two main categories. On the one hand, there were those who were persuaded by the Biafran arguments and believed that it was possible to resume night flights without Lagos's agreement. They even insisted within the Committee that, despite its president's statement, the ICRC should reserve the right to challenge the FMG's sovereignty if the latter used famine as a weapon of war or persisted in "remaining unreasonable".[72] On the other hand, there were those who wanted the ICRC to throw in the towel if the belligerents did not come to an agreement soon. Their view reflected the ICRC's growing feeling of annoyance in the past several months with the behaviour of the Nigerian authorities, whom the organisation saw as irresponsible and offloading their duties on its shoulders.[73] Moreover, this course of action was also favoured because of the financial situation of the organisation which once again required the support of the Swiss government to fund its activities in Nigeria–Biafra, since if it had drawn on its own funds, it could have gone bankrupt. This position gradually became the majority position within the ICRC during the negotiations it conducted in the last months of 1969. Indeed, the former president of the Swiss Confederation and member of the ICRC, Max Petitpierre, raised the possibility of resuming night flights during the Committee's plenary sessions of 21 and 28 August 1969. He wanted the Committee to inform public opinion that negotiations had failed and to once again exercise its freedom of action by resuming night flights.[74] This suggestion was particularly opposed by the organisation's director and president.

The ICRC therefore had to avoid a major institutional crisis and try to keep within the Committee "those who are ready to throw in the towel and those who focus on the fate of the Biafran victims and are therefore ready to resume flights without the parties' agreement".[75] To this end, continuing attempts to negotiate on daytime flights seemed the best solution. An agreement seemed to have been reached on 4 September 1969,[76] the terms of which were formally approved by the ICRC and the FMG on 13 September. These were immediately rejected by the Biafrans because they included a new clause stating "that the agreement will not prejudice Nigeria's military operations".[77] Although they had accepted the idea of daytime flights, the secessionists feared that the Nigerian air force could use relief flights as a cover to attack Biafra. They made their acceptance conditional on the following point: they wanted the FMG to undertake not to take advantage of relief flights to assault the Uli airstrip, and for this undertaking to be internationally guaranteed. In an attempt to get the Biafran authorities to be less intransigent, the ICRC sent a delegation to the province but the mission ended in yet another failure. Thus, at a plenary session held on 23 October 1969 the Committee decided to close the Fernando Poo and Cotonou bases since restarting the Red Cross airlifts seemed more and more unlikely with each day.[78] It seemed inevitable that the flights would come to an end, and those in favour of resuming them were increasingly marginalised. Final pressure and proposals from the US government also failed to persuade Ojukwu.[79]

Night flights were brought up one last time, before they were finally abandoned on 6 November 1969. The argument this time was that the host countries would no longer allow planes to take off from their territory without the FMG's permission. Discussions over daytime flights continued until Biafra's surrender on 10 January 1970, without an agreement ever being reached. The worsening situation in the province did not allow the ICRC to officially throw in the towel before that date but the measures it took with regard to its stocks showed that it had lost all hope. In October it began to transfer most of its food supplies to the French Red Cross and return its partners' donations so that they could be channelled via the FRC or JCA. On the other hand, it allocated the sum of 600,000 Swiss francs in support of the medical programme in Biafra, which consisted in particular of sending essential medicines and medical equipment via the FRC and JCA.[80]

The summer of 1969 marked not only the end of the ICRC's flights but also the end of its role as co-ordinator in Nigeria. On 30 June 1969, when it announced that the ICRC would no longer co-ordinate the relief programme in the federal area, the FMG seemed to be in a hurry to take the situation in hand. It was indeed a way to reassert its sovereignty over this programme by entrusting it to the National Rehabilitation Commission. The handover of the co-ordination of relief operations from the ICRC to local organisations showed, however, the ambivalence of the Nigerian authorities with regard to outside help from the West. It also reflected the legitimacy issues faced by the Nigerian Red Cross in its own country, where it was seen both as a Nigerian organisation and as being too closely associated with the International Red Cross Movement.

After the announcement made on 30 June 1969 the ICRC did not put up any particular resistance to the FMG's decision since it had itself already considered relinquishing this role on several occasions. It did, however, negotiate the conditions for handing over its activities to the Rehabilitation Commission. In particular, it was allowed to keep a delegation on site tasked with carrying out its traditional tasks, namely visiting prisoners of war, providing a tracing service[81] and promoting humanitarian law. It further negotiated a three-month period in which to organise the handover of its assistance activities to the Nigerians, with the deadline being set for 30 September 1969. To achieve this, it pointed out that if it was forced to stop its work in Nigeria at short notice, the funding for the whole operation, not least the Nigerian personnel involved, would also come to an end. Despite its firm stance, the FMG did not have the means to immediately take over all of the ICRC's activities. Thus, the financial argument seemed to convince the FMG of the need for "a more in-depth review and gradual handover of the organisation's responsibility to the Rehabilitation Commission, with whom the Nigerian Red Cross will work together".[82]

Thus, at the same time as negotiations on the air bridge were taking place, Enrico Bignami had the task of preparing the ICRC's handover with the federal government, the Rehabilitation Commission and the Nigerian Red Cross.[83] The discussions he conducted to this end were marked by tensions between the latter two organisations. The Rehabilitation Commission had been created in the spring of 1968 by the FMG in order to deal with the aid it provided to the civilian population either through the Commission or directly through the army, whose battalions were charged with distributing supplies until ICRC-co-ordinated humanitarian teams could reach the recaptured areas.[84] Under the FMG's new policy announced in July 1969, the Commission was responsible for overseeing the activities of all the organisations operating in Nigeria to ensure that they did not carry out "any operation that could threaten the security or undermine the sovereignty of Nigeria".[85] The NRC was therefore also subject to its authority, especially since it was linked to the International Red Cross and had to suffer the consequences of the ICRC's negative image in Lagos. Thus, in July 1969 the role of the Nigerian Red Cross in the new relief organisation was not self-evident. At first it was pushed aside by the authorities, who did not invite it to the initial discussions with the ICRC.[86] One of Bignami's tasks was therefore to insist that the NRC should take part in them to the greatest extent possible and in a relatively independent fashion. Indeed, it was not only the role of co-ordinator that was being handed over, but also all the goods (food, fleet of vehicles, medical equipment etc.) managed by the ICRC and provided by various donors who preferred to hand them over to the Nigerian Red Cross rather than directly to the FMG.[87] Despite this, the NRC's role in the new arrangements remained hypothetical.[88]

This had implications for the relationship between the ICRC and NRC. The latter criticised the Geneva-based organisation for not including it in its discussions with the FMG and for not having transferred responsibility for the assistance operation to it beforehand, which would have put it in a more favourable position vis-à-vis the Rehabilitation Commission.[89] These disputes attested to the struggles for influence between relief organisations within Nigeria, and showed the significant impact of international humanitarian aid on power relations between national organisations. In the end, the NRC's fears about the role played by the ICRC in its being sidelined appeared unfounded since the latter turned its assets over to the former and, to a certain extent, continued to support its activities. Whilst the Rehabilitation Commission did indeed gain control of the relief operations,[90] the fact that the Nigerian Red Cross inherited the ICRC's equipment meant that it had the leading role, being the one with the means to act. The NRC's gradual assertiveness caused some dissatisfaction among representatives of the Rehabilitation Commission who felt that it was taking too many initiatives with potential donors, but also in the field. One of the points of contention was the allocation of the NRC co-ordinator posts in the affected areas. The Commission's representatives were unhappy that these posts were not filled by people from the region but by people from the west, especially the Yoruba. In order to satisfy the Commission, the co-ordinators were replaced by local officials who were placed under the authority of and paid by the NRC.[91]

The tensions between the Nigerian bodies had implications for the funding of the operation. Until the summer of 1969 the ICRC had been responsible for raising the necessary funds and collecting aid from various donors, while it itself financed a part of it. Since the FMG had decided to dismiss it from its role as co-ordinator, these tasks were no longer its responsibility. Thus, beginning with 30 September 1969 the situation became critical for the Nigerian relief organisations. The NRC described the months of October and November 1969 as a period "characterised by a severe shortage of funds which did not allow even the minimum financial requirements to be met so the operation could run in a satisfactory manner".[92] The funds obtained during this period represented only half of the minimum amount required for the operation to be functional. Despite an appeal to governments on 2 October 1969 and a trip by the NRC President, Chief Ojo, to European capitals, support was not forthcoming. The League and National Societies seemed reluctant to get involved since the usual process for requesting support from the Red Cross community had not been followed.[93] The main problem lay in the confusion surrounding the independence of the Nigerian Red Cross from the Rehabilitation Commission. The latter was not deemed to be up to the task either in Nigeria[94] or by foreign donors. As Enrico Bignami pointed out, "until the division of responsibilities between the Rehabilitation Commission and the Nigerian Red Cross has been clearly established, the Nigerians will not receive any assistance".[95] Indeed, it was unthinkable that the Red Cross Movement should provide funding to the NRC which could then be used by the Commission. To this was added the problem of the distribution of funds. Most of the donations in Europe and the United States had so far been collected in order to alleviate the suffering of the "Biafran children". And since the Red Cross was no longer officially active in Biafra, donors were reluctant to support Nigerian entities that operated only on federal territory.

The lack of financial resources also affected the transport of food to the affected areas, resulting in a significant slowdown in the distribution of supplies. As the FMG claimed to be able to feed its population, the re-emergence of famine in the areas under its control prompted it to take steps to redress the situation. On the one hand, it provided means for the transport of goods, and on the other hand, it clarified the relationship between the Rehabilitation Commission and the Nigerian Red Cross, with the independence of the latter being recognised. In a statement issued on 9 December 1969 the FMG said that the Commission "will not in any way interfere in the recruitment of personnel, or the management of funds and equipment belonging to the Nigerian Red Cross".[96] The statement broke the deadlock, being followed by the immediate provision of financial support through the League, which made it possible to restart the distribution of relief supplies as the conflict was coming to an end.[97]

Ending the war, reclaiming the field

Beginning with the summer of 1969 the FMG's acquisition of additional weapons, its promises of reconciliation, as well as the further deterioration of the food situation in the province weakened Biafran resistance. As final peace talks held in Addis Ababa in December 1969 failed, a military victory by the federal army finally ended the conflict.[98] The city of Owerri fell on 10 January 1970. On 11 January Ojukwu went into exile in Côte d'Ivoire, and the next day Biafran Chief of Staff Philip Effiong ordered his troops to surrender. On 15 January, in Lagos, he informed General Gowon of Biafra's unconditional surrender.

Whilst the Western media no longer paid particular attention to the conflict, there was renewed interest in the region following the fall of Biafra. The announcement of the military victory by the federal troops rekindled fears about the fate of the Igbo population and provoked international reactions. The Pope publicly expressed his concern for the situation of the civilians who might fall victim to reprisals and massacres. Diplomatic initiatives were also being taken by French and American leaders at the UN in order to send a peacekeeping force or increase the presence of international observers. The associations that had mobilised in France and Great Britain during the conflict organised demonstrations to this end. Gowon was, however, able to provide sufficient assurances of his desire for reconciliation and the soldiers' good conduct to reassure the international community on this point.[99]

The food situation in the breakaway province also sparked great concern and the FMG was quickly overwhelmed by offers of collaboration from all sorts of organisations and governments. For example, the President of the United States, Richard Nixon, expressed his willingness to contribute to the relief effort by approving the allocation of 10 million dollars to support not only the activities of the Nigerian Red Cross but also those of the churches. Several political and civil-society figures also offered the services of foreign organisations in Nigeria. These were seen in Lagos as a reflection of the paternalistic attitude towards the FMG and its institutions, whose ability to manage the situation was clearly doubted. The Nigerian press and head of state were quick to react, echoing the policy of reappropriating the operations developed by the FMG since June 1969. Thus, General Gowon refused the assistance of any country that had supported Biafra, but also of organisations that had provided relief to the secessionists, and declared all the volunteers who had worked illegally in the enclave personae non gratae. Gowon prohibited the JCA from making its air fleet available for the transport of food into the former Biafra. The same applied to the ICRC, which only managed to send one plane loaded with medicines to Lagos. The Geneva-based organisation therefore decided to officially put an end to the operation in Nigeria–Biafra at its plenary session of 5 February 1970. Nevertheless, the delegation remained in Lagos until the end of March 1970 in order to see its traditional activities through and deal with the return to Nigeria of the dozens of seriously wounded who had been taken to Europe for treatment they could not receive in Biafra (Operation Medicairlift). The Nigerian government's stance had an impact on the speed of the delivery of relief supplies, with food and medicines failing to arrive in some areas.[100]

The FMG's particular distrust of humanitarian good intentions did not, however, exclude all foreign aid. For example, international organisations and governments which had supported it or had not expressed pro-Biafran sympathies were approached. However, the FMG, which was determined not to be dictated to by humanitarians it believed responsible for prolonging the conflict, laid down specific conditions with which governments and organisations wishing to become involved had to comply. The Uli airstrip, a symbol of Biafran resistance, was not opened for airlifts despite requests from voluntary organisations. Furthermore, while British and American leaders offered the use of their military logistics to deliver aid to the region, the FMG prohibited the use of any military assets, whether in the form of personnel or transport equipment. In line with what had been decided in June 1969, relief operations were co-ordinated by the Nigerian government. This time the task was assigned to the Ministry of Economic Development, reflecting the shift from emergency aid to reconstruction aid desired by the Nigerian leadership. The Rehabilitation Commission handled the allocation of donations from foreign governments, while the Nigerian Red Cross dealt with assistance proposals from volunteer agencies and conducted operations in the field, leaving little room for foreign organisations wishing to intervene directly.[101]

Nigerian organisations played a particularly important role in this context. Those who were part of international networks or federations and who could therefore provide the link between the international desire to act and the need to implement "Nigerian" operations did especially well. The changing role of the Nigerian Red Cross between the summer of 1969 and the beginning of 1970 attested to the function of go-between it performed. Being part of the International Red Cross Movement, it had the advantage of benefiting from foreign resources while remaining a Nigerian entity. These features made it a suitable interlocutor for both Western donors and the Nigerian government, which explains its emergence as a key player in late 1969, whereas in July 1969 it seemed rather marginalised within the FMG's new policy. Thus, at the beginning of 1970 it was the NRC itself that managed the relief effort since it provided most of the administrative personnel.[102]

An analysis of the work it carried out in the field and the means at its disposal makes it possible to qualify the FMG's stance against foreign aid. According to an NRC report, between 1 October 1969 and 31 August 1970 it received donations in cash, in kind and in the form of services (medical teams or technical advisers) from thirty-five Red Cross societies around the world, ten governments, UNICEF, Oxfam, Save the Children, the Quakers, the Salvation Army, as well as from international companies and banks.[103] Nigerian Catholic and Protestant organisations also contributed in the form of collections from Nigeria and above all international support they received.

Beginning with January 1970 the Nigerian Red Cross reported that it was facing a shortage of local staff for medical operations in the field. Whilst Biafran social and medical workers were initially encouraged to join the relief effort, the gradual normalisation of the situation led some of them, particularly those who had fled inside Biafra, to return to their home regions. Thus, various organisations provided teams made up of expatriates (see Table 6.1). Of the 139 people who made up the medical relief teams, only twelve were Nigerian (9 per cent), whereas 127 were foreigners, mostly from Britain, the US and Ireland.[104]

The strong British and American presence was not surprising since the FMG turned for help to the states that had supported it. However, the large Irish presence was more surprising and showed that the government's policy on accepting aid was more nuanced than stated. While the sending of volunteers by the Irish Red Cross was in line with the Red Cross societies' policy of supporting the Nigerian Red Cross, the presence of Irish missionaries in the Nigerian Catholic Secretariat's teams raised some questions given the FMG's stance towards them during the conflict. Because of their activities in the breakaway region, the Nigerian government had repeatedly accused

Table 6.1 Composition of medical teams involved in the relief effort in Nigeria by nationality, early February 1970

Members of medical teams involved in relief operations	Percentage	Provided by
54 British nationals	39	British Red Cross and the Salvation Army (9)
		Quakers (3)
		SCF (23)
		Oxfam (3)
		Christian Council of Nigeria (9)
		Catholic Secretariat (7)
27 US nationals	19	Christian Council of Nigeria (15)
		Catholic Secretariat of Nigeria (2)
		Quakers (10)
25 Irish nationals	18	Irish Red Cross (5)
		Catholic Secretariat of Nigeria (20)
12 Nigerian nationals	9	Catholic Secretariat of Nigeria (5)
		Christian Council of Nigeria (5)
		Quakers (2)
5 Swiss nationals	3.5	Swiss Red Cross (5)
5 Australian nationals	3.5	Australian Red Cross (4)
		SCF (1)
4 Austrian nationals	3	Austrian Red Cross
4 Japanese nationals	3	Japanese Red Cross
1 Indian national, 1 Swedish national, and 1 Italian national	2	Christian Council of Nigeria (2)
		Catholic Secretariat of Nigeria (1)
Total 139	**100**	

Irish missionaries, particularly those of the Spiritan order, of supporting the Biafran regime by sending relief supplies as well as weapons. Indeed, when Biafra fell some of them were detained by the federal authorities, and the Spiritans who had worked in Biafra were expelled.[105] However, this policy did not apply to all Irish missionaries. The FMG's tolerance of them was partly due to efforts by Irish diplomacy, but also to the important role they played in the country's social activities. Already during the conflict the Catholic Secretariat of Nigeria was working to obtain the authorities' agreement to restore its missions in the regions that were back under federal control. Local leaders were not systematically opposed to this since it allowed Catholic medical centres to reopen, for example in Nsukka and the Enugu area. This tolerance varied depending on the location and behaviour of the missionaries during the conflict. In the Port Harcourt area, for example, members of the Spiritan congregation were prohibited from returning.[106] However, the latter continued to play a fundamental role within the Nigerian Catholic Secretariat. The person in charge of social affairs and therefore relief work was none other than an Irish Spiritan, Desmond Byrne. Byrne then became the superior of the Spiritans in the areas retaken by the federal army and worked to enable his congregation to re-establish itself in the region. He was replaced in the Secretariat by another Spiritan, John McGuinness.[107]

Generally speaking, compared to the relief action conducted during the summer of 1968 on the federal side, the Red Cross Movement was less well represented, particularly in terms of the medical-social teams on the ground, the majority of whose personnel came from Catholic and Protestant religious organisations (see Table 6.2). Of the 139 people involved, the Catholic Secretariat, the Christian Council of Nigeria and the Quakers put together provided more than half (57 per cent), while the foreign Red Cross societies provided only 18 per cent.

Table 6.2 Composition of medical teams involved in the Nigerian Red Cross relief effort by organisation, early February 1970

Organisation	Number of individuals provided	Percentage
Catholic Secretariat of Nigeria	35	25
Christian Council of Nigeria	31	22
National Red Cross societies from other countries	26	19
Save the Children	24	17
Quakers	15	11
Others	8	6
Total	**139**	**100**

The Nigerian Catholic Secretariat and in particular its social-affairs department received support from Caritas Internationalis, who thus contributed to the relief programme co-ordinated by the ICRC and then the NRC in the federal areas since the beginning of the conflict. Its presence in the country independently of the crisis also allowed it to envisage longer-term activities, which probably also explains its substantial contribution to the programme immediately after the war.[108] The same was true of the Christian Council of Nigeria, which enjoyed the support of foreign Protestant organisations and the World Council of Churches. Like the Catholic Secretariat, it took part in the action run by the ICRC and NRC until June 1969. At the same time, though, because it was particularly critical of the ICRC, it set up its own relief and rehabilitation commission in order to make up for the shortcomings of the ICRC's operation in certain areas and prepare its involvement in the reconstruction work after the war.[109] However, the many administrative problems it faced and the lack of Nigerian personnel – at a time when the FMG limited the presence of foreign personnel – meant that the commission was barely operational in 1969.

Just as with the Nigerian Red Cross and Catholic Secretariat, the end of the war created a particularly favourable situation for this organisation which was both Nigerian and part of international networks. Since the aid agencies of foreign Reformed churches, some of which had been involved in Joint Church Aid, could not act directly, they worked with the Christian Council to provide relief. According to the latter, in 1970 they spent more than 4.5 million dollars on relief and rehabilitation activities by going through it. While taking part in the Red Cross programme the Council also developed its own activities, especially in areas where the Red Cross was said to be less active, with the latter concentrating its activities in the heart of former Biafra.[110] Indeed, the Christian Council of Nigeria was more specifically active in the West Central, Rivers and South East states, which had been recaptured by the federal forces several months earlier but where the return of the refugees was problematic.[111]

Overall, the situation around relief and reconstruction aid in Nigeria throughout 1970 and its suitability for the country's needs remain difficult to grasp. The international pressure exerted on the FMG at the end of the war did indeed have an impact on the way the situation was presented. Seeking to show that it had the problem well in hand, the FMG, for example, responded to the alarmist statements of Western relief organisations by painting an optimistic picture of the food situation in the former breakaway province. It was quickly supported in this sense by various international personalities who went to the area in mid-January for shorter or longer periods of time. The League's Secretary General Henrik Beer, UNICEF Director

Henry Labouisse, British relief co-ordinator Lord Hunt, UN Secretary-General U Thant and international observers all said that, despite some signs of malnutrition among the population, famine was not an imminent threat and could be stopped with the resources available in Nigeria. Their reassuring tone seemed to be at odds with reports from some of the journalists who went to the region in the second half of January and from humanitarians who left Biafra after it had fallen.[112]

Accounts of conditions differed not only immediately after the conflict but also throughout 1970. There were fresh concerns, for example, when Nigerian Red Cross operations came to a halt. After a difficult start, its work reached its peak in March and April 1970, when it claimed to have distributed aid to three million people. At the beginning of May, as the living conditions of the majority of the population had improved, it set up a selective programme for the most vulnerable groups, such as children for whom it organised milk distributions.[113] Government institutions were expected to take over, particularly by helping with co-ordination.[114] However, the Nigerian Christian Council and the Catholic Secretariat did not consider this to be sufficient and insisted on the need to continue the relief effort, but faced difficulties in finding the funds needed for reconstruction projects. The Christian Council complained that donation pledges had failed to materialise, while the Nigerian Catholic Secretariat struggled to fill its coffers despite a trip made by its secretary to meet with European donors. Indeed, although the fall of Biafra gave rise to strong international concern, this quickly dissipated and the situation in Nigeria no longer galvanised people into action. As for the UN entities that specialised in development aid, apart from their welcome participation in the programmes of early 1970, their contribution to the reconstruction of the former Eastern region remained, according to Emmanuel Urhobo, fairly negligible.[115]

By mid-1970 there were still many problems in the war-affected areas. Restoring health services in the former Eastern region was proving difficult. Hospitals were left to be run by religious orders who struggled to find the necessary resources, whether it was medical equipment or medicines. Catholic missionaries thus questioned the wisdom of their involvement in the Nigerian health system which allowed the FMG to offload this responsibility onto them.[116] In addition, the reconstruction of destroyed houses was delayed due to a lack of materials. In agriculture, the recultivation of crops was slowed down by the late arrival of seeds. The latter were provided by relief agencies but delivering them to the agricultural areas took time due to the poor state of the roads. Moreover, there was significant poverty in the region. Those who had chosen to flee within Biafra did not always find the possessions they had left behind. The transition from the Biafran currency, which was now worthless, to the Nigerian one accentuated this problem and many people no longer had any means of payment. Furthermore, those who went to the Nigerian central bank to exchange their Biafran money for Nigerian money were only given twenty pounds irrespective of the amount they brought in.[117] Finally, commercial activities were slow to pick up again.

Whilst this may be a normal state of affairs six months after the end of a conflict that had lasted over two and a half years, nevertheless, the secretary of the Christian Council of Nigeria criticised the FMG for not being committed enough to the reconstruction of the region. In November 1970 the Nigerian government announced it would invest three billion dollars into the country's development, of which only 240 million were earmarked for the states that had suffered the most damage (East Central, South East and Rivers).[118] This policy was explained by the Nigerian government's view of the causes of the conflict. It argued that the underdevelopment of the North was at the root of the war and in particular the 1966 massacres, and that in order to prevent this from happening again it was necessary to redress these inequalities.[119] This lack of investment in reconstruction was nevertheless a sore point with the Igbo population and contributed to the feeling among them that, despite a general amnesty that had been relatively well implemented, the central government was determined to make them pay for the war. This sentiment is still alive, especially in the Igbo diaspora, as evidenced by the writer Chinua Achebe, who in 2012 noted:

> There are tons of treatises that talk about how the Igbo were wonderfully integrated into Nigeria. Well I have news for them: The Igbo were not and continue not to be reintegrated into Nigeria, one of the main reasons for the country's continued backwardness, in my estimation. Borrowing a large leaf from the American Marshal Plan that followed World War II and resulted in the reconstruction of Europe, the federal government of Nigeria launched an elaborate scheme highlighted by the three Rs – for Reconstruction, Rehabilitation, and Reconciliation. The only difference is that, unlike the Americans who actually carried out all three prongs of the strategy, Nigeria's federal government did not. The administrator of East central state, Mr Ukpabi Asika, announced that Eastern Nigeria required close to half a billion pounds to complete the reconstruction effort. None of us recall that he received anything close to a fraction of the request.[120]

Other authors have further pointed out that the issue of the return of Igbo property has never really been discussed, that work on remembering the conflict and its consequences has barely started,[121] and they have argued that the Igbo's lack of representation in the Nigerian political system reflects their continued marginalisation in the country after the war.[122] Nevertheless, the consequences of the war were not limited to the Igbo. As Samuel Daly has demonstrated, the specific conditions of the secession and war also had a long-lasting impact on subsequent crime development in the country.[123]

The last months of hostilities and the postwar period illustrate particularly well the reactions to the international humanitarian operation, whether in terms of its perception by local authorities, its impact on the balance of power between local organisations or the questions raised by its replacement. The federal government's taking over the relief operations beginning with June 1969 was not without ambiguity. For the FMG this decision was above all a means of reasserting its sovereignty over its territory, a sovereignty which it believed had been flouted by the behaviour of foreign organisations, as represented by the ICRC in particular. Its implementation, however, suggested a more nuanced position. In the end, the FMG showed some flexibility towards the ICRC, who was backed by strong financial arguments, by granting it a three-month delay and allowing it to continue its traditional activities. Furthermore, international actors retained some influence in Lagos which was reflected in the balance of power between Nigerian relief agencies, with the Nigerian Red Cross gradually gaining the upper hand over the Rehabilitation Commission.

The predominant role gradually played by this National Society raised the broader question of the way in which National Red Cross Societies were viewed in the decolonised states. In Western countries they were particularly linked to the state and were sometimes seen as instruments of foreign policy, as the example of the French Red Cross, discussed in Chapter 7, shows. The Nigerian case illustrates a different configuration. Although it too had links to the government, it appeared to be more independent than other Nigerian organisations due to its membership of the International Red Cross Movement. Unlike Western Red Cross societies which were built in the late nineteenth century on a primarily national basis and in close connection with the state, the Red Cross societies of the decolonised countries maintained a close link with the League and the Western National Societies, which provided them with resources and helped to train and develop them. Thus, the Nigerian example highlights the role of interface between the national and the international that the Red Cross societies of decolonised countries played. These organisations were particularly well positioned to allay Western agencies' mistrust of organisations that emanated solely from African states, as well as the mistrust of African governments who sometimes saw the presence of foreign organisations as a challenge to their sovereignty.

Notes

1 Fassin, *La raison humanitaire*, p. 10.

2 Yala, "Les paradigmes coloniaux de l'action humanitaire", pp. 206–14.

3 C. Abu-Sada (eds), *Dans l'œil des autres. Perception de l'action humanitaire et de MSF* (Lausanne: Antipodes, 2011).
4 Fassin, *La raison humanitaire*, p. 311.
5 Dauvin, Siméant & C.A.H.I.E.R, *Le travail humanitaire*, pp. 276–85.
6 See, for example, J. Negrão, "Intervenants humanitaires du Nord et société civile mozambicaine", *Alternatives Sud: Interventions humanitaires?*, 11:3 (2004), 139–55.
7 Farré, *Colis de guerre*.
8 Hentsch, *Face au blocus*, p. 46.
9 AICRC, B AG 202 147-001, note from G. Hoffmann to the CICR, 7 June 1968.
10 AICRC, B AG 202 147-005, message from the CICR to J.-R. Pierroz, 28 May 1968.
11 TNA, FCO 38/304, "Relief supplies for Biafra: ICRC–Federal government relations", 26 September 1968, BHC, Lagos.
12 AICRC, B AG 202 147-005, telex from J-R. Pierroz to the CICR, 28 May 1968.
13 TNA, FCO 38/303, press release, Kwara State, 26 August 1968.
14 TNA, FCO 38/302, telegram from the BHC in Lagos (D. Hunt) to the CO, 16 August 1968.
15 TNA, FCO 38/303, telegram from the FO to the consulate in Geneva, 1 September 1968.
16 TNA, FCO 38/303, presse release, Nigeria House, London, 5 September 1968, reproducing the FMG declaration of September 2, 1968.
17 TNA, FCO 38/305, telegram from the BHC in Lagos (D. Hunt) to the CO, 28 September 1968.
18 TNA, FCO 38/305, memorandum "Lord Shepherd's visit to Nigeria", October 1968.
19 TNA, FCO 38/226, "Meeting with members of the International Observer Team".
20 TNA, FCO 38/305, copy of a telegram from the Americam Embassy in Lagos (Palmer) to the Department of State, 3 October 1968. On A. Lindt, see also D. P. Forsythe, *The Humanitarians: The International Committee of the Red Cross* (Cambridge: Cambridge University Press, 2005), p. 65; L. Marti, *Bonsoir mes victimes* (Geneva: Labor et Fides, 1996), pp. 149–53.
21 TNA, FCO 65/431, telegram from the FCO to the BHC in Lagos, 17 January 1969.
22 This opinion was shared by the US Embassy in Lagos: TNA, FCO 65/431, copy of a telegram from the US Embassy in Lagos to the Department of State, 8 January 1969.
23 TNA, FCO 65/432, telegram from the UK mission in New York to the FCO, 24 January 1969.
24 TNA, FCO 65/432, note by the BHC in Lagos, "Equatorial Guinea and the ICRC", 23 January 1969.
25 TNA, FCO 65/432, copy of a telegram from the American representative in Santa Isabel to the Department of State, 6 February 1969. During the negotiations, Equatorial Guinea demanded, among other things, that the ICRC staff be

reduced, that the airlift employ more Equatorial Guineans and, above all, that the ICRC pay airport taxes to Equatorial Guinea as well as a percentage of the amount it should have paid since the beginning of the operations.

26 TNA, FCO 65/431, telegram from the BHC in Lagos (D. Hunt) to the FCO, 9 January 1969.
27 TNA, FCO 65/431, telegram from the BHC in Lagos (D. Hunt) to the FCO, 9 January 1969.
28 TNA, FCO 65/431, telegram from the BHC in Lagos (D. Hunt) to the FCO, 14 January 1969.
29 AICRC, plenary sessions of the Committee, 9 and 14 January 1969; Presidential Council meeting, 23 January 1969. See also AVM 2005003-14/70.
30 TNA, FCO 65/432, telegram from the BHC in Lagos (D. Hunt) to the FCO, 4 February 1969.
31 AICRC, plenary session of the Committee, 21 December 1967.
32 AICRC, Directorate briefing note, 11 April 1968.
33 Croix-Rouge du Nigeria, *Action de secours au Nigeria, rapport de la Croix-Rouge du Nigeria, 1966–1970* (1970), p. 7.
34 AICRC, B AG 200 147-003.01, telegram from Lindt to Gallopin, 2 October 1968.
35 AICRC, B AG, 202 147-001, report by G. Hoffmann on his mission in Kampala and Lagos, 26 May–6 June 1968.
36 TNA, FCO 38/302.
37 AICRC, B AG 121 147-001, press release, 12 December 1968.
38 NAN, CWC 1/4/1, Organization of African Unity Observers, *No Genocide*, p. 9.
39 TNA, FCO 38/304, copy of a telegram from the US Embassy in Lagos to the Department of State, 20 September 1968.
40 AUN, cable from N.-G. Gussing to the Secretary-General and Rolz-Bennett, 19 August 1968.
41 Urhobo, *Relief Operations in the Nigerian Civil War*, p. 54.
42 AICRC, Directorate briefing note, 23 April 1968.
43 TNA, FCO 38/307, telegram from the BHC in Lagos (D. Hunt) to the CO, 6 July 1968; FCO 38/305, telegram from the CO to the BHC in Lagos, 8 October 1968.
44 AICRC, Directorate briefing note, 26 November 1968.
45 AICRC, plenary session of the Committee, 4–5 June 1969.
46 AICRC, Presidential Council meeting, 31 October 1968.
47 TNA, FCO 38/301, telegram from the BHC in Lagos (D. Hunt) to the CO, 12 August 1968.
48 AICRC, Directorate briefing note, 13 May 1969, report by G. Schürch.
49 AICRC, plenary session of the Committee, 9 January 1969, report by G. Schürch.
50 AICRC, B AG 121 147-001, letter from G. Schürch to the CICR, 5 November 1968.
51 Hentsch, *Face au blocus*, p. 170.
52 Draper, *Shadows*, pp. 174–7.

53 AICRC, plenary session of the Committee, 9 January 1969, report by G. Schürch.
54 AICRC, plenary session of the Committee, 4 and 5 June 1969.
55 AICRC, plenary session of the Committee, 19 June 1969, J. Freymond, "Note sur la politique à suivre dans la crise actuelle", 15 June 1969.
56 TNA, FCO 65/375, Radio Nigeria, 9 June 1969.
57 Hentsch, *Face au blocus*, p. 181.
58 TNA, FCO 65/376, note by J. E. Smallwood, BHC, Ibadan, 19 June 1969.
59 TNA, FCO 65/376, note by H. J. Arbuthnott, BHC, Lagos, 21 June 1969.
60 Thompson, *American Policy and African Famine*, p. 127.
61 AICRC, plenary session of the Committee, 19 June 1969, J. Freymond, "Note sur la politique à suivre dans la politique à suivre dans la crise actuelle", 15 June 1969.
62 TNA, FCO 65/376, note by D. C. Tebbit, "Nigeria and the International Committee of the Red Cross", 1 July 1969.
63 AICRC, plenary session of the Committee, 3 July 1969.
64 AICRC, A VM 2000078-0011.88, note by J. Freymond, "Appréciation de la situation au Biafra", 9 July 1969.
65 Hentsch, *Face au blocus*, p. 198.
66 AICRC, plenary session of the Committee, 30 July 1969.
67 Page, *Le Nigeria et la Suisse*, p. 258.
68 AICRC, A VM 2000078-0011.88, letter from J.-M. Rubli to J. Freymond, 16 June 1969.
69 *The Economist*, 19 July 1969, cited by T. Hentsch, *Face au blocus*, p. 198.
70 Hentsch, *Face au blocus*, pp. 202–3.
71 AICRC, plenary sessions of the Committee, 7 and 21 August 1969, Directorate briefing note, 4 August 1969, Presidential Council meeting, 14 August 1969.
72 AICRC, plenary session of the Committee, 30 July 1969.
73 AICRC, Presidential Council meetings, 26 September 1968 and 21 November 1968; BAG 280 147-002, Directorate meeting, 14 November 1968.
74 AICRC, plenary session of the Committee, 21 August 1969.
75 AICRC, A VM 2000078-0011.88.
76 AICRC, Directorate briefing note, 8 September 1969.
77 Hentsch, *Face au blocus*, pp. 204–6.
78 AICRC, plenary session of the Committee, 23 October 1969.
79 *Foreign Relations of the United States*, 1969–76, vol. E-5, Part 1, document 131.
80 AICRC, A VM 2000078-0011.88, "Décision concernant l'action du CICR au Biafra", 7 November 1969. See also the plenary sessions of the Committee and the Presidential Council meetings in October and November 1969.
81 The aim is to register prisoners of war and enable them to maintain contact with their families.
82 AICRC, plenary session of the Committee, 30 July 1969.
83 AICRC, Directorate briefing note, 11 August 1969.
84 Croix-Rouge du Nigeria, *Action de secours au Nigeria*, p. 8.

85 Croix-Rouge du Nigeria, *Action de secours au Nigeria*, annexe 2.
86 AICRC, plenary session of the Committee, 30 July 1969.
87 AICRC, AVM 2000 078-0011.88, "Note de la présidence pour la conduite future de l'action CICR au Nigeria", 4 August 1968.
88 AICRC, Directorate briefing note, 17 August 1969.
89 AICRC, AVM 2000 043-0003.11, letter from E. Bignami to M. Naville, Lagos, 19 August 1969; minutes of the meeting held on 16 August 1969 between the chairman of the NRC, the League's representative and the ICRC's head of delegation in Lagos.
90 AICRC, Directorate briefing note, 23 September 1969.
91 AICRC, AVM 2000078-0011.88, "Note à la présidence" by J.-P. Hocké, Lagos, 24 October 1969.
92 Croix-Rouge du Nigeria, *Action de secours au Nigeria*, p. 9.
93 AICRC, AVM 2000078-0011.88, "Note à la présidence" by J.-P. Hocké, Lagos, 4 November 1969.
94 Mohammed, "Relief Services in the Nigerian Civil War", p. 249.
95 AICRC, B AG 280 147-004, 6th meeting of the Consultative Commission, 31 October 1969.
96 AICRC, Directorate briefing note, 15 December 1969.
97 Croix-Rouge du Nigeria, *Action de secours au Nigeria*, p. 9.
98 Stremlau, *The International Politics of the Nigerian Civil War*, pp. 357–64.
99 Wiseberg, "The International Politics of Relief", pp. 426–7.
100 Schittly, *L'homme qui voulait voir la guerre de près*, p. 144. Of the 1,000 children in the Santana centre, half were transported to Port Harcourt in search of food and care.
101 Wiseberg, "The International Politics of Relief", pp. 427–32.
102 Croix-Rouge du Nigeria, *Action de secours au Nigeria*, annex 8. Some medical advisors or administrators were provided by USAID, the League, the ICRC and the German and Canadian National Red Cross, among others.
103 Croix-Rouge du Nigeria, *Action de secours au Nigeria*, annexes 5 and 6 bis.
104 Croix-Rouge du Nigeria, *Action de secours au Nigeria*, annex 7.
105 O'Sullivan, *Ireland, Africa and the End of Empire*, pp. 100–3.
106 ACSE, 11I1.12a3.1, letters from the administration of the East Central State to the Catholic Secretariat in Lagos, 27 December 1968, 9 January 1969, 16 June 1969.
107 ACSE, Nigerian Civil War: 1967–1970, Box 2, VIII AG 69 – SS – 12, "Relief and Rehabilitation Programme to Nigeria, General Report", Rome, 18 April 1969.
108 NAN, Roman Catholic Mission Papers, 1/174, reports by the Social Affairs Department of the Catholic Secretariat of Nigeria, 1970.
109 Urhobo, *Relief Operations in the Nigerian Civil War*, pp. 45–6.
110 Urhobo, *Relief Operations in the Nigerian Civil War*, pp. 50–1.
111 R. K. Udo, "Reconstruction in the War Affected Areas of Nigeria", *The Royal Geographical Society*, 2:3 (1970), 9–12.
112 Wiseberg, "The International Politics of Relief", pp. 433–62; Stremlau, *The International Politics of the Nigerian Civil War*, pp. 366–72.

113 Croix-Rouge du Nigeria, *Action de secours au Nigeria*, annex 6.
114 NAN, Roman Catholic Mission Papers, 1/174, reports by the Social Affairs Department of the Catholic Secretariat of Nigeria, 1970.
115 Urhobo, *Relief Operations in the Nigerian Civil War*, p. 56.
116 NAN, Roman Catholic Mission papers, 1/174, reports by the Social Affairs Department of the Catholic Secretariat of Nigeria, 1970.
117 Udo, "Reconstruction in the War Affected Areas of Nigeria".
118 Urhobo, *Relief Operations in the Nigerian Civil War.*
119 NAN, Roman Catholic Mission papers, 1/174, report by the Social Affairs Department of the Catholic Secretariat of Nigeria, 6 October 1970.
120 Achebe, *There Was a Country*, pp. 235–6.
121 The issue was addressed by the Commission of Inquiry into Human Rights Violations, better known as the Oputa Panel, in 2000. An unofficial report of the work of this panel is published on the website of the Nigerian NGO The Nigerian Democratic Movement, www.dawodu.com/oputa1.htm, accessed 4 August 2014.
122 Gould, *The Struggle for Modern Nigeria*, pp. 204–9.
123 Daly, *A History of the Republic of Biafra.*

Part III

Revisiting controversies

7

Humanitarian aid: the lifeblood of war?

The Nigeria–Biafra war has frequently been used to illustrate the perverse effects of aid and its impact on conflict situations. Beginning with the last decade of the twentieth century the focus on these aspects has reflected the loss of legitimacy suffered by humanitarian actions. In the early 1990s the responses to the crises in the former Yugoslavia, Somalia and Rwanda led to a process of reflection, particularly by the actors themselves, on the limitations and perverse effects of humanitarian action and, more broadly, on attendant political issues.[1] Research on this often focuses on two perspectives. Some place more emphasis on the question of the impact of humanitarian aid, particularly in situations of armed conflict.[2] Although at times these reflections are criticised for lacking a solid empirical basis or are accused of naivety, they have nevertheless sparked debates on issues that are often obscured by the good intentions professed by humanitarian organisations.[3] An analysis of the motives behind relief efforts is the second way in which the limitations of humanitarianism can be revealed. As expressed by Philippe Ryfman when speaking of the 1990s: "Humanitarian action, which was initially put on a pedestal, has been accused of ultimately being used by states or international organisations to further their own interests".[4] The increasing number of military-humanitarian interventions and the debates around the notion of the right to intervene have focused attention on the use of a humanitarian pretext to advance political or economic interests.[5]

Studies by historians have shown that these phenomena were not unique to the 1990s. Similar tensions have occurred repeatedly in the history of humanitarianism.[6] For example, the question of "perverse effects" was raised as early as the nineteenth century when the Red Cross was created, as some feared that the instruments intended to alleviate the evils of war would actually foster the latter. Although this was at first a mainly moral debate, it took on a more concrete and material dimension when humanitarian aid became quasi-industrial in nature during the two world wars. There were plenty of instrumentalisation and appropriation attempts by local authorities or belligerents. In 1921, for example, the Bolsheviks used the famine in their country and the Western aid provided to strengthen their position and gain some form of legitimacy on the international stage.[7] The same goes for actors' motivations. Studies on *interventions d'humanité* have shown how humanitarian motives and geopolitical interests combine in European states' decisions on whether or not to intervene when civilians are being massacred in other states.[8] There are also many examples of assistance programmes driven by ideological, religious or political imperatives. We can thus cite the American aid deployed through the American Relief Administration in Europe after the First World War, which was conceived primarily as a means of curbing the advance of communism.[9]

As far as the Nigeria–Biafra conflict is concerned, several authors have concluded that the airlifts run by the churches and Red Cross societies provided the Biafran regime with primarily economic means to survive.[10] Some organisations were also strongly suspected of having transported arms for the secessionists and of having knowingly lent the latter's cause real support. Although in hindsight it is easy to point out that outside aid partially provided the resources that helped prolong a conflict, it is nevertheless difficult to gauge the exact extent to which it did. Above all, there has been little analysis of humanitarian actors' views on these issues, even though they shed light on the ways in which they perceived and dealt with the political issues that attached to their work.

The first and second sections of this chapter examine the way in which humanitarian aid was perceived as a significant symbolic, economic and military resource by belligerents and their supporters. I look at the arguments used to highlight the impact of relief operations on the prolongation of the war and show how this issue emerged during the conflict. I also address the various humanitarian actors' questions about the validity of their activities. In the third section, I study the links between humanitarianism and politics through the lens of the programme developed by the French government. I show how this state conceived its humanitarian programme as a foreign-policy tool for supporting Biafran independence and raise the question of the relationship between this specific operation run by the French Red Cross and those co-ordinated by the ICRC.

Reassessing the symbolic and economic impact of aid

In a war of secession where one side seeks independence from a central government without having many resources at its disposal, humanitarian aid can represent a crucial symbolic, economic and military contribution. In the Biafran case the symbolism crystallised around the conditions for the delivery of relief supplies. The Biafran authorities attached particular importance to this aspect, which helps us better understand their attitude during negotiations. In their view, these conditions had to reflect Biafra's independence from Nigeria, which explains why they categorically rejected the idea of relief planes passing through Lagos. Furthermore, during discussions they demanded to be treated on an equal footing with the Nigerian government. Making their views known in this process allowed them to gain some form of international recognition and legitimacy, which was necessary for the leaders of a republic that claimed to be independent. These issues aside, humanitarian aid helped break the isolation of Biafra and boost the morale of the population. This is a little-studied aspect which remains difficult to perceive.

The economic dimension of humanitarianism is much better documented. Critical studies on the impact of international aid distinguish three ways in which, by feeding "war economies in situations of scarcity and heightened competition", humanitarian aid helps prolong conflicts.[11] "Predation", which is the direct reappropriation of aid by belligerents particularly through looting or misappropriation, is probably the most visible phenomenon since it is often reported by the media. But the arrival of financial or material aid in a given place is also accompanied by "economic knock-on effects", which are particularly noticeable in situations where it represents one of the main inputs to the economy, as in the case of a siege or blockade. Finally, aid strengthens belligerents in an indirect way: by taking over relief tasks that could or should be their responsibility, humanitarians allow them to allocate maximum resources to military activities.

Even before the war began, economic matters were central to the Biafran conflict. In the early part of 1967 the issue of oil royalties helped fuel tensions. Ojukwu demanded that these be paid directly to the East, whereas Gowon insisted that they be paid to the federal government.[12] Once independence was declared, the economic suffocation of the region was the first strategy used to end the secession, as evidenced by the blockade imposed by the FMG. In doing so, the latter deprived Biafra of its revenues from the export of oil and palm oil.[13] In late December 1967, in order to render the funds held by the Biafrans – estimated at 48 million Nigerian pounds – unusable, the Nigerian central bank issued new banknotes, and at the end of January 1968 it declared the previous ones obsolete.[14] The secessionists then decided to free themselves financially from Nigeria by creating their own currency. Meanwhile the Biafran economy, which was closed by the blockade and the fact that its independence was not recognised internationally, was still facing serious difficulties. In this context, the contribution of humanitarian operations was essential.

The mere presence of hundreds of Europeans on the ground, who had better resources than most of the local population, had a knock-on effect on the Biafran economy. Their purchasing power also allowed them to buy supplies from within Biafra, despite soaring prices. The food brought in by humanitarian organisations or the goods, such as alcohol or cigarettes, that some expatriates had sent over especially[15] also kept the economy running. These would sometimes be stolen and resold on the black market. Gloria Chuku explains, for example, that the proximity of Uli airstrip benefited the economic and commercial activities in the towns of Ihiala, Orlu and Nkwo-Nnewi.[16] The illegal trade in relief goods was part and parcel of various trading and trafficking strategies both inside Biafra and across its borders. Developed by Biafran women in particular, these strategies helped the population survive during the years of conflict.[17]

But it was mainly by providing foreign currency that the relief operations contributed to the secessionist regime's military investments. Being essential for the purchase of arms, it was not easy for the secessionists to get it. Beginning with April 1967, even before issuing new notes, the FMG restricted the exchange of Nigerian currency abroad.[18] Whilst the Biafran authorities were still able to sell the Nigerian pounds they had on the European black market at a lower exchange rate, acquiring around fifteen million dollars,[19] the introduction of the new Nigerian currency limited this possibility. Creating the Biafran currency did not solve the problem as it had no international value. Other means were therefore put into play. The French oil company Safrap, which hoped to gain some benefits from Biafra's independence, provided the secessionists with foreign currency before apparently adopting a more wait-and-see strategy.[20] The secessionists also found a source of income in the authorities' contributions to the relief efforts.[21] For example, Biafran leaders opened an account with the Union Bank of Switzerland supposedly in order to receive donations to improve the plight of the refugees.[22] The account allowed various entities who supported Biafran independence – associations from the diaspora, companies, special services – to deposit money which the secessionists then used as they saw fit.

The main relief organisations had less recourse to these types of practices and sought to maintain control over the money they used. However, by developing their activities they also injected foreign currency into the secessionist economic system. On the one hand, in order to be able to work in the province, they needed Biafran currency, which they therefore exchanged for foreign money. On the other hand, the relief provided was not always made up of food supplies, sometimes taking the form of financial aid. For example, the representative of the World Council of Churches who went to Lisbon in the spring of 1968 reported that Das Diakonisches Werk organisation was sending large sums of money directly to Biafra.[23] At the time, the amount of food brought into the province was not enough for all the mouths that needed feeding. The wife of Reverend Somerville confirmed this practice when mentioning that the hundred or so refugees her husband was looking after had not received any of the food aid sent from Europe, but that he was able to give them a little money so that they could buy food despite soaring prices.[24]

This practice continued despite the increase in the relief sent from September 1968. Donors would sometimes explicitly wish some of the money to be used for local needs. In 1969 the Bishopric of Chur, Switzerland, sent donations to the Spiritans to help fund their activities and especially their "specific needs" on the ground. These were used to buy various products inside the province.[25] A World Council of Churches representative visiting Biafra in November 1968 estimated, with some unease, that so-called "WCC" operations were spending around 200,000 pounds a month locally so they could run.[26] John Stremlau offers other examples of aid provided in monetary form by various organisations in order to acquire food or equipment to house refugees.[27] It is difficult to know exactly how much control they had over the use of these funds, especially when they were transferred to local committees. Moreover, by helping to feed the population and care for displaced individuals, they allowed the Biafran authorities to reduce their expenditure in these areas. The money thus saved could then be allocated to military investments.

The contribution of relief operations to the war economy was highlighted in the autumn of 1968 by Kennedy Lindsay, a history lecturer at the University of the West Indies, who was familiar with Nigeria, where he had taught from 1962 to 1964. Looking into the sources of funding that enabled the Biafrans to support the war effort, he pointed to, on the one hand, the salaries received by missionaries in Biafra, and, on the other hand, the financial support provided by organisations for certain projects. He then advised humanitarian agencies to focus their activities on sending goods in order to minimise the exchange of foreign currency for the Biafran currency. His findings, published in *West Africa* magazine and later reprinted in the Nigerian newspaper *Daily Time*,[28] the Canadian Toronto newspaper *The Globe and Mail*[29] and then the British newspaper *The Observer*,[30] put the amount of foreign currency provided by the relief organisations at 613,000 pounds sterling between April and September 1968, which was more than half of the province's external income.

Whatever the reliability – difficult to assess – of the method employed, this article made an impact in the circles concerned with these issues. In Lagos it helped fuel the suspicion of the population and authorities towards the ICRC, which had already been accused by the press of exchanging very large sums of money for Biafran currency to make local purchases. At the UK's Foreign Office the article aroused great interest and led British officials to investigate the issue further. A report on Biafra's sources of funding paradoxically seemed to reach more nuanced conclusions. It particularly distinguished the ICRC from other organisations since from the outset the former proved less inclined than the churches to provide aid in financial form. There still remained the problem of the payments to the staff on the ground, but the sums involved appeared limited. Thus, in August 1968 August Lindt assured American diplomats in Lagos that most of the goods needed by the teams were brought in directly from abroad and that up until then only 14,000 dollars had been spent in the province.[31]

Protestant and Catholic organisations followed a much less strict policy in this respect. Sending money to Biafra was common practice, as the examples mentioned above attest, but it is particularly difficult to determine the precise amounts involved. In 1970 the Secretary General of Caritas Internationalis, Carlo Bayer, indicated that during the entire war the amount of currency exchanged for Biafran money was close to six million dollars, which helped fund the activities of the Catholic (three million dollars) and Protestant (three million dollars) missions.[32] Among these groups, Lindsay's article led organisations to reflect on the consequences of their practices, without actually changing them. The WCC reacted by producing an overview of the funds sent directly to Biafra.[33] The author of the report, Burgess Carr, concluded that these sums – relatively small since the Council did not represent all the Protestant activities in the province – did not constitute a substantial contribution to the Biafran economy. Among Catholics, the article did not seem to call their operations into question either. However, the accusations it helped spread caused a major stir within the Vatican and Caritas Internationalis at the end of the war.

These tensions, which crystallised around Caritas Secretary General Carlo Bayer and resulted in his dismissal, provide a better understanding of how the political consequences of relief operations were perceived by those who decided on them. After ordering an investigation into Carlo Bayer, the Cardinal Secretary of State's deputy, Giovanni Benelli, learned that Caritas had provided money directly to Biafra and had paid some of the bills of the secessionist regime. In July 1970 Benelli summoned Bayer and Jean Rodhain, the President of Caritas, and asked them for an explanation during a heated conversation. The problem revolved around the amounts of money that had been spent in the province and the way in which they had been provided. Benelli seemed to have discovered that Caritas had not only sent food and medicine to Biafra but also money. He maintained that if he had been informed, he would have opposed it. Paradoxically, Bayer justified this practice by the need to control and organise food distributions:

> Do you mean to say that you thought that Caritas just dropped the food and medicines on the airstrip in Uli and did not bother what happened to it after that? It would have been used to feed the soldiers; it would have never

> reached the children or the destitute. Money had to be given to enable Bishop Whelan and all the missions to transport the relief, to organize the myriad village kitchens, to supervise the food until it reached the mouths of the starving civilians.[34]

The biggest point of contention was the way in which the money had been transferred. Indeed, Bayer admitted to having paid some of the bills for printing Biafran banknotes in Switzerland and Lisbon. The equivalent of the amount paid had been issued in Biafran currency, which was used for activities on the ground. For Benelli this was unacceptable:

> Monsignor Benelli then told Bayer how serious this matter was; that the Pope had not slept the night after he heard it; that the Pope and Benelli had assured the world and the Governments, including Nixon, that the Church was not involved politically by this action of Monsignor Bayer. For to create a separate currency is an act of sovereignty. And in paying for the printing of the Biafran banknotes Caritas, and therefore the Pope and the Church were collaborating in an act of rebellion.[35]

In justification of his decision, Bayer argued that helping to pay for the currency was paradoxically one of the surest ways of controlling the use of Caritas funds. In his view, other methods such as sending dollars exchanged directly in the province, or depositing money into a European account designated by the Bank of Biafra, were no more satisfactory; quite the contrary. In both cases, Bayer explained, the money could have been used to buy weapons, whereas by paying the bills for the issuance of Biafran currency he ensured that it was not used for military purposes. He added:

> My conscience is perfectly clear on that particular way of transferring the money. If I could have done so I would have arranged to pay all Biafra's non-military bills, e.g., travel expenses of their diplomats. It was my own decision. I informed nobody how I was transferring the money. I took the risk and I am ready to take any consequences. I am not afraid even to face the Nigerian Government and answer for what I did.[36]

Thus, humanitarians did not deny the political effects of some of their practices, but justified them by the imperative of helping a civilian population in the grip of famine – an imperative that could be explained in the initial emergency phase, but which became more difficult to legitimise in the long term. In defence of his position, Bayer also pointed out that these transfers represented only a minimal contribution to the Biafran economy, which on its own would not have been enough to finance the prolongation of the war. During the conflict the focus on the foreign currency injected by the relief operations obscured the various sources of funding available to Biafra, be it support from other states or, to a lesser extent, the trade with other parts of Nigeria which developed despite the blockade.[37]

The issue of humanitarians' control over what they provided was not only in relation to money but also goods. Indeed, whilst the medical equipment sent by the ICRC in support of the local Red Cross societies was used to treat wounded civilians or soldiers, the distribution of food supplies in the context of a blockade was authorised only for civilians and was not supposed to be used to supply the army.[38] However, in a region at war and suffering from shortages, the temptation for the regime to appropriate the resources provided by humanitarian workers was great.

During the war the military had priority over the local food within the province. The food grown by the Biafra Land Army was primarily intended for them, which explains why at first the pressure on the goods imported by humanitarians seemed moderate. However, as the situation gradually deteriorated, predation attempts became more frequent and food convoys were sometimes attacked. Organisations then strengthened their control systems to ensure that goods leaving the airport reached the distribution and feeding centres in the various provinces.[39] From the summer of 1969 pressure increased sharply, leading to deteriorating security conditions and a rise in looting. Indeed, although combatants were given preferential treatment, the shortage of food also affected them, as described by Reverend Somerville:

> Unfortunately with the worsening food situation the amount of pilfering during the unloading operation at the airport is increasing alarmingly. ... You get hoards of soldiers walking around every plane and it is very difficult to keep some kind of order – they are far too many for efficiency and honesty.[40]

He also reported that during the same period his residence had been attacked, probably by hungry soldiers. Food was not the only thing the Biafran army was interested in. The petrol brought in by airlifts to enable the transport of food supplies within the province was equally coveted.[41]

Whilst humanitarian sources allude to such theft or looting by soldiers, it is less common to find evidence of the army systematically poaching resources. It seems, however, that there was some control over the distributions. And the Biafran authorities helped in this respect by asking police officers to accompany aid workers on their food deliveries. Indeed, if the secessionist leaders wanted the relief operations to continue, these would have to be more or less respected by the military. However, this did not preclude officials involved in food distributions from helping themselves to the goods being transported.[42] This raises the question of the aid workers' leniency towards and even approval of these practices on the ground. The enthusiasm of some staff for the Biafran cause makes this a possibility. In religious operations in particular the need for neutrality was less important and some missionaries' commitment to Biafra was total. Some went beyond providing assistance to civilians, with Catholic and Protestant networks accusing each other of feeding soldiers.[43]

As far as the ICRC was concerned, its teams were expected to respect the principle of neutrality and not take a stand directly in favour of the side on which they operated. One could, however, wonder how aware their members were of this principle, since some volunteers went into the field without having received any training. In any event, in the eyes of the Geneva-based institution the air bridge and attendant distribution system on the ground remained the best means available to deal with the problem of controlling food supplies. It was thus chosen over other possibilities which would have allowed transporting food more cheaply and in greater quantities, but which were discarded. For example, from August 1968 the ICRC considered dropping food by parachute over Biafra. Although the material conditions for such an operation were virtually in place and different relief organisations seemed convinced that it was a good idea,[44] the fact that it was impossible to control the use of the parachuted supplies finally put paid to the project.[45]

A significant contribution to the military operations?

Over and above the economic contribution it may have made, humanitarian aid is also thought to have provided cover for the delivery of weapons to Biafra via airlifts. This remains a thorny issue on two levels. Did relief organisations deliberately transport military equipment for the benefit of the Biafran regime? Whilst most humanitarians denied this, in Nigeria this belief – alive to this day – became part of the collective memory very soon after the conflict. The report of two ICRC delegates who visited Nigeria in 1974 attests to this. The aim of their mission was to re-establish contact with the Red Cross and Nigerian government. During a public meeting in Ibadan, the answer to the question "do you think the ICRC transported arms for the benefit of the secessionists during the conflict?" elicited the following reflections on the part of the ICRC delegates:

> The clear and unanimous answer, which could be read on people's faces before being voiced, was immediate: yes, the ICRC did transport weapons. Perhaps it had been unaware of it, perhaps the weapons had been slipped onto the planes by temporary staff who were not well known to the organisation, perhaps they were hidden in sealed bags whose contents Geneva did not know, but as for the fact itself there was no doubt: as far as our interlocutors were concerned, the ICRC had delivered arms to the enemy. So this myth, which we came across so often in several other African countries, was strongly rooted in the minds of the Nigerians, at all levels. I had heard it from the mouths of a Nigerian OAU Under-Secretary General and African diplomats; the Chief of Staff, a Major-General, had alluded to it during our conversation; and now we had it confirmed by "the masses". I relate this anecdote in detail in order to explain why we chose this "soft sell and low

> profile" policy for this initial resumption of contact between the ICRC and Nigeria since the "Biafra" affair ... a taboo word which the diplomats posted there have never heard uttered since the end of the civil war, nor did we in the course of our week-long mission.[46]

The persistence of this belief in several African states still marred their relations with the ICRC in the mid-1970s.[47] It even raised doubts within the ICRC, which commissioned a member of its staff to shed light on the matter. The Geneva-based organisation concluded this had not occurred, but other charities frankly admitted to having transported weapons. The discrepancies between accounts make it impossible to paint an accurate picture of what happened. To this first question is added a second one: to what extent did the airlifts facilitate arms deliveries by arms carriers or secessionists? Whilst the distinction between these two issues may seem tenuous, nevertheless, the humanitarian actors' responsibility differs in each case.

The logistics involved in the airlifts provide a better understanding of the Nigerian accusations against the ICRC. The complexity of organising flights from the Fernando Poo base to Biafra was a first cause for suspicion. In July 1968, before the negotiations to keep the airport on the Spanish island open till late, planes could not take off at night from there. They were therefore loaded during the day with relief supplies stored in Fernando Poo, and then travelled to São Tomé, from where they set off for Biafra in the evening. Since São Tomé also served as a base for arms carriers, this manoeuvre fuelled suspicions among the Nigerians who, despite the ICRC's denials, were convinced that the planes flew to the Portuguese island to load military equipment.[48]

More generally, the Nigerians accused relief organisations, and in particular Joint Church Aid, of sending cargo to Biafra that contained both weapons and food. According to an investigation conducted by the British, who were trying to find out what concrete evidence these accusations were based on, it appeared that these were mainly the result of statements made by church leaders in the summer of 1968. Indeed, during this period religious organisations admitted to using Wharton's airline, which at the time was also transporting weapons for the secessionists. They would thus either charter planes solely for the food and medicines they sent, or buy space on aircraft meant to carry military equipment. This was also, to a lesser extent, the strategy adopted by the ICRC during the same period. Although humanitarians were not proud of these practices, they nevertheless accepted them. They justified them by arguing that, given the needs on the ground, any means could be used to get even a few tonnes of aid to Biafra.[49] According to the British report, these statements, coupled with revelations about the foreign currency provided to the secessionists and the pro-Biafra comments made by some of the volunteers, naturally led Nigerians to believe that these organisations were themselves prepared to transport arms and that, although they would not admit to it, they were definitely engaging in this practice.[50]

While this British survey provides a better understanding of how the Nigerians came to their belief, for each airlift there were varying degrees of uncertainty. Although the ICRC tried to ensure maximum control over its shipments by suggesting to the Nigerian government that it check the loads and by providing it with the flight schedules, nevertheless, it was not safe from some irregularities. In the autumn of 1969 former employees involved in the airlifts from Cotonou claimed that these had been used to bring in weapons.[51] These accusations, which remained isolated phenomena, were denied by the ICRC, which attributed them to workers who bore a grudge against the organisation.[52] When in the mid-1970s the ICRC was confronted with persistent criticism over its role in transporting weapons, it concluded that it could not entirely rule out the possibility that temporary staff might have occasionally broken the organisation's rules, but that there was no evidence of a widespread practice.

Ironically, one of the rare episodes in which it was established that a Red Cross plane had been carrying weapons took place on the federal side. Thus, in the summer of 1968 the ICRC chartered aircraft from the Nigerian airline Pan African to bring the food supplies that had been shipped to Lagos by boat closer to the front lines. These planes were marked with a red cross, but this did not prevent the Nigerian army from requisitioning them to transport equipment or troops to the east, without completely obscuring the emblems.[53] The aim of such a decision was probably not to deceive the enemy by using the Red Cross sign, but to quickly and simply use the means of transport available. It did, however, show the Nigerian army's lack of respect for this symbol, which also explains why the FMG was particularly suspicious of the ICRC's neutrality.

For the reasons mentioned above, there were also widespread suspicions about weapons being delivered via airlifts organised by the churches, although it remains difficult to determine the truth. The French ambassador to Nigeria, for example, reported that one of those in charge of the air bridge had hinted in the spring of 1969 that relief flights might have been completed with weapons, and that he had subsequently had to set the record straight.[54] The vagueness surrounding this episode makes it impossible to determine whether it was the same practices mentioned earlier in relation to Wharton's airline, or a deliberate policy by the relief agencies to make room in their planes for military equipment. Once again, there were strong denials from the organisations themselves.[55] Among them, the group suspected of engaging in the most pro-Biafran activities was the Irish Spiritan missionaries, which posed problems for the Irish government, which itself followed a policy of non-engagement in the conflict.[56] The fact that some of them had helped set up Africa Concern and were involved in its activities aroused many suspicions. Indeed, the first ship sent by this NGO to São Tomé was suspected by the Irish authorities of carrying weapons. Initially, the goods it sent were to be transported by the JCA, but it then set up its own air bridge from Gabon's capital, Libreville. To this end, Africa Concern used a Belgian company, Belgian International Air Service, which also transported arms for the secessionists. This further convinced its critics that it engaged in activities providing military support to the Biafran regime.[57] Other actors seemed to confirm these suspicions. In a documentary which touched on France's support for Biafra, the French ambassador to Libreville, from where the operation to send supplies to the province was run, recounted his meeting with an Irish priest who had come to ask him for weapons which his organisation would then transport to Biafra.[58] Ambassador Delauney did not name the organisation, but the presence of Africa Concern in Libreville makes the latter a possibility.

The accusations against the humanitarians related not only to the transportation of weapons but also to the way in which their airlifts facilitated the coming and going of planes supplying Biafra with military equipment. After the fall of Port Harcourt in the spring of 1968 the province's main airport was in Uli, which was actually an airstrip set up on a stretch of road. Landing and taking off on this poorly lit and poorly equipped airstrip was particularly dangerous and its reception capacity was low. Thus, in August 1968 the churches began to improve the site so as to increase their airlift potential. They brought aluminium plates to enlarge the aircraft aprons, a technician and radio equipment to facilitate communications between planes and the control tower, which could only light up the airstrip at the last moment, otherwise it risked being spotted by Nigerian bombers.[59] In March 1969 Nordchurchaid sent another air-traffic controller to Uli to train Biafran teams. These few examples attest to the churches' commitment to improving the capacity of the Biafran airport, which received not only aid but also military equipment. Humanitarian organisations justified the need for these practices by the fact that the Biafran authorities prioritised arms flights. Thus, if they wished to acquire more space and facilities for their own planes and bring the amount of food needed by civilians, they had no option but to help improve Uli airport. In practice, these improvements to the Biafran air transport system as a whole benefited military carriers as well.

However, the main problem lay elsewhere. The airlifts were first and foremost accused of facilitating the passage of aircraft loaded with weapons to Biafra. This problem started with the first relief flights carried out by the ICRC in the winter of 1967–68. According to Michael Draper, during the short period in which the FMG agreed to the organisation bringing food supplies to Biafra, the number of flights carrying military equipment to the province increased, as they slipped behind ICRC aircraft and thus avoided the risk of being attacked by the Nigerian army, which could not, at night, distinguish them from the relief planes it was supposed to spare.[60] As mentioned in Chapter 6, this issue crystallised tensions between the Geneva-based organisation and FMG, especially once the ICRC began its night airlifts in September 1968, since it was undeniable that the airlifts that ran at night benefited the transportation of weapons to Biafra. The latter intensified considerably from that period onwards, particularly due to an increase in French military involvement in support of the secessionists. This situation led to growing frustration in Nigeria with humanitarians in general. This was reinforced by the fact that those involved in the airlifts sometimes wore two hats, like Count von Rosen who worked for Nordchurchaid in the summer of 1968 and then carried out military air operations for the secessionists. This overlap persuaded the Nigerian government of the negative impact of humanitarian operations on the war, and shows the porosity of the boundary between the humanitarian and military worlds.

On the churches' side, it was not until the end of the conflict that some of the organisations involved in the JCA publicly expressed their doubts about the implications of their airlifts in terms of the continuation of the war. After the attack on the Red Cross plane in June 1969, the JCA resumed its night flights to Uli. This did not make the ICRC's task any easier since it thus had no means of putting pressure on the secessionists as long as others kept sending supplies at night. In late 1969 one of the bodies involved in the JCA, the World Council of Churches, publicly raised questions about the harmful effects of the stance of the JCA, which continued to send aid in conditions set by the secessionists without considering the consequences. This was in line with the WCC's policy of prudence with regard to the activities undertaken by the churches. From the outset it had favoured taking part in the ICRC's action, which was considered legal since it was carried out by seeking the consent of the belligerents.[61] Nevertheless, in order to be able to contribute to relief operations in a continuous fashion, the WCC turned to the JCA when the ICRC was bogged down in protracted negotiations. It was in this context that in December 1969 the WCC's Inter-Church Aid Division issued a statement asking the JCA to look at the future conduct of its action. In it "it expressed its deep concern about the ambiguous position in which the huge effort undertaken had placed Christians, churches, and relief organisations because of its indirect political repercussions. In particular, these indirect repercussions left the churches open to the accusation of prolonging the war and increasing people's suffering".[62] The JCA's response followed a barely changed line of argument:

> The organizations participating in Joint Church Aid all recognize that relief work has political side effects. This is true of relief work in Nigeria as in Biafra, but they do not see that they are left with any choice. Joint Church Aid has supported directly and indirectly all initiatives to establish more regular and effective alternatives to night flights. To stop the airlift now would not only have political consequences, but also result in the death of millions of civilians. It would establish starvation not only as a legitimate weapon of war but also as a partisan tool in the hands of groups pursuing their own motives.[63]

Once again, the churches chose to accept the political effects of their airlifts rather than change their stance, which they believed would have more disastrous consequences for the civilian population. The controversy between the JCA and WCC did not last long, since Biafra's capitulation in January 1970 and FMG's eviction of all the bodies who had provided relief to the province put an end to it. This episode, however, attests to the cracks that had started to show among the churches after several months of running increasingly controversial night-time air operations.

The Nigerian government also gained some strategic advantages from the humanitarian crisis and the relief operations set up on its side of the front line. As a *Nigerian Opinion* journalist pointed out in 1970, if the FMG had had to meet the needs of the civilian population by itself, the war would have cost it much more.[64] At little cost, humanitarian aid reassured the inhabitants and allowed life to resume in the provinces that were back under Nigerian control. This advantage was clearly recognised by the Biafran authorities who, showing no more regard for the Red Cross sign than their Nigerian counterparts, did not hesitate to send soldiers to attack or intimidate relief operations or those involved in them in order to prevent these areas from returning to normal.[65]

There were also some instances of aid being exploited on the Nigerian side. Thus, the policy of "Nigerianising" the ICRC's action caused problems, particularly with regard to its service for tracing prisoners of war. The latter was provided by the ICRC during armed conflicts and consisted of obtaining lists of the prisoners of war held by both sides in order to record them and thus ensure their protection and contact with their families. Entrusting this task to the Nigerians seemed to pose a problem since "on several occasions the FMG's security services tried to take advantage and interfere in the conduct of what was traditionally an ICRC activity".[66] Controlling the distribution of food also proved difficult, especially during the deployment of operations in the federal area in the spring of 1968 when there was still not enough personnel. The ICRC could not guarantee that the aid sent on the ground was actually delivered to those for whom it was intended and was not appropriated by the Nigerian army. The fact that it was impossible to effectively monitor distributions as long as there was a considerable risk of food being diverted prevented National Societies from getting involved.[67] Subsequently, soldiers helped aid workers distribute relief (Figure 7.1). While on the whole this went relatively well, the former also derived some benefits. For example, a participant in the ICRC's action stationed in the Uturu area in October 1969 explained that, by welcoming the Red Cross, the military hoped to reduce the population's hostility towards them, and that they sometimes offered help with storing food which they then appropriated.[68]

The ICRC was not the only organisation dealing with the potential strategic advantages that the federal government could gain from the relief effort. This was also the case of the US Agency for International Development (USAID). The agency, which had been present in Nigeria since its creation in 1961, had to consider the potential politico-military implications of its projects when the war broke out. Firstly, it was concerned that the trucks and construction equipment it supplied – such as graders – which were initially intended to facilitate the transport of relief supplies, could also be used by the federal army to move more quickly along roads that had been damaged by the secessionists in an attempt to slow them down. Furthermore, the construction of a road from Calabar to Ikom, which had already been decided in 1963 but suspended in the early months of the war, could have helped the Nigerian advance towards Biafra. For the American officials the actual

Figure 7.1 N'Kalagu, distribution centre, federal soldiers helping to maintain order, V-P-NG-N-00039-09 (© ICRC / R. Burgy)

military value of such a project seemed minimal since the road was almost unusable and the front in that area was not very active.[69] Nevertheless, the Biafrans seized on this project to denounce the United States' pro-FMG leanings. This raised concerns in Washington about the safety of American employees working there. The emergence of this controversy concerning the project's potential military implications in the US press and then the Senate led officials to suspend it until the conflict was over.[70]

Finally, from the point of view of the FMG's allies, humanitarian issues seemed to be a good way to provide Nigerians with some strategic advice on the conduct of the war. Among international observers, the British representative General Alexander played a special role in this respect. He took advantage of his mission to observe the troops' conduct towards civilians, in order to gather intelligence for the British government and enable it to adjust its strategy of supporting its federal ally. Thus, some of the issues that were to be discussed with Alexander on his return to London from one of his trips to Nigeria were:

> 3. How can we help the Nigerians to improve their fighting capability by
>
> (a) providing additional arms and ammunition – types
>
> (b) providing additional equipment – transport and communications equipment – river crafts etc.
>
> (c) giving organizational or tactical advice
>
> (d) advising particularly how to neutralize the remaining Biafran airstrips.
>
> 4. What is the state of discipline in the Federal Army.
>
> 5. Has the Federal Army the capability to win the war?[71]

Thus, the British saw the monitoring of humanitarian problems as an opportunity to send a high-ranking army officer to the area without provoking the ire of public opinion. However, this tool had to be handled subtly so as not to discredit the observers' missions and complicate relations with the Nigerian government, who welcomed their presence but also sometimes found it too intrusive.

Reconsidering French ambitions: aid as a foreign-policy tool

It was in Biafra that humanitarian aid was most blatantly exploited by a state for political purposes, French relief operations being a paradigmatic case in point. Chapter 2 has highlighted the way in which public authorities influenced French opinion in order to get the population involved in sending aid to Biafra. This section focuses on French policy towards the conflict.

I examine the role that humanitarian aid played in the Élysée's measures of support for Biafra. I demonstrate how relief operations were conceived as a means of encouraging Biafran secession and, reversing the perspective, how humanitarian actors viewed the political use of aid.

France's support for Biafra was part of its policy of asserting its role on the international stage during the Cold War, a policy developed by General de Gaulle during his years as President of the Fifth Republic.[72] In this respect, maintaining real influence on the African continent despite the decolonisation process was a major challenge. To this end, the President relied on the Secretariat for African and Malagasy Affairs headed by Jacques Foccart, who had been one of de Gaulle's early followers.[73] Foccart ensured that French interests in Africa were safeguarded by using intelligence services – particularly the Service de documentation extérieure et de contre-espionnage (SDECE) (External Documentation and Counterintelligence Service) – to carry out all sorts of missions, but also by cultivating special links with a Francophile and conservative African elite on a continent that was coveted by the two superpowers: the United States and Soviet Union.

In this context, the conflict presented France with an opportunity to extend its influence in the region at the expense of Britain. A large English-speaking country richly endowed with natural resources, Nigeria seemed destined for a bright future, holding sway over West Africa. Its relations with France had been very tense from the beginning of its independence: the young state had protested against the nuclear tests that the former had carried out in the Sahara in 1960, breaking off diplomatic relations between 1961 and 1965.[74] As Foccart related with reference to one of his conversations with de Gaulle: "We should neither intervene nor give the impression of having chosen. But, on balance, the break-up of Nigeria is desirable and, if Biafra succeeds, it will not be a bad thing".[75]

The prospect of the weakening of West Africa's English-speaking giant also appealed to the president of one of its neighbouring countries, Côte d'Ivoire.[76] A pillar of French influence on the continent, Félix Houphouët-Boigny was an early advocate of the Biafran cause with the French leadership. Although the Soviet presence in Lagos never really threatened Nigeria's ties with the West, Houphouët-Boigny did not hesitate to brandish the fight against "communism's dangerous implantation in Africa" – a pet subject of the Élysée Palace – to convince de Gaulle of the need for his support.[77] The anti-communist argument also helped win over to the Biafran cause the South African government, which at the time was being ostracised on the continent because of its apartheid policy, and which took advantage of this opportunity to forge links with the heads of state of Côte d'Ivoire and Gabon.[78]

Houphouët-Boigny therefore did not need France's encouragement to recognise Biafra's independence on 14 May 1968. But the situation seemed to be different with President Bongo, who had just come to power in Gabon with the support of Foccart's networks, whose support he still needed. Whilst he invoked humanitarian considerations to justify his decision, he seems to have chosen to recognise Biafra "perhaps to follow Houphouët, but above all", Jacques Foccart explained, "because he sensed it was what we wanted".[79] He had thought that France would follow suit and support his decision, and made his resentment known when he realised that this was not going to happen:

> By taking this initiative in spite of warnings and pressures of all kinds, we accepted with serenity the break with the Federation of Nigeria and the enmity of this state which is considered the most powerful in Africa, because we hoped that our example would be followed. But this has not happened and we look reckless and unrealistic in the face of the silent but real disapproval of many African states, whether they approve of Nigeria, or remain neutral and reserved, or confine themselves to humanitarian statements.[80]

The Gabonese president seemed to be left with bitter memories of this situation, which led him to officially recognise Biafra and to host on his country's territory most of the operations organised by France in support of the secessionists, thus jeopardising relations with one of the most powerful states in the region.[81]

Nigerian subsurface resources were an additional factor in French involvement in Biafra. The large oil reserves, which were located mainly in the territory claimed by the secessionists, particularly the Niger Delta, attracted interest and played a major role in the internationalisation of the conflict. Michael Gould points out that they contributed to Britain's determination to preserve Nigeria's unity, as London had received a secret report just before the war broke out confirming the extent of untapped resources in the area.[82] These reserves were coveted by major British oil companies such as Shell, but also by American and French ones. This was particularly the case of Safrap, a subsidiary of the Elf company, which unlike its Anglo-Saxon competitors was not very well established in the region. Thus, French support for Biafra could, in the event of a Biafran victory, enable it to obtain authorisation to exploit some of the deposits in the area.[83] This reason was obviously crucial but should not be overestimated and lead to an analysis of the conflict in which all strings were pulled by "Foccart's networks", which were made up of African heads of state (Félix Houphouët-Boigny and Albert-Bernard Bongo), members of the intelligence services (Maurice Robert), French mercenaries (Roger Faulques, Bob Denard) and Elf directors (Pierre Guillaumat). Whilst French engagement in support of the secessionists did occur partly through these actors, such a perspective seems to somewhat overestimate the influence of the former colonial power in this conflict, ignoring Nigerian national issues. It also gives prominence to the oil issue, which was certainly an important factor in France's support for Biafra, but does not explain either its persistence in championing the secessionist cause when the areas richest in hydrocarbons were lost in the early months of the war, or the French desire to also extend its cultural and linguistic influence.

The Élysée's support for the Biafran regime came in various guises, most of which were not part of the traditional and official foreign-policy channels. At the centre of it all, Jacques Foccart played a special role since his position as Secretary General for African and Malagasy Affairs and his contacts in various circles – notably the world of intelligence – placed him at the interface between the different dimensions of French support that were deployed in the military, political, cultural and humanitarian spheres. Since Biafra's independence was never going to be recognised, the government officially endorsed only the humanitarian aid provided. Far from meeting the neutrality requirements of the Red Cross Movement,[84] to which the French Red Cross (FRC) – the main actor in French relief operations – belonged, this aid was very much seen by the executive as a means of supporting the secessionists and was part of a system in which military, political and humanitarian issues co-existed, on both French and Biafran soil.

The food crisis and the suffering of the Biafran population were first used – not without hypocrisy – to advance more political demands and convince people that independence was worth defending, as illustrated by this speech by the French Foreign Minister, Michel Debré, before the UN General Assembly in 1968:

> How can we not denounce the Biafran tragedy, the martyrdom of the Ibo people, this tragedy that the world community watched and commented on – indeed, it is still watching and commenting – without trying to put an end to it? Food and medicines must of course reach those places where they are sorely needed as quickly as possible, and the obstacles that still stand in the way of aid delivery should be strongly denounced. But even more importantly, we need to put a stop to the sending of weapons that prolong the fight. Over and above this, we have to note that, despite the imbalance between the opposing forces, the will of the Biafrans has not wavered. It becomes clearer with each day that only a solution that takes into account the personality of this people, and is in accordance with the principle of self-determination enshrined in our Charter, can solve this painful problem. The French government would be in favour of such a solution.[85]

During the three years that the conflict lasted, the situation in Nigeria was never on the agenda of the UN General Assembly; however, these meetings provided an opportunity for the countries supporting the Biafran cause to try and rally other members of the international community to their position. Nevertheless, this strategy did not work since the UN never really got involved in resolving the conflict and only Haiti joined, in 1969, the four African states who had recognised Biafra in the spring of 1968.

These political considerations aside, above all the crisis made it possible to set up a French humanitarian operation in support of the province. Although it was run mainly through the French Red Cross, it enjoyed considerable autonomy from the Red Cross Movement operation which was co-ordinated by the ICRC. It originated with General de Gaulle's desire to help the population, but also to obtain information on the situation in the region and to get the Nigerian army to show more leniency towards civilians.[86]

It was launched in May 1968 when the Quai d'Orsay turned to the French Red Cross, who had also already received the appeal from the ICRC but did not yet have sufficient means to send aid. The first humanitarian aid shipments were funded by the French Foreign Ministry to the tune of 20,000 and then 75,000 francs, to which de Gaulle added 30,000 francs from his "personal funds".[87] They were transported either from Libreville by an unofficial Biafran representative, or by the ICRC, which was instructed that the aid was specifically for Biafra and not Nigeria. At first no relief workers were sent to the area, since the Biafrans were mainly asking for medical equipment and medicines and the Quai d'Orsay feared that the Nigerian army would consider them mercenaries.[88]

As the situation deteriorated and aroused strong emotions in the summer of 1968, this solution was no longer satisfactory. The Élysée felt it was becoming necessary to put in place a real humanitarian aid operation led by France. Beginning with September 1968 a group made up of representatives of the Secretariat for African and Malagasy Affairs, Ministry of Foreign Affairs, Ministry of the Armed Forces, Ministry of Transport, French Red Cross, Order of Malta, Comité catholique contre la faim and Secours Catholique met regularly to elaborate and co-ordinate the various aspects of a real policy of providing humanitarian aid to Biafra. The French operations were of major psychological importance as they were intended to show France's support for the Biafran people and their struggle. The source of the aid had to be clearly identifiable, which meant that it had to be distributed by French personnel. For de Gaulle, therefore, sending volunteers on the ground was the first element of this operation which was not, under any circumstances, to be left in Swiss hands.[89]

Paradoxically, this imperative set by the French head of state coincided with the needs of the ICRC, which was seeking to strengthen its presence on the ground and appealed to the National Red Cross Societies to provide volunteers. Thus, in September 1968 the French Red Cross sent two medical teams to Biafra. They were based in Awo-Omamma and Santana, and the volunteers who made them up stayed for around two months before being replaced. Among them were some of the future founders of Médecins Sans Frontières. While in the province, the teams operated under the ICRC's responsibility for insurance and security reasons,[90] since the personnel were theoretically better protected by the Committee's neutrality.

Whilst the distribution of aid on the ground had to therefore be done by French nationals, the delivery of supplies to the breakaway province also had to be independent and clearly associated with France. As de Gaulle pointed out to Foccart: "It is out of the question that our aid to Biafra should go through international bodies. We must provide direct aid to Biafra through the French Red Cross, and not the International Red Cross".[91] This translated into the French Red Cross setting up an air bridge between Libreville and the breakaway province in September 1968. This was the second element of the operation. This undertaking was funded by launching a national public collection in early August 1968. It helped raise 13,245,000 francs and pay for airlifts that cost more than 300,000 francs a month just to transport food between Libreville and Biafra.[92] Two planes flew to Biafra and back, at night, three times a week at first, and then up to ten times from September 1969. They mainly supplied the French Red Cross teams on the ground. According to Ambassador Delauney, 2,861 tonnes of aid and medicines were shipped during 475 missions which were conducted between September 1968 and January 1970.[93] Compared to the tens of thousands of tonnes transported by the churches and the ICRC, these quantities were relatively small, but this air bridge became crucially important once the ICRC airlifts stopped in 1969.

Beginning with September 1968 planes often brought severely malnourished Biafran children back to Libreville. Transporting and caring for these children was the third element of the French humanitarian aid provided to Biafra. The health service of the Ministry of the Armed Forces set up a military hospital in Gabon in order to provide them with care as soon as they arrived. The most critical cases were treated on site, while those whose health allowed it were sent to Gabonese reception centres run by local authorities, Secours Catholique and the Order of Malta. This initiative caused tensions with Ojukwu, who was initially opposed to it because he did not want the children to be taken out of Biafra.[94] He finally agreed at the insistence of the Gabonese head of state,[95] who set up a relief committee for Biafran children to co-ordinate their care. This task, however, seemed to quickly fall to the French embassy in Libreville, which also provided funds to help run the Gabonese centres.[96] As the latter reached saturation by the end of 1968, some children were then sent by the Order of Malta to Côte d'Ivoire, where they were taken into care by four centres set up in Bouaké, Yamoussoukro, Cocody and Grand-Bassam. As before, this initiative had to be clearly associated with France's support for Biafra. It was therefore preferable to leave it in the hands of French organisations, which caused tensions with other associations who wished to take part. For example, the Swiss NGO Terre des Hommes was able to get involved only after tough discussions.[97] The debates around whether or not to keep the military hospital reflected the same concern. The facility was particularly expensive compared to the number of patients that could be treated there (around 200), which led the president of the French Red Cross to ask that a less costly solution be considered. The Foreign Minister was opposed to this since, in his view, it was essential to maintain the three elements of French humanitarian aid for "both psychological and political reasons".[98]

Designed as a way to show the Biafrans that France supported their struggle without formally recognising them, the humanitarian operations also served other (military and media) purposes in support of secession. Firstly, the airlifts aroused many suspicions about the goods carried. Apart from the fact that Libreville was used as a base for the arms deliveries organised by the French services, the actors at the centre of the military and humanitarian airlifts were sometimes the same people. As the planes took off from the same airport, it is likely that some flights carried mercenaries and that the cargoes were sometimes mixed,[99] albeit the arms supplies were organised independently. The humanitarian aid sent to Biafra also provided a good pretext for sending technicians and equipment to the province to set up a landing strip meant solely for French relief planes,[100] but the project never seemed to materialise. Furthermore, like the other airlifts, the FRC flights facilitated the passage of aircraft carrying weapons, which could fly behind them at night to avoid Nigerian anti-aircraft fire. The French authorities were well aware of this and when, in 1969, the ICRC asked them again to help it persuade Ojukwu to accept daytime instead of night-time flights, the Secretariat preferred to turn it down since it believed that pushing for such a solution would be tantamount to "abandoning the Biafrans".[101]

Secondly, the use of funds allegedly intended for French humanitarian operations raised questions. There were strong suspicions that they went directly to helping the Biafran war effort. Witnesses stated that some of the money was simply handed over to the Biafran Red Cross which then used it as it saw fit.[102] More generally, there was the issue of the use of funds collected from the public for humanitarian purposes. To what extent were they used to finance French military support for the secessionists? For example, Maurice Delauney asked that part of the money collected be made available to his military adviser at the embassy in Libreville in order to pay for the expenses incurred by the relief operations in Biafra.[103] Although he indicated that a report on the spending of this money would be forwarded to the Red Cross, it is easy to see how it could be used to pay for other activities which the embassy's military adviser also dealt with. The rapidity with which these funds diminished in the autumn of 1968 seems to confirm this hypothesis. Indeed, those in charge of the operations estimated that by December 1968 only two million francs would remain of the thirteen raised in August 1968, whereas the total monthly expenditure was estimated at 1,117,000 francs on average.[104] Thus, funds meant for humanitarian aid were undoubtedly diverted but not, it seems, in a systematic fashion, and some people even made a point of taking precautions to avoid this becoming a widespread practice. For example, officials in charge of aid for Biafra refused to allow donations to be given directly to the Biafran Red Cross since the latter could make them available to the military. While there were those, particularly within the Secretariat, who were in favour of directly providing aid to this Society, it was also recognised that this should come from funds other than those raised from the public.[105] There were similar discussions around the construction of the landing strip allegedly reserved for Biafran relief: it was pointed out that "it had not been planned nor did it seem possible to use funds raised from the public to pay for it, since building an airfield was not normally part of the humanitarian assistance for which the collection had been intended".[106] These hesitations about the use of the money raised show that, even when it was seen as part of a state's support for a very specific cause, the exploitation of humanitarian aid posed a number of moral dilemmas for those involved in these processes, which led them to seek a middle way. These subtleties, however, were lost on the Nigerian government, for whom the French initiatives helped discredit the action of the Red Cross Movement as a whole.

Thirdly, the role played by French medical volunteers involved in ICRC operations also raised questions. Indeed, relief teams could provide opportunities to send intelligence operatives into the field. Thus, in the last weeks of the war, Louis Schittly suspected the logistician based in Santana of being "a soldier in civilian clothes, the eyes of National Security, one of Foccart's moles".[107] More generally, despite the ICRC's rules of neutrality, French medical staff maintained close links with the French embassy in Libreville, which played a major role in co-ordinating all kinds of French support in Biafra. While there, they frequently travelled to Libreville, where they provided information on the situation. Through Delauney, they informed those in charge of providing support to Biafra about the morale of the population and troops.[108] At the request of the French authorities, they also sometimes provided material to be published in the press,[109] and did not hesitate to use the attention they were given in Libreville to relay their humanitarian concerns in high places.[110] To some this was not incompatible with the duty of neutrality of the International Committee of the Red Cross since other volunteers were on the other side of the front line and probably also felt some empathy with the opposing side.[111]

This view seemed to be shared by the ICRC, which maintained an ambiguous relationship with the French Red Cross throughout the war. As for the teams it provided, they were made up of quality personnel, something which the ICRC struggled to find during the conflict. These volunteers were therefore welcome and Geneva seemed to accept their pro-Biafran sympathies. The FRC's air operations were more difficult for the ICRC to come to grips with. Initially, in the autumn of 1968, there were plans for the French airlifts to be integrated into the efforts co-ordinated by the ICRC.[112] This solution was dropped, probably because of the political and military implications of these activities, but also because of a certain reluctance on the part of the French leadership, who wished to maintain the national character of the operation. However, beginning with June 1969, when the ICRC ended its airlifts, those run by the French Red Cross took on a new importance for the Geneva-based organisation since it enabled it to supply its staff inside the province and continue to provide some relief. It discreetly gave part of its food stocks intended for the Biafrans to the French Red Cross and helped financially to increase its round trips between Libreville and Biafra.[113] The ICRC's involvement in the FRC's airlifts was due in particular to the tensions within the Geneva-based organisation, where not everyone supported the decision to end the airlifts in the summer of 1969. In this context, discreetly using the French Red Cross to deliver the food still available to the Biafran population was a compromise solution. Moreover, the organisation saw this solution as a way to continue its work on both sides of the front line and thus, paradoxically, observe the Red Cross principle of impartiality.

Analysing the impact and exploitation of the relief operations through the prism of humanitarian actors' reflections helps show the complexity of this issue. Because of the urgency of the situation, organisations had to demonstrate a certain pragmatism which varied according to the media pressure they felt, their own moral imperatives, but also the more or less close links they had with the breakaway province. The interplay between these different factors did not produce the same results for all organisations, but led them to make decisions for which they were prepared to accept the consequences. This perspective makes it possible to nuance a sometimes simplistic view of the conflict whereby they were unwittingly exploited by Ojukwu's ambitions. The impact of humanitarian aid on the prolongation of the hostilities, however, remains particularly difficult to gauge because of the way it was used in the Nigerian discourse. Indeed, the emergence of the debate around the impact of the relief effort was of some interest to the proponents of Nigerian unity – particularly the British government – who were quick to point out the unscrupulousness of the Ojukwu regime who used Western generosity to continue the war.

Conceived from the outset as a means of helping Biafra achieve its independence, the French relief operations are a paradigmatic example of the possible political uses of humanitarian aid. However, here too the reactions of the organisations concerned were pragmatic. While the French Red Cross was part of the Red Cross Movement whose principles of neutrality and impartiality it theoretically had to respect, its pro-Biafran stance was to some extent seen as an opportunity by the ICRC, at a time when it could no longer act directly. This pragmatism on the part of the Geneva-based organisation did not apply only to the activities of the French Red Cross but also to the personnel that the latter provided.

Notes

1 Ryfman, *La question humanitaire*, p. 164.
2 M. Anderson, *Do No Harm: How Aid Can Support Peace – or War* (Boulder: L. Rienner, 1999); see also M.-A. Pérouse de Montclos, *Aide humanitaire, aide à la guerre?* (Brussels: Éditions Complexes, 2001).
3 F. Terry, *Condemned to Repeat? The Paradox of Humanitarian Aid* (Ithaca: Cornell University Press, 2002), p. 16 and p. 224.
4 Ryfman, *La question humanitaire*, p. 164.
5 One of the most emblematic cases is probably Operation Turquoise, deployed by France in Rwanda; see L. de Vulpian & T. Prungnaud, *Silence Turquoise, Rwanda, 1992–1994, responsabilité de l'État français dans le génocide des Tutsi* (Paris: Don Quichotte, 2012).
6 J. Paulmann (ed.), *Dilemmas of Humanitarian Aid in the Twentieth Century* (London: Oxford University Press, 2016).
7 J.-F. Fayet, *VOKS, le laboratoire helvétique. Histoire de la diplomatie culturelle soviétique durant l'entre-deux-guerres* (Geneva: Georg Editeur, 2014), pp. 101–25.
8 Rodogno, *Against Massacre*; Simms & Trim (eds), *Humanitarian Intervention.*
9 Farré, *Colis de guerre.*
10 For example: M.-A. Pérouse de Montclos, "Humanitarian Aid and the Biafra War: Lessons not Learned", *Africa Development*, 34:1 (2009), 69–82; De Waal, *Famine Crimes*, pp. 72–7; Stremlau, *The International Politics of the Nigerian Civil War*, pp. 215–52.
11 M.-A. Pérouse de Montclos, *Les humanitaires dans la guerre, des idéaux à l'épreuve de la politique* (Paris: La Documentation française, 2012), pp. 28–30.
12 S. Adejumobi & A. Aderemi, "Oil and the Political Economy of the Nigerian Civil War", in Osaghae, Onwudiwe & Suberu (eds), *The Nigerian Civil War and Its Aftermath*, pp. 196–7.

13 Stremlau, *The International Politics of the Nigerian Civil War*, pp. 220–1.
14 C. Uche, "Money Matters in a War Economy: The Biafran Experience", *Nationalism and Ethnic Politics*, 8:1 (2002), 29–54, at 38.
15 Farmar, *Believing in Action*, p. 26.
16 G. Chuku, "Women under Fire", in Osaghae, Onwudiwe & Suberu (eds), *The Nigerian Civil War and Its Aftermath*, pp. 220–1.
17 Chuku, "Women and the Nigeria–Biafra War", p. 329–59.
18 Uche, "Money Matters in a War Economy", p. 35.
19 Stremlau, *The International Politics of the Nigerian Civil War*, p. 221.
20 J. Foccart, *Journal de l'Elysée, t. 1: 1965–1967: tous les soirs avec de Gaulle* (Paris: Fayard, 1997), pp. 728–9; J. Foccart, *Journal de l'Elysée, t. 2: 1968–1969: le Général en mai* (Paris: Fayard, 1998), p. 87; Uche, "Money Matters in a War Economy", p. 42.
21 Stremlau, *The International Politics of the Nigerian Civil War*, p. 242.
22 FNA, 5 AG FPU/686, notes from V. Balési to J. Foccart, 12 and 15 September 1969.
23 AWCC, General Secretariat, 42.003.07, memorandum by H. Reuschle, 26 April 1968.
24 NLS, Papers of Rev. A. G. Somerville, file 5, letters from W. and A. Somerville, 1 April 1968 and 20 August 1968.
25 ACSE, 11I1.12a3.2, letter from C. Wencker to D. O'Sullivan, 13 March 1969; 11I1.12a4.1, letter from D. O'Sullivan to the bishop of Chur.
26 AWCC, DICARWS, 425.04.057, "Commentary on Diary".
27 Stremlau, *The International Politics of the Nigerian Civil War*, p. 241.
28 TNA, FCO 65/311, copy of a telegram from the US Embassy in Lagos to the Department of State, 26 October 1968.
29 K. Lindsay, "Biafra: How a Poor Country Found the Money to Fight Its War of Independence", *The Globe and Mail*, 9 November 1969.
30 TNA, PREM 13/2827.
31 TNA, FCO 65/311, copy of a telegram from the US Embassy in Lagos to the Department of State, 26 October 1968.
32 ACSE, 11I1.12a5.1, "Sequel to report of Fr O'Sullivan to General Council", 10 October 1970.
33 AWCC, General Secretariat, 42.3.008, memorandum from B. Carr to A. Booth, 16 December 1968. At this moment, Carr calculated that since the start of the relief effort, approximately $45,000 and £7,500 had been sent to Biafra.
34 ACSE, 11I1.12a5.1, "Sequel to report of Fr O'Sullivan to General Council", 10 October 1970.
35 ACSE, 11I1.12a5.1, "Sequel to report of Fr O'Sullivan to General Council", 10 October 1970.
36 ACSE, 11I1.12a5.1, "Sequel to report of Fr O'Sullivan to General Council", 10 October 1970.
37 AWCC, CCIA, 428.6.26, letter from K. Lindsay to A. Booth, 12 December 1968.
38 Article 23 of the Fourth Geneva Convention relative to the Protection of Civilian Persons in Time of War, 12 August 1949.

39 AICRC, plenary session of the Committee, 3 April 1969.
40 NLS, Papers of Rev. A. G. Somerville, file 8, letter from Somerville, 10–17 July 1969.
41 FNA, 5AG FPU/686, letter from the Secretariat for African and Malagasy Affairs to the French President, 28 February 1969.
42 Stremlau, *The International Politics of the Nigerian Civil War*, pp. 247–50.
43 ACSE, 1111.12a4.1, "Iheoma relief activities".
44 AICRC, plenary session of the Committee, 8 August 1968, Presidential Council meeting, 26 September 1968; TNA, FCO 38/308, "Note of a meeting between the Secretary of State and representatives of the major relief bodies in the UK", 20 September 1968.
45 TNA, FCO 38/312, telegram from the BHC in Lagos (D. Hunt) to the CO, 21 September 1968; FCO 38/305, "Lord Shepherd's Visit to Geneva", October 1968.
46 AICRC, B AG 202 147-009, mission report by J. Moreillon and D. Delapraz, 8–13 September 1974.
47 AICRC, B AG 202 147-009, note by D. Delapraz on the CICR in the African public opinion, 12 March 1976.
48 Draper, *Shadows*, pp. 116–17.
49 TNA, FCO 60/350.
50 TNA, FCO 60/350, letter from the BHC in Lagos (D. Hunt) to the FCO, 17 January 1969.
51 AICRC, B AG 202 147-001, telex from Bignami to the CICR, 14 November 1969.
52 TNA, FCO 60/350, letter from the consulate in Geneva to the FCO, 4 December 1969.
53 AICRC, Lagos delegation's papers. This episode is recounted in C. Brovelli's book; J. Wolf, *La guerre des rapaces: la vérité sur la guerre du Biafra* (Paris: Albin Michel, 1969), pp. 162–4.
54 FNA, 5 AG FPU 687, telegram from the French Embassy in Lagos (Barbey) to the MAE, 14 January 1970.
55 Press release by Joint Church Aid, 19 December 1968.
56 O'Sullivan, *Ireland, Africa and the End of Empire*, pp. 83–106.
57 O'Sullivan, *Ireland, Africa and the End of Empire*, pp. 122–3.
58 Interview of M. Delauney in J. Calmettes's documentary, *Histoires secrètes du Biafra*, 54'.
59 Lloyd, Mollerup & Bratved, *The Nordchurchaid Airlift to Biafra*, pp. 23–32.
60 Draper, *Shadows*, p. 118.
61 On the WCC policy, see A. Booth, "The Churches in the Nigerian War", *The Round Table*, 60:238 (1970), 121–8; Wiseberg, "Christian Churches and the Nigerian Civil War", pp. 297–331.
62 AWCC, General Secretariat, 42.3.009, declaration by the DICARWS Committee, 5 December 1969.
63 "Joint Church Aid statement on Nigeria/Biafra", in Lloyd, Mollerup & Bratved, *The Nordchurchaid Airlift to Biafra*, p. 232.
64 Mohammed, "Relief Services in the Nigerian Civil War", p. 249.

65 AICRC, B AG 202 147-001, letters from G. Schürch to the CICR, 5 and 23 December 1968; letter from H. Egli to the CICR, 10 January 1969.
66 AICRC, Directorate briefing note, 20 May 1969.
67 TNA, FCO 38/300, telegram from the BHC at Lagos (E. G. Willan) to the CO, 29 May 1968.
68 AICRC, B AG 200 147-003.02, report by P. A. Reardon, 6 October 1969.
69 *Foreign Relations of the United States*, 1969–76, vol. E-5, Part 1, document 146.
70 Thompson, *American Policy and African Famine*, p. 143.
71 TNA, FCO 65/167, "Points of discussion with General Alexander on Tuesday", 29 October 1968.
72 M. Vaïsse, *La Grandeur. Politique étrangère du général de Gaulle (1958–1969)* (Paris: Fayard, 1998).
73 J.-P. Bat, *Le syndrome Foccart. La politique française en Afrique de 1959 à nos jours* (Paris: Gallimard, 2012), pp. 126–39; F. Turpin, "Jacques Foccart et le secrétariat général pour les affaires africaines et malgaches", *Histoire@Politique*, 8:2 (2009), 85–98.
74 D. Bach, "Le Général de Gaulle et la guerre civile au Nigeria", *Canadian Journal of African Studies / Revue Canadienne des Études Africaines*, 14:2 (1980), 259–72.
75 J. Foccart & P. Gaillard, *Foccart parle, entretiens avec Philippe Gaillard*, Vol. 1 (Paris: Fayard, 1995), p. 342.
76 J. Baulin, *La politique africaine d'Houphouët-Boigny* (Paris: Éditions Eurafor-Press, 1980), pp. 87–119.
77 FNA, 5 AG FPU/2432, letter from Houphouët-Boigny to de Gaulle, 9 February 1969.
78 FNA, 5 AG FPU/695, telegram from the French Embassy Libreville (Delauney), 28 October 1969. See also A. Konieczna, "L'Afrique du Sud: un partenaire particulier pour le 'dialogue'", in J.-P. Bat, O. Forcade & S. Mary (eds), *Foccart: archives ouvertes (1958–1974). La politique, l'Afrique et le monde* (Paris: Presses Universitaires de Paris-Sorbonne, 2017), chapter 21.
79 Foccart, *Journal de l'Elysée, t.* 2, p. 331.
80 FNA, 5 AG FPU 574, letter from President Bongo to de Gaulle, 30 August 1968.
81 M'Bokolo, *Médiations africaines*, pp. 92–102.
82 Gould, *The Struggle for Modern Nigeria*, p. 220.
83 F.-X. Verschave, *La Françafrique: le plus long scandale de la République* (Paris: Stock, 2003), pp. 137–53; Monsieur X & P. Pesnot, *Les dessous de la Françafrique* (Paris: Nouveau monde éditions, 2008), pp. 27–36.
84 J. Pictet, *Les principes de la Croix-Rouge* (Geneva: CICR, 1966).
85 AMAE Nantes, French permanent representation to the UN in New York, box 214, "discours du ministre des Affaires étrangères, M. Debré, à la XXIIIe session de l'Assemblée générale des des Nations unies", 7 October 1968.
86 Foccart, *Journal de l'Elysée, t.* 2, p. 88.
87 Foccart, *Journal de l'Elysée, t.* 2, p. 95.
88 FNA, 5AG FPU/346, note from the MAE to the Secretariat for African and Malagasy Affairs, 7 May 1968.

89 Foccart, *Journal de l'Elysée, t. 2*, p. 323.
90 AFRC, INT 23 Biafra, 01/16 and 04/16.
91 Foccart, *Journal de l'Elysée, t. 2*, p. 310.
92 FNA, 5 AG FPU/689, co-ordination meeting, 29 July 1969.
93 FNA, 5 AG FPU/2181, note from M. Delauney to J. Foccart, 24 June 1970.
94 More broadly on the evacuation of children, see G. N. Njung, "Playing Politics: The Saga of the Biafran Child Refugees in Gabon and Côte d'Ivoire during the Nigerian Civil War, 1967–70", *Africa Today*, 69:1–2 (2022), 110–33. The fact that children and youth were heavily mobilised during the conflict might explain Ojukwu initial reluctance. S. Hynd, "Biafran Childhoods, Youth Mobilization, and Child Soldiering in the Nigerian Civil War 1967–70", *International Journal of African Historical Studies*, 58:1 (2025), article 16.
95 FNA, 5 AG FPU/574, co-ordination meeting, 24 August 1968; interministerial meeting, 12 September 1968.
96 FNA, 5AG FPU/689, letter from the French Embassy in Libreville (Posier) to the MAE (Debré), 7 January 1969.
97 FNA, 5AG FPU/689, notes from V. Balesi to J. Foccart, 27 September 1968, 15 October 1968, note by the SDECE 5769 II B, 19 November 1968, note by the SDECE 5951 II B, 10 December 1968. On Terre des Hommes, Y. Denéchère, "Nouvel acteur et nouveau phénomène transnationaux: Terre des Hommes et l'adoption internationale (1960–1980)", *Relations internationales*, 142:2 (2010), 119–36.
98 FNA, 5 AG FPU/689, handwritten notes by V. Balési, January 1969; note for the attention of J. Foccart, 17 January 1969.
99 Interview with the pilots A. Gréard (25 July 2009) and E. d'Herbès (30 October 2009). The latter remembered the chaos at Libreville airport.
100 FNA, 5 AG FPU/689, note from V. Balési to J. Foccart, 7 October 1968.
101 FNA, 5 AG FPR/799, note for the French President, 11 September 1969.
102 Calmettes, *Histoires secrètes du Biafra*.
103 FNA, 5 AG FPU/574, telegram from the French Embassy in Libreville (M. Delauney) to the MAE, 28 August 1968.
104 FNA, 5 AG FPU/689, note from V. Balési to J. Foccart, 25 October 1968; co-ordination meeting, 29 July 1969.
105 FNA, 5 AG FPU/689, notes by V. Balési, January 1969.
106 FNA, 5 AG FPU/689, note from V. Balési to the Secretary General, 7 October 1968.
107 Schittly, *L'homme qui voulait voir la guerre de près*, p. 106.
108 FNA, 5AG FPU/688, telegram from the French Embassy in Libreville (Posier) to the MAE, 7 February 1969.
109 FNA, 5AG FPU/689, letter from J. Foccart to M. Schumann, 17 October 1969.
110 FNA, 5 AG FPU/688, telegram from the French Embassy in Libreville (M. Delauney) to the MAE, 20 September 1969.
111 Interview of P. Grellety-Bosviel by J. Calmettes, *Conversations avec les hommes du Biafra*, documentary, 7×26', Histoire, 2001.
112 AICRC, B AG 280 147-002, Directorate meeting, 16 September 1968.
113 FNA, 5AG FPU/2181, note from M. Delauney to J. Foccart, 24 June 1970.

8

MSF versus the ICRC: the ingredients of a myth

On 22 December 1971 Jacques Bérès, Philippe Bernier, Raymond Borel, Pascal Grellety-Bosviel, Jean Cabrol, Marcel Delcourt, Gérard Illiouz, Bernard Kouchner, Gérard Pigeon, Vladan Radoman, Max Récamier and Jean-Michel Wild founded Médecins Sans Frontières.[1] Although it was created two years after the end of the Nigeria–Biafra war, in collective representations it remains unquestionably associated with this conflict, not least because of the link established between some of its future members' experience in Biafra and the need to form their own emergency aid organisation on their return. Bernard Kouchner has repeatedly emphasised the impact that the conflict had on his conception of humanitarianism, which is based on the notion of bearing witness and the duty to intervene. In his 1986 book *Charité business* he writes:

> The few doctors who were in Biafra were screaming to general indifference. As an activist accustomed to and even spurred by rebuffs, I did not give up. In order to be accepted into ICRC teams, volunteers agreed to never talk about what they had seen during their missions. I signed up to this and I broke my word. As soon as I returned to France, seeing the lack of response to my political meetings, I set up an International Committee against Genocide in Biafra. My reasoning was simple: I did not want to make the same mistake as the ICRC who, during the war of 1939–45, had not denounced the Nazi extermination camps. That is how Médecins Sans Frontières and Médecins du Monde came into being.[2]

This account of the crisis has evolved in Kouchner's writings over time depending on the context and his political trajectory. In the mid-1980s the conflict was the point where the break with the ICRC's silence happened and the principle of speaking out and "bearing witness" was put into practice; then, in the early 1990s, in *Le malheur des autres* (The misfortune of others), Biafra still represented the "breaking of the silence", which this time was associated with the notion of intervention.[3] Beginning with the 1990s authors such as Rony Brauman and Anne Vallaeys revisited the

Biafran episode, highlighting the perverse effects of the doctors' statements which, by denouncing a genocide that had not taken place, had apparently helped prolong the war.[4] Vallaeys also noted the role that those who had not been involved in Biafra had played in setting up the organisation.[5] For Denis Maillard this reappraisal of the Biafran episode was closely linked to the split between the "Biafrans" who left with Kouchner to found Médecins du Monde in 1980, and the "*soixante-huitards*" who remained at MSF with Claude Malhuret and Rony Brauman. Maillard echoed the view of Patrick Aeberhard, a former "Biafran", for whom Brauman's and Vallaeys's analyses "represent the latest charges against Kouchner and the original MSF staff who were driven away or withdrew at the time of the split in 1979".[6]

By drawing on primary sources that are often absent from the accounts of the various protagonists, this chapter revisits the founding myth of MSF by putting the French doctors' stances in the wider context of the ICRC's attitude towards violations of humanitarian law and allegations of genocide. It examines how narratives about violence witnessed by humanitarians in "extreme crises" are constructed. In this respect, NGOs are privileged observation points because, by being present on the ground, they play the role of whistle-blowers and can, for example, help disseminate and legitimise the use of the term genocide.[7] Debates often crystallise around the use of this term because of the legal and moral obligations it entails. Indeed, the Convention on the Prevention and Punishment of the Crime of Genocide adopted in 1948 made genocide a crime under international law. Although it is rarely enforced,[8] the obligations it gives rise to explain the gradual polarisation of attitudes towards this term in the decades that followed the Second World War. In cases of mass violence, states, but also intergovernmental organisations and especially the UN, are particularly reluctant to use it so as not to be obliged to intervene.[9] Conversely, from the 1960s it was frequently used by various civil-society groups as a means of attracting attention, as in the case of Biafra.[10] This raises the question of the meaning that actors of the time ascribed to this term. As Dirk Moses pointed out in relation to the situation in East Pakistan (now Bangladesh) in 1971, the word genocide was very widely used by the press, Indian politicians and some Western diplomats to describe the atrocities committed by Pakistani soldiers. However, UN representatives on the ground remained unaware of the legal implications of its use.[11]

In the case of Biafra, MSF's founding myth says little about the meaning that Western actors ascribed to the term genocide which they used, and focuses on staging the opposition between the French doctors speaking out and an ICRC presented as monolithic and silent. To understand the ICRC's stance towards the violence it observed, the first section of this chapter analyses not only its guiding principles, but also its knowledge of the situation on the ground. While during the first year of the war violations of the Geneva Conventions mainly concerned the Biafran civilian population, beginning with the summer of 1968 the ICRC staff, who had become more numerous on the ground, were directly confronted with them. This change and its implications are analysed in the second section. The tensions that arose between headquarters and field teams around the violence that the latter were victims of provide a better understanding of the context in which the French doctors' positions were taken. The third section examines the elements of the founding myth of Médecins Sans Frontières – namely speaking out and *sans-frontiérisme* – and concludes with the creation of the organisation in 1971.

The ICRC and the violations of humanitarian law

In the summer of 1967, just after the start of the conflict, the ICRC headquarters received the first reports from delegates who had made it to Biafra. They contained frequent references to alleged abuses committed against Biafran civilians, raising concerns in Geneva. Delegates described the fear they perceived among the population and did not hesitate to use the term genocide. Thus, Paul Reynard, sent on a mission to Biafra for a few weeks in September 1967, reported his conversation with an Anglican bishop who made it clear that "if the Federals win, there will be genocide".[12] According to Reynard this fear was widely shared among the population. He took it seriously and wrote to the ICRC that it should prepare for such an eventuality:

> Everyone here is convinced that falling into the hands of the federals would be a death sentence. They hardly ever mention prisoners of war. They think people are not captured but exterminated. So it is understandable that in this hateful war between not just armies but race groups the civilian population should flee from the enemy. … In the event that Biafra is invaded, there should be a minimum of protection for the Ibos who could particularly be the target of genocide.[13]

In November 1967 Reynard was replaced by Karl Heinrich Jaggi as head of the ICRC delegation in the breakaway province. Jaggi expressed the same concerns as his predecessor. He wrote that the most serious aspect of the war was the danger of genocide and expressed relief that the Igbo were fleeing from the advancing federal troops, otherwise the region would have looked like "Europe thirty years ago".[14] He made a point of informing his superiors of this situation, which he described as serious and grave. Other sources such as missionaries and doctors confirmed the fears of the Biafran population and took the allegations of genocide very seriously.[15] The situation also concerned UNICEF representatives in Nigeria, who alerted the organisation's offices in Paris and New York to the possibility of genocide. The latter then turned to Geneva to check their information with the ICRC, who was considered the most likely actor to have first-hand information about the situation.[16] As these different examples suggest, those present on the ground used the term genocide to alert ICRC headquarters to the seriousness of the problem, without thinking about its precise definition and legal implications.

The arrival of these reports at ICRC headquarters raises the question of how information gathered in the field should be used, particularly in the case of massive violations of humanitarian law and human rights.[17] In his book on the ICRC, François Bugnion provides a detailed analysis of the organisation's policy on non-compliance with humanitarian rules in the various conflicts it has faced since its creation.[18] The author distinguishes between violations reported to it by the National Red Cross Societies or belligerents, and those that it observes directly or for which the facts are indisputable. In the first case, it passes on the complaints it has received to the other party and asks for an investigation to be launched. As the author points out, this procedure has rarely produced results. In the second case, the ICRC prefers holding discreet discussions with the parties to get them to change their behaviour. It can also take a public stance on these violations. Nevertheless, silence has generally prevailed, as shown in particular by its decision not to speak out against the abuses committed by the Nazi regime during the Second World War.

François Bugnion notes the Committee's increased tendency beginning with the late 1960s to take a public stance, which would indicate a change of direction on this point. However, this was not preceded by a change in doctrine. On the contrary, the policy of silence was reiterated by the former president and member of the Committee Léopold Boissier in an article published in the *International Review of the Red Cross* and reprinted in the Genevan press in January 1968.[19] His argument ran as follows: the ICRC preferred discretion to noisy denunciations because victims' interests were better protected by silence attended by an active presence on the ground than by public denunciations that could lead to its expulsion. Whilst this position generally prevailed within the Committee, dissenting voices sometimes succeeded in imposing a different point of view, as attested by the two statements issued by the ICRC on the use of poison gas in Yemen in early 1967. A few months later there were also debates about the attitude that should be adopted in relation to the ICRC's activities in Greece. Jacques Freymond insisted that the ICRC should "provide as much information as possible about what our delegates have done and seen" in order to make the public understand that it is taking action. But this suggestion did not arouse much enthusiasm, with some, including Léopold Boissier and Hans Bachmann, pointing out that "the ICRC's established practice has always been to never publish the findings of its delegates" and that "the Committee's sole concern should be to make findings with a view to improving the lot of the victims rather than seeking publicity".[20] A few days later the killing of prisoners in Nigeria prompted the Committee to address the same type of question.

> Mr Gallopin let it be known that a message had been prepared for the attention of the council, indicating that the ICRC was speaking out against these killings. In reply to Mr Boissier who noted that the ICRC had very often refrained from protesting against such killings and wondered whether this was an extension of its purview, Mr Siordet stated that the Committee could not protest against alleged violations which it had not witnessed. However, in the present case, it had been a witness. And it therefore had to protest. Mr Gallopin also drew the council's attention to the fact that the word "protest" should be avoided so that there wouldn't be any criticism later that a protest had been made. "We are strongly opposed", that was the phrase to be used. For Mr Pictet this was a question of words. This statement was not very different from those the ICRC had already made on the subject of, for example, the use of gas in Yemen or the prisoners of war in northern Vietnam. On the other hand, these representations to Nigeria would have to be made public since publicity was ultimately the only thing those people feared.[21]

These discussions show that the issue of publicising the observations of ICRC delegates did not follow a clearly established policy. Whilst in the case of Greece this issue gave rise to debates, in the case of Nigeria the Committee was more inclined to favour a certain degree of publicity. Lodging protests with governments did not seem to be a unanimously endorsed practice either. It did, however, tend to gain ground, as shown by the references to the conflicts in Yemen and Vietnam, and followed certain rules. The ICRC, via its delegates, had to have witnessed the violation committed. This condition required the organisation to have good knowledge of the situation, something which its weak presence on the ground did not always allow for. Thus, in the case of the prisoners killed in Nigeria, the ICRC had to drop its protest a few days later since its delegate had not actually witnessed the execution. However, it did make a public appeal to the belligerents in which it referred directly to the incident:

> Deeply alarmed by the summary execution of three prisoners, of which its delegation in Nigeria has been made aware, and by reports of civilians being massacred, the International Committee of the Red Cross has strongly appealed to the belligerents to comply strictly with the provisions of humanitarian law, and in particular Article 3 of the Geneva Conventions.[22]

Making public appeals was not something new for the ICRC, which had already used this method during the First World War to urge belligerents to respect humanitarian law. The problem, however, was deciding to what extent these appeals implied a degree of denunciation of the belligerents' behaviour, which might lead the ICRC to depart from its policy of neutrality. These different factors explain why the organisation's practice did not always seem consistent. In May 1968 a document drew up a list of the protests lodged by the ICRC with the Nigerian government.[23] It enumerated around ten, most of which were related to indiscriminate bombings by the Nigerian air force. These were for the most part attested by the organisation, but it seems that this was not always the case as the document also contained a list of protests received from the Biafran Red Cross and passed on to the Nigerian government between September 1967 and May 1968. These actions were not systematically publicised but were sometimes reported in the press, which inevitably provoked the anger of the FMG.[24] The appeal made from Kampala in May 1968, urging belligerents to lift the blockade and spare the civilians, was thus perceived by the FMG as a denunciation of its attitude, which helped worsen their relationship.

At the same time, the ICRC was looking for other ways to share its concerns and raise the alarm about the plight of civilians. Even before the start of the conflict, the killings perpetrated mainly against the Igbo population were the subject of discussions between the UN and ICRC. The ICRC official dealing with the situation in Nigeria, Thérèse Mathez, warned the UN of the risk of new massacres and even the outbreak of a civil war.[25] In the autumn of 1967 the delegate general for Africa, Georg Hoffmann, envisaged more substantial action being taken on the basis of the information available to him. He wished the ICRC to contact the UN and OAU to offer to mediate between belligerents. This scenario, which would have meant involving the ICRC in the political settlement of the conflict and thus violating the principle of neutrality, was rejected by Committee members and strongly discouraged by the Swiss ambassador to Lagos, Fritz Real.[26] This did not stop some ICRC staff from finding roundabout ways to raise awareness of the situation in Biafra. For example, the person dealing with the Nigerian situation at the ICRC's headquarters encouraged UNICEF officials to disseminate the information they had "in order to build up a groundswell of public opinion that could influence the behaviour of the federal troops".[27] The numerous air attacks and the deteriorating situation in Biafra during the spring of 1968 led delegates on the ground to insist that "organisations with a mandate to protect humanity" should be alerted.[28] In March 1968 the Committee decided to "contact the competent international body, such as the UN Commission on Human Rights, in order to draw its attention to the dramatic situation of the civilian population resulting from the unacceptable manner in which this war is being conducted".[29] In June 1968 it reiterated its decision and wished to

> inform the UN Secretary-General of the situation in Nigeria and Biafra, such as it is known to the ICRC from the many reports it receives from its delegates, and to express its deep concern about the situation in that part of Africa at the Labour Conference currently being held in Geneva.[30]

The aim of the first course of action was to alert the highest UN official, who in turn could draw the attention of Security Council members to a situation that threatened international peace and security. Thus, the ICRC was seeking to "urgently ensure the humanisation of the conflict so that the killings would stop".[31] The second course of action seems a bit more surprising but probably reflected its desire to make its concerns known on the international stage. The International Labour Conference, which every June brought together government, employer and worker delegates from the member states of the International Labour Organization, was probably a good opportunity to alert many governments as well as other circles such as employers' and workers' organisations.

It is difficult to grasp the results of these approaches. They did not seem to elicit any particular reaction from the UN Secretariat, which did not perceive the situation in the same way. On the contrary, the United Nations helped spread the opposite view since, in September 1968, the Secretary-General's representative in Lagos, Nils-Göran Gussing, was already a member of the international group of observers set up at Britain's suggestion to confirm that the Nigerian government was not committing genocide. It is true that the Secretary-General tried to ensure the independence of his representative's observations by attaching certain conditions to his involvement. For U Thant it was important that the mission be carried out by a civilian – who was better able to judge the treatment of civilians than a military official – which went against the wishes of the Nigerian government. Moreover, Gussing was not to be part of the team of national observers, rather, he was to conduct his own investigation and compile his findings separately to ensure their independence.[32] In practice, these precautions had no real effect since the FMG organised all of the observers' trips on the ground.

During the first year of the conflict the ICRC's various positions and approaches confirmed that it took the threat of genocide seriously, at least initially. It sometimes expressed its concerns in the media but did not follow a systematic policy in this respect as the violations it denounced could be alleged or attested by delegates, and reported in the press or not. The lack of a systematic approach was seized upon by the FMG, which accused it of repeating the Biafran discourse. Ironically, this trend was reversed in the autumn of 1968, with its own staff criticising it for being too cautious in the face of the Nigerian army's abuses.

An erratic ICRC: tensions with field teams and National Societies

In the summer of 1968 the ICRC's main concern became finding a way to deliver food. Thus, the issue of the conduct of hostilities was relegated to the background, although its leadership did point out that "the problem of the behaviour of Nigerien [*sic*] troops exterminating the Igbo must not be forgotten".[33] This issue was quickly raised by the growing number of Western humanitarian volunteers working in the province, who were therefore directly confronted with it. Indeed, the organisation's operations and personnel would sometimes fall victim to the violence of the federal offensive, which posed a concrete problem in the sense that the Red Cross emblem was not respected, but also – though this was never spelled out – because of the implicit inequality between Western lives and the lives of the local population.[34]

In the context of the advance of federal troops at the end of the summer of 1968, the Geneva-based organisation pondered the instructions it should give its delegates. Should it ask them to remain in the medical centres where they worked in order to ensure continuity of care and thus demonstrate the neutrality of Red Cross staff who could work equally well under both Biafran and Nigerian rule? Or should they retreat with the Biafran population and the patients trying to flee inside Biafra? After many debates within its headquarters, the ICRC decided to ask its delegates to stay put and wait for the arrival of the federals.[35] This decision seems to have been motivated by several considerations: it wished, on the one hand, to ensure continuity of care and, on the other hand, to show the Nigerian government, who had accused the ICRC of favouring the Biafrans, that its teams would stay on regardless of the evolution of the conflict. The organisation notified the FMG of the composition and position of its teams and was promised that they would not be attacked. Nevertheless, the field staff did not feel reassured. They agreed to stay but asked in return that the situation in which they found themselves be publicised.[36] On 23 September 1968 a collective message from the ICRC teams in Biafra, approved by their head of delegation on the ground, Karl H. Jaggi, was sent to August Lindt and then forwarded to the headquarters in Geneva. In it, the medical personnel demanded that public opinion be told about the killings taking place in Biafran hospitals when surrounded by Nigerian troops, and announced that one of their number would be sent as an emissary to Geneva to hold a press conference. Lindt strongly advised against this but did recommend that the ICRC make a public statement.

> This statement would inform public opinion of the teams' voluntary and courageous decision to stay on in accordance with Red Cross principles, to serve the victims regardless of the authorities in charge. ... It would mention that the Nigerian government has assured us of its co-operation and would express confidence. In my opinion this approach is much more effective.[37]

Thus, on 26 September 1968 an article was published in the *Journal de Genève*. It made reference to the statements by Karl Jaggi and by Max Récamier, the leader of the French team stationed in Awo-Omamma which would theoretically be the first to face the advance of the federals. In it, Jaggi explained the ICRC's position and the assurances received from Lagos, while stressing the voluntary nature of the doctors' presence in the field, as well as their fears.[38]

The decision to keep the teams in the medical centres was immediately called into question because of events that occurred a few days later. On 1 October 1968 four volunteers – two Yugoslav and two British – working in Okigwe for the humanitarian operations run by the ICRC and "WCC" respectively were murdered by federal soldiers. It therefore became out of the question that the teams should stay in the event of an offensive by the Nigerian army. At the same time, neutralised hospitals marked with the Red Cross emblem were again attacked by the air force in the autumn of 1968 and winter of 1968–69. These events, which were confirmed by delegates, caused considerable tensions within the ICRC and in particular between the organisation's headquarters and field staff. The volunteers felt that the ICRC's protests, although mentioned in press releases,[39] lacked vigour and visibility, a sentiment that was ultimately shared by Lindt.[40] They did not hesitate to express their dissatisfaction in the media, thus breaking the agreement they had signed up to not to divulge anything they did or saw while on an ICRC mission.[41] For example, on 7 October the *Journal de Genève* picked up an Agence France-Presse (AFP) report with the headline: "Nigeria–Biafra: anger among relief agencies' representatives after the killing of four Europeans".[42]

The field staff's discontent was exacerbated by the leadership's inconsistency about its denunciation policy. Their hesitation was not only due to the Committee's desire for discretion. The preparation by delegates of detailed reports about incidents and their transmission to Geneva also helped delay the process. There were also strategic considerations. The prevarications that followed the bombing of the hospital in Aboh on 19 October 1968 (Figure 8.1), where an ICRC team was working, are a good example of the interplay of these various factors. August Lindt informed the Committee

Figure 8.1 Aboh, crater of a bomb next to the hospital, V-P-NG-N-00016-18A (© ICRC / H. D. Finck, October 1968)

about the attack on the same day, having been witnessed by a delegate, and stated that "a public protest about this violation of the conventions is needed as quickly as possible".[43] A few days later, when Lindt reproached the Committee for remaining silent, the latter replied that it could lodge a protest with the FMG, but that it was waiting to receive the report of the delegate who had witnessed the violation before making it public.[44] However, taking into account the important negotiations that were at the time taking place between the FMG and ICRC on the subject of the air bridge, Lindt finally decided to postpone his proposed approach. He put off lodging his protest with the FMG until 1 November and gave up on making it public since it would have come too late after the events.[45] This erratic handling was not limited to denunciations but characterised the ICRC's entire communication policy, which on the whole did not receive the attention it deserved.

The personnel sent by the French Red Cross were particularly involved in these various events. An initial medical team, made up of six people and led by Max Récamier, left Paris for Biafra on 3 September 1968 and was quickly joined by other volunteers. Overall, more than sixty individuals (mostly men) took turns working one or more times as part of the French Red Cross medical teams between September 1968 and January 1970.[46] As soon as they arrived on the ground in September 1968, the volunteers were confronted with the advance of the federal army and feared for their lives. Thus, some of them became particularly active in denouncing the violence that ICRC teams had to face. Max Récamier and Pascal Grellety-Bosviel, two of the individuals involved in these operations, had already come up against this problem during a mission to Yemen, where they had helped relay the concerns of personnel on the ground about the use of gas, leading headquarters to publicly denounce it. In Biafra, the envoy mentioned in the ICRC teams' message was none other than Bernard Kouchner who, because of August Lindt's reaction, had to cut his journey short in Santa Isabel and return to the Biafran region, before going back to Paris in mid-October.[47]

Moreover, one of the places where French volunteers worked, the hospital in Awo-Omamma (Figure 8.2), was bombed several times during the winter of 1968–69. They were exasperated by the ICRC's lack of responsiveness and forcefulness in its protests, which did nothing to change the behaviour of the Nigerian air force. Thus, following the attack on 9 December 1968, one of the doctors, Pascal Grellety-Bosviel, asked the embassy in Libreville to inform the French media.[48] The news appeared in the newspapers two days later through AFP, who reported that humanitarian circles were aware that a Red Cross hospital had been bombed.[49] The ICRC press release was

Figure 8.2 Awo-Omamma hospital with Red Cross flags, V-P-NG-N-00049-18 (© ICRC / Max Vaterlaus)

not issued until the following day,[50] again showing the organisation's lack of responsiveness.

This bombardment, one of several such attacks, also provoked a reaction from the French Red Cross, which let the ICRC know of the emotions provoked within French circles. The vice-president of the French Red Cross added that, given the situation of insecurity in which the doctors found themselves, it was becoming difficult to recruit personnel. This problem was confirmed by Max Récamier when visiting the headquarters in Geneva. He explained that several volunteers who had been ready to go had withdrawn because, in the current circumstances, they "no longer felt sufficiently 'covered' in case of an incident". On 5 January 1969 the federal air force attacked Awo-Ommama again, reinforcing the exasperation of the doctors present there. They called for "an immediate and vigorous formal protest against this deliberate attack on a hospital which displays the Red Cross sign of neutrality on all of its buildings". The ICRC sent a message to that effect on 6 January 1969, which it made public the following day in a press release.[51]

The attitude of the French doctors was part of a context in which a rift was developing between the leaders of the operation, who were mostly based at the organisation's headquarters, and the workers in the field, who were confronted with violence on an almost daily basis. The medical teams – not only the French doctors – did not hesitate to make their concerns and discontent known to the ICRC. Their stances prompted headquarters to reflect on the way it dealt with the bombings. Thus, the first strike in Awo-Ommama led to the development of a new procedure, meant to be more rigorous, concerning any attacks on the Red Cross. Paradoxically, in order to improve the effectiveness of its actions, the ICRC decided to stop protesting when Biafran civilian infrastructure was affected, as it had sometimes done in the previous months. On the other hand, when sites bearing the Red Cross sign were targeted, it would systematically and immediately lodge a protest with the Nigerian Foreign Ministry. Depending on the situation, the commissioner general, August Lindt, and the ICRC Director, Roger Gallopin, would decide together whether to make this public or not.[52] Despite this change in practice, behind the scenes, some staff in Geneva still had doubts about the effectiveness of the procedure put in place.[53]

Whilst up until then the organisation's headquarters had been receptive to the volunteers' complaints, in the first few months of 1969 a change in attitude could be detected. Thus, on 26 January 1969 Jaggi demanded that the ICRC strongly condemn air attacks carried out on markets. This time headquarters replied that public condemnations were not the organisation's policy.[54] The reactions from the FMG, who almost systematically rejected its protests by claiming that they were merely the expression of

Biafran propaganda,[55] may have prompted the ICRC to be more cautious and question the reliability of the information it received, as shown by the clarifications it requested when the next bombing occurred. Thus, on 10 March 1969 the delegate Robert Jenni sent a message to Geneva reporting the attack on a hospital clearly marked with a red cross, which in his view justified making a vigorous and public protest. The ICRC then explicitly asked its representative not to speak publicly on the matter and to investigate in order to ensure that there were no military targets in the area. It further added that the delegate had to "understand that the ICRC's operations in Nigeria are part of a broader set of actions in Vietnam and the Middle East".[56]

This reference to the organisation's multiple fields of action provides another key to explaining the ICRC's taking a stricter stance on protests. Indeed, it had begun to be criticised by various members of the Red Cross Movement who looked at and compared the organisation's attitudes in the different conflicts in which it was involved. Thus, at a regional seminar held in Kuwait, Red Crescent Societies criticised the ICRC for not denouncing violations of the Geneva Conventions in the Middle East – particularly with regard to Israel – as vigorously as it did in Nigeria. The ICRC feared that this issue would acquire considerable importance at the 21st Red Cross Conference to be held in Istanbul in September 1969. For some within the Committee its approach to protests was in fact well established – it publicly spoke out against attacks on sites marked with the Red Cross, but did not protest against bombings in general – and it was the indiscipline of the delegates in Biafra who did not always follow instructions that explained this criticism.[57] As the previous sections have shown, the reality was more nuanced, particularly as far as the first year of the war was concerned.

In any event, to avoid ending up in a difficult position in Istanbul, the ICRC president asked the organisation's lawyers to study the matter in detail. The latter concluded that the doctrine on taking public stances was as follows: "In principle, the ICRC only takes a public stance in exceptional cases, for good reasons, and on the basis of complaints made by its delegates".[58] The possibility of going public was seen as an evolution of ICRC doctrine:

> Whereas in the past the rule for the ICRC was to, in principle, observe total discretion, in the past few years it has sometimes gone public in order to make its work more effective in the interests of the victims themselves. The classic example is the use of gas in Yemen. Recourse to this approach depends on the circumstances of each case and, consequently, it is inevitable that there will be an imbalance in the degree of publicity the Committee gives to the steps it takes in order to put an end to violations: some of them will be made public,

> while others will not. This situation seems inevitable unless we return to the rule of absolute discretion.[59]

There seemed to be confusion about the criteria for applying this doctrine which depended above all on circumstances. It was not until 1981 that the ICRC published a document setting out the conditions in which it could decide to take a public stance on violations of humanitarian law.[60] Nevertheless, the legal opinion issued in March 1969 allowed the ICRC to retrospectively make its approach more consistent and thus answer its critics by showing that its line of conduct was in fact well established. It reflected the difficulties the organisation faced in dealing with these violations and the slightly stricter policy it was implementing on this point.

Paradoxically, other methods appeared to be more effective in improving the lot of the population on the ground. For example, international observers also seemed to be quietly helping to change the situation of prisoners of war and civilians. They used their position to make very concrete recommendations in the areas retaken by the federal army. As noted by an ICRC delegate in the autumn of 1969: "Although their visits were less systematic and less thorough than those conducted by the ICRC, they nonetheless helped to a good extent to improve the conditions of detention of prisoners of war".[61] More generally, despite major reservations expressed about the reports produced by the observers, who were deemed to be too complacent, ICRC officials emphasised the positive effects of their missions on the ground which reassured the civilian population:

> Although the observers' investigations sometimes seem rather superficial and some of their conclusions hasty, it needs to be acknowledged that their intervention in the current conflict has a positive influence on the behaviour of the military authorities. The Nigerian government has taken their recommendations into account and has already acted on them in several cases. For example, some Nigerian officers whose behaviour was formally criticised by observers have reportedly been replaced. On the other hand, their periodic inspections in areas close to the front certainly help limit the number and severity of abuses committed by the armed forces.[62]

The French doctors' stance: rebelling against the Swiss institution?

It was in this context of debating available means to put an end to belligerents' violations of humanitarian law that the tensions between the future founders of MSF and ICRC crystallised. In addition to the sending of a messenger to Geneva to give a press conference, other events have been used in accounts about MSF to attest to the desire of French doctors to break with humanitarianism as conceived and practised by the ICRC. Comparing the doctors' decisions with their views of the Geneva-based organisation is essential for understanding how the conviction that a new humanitarianism was emerging, with Bernard Kouchner as its spokesperson, was forged. The many accounts and testimonies about the role played by French doctors during the conflict and in setting up Médecins Sans Frontières make it possible to identify two main areas around which the split occurred. Bearing witness and using the media to convey a discourse in support of the "victims" was one. In the words of Didier Fassin, it was a case of acting as spokespersons for the voiceless, which further raised questions about the humanitarians' perception of the "victims".[63] The other area had to do with the commitment of the future MSF founders who went or remained in the field at the risk of their lives, whereas others, notably the ICRC but more generally the international community, were presented as failing to mobilise.

In addition to the stances discussed above, two further events are cited to justify the new policy adopted by the French doctors in terms of bearing witness and speaking out: the publication of an article in *Le Monde* newspaper in 1968, and the creation by Bernard Kouchner of the International Committee for the Fight against Genocide. The first episode took place on 27 November 1968 when Bernard Kouchner and Max Récamier published an account of their first trip to Biafra.[64] The article took the form of a story in which the two doctors described what they had seen and done in Biafra. This act of speaking out is sometimes seen as the moment when the French doctors broke with the ICRC by violating its rule of silence. Whilst not questioning the importance that such a gesture may have had for its authors, reconstructing the ICRC's point of view at the time of the article's publication leads us to qualify its subversive character. Within the Committee, the *Le Monde* piece did not provoke indignation; on the contrary. At first it was described as excellent in the press review that accompanied the management's monthly newsletter to Committee members, and was later reprinted in the January 1969 issue of the *International Review of the Red Cross*.

The article therefore did not mark a break with the ICRC but, paradoxically, seemed to suit the communication policy that the organisation was trying to put in place by paying attention to its public relations.[65] From the summer of 1968 this was all the more necessary as its every move was commented on.[66] To this end, the ICRC sent an "audiovisual information specialist" on a mission to Biafra to produce a series of reports designed to publicise its work. In the last days of September, Bernard Kouchner was interviewed by this journalist.[67] As with the article of 27 November, the tone remains relatively neutral except when Kouchner explains about the flight of Biafran patients on the arrival of Nigerian troops. He uses the word "enemy" several times. Aware of how this looks, he corrects himself and says that he has picked up Biafran terminology since he works on the Biafran side. In the background, other French doctors can be heard saying: "Ah no, no, you can't say that, you must be kidding". The journalist intervenes saying he will cut the passage. Kouchner ends the interview by pointing out that the Red Cross treats "all sides" and that wounded Nigerians have recently been admitted to Awo-Omamma. This episode illustrates two things. On the one hand, it shows that attention was being paid to the Red Cross rules of neutrality, which the doctors sought to observe. On the other hand, it shows the impact of the environment in which humanitarians worked on their perception of the conflict. This second observation applies especially to volunteers who went to Biafra and described being particularly affected by its people and their struggle. As expressed by Pascal Grellety-Bosviel: "I don't know one person who has been to Biafra and has not been struck by the horror of the situation and the courage of its people".[68] This attitude was not unique to French doctors. Thus, the head of the ICRC delegation in Nigeria, Gerhart Schürch, explained that it was impossible to get teams who had served in the breakaway province to then work in the federal area:

> Those who have worked on the other side feel sympathy towards the people they have helped – which I can understand – even though they are as neutral as possible and do their best to remain neutral. It is therefore inevitable that they will say things which the Nigerians will find provocative and then they will think that they are Ojukwu's agents.[69]

Within the French teams, the violence experienced directly on the ground and the fears felt by patients who fled at the slightest rumour of the federal troops' arrival helped radicalise some members of the medical personnel, who gradually wanted to take a public stand. Thus, during a meeting attended by Récamier at the ICRC headquarters in late 1968, it became clear that some doctors no longer wished to simply "bear witness" as described in the article published on 27 November, but actually side with the Biafrans:

> While, according to Dr Récamier, Africans and Europeans on the ground are wondering whether the Red Cross has become a target rather than a protection, French doctors who would be prepared to assist the Biafran victims of the conflict are beginning to question the usefulness of preserving the neutrality of the Red Cross and are even wondering whether they should offer their services independently of the Red Cross, who no longer protects them and prevents them, on their return, from publicly expressing their sympathy for one side of the conflict.[70]

It seems that their decision had already been made, since in mid-December doctors, technicians and pilots set up the International Committee for the Fight against Genocide in Biafra.[71] This association sided with the Biafrans in the way it presented the belligerents: "The Biafran people are confronted with an ambiguous and murderous coalition of the British, Soviet, American, and Egyptian governments; they are putting up fierce, unanimous, and desperate resistance against the bombing and extermination of civilians".[72] By simply contrasting victims and aggressors, regardless of their political affiliation, the authors distanced themselves from the third-worldist thinking that was very influential at the time.[73] Bernard Kouchner further published an article along these lines at the end of the conflict. He denounced the idea that there were good and bad victims which explained the lack of mobilisation in support of the Biafrans, who did not fight against imperialism and therefore did not benefit from the support of third-worldist or left-wing movements.[74] The newly formed committee called for a political solution to the conflict as it stated that "there is no 'humanitarian' solution to this political problem",[75] stressed the need to alert public opinion and explicitly drew a comparison with the Jewish genocide. Its founders explained their approach as follows:

> As direct witnesses who have returned from this country in conflict, we cannot remain silent: we have decided to set up a committee to provide information and seek solutions that could help protect these millions of people by restoring peace, irrespective of the means used.[76]

A few weeks later, on 12 February 1969, its members published an open letter in *Le Monde*, signed by some thirty doctors, pilots and journalists, denouncing the genocide in Biafra.[77] The signatories refuted the findings of the international observers, who had stated that there was no genocide. However, the committee's efforts to raise awareness of the Biafran cause remained limited in reach.[78] It organised public meetings but was hardly visible in the media and its message remained vague. Paradoxically, although it advocated a political solution to the conflict, the Foreign Ministry officials who identified the French organisations actively engaged on this matter considered it a group with "essentially or exclusively humanitarian" ambitions.[79] However, in November 1969 it merged with the France–Biafra association, a pro-Biafran body created by French politicians, forming the Movement for Peace in Nigeria–Biafra (Mouvement pour la paix au Nigeria–Biafra). Thus, to a certain extent, it lost its specificity as an organisation established by humanitarians, blending more generally into French expressions of sympathy for Biafra.[80]

It is in these documents, much more than in the article of 27 November, that we find some of the main elements around which the founding myth of Médecins Sans Frontières was built. As Anne Vallaeys points out, the ICRC was not directly criticised with the exception of an anonymous article, probably written by Kouchner, which was published in the Libreville gazette.[81] The doctors themselves maintained an ambiguous relationship with the organisation and continued to occasionally work with it during and after the conflict. One of the MSF founders, Pascal Grellety-Bosviel, worked as a medical co-ordinator of ICRC emergency missions for ten years from 1971.[82]

On the ICRC side, the creation of the Committee for the Fight against Genocide in Biafra by doctors that worked for the international organisation did not seem to lead to any specific dismissals or sanctions. In December 1968 the management's press review briefly mentioned it,[83] but the event apparently did not elicit any particular reaction from within the ICRC. The publication of the open letter denouncing the genocide did not seem to lead to any specific response either, nor did the doctors' other articles or statements which appeared in the French press.[84]

Several hypotheses could explain this relative indifference. The first one is related to the content of the doctors' statements. Apart from the press releases of the International Committee for the Fight against Genocide in Biafra, the other articles, including those published by Récamier and Grellety-Bosviel, were less politically committed and did not directly call for Biafra to be recognised. They were more in line with the article of 27 November.[85] Furthermore, whilst at first the term genocide was vehemently embraced, later there was less agreement on how it should be used. Thus, in May 1969 Max Récamier published an article in the *Droit et liberté* journal in which he wrote:

> They are above all the victims of this war and it is in relation to them that we can speak of genocide. Is it genocide? No, it is not, if by that we mean a coldly decided extermination in the Nazi fashion. Yes, it is, if one considers the sequence of circumstances, the particular conditions of this blockade, and perhaps the difficulty in controlling overzealous or mercenary troops and pilots.[86]

This quote reveals a shift in the stance of the French doctors. The intentional element, which is normally part and parcel of the definition of genocide, is virtually absent here. This shift was probably due to the gradual questioning of the way in which the conflict was presented on the international stage. The Biafran leadership's stubbornness was leading more and more observers to wonder about the role played by each warring party in the continuation of the war and the famine. Thus, Olivier Weber recounts Max Récamier's indignation when he discovered a camp reserved for the press, filled with starving people, where doctors could not enter.[87] This shift also illuminates the way in which the term genocide was used. It did not denounce an intentional policy of extermination but referred to the disappearance of a group, without actually naming those responsible for the situation. Indeed, at the end of the conflict opinions were less clear-cut and French doctors were divided. While some continued to denounce a genocide, others took the opposite view.[88]

Whilst the diversity of the positions taken may be one of the reasons for the ICRC's indifference, other factors seem more decisive in understanding its tolerance. First of all, these instances remained relatively rare and less visible compared to the intense media coverage of the crisis in the summer of 1968. Given the many criticisms levelled at the ICRC,[89] the French doctors' statements were nothing special. Secondly, they occurred at a time – the winter of 1968–69 – when the ICRC had other problems to deal with, such as reorganising its airlifts from Equatorial Guinea. Furthermore, it still had difficulties in finding competent personnel and the French Red Cross teams remained indispensable to its operation in Biafra. It was likely more concerned about its recruitment problems than the creation of the International Committee for the Fight against Genocide in Biafra.

Finally, the volunteers' nationality as well as their link to the French Red Cross, whose pro-Biafran activities were well known, probably led the ICRC to somewhat relax its rules of neutrality in relation to these particular teams. In the organisation's thinking at the time, its neutrality was closely associated with the Swiss nationality of the Committee members and more generally of its personnel.[90] Indeed, the head of the ICRC's delegation in Nigeria was surprised to discover that the Swiss nationality of its employees was not enough to convince the Nigerians of the organisation's neutrality.[91] This very close association between Swiss nationality and neutrality explains why the statements of the French doctors were tolerated, while those of Swiss delegates were frowned upon.[92] Jaggi's statements about a possible food drop inside Biafra at the same time as the publication of the article on 27 November seemed to raise more concerns within the organisation, which decided to remind him "that he should not give a press conference without the ICRC's permission".[93] Again in January 1969, it was the statements made to the media by a Swiss doctor, Dr Pidermann, which were explicitly cited as a problem by the Committee. The issue resurfaced again three weeks later in the context of questions raised about the quality of training provided to delegates before their departure or in Lagos. Thus, a Committee member deplored the fact that not all delegates honoured their commitment to remain silent on their return, although this time his comment was in reference to personnel working in the federal area.[94]

It was not until July 1969 that field volunteers really took a stand against the policy set by the ICRC's headquarters. The delegations in Biafra and Cotonou publicly contradicted the organisation's president who, at a press conference on his return from Lagos, had stated that the situation was not disastrous. This time, the head of the Nigeria–Biafra Office in Geneva, Hans Schaedler, wrote the following message to the delegations:

> In the past few days Geneva has received requests from delegations to resume the relief action. I am perfectly aware of the efforts required to put an end to the current latent situation. ... During the whole time while the action ran, the Geneva headquarters fully supported its delegations, giving them the right of initiative. I expect them now to reciprocate.[95]

During this episode the future founders of Médecins Sans Frontières were not particularly at the forefront of the revolt, although some of its future members were among the sixty or so people taking part in the ICRC's operations in Biafra at this time.[96] Moreover, Karl Jaggi went to Geneva in early August to express the impatience of the teams in Biafra and to insist that the ICRC resume flights, or that stocks be released and delivered by other organisations.[97] The trip made by the head of delegation shows that he was annoyed with the policy adopted by headquarters. These episodes highlight the many dividing lines that existed between the ICRC and the personnel who worked for it, and make it possible to qualify the opposition that developed between the ICRC and the French doctors during the Biafra conflict.

The second aspect of the myth of the French doctors' exit is their refusal to follow instructions on the ground. It appears less frequently in the literature but explains particularly the *sans-frontiérisme* element which relates to the willingness to act irrespective of the view of the authorities and governments. The attitude of the ICRC, described as legalistic, overly attentive to humanitarian law and the will of states, serves as a counterpoint to this narrative.[98] Two episodes from the Biafran conflict are cited – differently by different authors – to demonstrate the French doctors' appetency for this type of attitude.

The first episode, already mentioned, concerns the killing of two ICRC staff by Nigerian soldiers on 30 September 1968 in Okigwe. Following these murders, the organisation allegedly issued a withdrawal order which was ignored by the French doctors. The ICRC archives provide a different version of this episode: the organisation did not decide to withdraw all of its volunteers from Biafra, rather, it initially let teams decide whether or not to remain on the ground given the dangers they faced. Whilst a gradual reduction in personnel did begin in October 1968, this was not solely due to the Okigwe killing. It was also the result of broader reflections on the humanitarian action under way, whose magnitude seemed to overwhelm the ICRC. This translated especially into the non-replacement of teams who had completed their mission at the end of 1968. However, this did not include medical personnel, who were not deemed redundant and whom the ICRC kept on the ground throughout the conflict. Thus, the hospital in Awo-Omamma remained operational until the very end of the war, also because it was part of the support system set up by the French Red Cross in Biafra.

The second episode cited in support of the French doctors' courage in contrast to the ICRC occurred at the end of the war.[99] As previous chapters have shown, the ICRC's position in this final phase of the conflict was more complex than at first sight. Although it could no longer resupply its teams via its airlifts which had ground to a halt, it sought to maintain a presence in Biafra by continuing and even reinforcing its medical activities. In January 1970, during Biafra's final moments, the fate of the European personnel on the ground was a cause for concern. Jean-Pierre Hocké, the ICRC delegate in Lagos, informed the Nigerian Defence Ministry of the composition of the Red Cross teams still in Biafra and was assured that precautions were being taken to avoid any accidents. Nevertheless, the Permanent Defence Secretary, Alhaji Gobir, could not absolutely guarantee this and confirmed that the ICRC representative in Biafra, Jaggi, needed to "leave any area where federal troops might go in the near future".[100] Indeed, Jaggi, who had led the ICRC delegation in Biafra since 1967, was accused by the Nigerian government of bias and of helping to give credence to the Biafran point of view within the ICRC and in the world.[101] In these circumstances, the ICRC evacuated its volunteers on the nights of 10 to 12 January. Eight people stayed behind.[102] They were members of the Awo-Omamma and Santana teams: doctors Max Récamier, Bernard L'Huillier, Louis Schittly, Vladan Radoman, Dominique Benoît, administrators Samuel Andres and Jean-Claude Dantillo, as well as Jean-Pierre Gontard, who liaised between the ICRC and French Red Cross.[103] They were repatriated to France after passing through Lagos, clandestinely in some cases, followed by a quick trial in others.[104] The behaviour of this small group, led by Récamier, was described by the ICRC as "remarkable during these last days of crisis".[105]

The accounts of the events leading up to this decision vary according to the different protagonists. In Kouchner's writings, this episode, in which he was not involved, is barely mentioned.[106] Anne Vallaeys takes up Récamier's version, who recounted staying behind with his comrades to try to look after the sick for as long as possible, and then going to Uli with the Biafran children who were in their care. The situation there was chaotic because of the imminent arrival of Nigerian soldiers and the dignitaries of the secessionist regime who were scrambling to board the last remaining planes. Récamier was thus unable to board the Red Cross aircraft with the children.[107] Drawing on this account, Vallaeys highlights one of the things that are said to have characterised the attitude of the French doctors in Biafra: their heroism. Since the children could not come with them, the doctors refused to abandon them to certain death and decided to stay behind despite the arrival of the federal troops. Olivier Weber places particular emphasis on the courage shown by Max Récamier, who refused to board the Red Cross "helicopter".[108] Louis Schittly's published memoirs also contain plenty of details about this final moment. Schittly provides a vivid description of the opposition between the French doctors and the rest of the ICRC personnel, which serves to reinforce the heroic attitude of the former. He recounts his decision not to abandon the children in their care and to collect them from Santana and bring them to Uli so that they could board the Red Cross planes. Faced with the pilot's refusal to take them on board and the panic caused by the arrival of Biafran high dignitaries who rushed to get onto the last planes leaving Biafra, he chose to stay behind with the children.

This type of narrative, which highlights the heroism of the French doctors, takes many forms, from refusing to abandon children at the airport to refusing to abandon a patient in the operating room. Thus, Schittly relates the experience of another doctor, Bernard L'Huillier, at the time of Biafra's fall:

> He came on board, still laughing, and told me his story: when Max [Récamier] came back from the ICRC Headquarters to gather his team, L'Huillier was in the operating room. "Bernard, we're getting out of here. Hurry up!" somebody cried out. And everyone left, he explained, except the Biafran nurse anaesthetist, himself, and of course the patient on the operating table. "A surgeon does not leave a belly open!" So he kept working silently. His nurse said to him: "Doctor Bernard, if you stay, I stay". They both stayed there, closed up the wounded patient, waited for him to wake up, and then carried him on a trolley to the ward with the other wounded, where he had some friends.[109]

This episode was related differently by Olivier Weber, according to whom Max Récamier and Vladan Radoman came to fetch L'Huillier, who was impassive in the operating room. He made his two colleagues wait while he stitched up his patient. He then left with them after exclaiming: "Had to stitch up my guy!"[110] These anecdotes, whose versions vary, always underline the courage of one of the doctors who was not afraid to put his life in danger to save his patient(s). This emphasis on risk-taking remained a fundamental characteristic of MSF founders, but also of emergency workers in the 1990s.[111]

In these accounts the heroism of the French doctors stands out in contrast to the attitude of other humanitarians, particularly those working for the ICRC. Bernard Kouchner, Olivier Weber or Louis Schittly all emphasise the difference with the Red Cross personnel, who are presented as having a civil-servant mentality and being insensitive to the suffering of the Biafran population. Bernard Kouchner writes, for example: "When we opened up about our fatigue to local ICRC officials we were told, 'there's nothing more we can do, you have to turn away the wounded!' As if a doctor could turn away wounded patients!"[112] He calls Red Cross delegates "Red Cross minions", "in a hurry to get out of dangerous places". Olivier Weber also sheds light on the differences between the ICRC and future members of MSF: "The two men stare at each other. One is a former revolutionary from a small Central American country; the other was a Peugeot and Mercedes dealer in Nigeria, who had converted to charity work".[113] The description of the confrontation between the French and Swedish teams works in a similar way:

> Pascal Grellety-Bosviel had to endure the rigidity of the Red Cross. Overzealous civil servants adhered to strict working hours, deferred to Geneva's decisions, and refused to improvise when faced with an emergency. ... That day he had to collect medicines from a Red Cross warehouse run by a Swede, General Brucellius. After an hour's drive in a Jeep, accompanied by Minor Hernandez, he could finally see the building ... It was noon. He knocked. A sleepy Scandinavian half-opened the door: "It's closed, it's siesta time". "It's urgent, it's for the hospital in Awo Omamma!" explained the two doctors. "I'm telling you it's closed. Come back in two hours". And the Scandinavian shut the door.[114]

The story continues with Grellety and Hernandez taking everything they could get from the warehouse "as the Swedish general looked on in amazement". In his memoirs published in 2011, Louis Schittly offers his own account of the opposition between the French doctors and the "ICRC":

> I'm going around in circles. The unease about our flight tortures me. And these ICRC "permanent staff" – former blue helmets according to rumours – with their mountains of luggage, ugly faces, and whisky bottles that go around, disgust me deeply. I have nothing to do with this kind of bastards, overdressed, overpaid, lily-livered charity functionaries.[115]

Dazed and drunk, lost because of their poor knowledge of the roads, more concerned about their luggage and personal belongings than the children, "the Swiss and the Swedes" described by Schittly, like those portrayed by Weber and Kouchner, were the ideal counterpoint for highlighting the values of courage, altruism, selfless commitment to the victims, sacrifice, as well as the ability to adapt and respond, which were claimed especially by some French doctors.

The incompatibility of values and behaviour between the French doctors and ICRC allows the creation of Médecins Sans Frontières to be retrospectively rooted in the Biafran experience. Moreover, it offers the possibility of establishing a continuity between the identity gradually acquired by MSF and the values claimed by its founders: as Anne Vallaeys has shown, the organisation which came into being in December 1971 did not initially advocate humanitarian intervention or speaking out, let alone political involvement. Its statutes stipulated that

> the members of the association are prohibited from making statements, written or oral communications in reference to the association or relating to the interventions it carries out, has carried out, or will carry out, unless specifically

> authorised to do so by the collegial management committee. Any infringement of this prohibition will be sanctioned with immediate exclusion.[116]

Thus, the organisation was not solely the result of the doctors' break with ICRC principles, and it is necessary to look back at the two years between the end of the conflict and its creation to understand its genesis.

On their return from Biafra the doctors founded the GIMCU – Groupe d'intervention médicale et chirurgicale d'urgence (Emergency Medical and Surgical Intervention Group) – which brought together most of those who had been to Biafra[117] and who were joined by Jacques Bérès, whose assignment in Biafra had been cancelled, and Xavier Emmanuelli, who had studied with Kouchner. The GIMCU served as an emergency unit of the French Red Cross. As part of this, the doctors carried out a mission following the earthquake in Peru in the summer of 1970, and then in Jordan during the events of Black September.[118] However, they were not happy with this way of working as they were dependent on the goodwill of the French Red Cross who, for example, did not let them go to East Pakistan in 1971. In November 1971 they came across an appeal launched by the journalists Philippe Bernier and Raymond Borel in *Tonus*, a weekly magazine mainly read by general practitioners. The two wanted to bring together medical personnel ready to carry out some missions "where needed", on a voluntary basis. Over one hundred volunteers answered the journalists' call, including the GIMCU doctors. This led to the founding of MSF on 22 December 1971 and explains why, of the twelve people present at the initial meeting on 22 December 1971, only four doctors had been to Biafra. They were Pascal Grellety-Bosviel, Bernard Kouchner, Max Récamier and Vladan Radoman. However, they were quickly joined by the other GIMCU members.

Two months after it was set up the association had fifty-four members. During its first year of existence MSF served mainly as a pool of qualified personnel for the Red Cross and NGOs who needed doctors for the programmes they developed in the Third World. The December 1972 earthquake in Nicaragua, a year after the organisation was founded, provided it with the opportunity to conduct a mission under its own name. This experience led to many criticisms, particularly from the French Red Cross, which did not agree with its former doctors becoming independent, and from the army's emergency response teams, which did not appreciate the presence of MSF volunteers. Furthermore, the various influences that presided over its birth were reflected in the fact that the organisation was struggling to find its identity. In the early 1970s it still hesitated between emergency medicine and developing access to health care in the Third World, although the GIMCU's ideas gradually prevailed.[119] Johanna Siméant has thus shown how by examining the common points in the biographies of the MSF founders – in the broader sense of term – whether it be their relationship to violence, politics or medicine, we can better understand the types of interventions they subsequently promoted within the organisation:

> Thinking up emergency humanitarian work (i.e. short missions) which allowed one to play the role of an enlightened amateur engaging in adventurous activities in the service of an ideal, and to take a public stand in the name of this engagement (not all professions provide resources as important as medicine to allow them to make moral judgements), clearly suited the founders' social attributes.[120]

As for the Biafran episode, although it undeniably had a socialising effect on the doctors involved, this was not so much because of their declared opposition to ICRC principles as the fact that they had shared a particularly trying experience due to the violence they had faced and the emotions aroused by the suffering and courage of the Biafran population. By placing the stances taken by the French doctors in the broader context of the relief operations taking place in Biafra, it is possible to show that they were not the only ones to raise the issue of bearing witness and making public denunciations, and to highlight the erratic way in which the ICRC operated in this respect. Paradoxically, while most French doctors went relatively easy on the Geneva-based organisation in their public statements during the conflict, others did not hesitate to point out the inadequacy of the ICRC's response to the crisis. The body was not criticised by the MSF founders but especially by its direct partners, such as the National Red Cross Societies, or by its competitors, the religious charities, and by journalists. The widespread criticism it received led it to rethink its way of working and made Biafra a pivotal moment in its history.

Notes

1 On the MSF France website, X. Emmanuelli is added to this list from coming from the French *Journal officiel*; www.msf.fr/decouvrir-msf/notre-histoire, accessed 9 June 2025. On MSF, see also P. Redfield, *Life in Crisis: The Ethical Journey of Doctors Without Borders* (Berkeley: California University Press, 2013); R. C. Fox, "Medical Humanitarianism and Human Rights: Reflections on Doctors Without Borders and Doctors of the World", *Social Science and Medicine*, 41:12 (1995), 1607–26.
2 Kouchner, *Charité business*, p. 217.
3 Kouchner, *Le malheur des autres*, p. 113.
4 Brauman, "Les liaisons dangereuses du témoignage humanitaire et des propagandes politiques", pp. 188–204; R. Brauman, "MSF et le CICR: questions de principes", *Revue internationale de la Croix-Rouge*, 94:2, sélection française (2012), 345–57.
5 Vallaeys, *Médecins sans frontières*, p. 108.

6 Maillard, "1968–2008: le Biafra ou le sens de l'humanitaire"; P. Aeberhard, "A Historical Survey of Humanitarian Action", *Health and Human Rights*, 2:1 (1996), 30–44.

7 Le Pape, Siméant & Vidal, *Crises extrêmes*, pp. 11–18. For other cases, C. Bob, *The Marketing of Rebellion: Insurgents, Media, and International Activism* (Cambridge: Cambridge University Press, 2006).

8 D. O. Pendas, "Toward World Law? Human Rights and the Failure of the Legalist Paradigm of War", in S.-L. Hoffmann (ed.), *Human Rights in the Twentieth Century* (Cambridge: Cambridge University Press, 2011), pp. 215–36, at p. 228.

9 Smith, *Genocide and the Europeans*, pp. 1–29; S. Power, *"A Problem from Hell": America and the Age of Genocide* (London: Flamingo, 2003).

10 Prior to Biafra, it was used, for example, by some activist groups or political opponents to describe the situations in Tibet, the Dominican Republic and Vietnam. See, for instance, articles in the newspaper *Le Monde* during the 1960s.

11 D. Moses, "War Crimes/Genocide Trials for Pakistani Soldiers", in Hoffmann (ed.), *Human Rights in the Twentieth Century*, pp. 258–79.

12 AICRC, B AG 200 147-002.02, report by P. Reynard, 26 September 1967.

13 AICRC, B AG 200 147-002.02, telex from P. Reynard to G. Hoffman, 16 October 1967.

14 AICRC, B AG 200 147-003.01, letter from K. H. Jaggi to the ICRC's President, 31 January 1968.

15 AICRC, Directorate briefing notes, 8 September 1967, 9 February 1968.

16 AICRC, Presidential Council meeting, 15 November 1967; AICRC, B AG 202 147-001, minutes of phone calls between T. Mathez, V. Martin (Bern) and Dr Sicault (UNICEF Paris), 14 and 15 November 1967.

17 For an idea of the ICRC's attitude towards massacres during the twentieth century, see I. Herrmann & D. Palmieri, "Humanitaires et massacres, l'exemple du CICR, 1904–1994", in J. Sémelin, C. Andrieu & S. Gensburger (eds), *La résistance aux génocides, De la pluralité des actes de sauvetage* (Paris: Presses de Sciences Po, 2008), pp. 235–45.

18 Bugnion, *Le CICR et la protection des victimes de la guerre*, pp. 1077–109.

19 L. Boissier, "Les silences du Comité international de la Croix-Rouge", *Journal de Genève*, 19 January 1968.

20 AICRC, plenary session of the Committee, 5 October 1967.

21 AICRC, Presidential Council meeting, 19 October 1967.

22 ATS, "Respectez les règles humanitaires", *Journal de Genève*, 24 October 1967, p. 5.

23 AICRC, B AG, 202 147-008.01, M. Borsinger, note to the file, 15 May 1968.

24 Wiseberg, "The International Politics of Relief", p. 175.

25 AICRC, B AG 200 147-001, message from G. Palthey to T. Mathez, 24 February 1967.

26 AICRC, B AG 200 147-002.02, telex from the CICR to G. Hoffmann, 29 November 1967; B AG 202 147-001, conversation between T. Mathez and the Swiss Ambassador in Lagos, 15 November 1967.

27 AICRC, B AG 202 147-001, conversation between Mme Mathez and V. Martin, 14 November 1967.
28 AICRC, B AG 202 147-008.01, letter from K. H. Jaggi, 27 April 1968.
29 AICRC, plenary session of the Committee, 6 March 1968.
30 AICRC, plenary session of the Committee, 5 June 1968.
31 AICRC, B AG 202 147-001, note by P. Gaillard, "Conflit Nigeria/Biafra", 6 June 1968.
32 AUN, S-0303-0005-04, cable from the Secretary General to N.-G. Gussing, 29 August 1968.
33 AICRC, B AG 280 147-002, Directorate meeting, 23 August 1968.
34 See D. Fassin's analysis in terms of an "unequal humanity": "To some the freedom to sacrifice themselves for a just cause. To others, the condition of being sacrificeable in a dirty war"; Fassin, *La raison humantaire*, pp. 291–7.
35 AICRC, B AG 202 147-001, from R. J. Wilhelm to J. de Heller, 13 September 1968.
36 Kouchner, *Charité business*, pp. 215–16.
37 AICRC B AG 202 147-001, telex from A. Lindt to the Comité, 24 September 1968.
38 AFP, "Les équipes du CICR ne reculeront plus devant les Nigérians", *Journal de Genève*, 30 September 1968.
39 AICRC, B AG 202 147-006, press release, 4 October 1968.
40 AICRC, B AG 202 147-006, telex from A. Lindt to the CICR, 24 October 1968.
41 The contract of engagement signed by volunteers carrying out a mission for the FRC and under the supervision of the ICRC stipulates that they undertake "to exercise the utmost discretion and, in particular, not to publish anything about the work of the Red Cross in Biafra without the agreement of the French Red Cross and the ICRC"; AICRC 2000.038.0003, "Contrat d'engagement, personnel bénévole".
42 AFP, "Nigeria–Biafra: après le meurtre de quatre Européens, colère chez les délégués des organismes de secours", *Journal de Genève*, 7 October 1968, p. 24.
43 AICRC, B AG 202 147-008.06, telex from A. Lindt to R. Galopin, 19 October 1968.
44 AICRC, B AG 202 147-006, telex from A. Lindt to the CICR, 24 October 1968, and reply from the ICRC's headquarters, same day.
45 AICRC, B AG 202 147-008.06, file "bombardement de l'hôpital d'Abo".
46 AFRC, INT 23 Biafra, 04/16, lists of medical staff sent to Biafra.
47 Kouchner, *Charité business*, pp. 215–16.
48 FNA, 5 AG FPU/689, telegram from the French Embassy in Libreville to the MAE, 10 December 1968.
49 AFP, "Biafra, un hôpital de la Croix-Rouge bombardé", *Journal de Genève*, 11 December 1968.
50 AICRC, B AG 202 147-008.08, ICRC press release, 12 December 1968.
51 AICRC, B AG 202 147-008.08.
52 AICRC, B AG 202 147-008.01, note from A. Lindt to R. Gallopin, 20 December 1968.

53 AICRC, B AG 202 147-008.08, note from R. J. Wilhelm to J. de Heller, 27 December 1968.
54 AICRC, B AG 202 147-008.01, telex from K. H. Jaggi, 26 February 1969, and reply from the headquarters, 2 March 1969.
55 AICRC, B AG 202 147-008.02, reply from the FMG (11 March 1969) to ICRC's telegram (4 March 1969).
56 AICRC, B AG 202 147-008.01, correspondence between R. Jenni and the ICRC's headquarters, March 1969.
57 AICRC, plenary session of the Committee, 4 and 5 March 1969.
58 The term "delegate" is somewhat ambiguous, as the ICRC does not always consider the staff of Societies made available to it by national Red Cross or other organizations to be true delegates; see B. Troyon & D. Palmieri, "Délégué du CICR: un acteur exemplaire?", *Revue internationale de la Croix-Rouge*, 89 (2007), 67–88.
59 AICRC, plenary session of the Committee, 30 April and 1 May 1969, "compte rendu de l'étude du groupe des juristes sur la question des protestations".
60 Bugnion, *Le CICR et la protection des victimes de la guerre*, pp. 1106–7.
61 AICRC, B AG 200 147-003.02, note from Martin, Lagos, to the CICR, "Concerne mission des observateurs internationaux", 15 October 1969.
62 AICRC, B AG 200 147-003.02, note from Martin, Lagos, to the CICR, "Concerne mission des observateurs internationaux", 15 October 1969.
63 Fassin, *La raison humanitaire*, p. 266.
64 B. Kouchner & M. Récamier, "De retour du Biafra, deux médecins français témoignent", *Le Monde*, 27 November 1968.
65 AICRC, plenary session of the Committee, 23 October 1968, report by K. H. Jaggi.
66 AICRC, B AG 280 147-002, Directorate meeting, 1 October 1968.
67 AICRC, Audiovisual archives, VS 14606-M-A-04, interview of B. Kouchner.
68 P. Grellety-Bosviel & S. Boquillon, *Tout une vie d'humanitaire, 50 ans de terrain d'un médecin-carnettiste* (Bordeaux: Elytis, 2013), p. 86.
69 AICRC, plenary session of the Committee, 9 January 1969, report by G. Schürch.
70 AICRC, B AG 202 147-008.08, note by M. Veuthey, 27 December 1968.
71 "Création à Paris d'un Comité de lutte contre le génocide au Biafra", *Le Monde*, 14 December 1968.
72 AFRC, INT 23, Biafra 14/16, "Appel du Comité international de lutte contre le Génocide au Biafra".
73 Davey, *Idealism Beyond Borders*.
74 "Un médecin accuse", *Nouvel Observateur*, 19 January 1970.
75 AFRC, INT 23, Biafra 14/16, document produced by the Comité international de lutte contre le génocide au Biafra.
76 AFRC, INT 23, Biafra 14/16, "Appel du Comité international de lutte contre le génocide au Biafra".
77 "Une trentaine de médecins, pilotes et journalistes dénoncent 'le génocide au Biafra'", *Le Monde*, 12 February 1969.

78 Kouchner, *Le malheur des autres*, p. 115.
79 AMAE Nantes, French Embassy in London, Box 1456, note by Pierret, 10 March 1969.
80 "M. Buron annonce la création d'un nouveau Mouvement pour la paix au Nigeria", *Le Monde*, 14 November 1969.
81 Vallaeys, *Médecins sans frontières*, p. 76.
82 Grellety & Boquillon, *Tout une vie d'humanitaire*, p. 89.
83 AICRC, Directorate briefing note, 17 December 1968, press review 14–16 December 1968.
84 P. Decraene, "Tumulte à la Mutualité ou solitude du Biafra", *Le Monde*, 14 March 1969; P. Grellety-Bosviel, "Bloc-notes d'un médecin au Biafra", *La Croix*, 14 March 1969; M. Récamier, "Le cessez-le-feu viendra-t-il trop tard?", *Le Figaro*, 15 March 1969; M. Récamier, "Le Biafra sous les bombes", *Droit et Liberté*, May 1969. Most of these articles were part of the week of support for Biafra orchestrated by the French government.
85 AFRC, INT 23 Biafra 14/16.
86 Récamier, "Le Biafra sous les bombes".
87 Weber, *French Doctors*, pp. 37–8.
88 Lavoinne, "Médecins en guerre", p. 124.
89 See also J. de Saint Jorre in *The Observer*, 7 September 1969.
90 J. Freymond, *Guerres, Révolutions, Croix-Rouge* (Geneva: Institut universitaire de hautes études internationales, 1976), pp. 3–35.
91 AICRC, plenary session of the Committee, 9 January 1969, report by G. Schürch.
92 Troyon, Palmieri, "Délégué du CICR".
93 AICRC, B AG 280 147-002, Directorate meeting, 3 December 1968.
94 AICRC, plenary sessions of the Committee, 14 January 1969 and 6 February 1969.
95 AICRC, Directorate briefing note, 21 July 1969.
96 J.-F. Casteres, P. Sargos, B. L'Huillier and L. Bravo-Salvador.
97 AICRC, Directorate briefing note, 4 August 1969.
98 For example, C. Zorgbibe, *Le droit d'ingérence* (Paris: Presses universitaires de France, 1994), p. 92.
99 Weber, *French Doctors*, pp. 60–6; Vallaeys, *Médecins sans frontières*, p. 88; C. Zorgbibe, *Le droit d'ingérence*, p. 92.
100 AICRC, B AG 200 147-003.02, note by J.-P. Hocké for the Nigeria–Biafra office, 9 January 1970.
101 The ICRC is accused on several occasions of being intoxicated by Ojukwu through K. H. Jaggi. This was the case, for example, after the appeal made from Kampala, but also during the series of bombings in the winter of 1968–69.
102 AICRC, plenary session of the Committee, 15 January 1970.
103 "Les médecins et administrateurs européens restés à leur poste sont en bonne santé", *Le Monde*, 16 January 1970.
104 Schittly, *L'homme qui voulait voir la guerre de près*, pp. 153–7.
105 AICRC, plenary session of the Committee, 5 February 1970.
106 Kouchner only briefly refers to it in his book *Le malheur des autres*, p. 116.

107 Vallaeys, *Médecins sans frontières*, pp. 88–9.
108 Weber, *French Doctors*, pp. 62–3.
109 Schittly, *L'homme qui voulait voir la guerre de près*, p. 113.
110 Weber, *French Doctors*, p. 62.
111 Siméant, "Entrer, rester, en humanitaire", p. 56.
112 Kouchner, *Charité business*, p. 216.
113 Weber, *French Doctors*, p. 32.
114 Weber, *French Doctors*, p. 43.
115 Schittly, *L'homme qui voulait voir la guerre de près*, p. 110.
116 Vallaeys, *Médecins sans frontières*, pp. 124–5.
117 B. Kouchner, M. Récamier, V. Radoman, M. Hernandez, A-M. Barbé, A. Marty-Lavauzelle, P. Aeberhard, L. Bravo-Salvador, D. Benoît, L. Schittly, B. L'Huillier, D. Tarantola, P. Sargos, P. Fyot and P. Grellety-Bosviel.
118 Vallaeys, *Médecins sans frontières*, pp. 102–3.
119 Vallaeys, *Médecins sans frontières*, pp. 127–55.
120 Siméant, "Entrer, rester en humanitaire", p. 55.

9

Biafra and the birth of the "modern ICRC"?

In the late 1960s the increase in the number of non-governmental organisations engaging not only in fundraising but also in field operations, the importance given by the media to humanitarian crises, and the postcolonial context in which relief operations were taking place raised questions about the practices of emergency-aid actors, particularly the ICRC.[1] Thus, for this leading humanitarian-aid organisation in situations of armed conflict, the Nigeria–Biafra war represented a very important moment.[2] As one former ICRC delegate pointed out, it may even be considered a real turning point:

> the modern ICRC was born in Africa, in the late 1960s, among the smouldering ruins of Biafra. It was there that the new ICRC came into being in a new humanitarian era when a huge operation to rescue hundreds of thousands of victims of the Nigerian civil war was set up.[3]

This particular emphasis on the conflict was due to the nature of the intervention scenario which was relatively new to the ICRC, but also because in the long run it shook up an organisation which, as David Forsythe writes, was generally reluctant to change and only did so when it foresaw negative consequences if it did nothing.[4] Indeed, a book on the ICRC covering the period from 1945 to 1980 notes important developments after the Biafra conflict. The authors point out that it represented a key moment in the ICRC's assistance policy.[5] The latter was subsequently directed more and more towards non-European areas, in particular Africa and South America, growing in scope and scale to a level it would then maintain. Furthermore, there was a significant increase in the ICRC's budget and personnel beginning with this period.[6] Its institutional structure was also transformed between 1970 and 1974 when the results of the Nigeria–Biafra operation were assessed.[7]

In order to understand the specific role played by this conflict, this chapter demonstrates that the operation underscored the ICRC's weaknesses and led to a process of change. These weaknesses were particularly noticeable in three areas. First of all, questions were raised about the way in which the organisation itself worked and its ability to handle a large-scale operation. Secondly, its relations with other actors – whether governments, various humanitarian organisations or the media – were criticised. Finally, the difficulties encountered by the ICRC in recruiting and training competent personnel pointed to a new challenge it had to face: becoming a more effective actor in the field. This set of problems required the Geneva-based organisation to demonstrate flexibility and initiative in order to be able to carry out an operation whose complexity has been shown in the previous chapters. The aim therefore is to understand how a series of emergency measures, which may or may not have worked, were part of a wider reform process that profoundly shaped the ICRC in the years that followed. More generally, an analysis of this process of change illuminates the way in which actions on the ground led to changes in the internal structure of the humanitarian organisations themselves. It also provides an insight into how the ICRC actually worked.

The ICRC on the eve of the Nigeria–Biafra operation

In the mid-1960s the ICRC had not yet fully recovered from the difficulties it had experienced after the Second World War, when a decrease in its activities led to a drastic reduction in its budget and personnel. Its failure to act on behalf of the victims of the genocide perpetrated by the Third Reich and of the Soviet prisoners on the Eastern Front earned it much criticism, and the organisation had to fight for its survival.[8] The ICRC managed to gradually re-establish its position within the Movement and on the international stage, particularly with the adoption of the four Geneva Conventions in 1949. Nevertheless, in the mid-1960s its situation remained precarious. Whereas 315 people worked at the Geneva headquarters in 1949, by 1967 the number had dropped to 146.[9] Between 1955 and 1965 the ICRC carried out important actions but on the whole these required relatively few resources. Consequently, during the conflicts in which its intervention was required, the ICRC concentrated mainly on its traditional tasks, namely its activities for the benefit of detainees – whether prisoners of war or civilian internees – and supporting National Red Cross Societies in times of unrest. Whilst it did take part in important operations helping civilians,[10] this type of activity, which required considerable resources, remained secondary and, more often than not, it sought to avoid it.[11] François Bugnion and Françoise Perret sum up the ICRC's situation as follows:

> since it lacked the means to conduct its policy, the ICRC was reduced to conducting a policy based on its means. In the absence of adequate resources, too

> often it had to cut back on its programmes, even discontinue an action, while the victims' needs remained unmet.[12]

In the late 1960s this lack of resources was exacerbated by an increase in the number of ICRC's fields of action. Besides the Nigeria–Biafra operation, the organisation's resources were also occupied by Vietnam, the Arab-Israeli and Yemeni conflicts, as well as the situation of Greek political prisoners. This period was therefore characterised by an increase in activities and a diversification of geographical areas of intervention.[13] The Geneva-based organisation was not only working in Europe, the Middle East and Asia, but also in sub-Saharan Africa, a region which the ICRC had long approached with colonial lenses and had little direct experience of.[14]

The increase in the number of potential fields of action and the difficulties encountered by the ICRC underscored the inadequate way in which it worked:

> As noted by Mr Freymond, the ICRC's current weakness not only in Africa but elsewhere, including in South-East Asia, often stems from the fact that the competent authorities make it impossible for it to act (by refusing to apply the conventions), but also, and to an equal extent, from its slowness to act or react. All this means that the institution's working methods need to be revisited and revised.[15]

This comment is particularly interesting insofar as the argument of a lack of a legal basis was frequently used by the ICRC to explain its failures. It opened the way for a debate on the way the organisation worked, something which had already been on the agenda for several years but was catalysed by the late 1960s. Initially, this examination centred on the decision-making and executive bodies. The composition, role and delimitation of the remit of the Committee (now the Assembly), Presidential Council and Directorate were the main focus. In 1967 the Committee was made up of seventeen members co-opted from among Swiss nationals who mostly came from the liberal professions, higher education, banking, senior administration or the diplomatic service. Generally speaking, and especially during the years the conflict unfolded, legal experts were particularly well represented (see Table 9.1).

Committee members met in plenary session once a month, when they decided on the ICRC's general policy, budget and overall direction. The importance of this body, which was often criticised for its being essentially Swiss, was the ICRC's distinguishing feature.[16] In order to ensure that ongoing matters were followed up on, a reduced version of the Committee, the Presidential Council, met every fortnight between plenary sessions. It consisted of the president, two vice-presidents (elected by all the members) and a few other ICRC members. Finally, the Directorate, made up of two

Table 9.1 Composition of the ICRC's Committee during the conflict, 1967–70

Name (place and date of birth)	Education and profession	Committee member	Other ICRC roles
Jacques Chenevière (Paris, 1886)	Arts degree Novelist	1919–69	Worked with the ICRC from 1914; served on all ICRC governing bodies
Martin Bodmer (Zurich, 1899)	Philosophy studies Person of private means, collector and philanthropist	1940–71	In charge of intellectual relief during the Second World War; Vice-President several times between 1947 and 1964
Léopold Boissier (Geneva, 1893)	Doctor of Law Diplomat, Secretary General of the Inter-Parliamentary Union, then professor of law	1946–68	ICRC President 1955–64; Vice-President 1950–53, and then in 1955; led the ICRC's legal commission, as well as a group working on ICRC principles
Paul Ruegger (Lucerne, 1897)	Doctor of Law Diplomat, member of the Permanent Court of Arbitration	1948–72	Worked with the ICRC in 1943 (dealing with delegations); ICRC President 1948–55
Rodolfo Olgiati (Lugano, 1905)	Mathematics degree Worked for aid and support organisations (e.g., former director of Le Don Suisse)	1949–70	Member of the Relief and Social Affairs Commission
Frédéric Siordet (Geneva, 1900)	Law degree Diplomat and lawyer	1951–69	ICRC advisor 1943–51; President of the Delegations Committee 1944–46; Vice-President several times between 1953 and 1968

(continued)

Table 9.1 (Cont.)

Name (place and date of birth)	Education and profession	Committee member	Other ICRC roles
Marguerite Gautier-Van Berchem (1892)	École du Louvre et des Hautes Études Archaeologist	1951–69	Head of the German Service of the International Prisoners of War Agency 1914–18, and Head of the Colonial Service of the Central Prisoners of War Agency during the Second World War
Guillaume Bordier (Geneva, 1901)	Engineering degree, Master of Business Administration Banker	1955–72	Vice-President 1966–67
Adolphe Franceschetti (Zurich, 1896)	Doctor of medicine Medical doctor and professor	1958–68	Member of the Joint Relief Commission of the International RC 1943–46
Hans Bachmann (Winterthour, 1912)	Doctor of Law Lawyer	1958–75	ICRC Secretary 1942–45; member of the Joint Relief Commission of the International RC; Vice-President 1964–65 and 1968–70
Jacques Freymond (Lausanne, 1911)	Doctor of Letters Professor and historian Director of the Institut Universitaire de Hautes Études Internationales (Graduate Institute of International Studies)	1959–72	Vice-President 1965–66, then 1969–70, and interim president January–June 1969

Dietrich Schindler (Zurich, 1924)	Doctor of Law Legal expert and professor	1961–73 and 1980–94	Served on the Legal Commission and the Commission for the Study of the Doctrine, Activities, Methods, and Organisation of the ICRC
Hans Meuli (Nufenen, 1897)	Doctor of medicine Medical doctor and soldier	1961–70	
Marjorie Duvillard (1911)	Diploma in nursing Nurse, Head of "Le Bon Secours" nursing school	1961–75	President of the Commission for the Florence Nightingale Medal and of the Medico-Social Commission
Max Petitpierre (Neuchâtel, 1899)	Doctor of Law Lawyer, notary, professor and politician (former President of the Confederation)	1961–76	
Samuel Gonard (Neuenburg, 1896)	Law degree, graduate of the École Supérieure de Guerre de Paris Soldier and professor	1961–69	President 1964–68
Adolphe Graedel (Sonvilier, 1902)	Trained as a sheath maker Sheath maker, trade unionist, and politician	1965–74	
Denise Bindschedler-Robert (Saint-Imier, 1920)	Doctor of Law Legal expert and professor	1967–90	

(*continued*)

Table 9.1 (Cont.)

Name (place and date of birth)	Education and profession	Committee member	Other ICRC roles
Jacques de Rougemont (1918)	Doctor of medicine Medical doctor	1967–86	Carried out various ICRC missions after the Second World War (Poland, Greece)
Marcel Naville (Genthod, 1919)	Arts degree Banker	1967–83	Part of the ICRC's legal division after the Second World War; President 1969–73
Waldemar Jucker (Canton, China, 1924)	Doctor of Law, economics degree Trade unionist (Secretary of the Swiss Trade Union)	1967–76	
Roger Gallopin (Geneva, 1909)	Doctor of Law ICRC official	1967–79	Joined the ICRC in 1936; member of the Secretariat 1942–46, then of the Directorate from 1946; Executive Director and Director General of the ICRC from 1950, resigned late 1969; President of the Executive Council 1973–76
Jean Pictet (Geneva, 1914)	Doctor of Law ICRC official and legal expert	1967–84	Joined the ICRC in 1937, member of the Secretariat 1939–46, then of the Directorate from 1946; ICRC Director General 1966–69, and Vice-President 1971–79

directors general (Roger Gallopin and Jean Pictet)[17] and a director (Claude Pilloud), handled the ICRC's day-to-day activities and administration.

A critical assessment of the way in which these bodies operated in late 1967 highlighted a number of factors that could to a certain extent explain the ICRC's lack of initiative in developing its actions.[18] On the whole, Committee members were not sufficiently invested in their role. Their assiduity and knowledge of the cases at times seemed inadequate, despite briefing notes that were specially prepared for them. In order to improve its dynamism, it also appeared necessary to diversify and rejuvenate the Committee, whose average age was around 65 before the co-option of four new members in late 1967 and the granting of membership to the organisation's two directors general.[19] Furthermore, the distinction between the Presidential Council and the Committee was unclear and the subject of debate. The plenary sessions dwelt too much on the details of the implementation of the ICRC's policy, which was mainly the responsibility of the Presidential Council or the Directorate. Finally, it also appeared necessary to reinforce the Directorate by appointing one or more assistants.[20]

Whilst these deficiencies were not particularly related to the action in Nigeria–Biafra, they did have repercussions for it. Indeed, the ICRC was slow to really take charge of the operation and Thierry Hentsch interpreted the first difficulties he came up against in the negotiations with the belligerents as the consequence of a certain casualness. The situation in Nigeria–Biafra was not initially of particular interest to the Committee. Poorly informed, it relied mainly on information from Swiss diplomats in Lagos, where there was a widespread belief that the federal army would quickly defeat the secessionists.[21] In Geneva the conflict was not given the attention it deserved, leading the ICRC to make blunders in its interactions with the Nigerian and Biafran authorities. Moreover, it failed to give its representations to the belligerents the full weight they needed, for example by sending one of the Committee's members on the ground in the very first months of the conflict.[22]

The Swiss Confederation and the International Red Cross Movement: short-term solutions

In order to be able to handle an operation of this scale, the largest it had had to carry out since the end of the Second World War,[23] the ICRC was quickly forced to call on considerable external support in terms of recruiting personnel, raising funds and managing the operation. To this end, it turned to both the Swiss Confederation and the other members of the Red Cross Movement. During the first year of the Nigeria–Biafra conflict most of the

ICRC's activities consisted of sending medical personnel and equipment to the war-torn areas. It was therefore in this area that its recruitment difficulties were initially most felt. The ICRC first asked the Swiss Red Cross to provide teams with financial support from the Swiss government,[24] but results were relatively inconclusive. Finding new recruits was difficult. Two doctors, Guido Pidermann and Edwin Spirgi, who had already worked for the organisation on several occasions, finally got the first two medical teams set up in Nigeria and Biafra. Soon, Swiss personnel were no longer enough and the ICRC was obliged to internationalise its operation by asking various National Societies to provide medical teams, which to some extent was reminiscent of its interventions in Congo and Yemen.[25] It also accepted support from other organisations, including religious ones such as the World Council of Churches. However, these collaborations were still not enough. On the one hand, some National Societies were sometimes slow in making them happen, and on the other hand, they were hampered by the ICRC's difficulties in getting volunteers on the ground.[26] Thus, between January and July 1968 it was unable to set up a medical team in Biafra, while in Nigeria the teams were understaffed.[27] Media coverage of the crisis in the summer of 1968 finally brought solutions as volunteers responded to its appeals, and by October 1968 more than 400 expatriates of various nationalities were involved in its field operations (53 in Santa Isabel, 140 in Biafra and 229 in Nigeria).

This international opening in terms of medical and technical personnel contrasted with the organisation's recruitment policy for the key positions of the operation, which was primarily Swiss. Nevertheless, it experienced similar mobilisation problems. After the Second World War its resources were drastically reduced and it was forced to lay off most of its headquarters personnel and field delegates. In 1965, in order to carry out its actions abroad, it relied mainly on a small team of a dozen or so delegates who moved from one operation to another.[28] Faced with this reduction in personnel, an International Mission Group (IMG) set up in Bern in 1963 was supposed to enable the ICRC to enlist members of the academic community, army, civil service and industry, who would be on call for missions lasting two months.[29] However, this solution was rarely used, probably because IMG volunteers were only available for very short periods of time. The increase in the organisation's activities in the late 1960s led it to look for other recruitment strategies, but still within the Swiss Confederation.

The lack of Swiss personnel willing to spend time in the field was evident from the start of the conflict, particularly in Biafra, where the ICRC struggled to even send a delegate. A few people were considered but encountered obstacles in the breakaway region, which was difficult to get into and where they were met with suspicion, since in the summer of 1967 humanitarian issues were not the Biafran authorities' main concern. Moreover, some delegates did not seem particularly enthusiastic about going there, while others still harboured many prejudices about the African continent and even questioned the usefulness of the ICRC's involvement in the conflict: according to some, it would be "impossible to achieve anything in Africa in times of unrest from a humanitarian point of view".[30]

The ICRC then decided to appoint a simple correspondent on the ground in the person of Karl Heinrich Jaggi, a Swiss national who was based in what became Biafra as a representative of the Swiss Union Trading Company. He was described as someone who knew nothing about Red Cross principles but who was well acquainted with Biafran circles. Using Swiss expatriates was a relatively common ICRC practice. However, they were mostly the organisation's "correspondents" abroad, whose task was to occasionally act as its representatives to governments. It was less common for them to have to mount a humanitarian operation during a civil war. Jaggi seems to have been a good choice, since this measure, which was initially meant to be temporary, remained in place. After a trip made by another delegate, Paul Reynard, in the autumn of 1967, Jaggi became the ICRC's head of delegation in Biafra at the end of 1967, a role which he performed until the end of the conflict.[31]

In Nigeria the situation was similar. In the early months of the war the ICRC's delegate general for Africa, Georg Hoffmann, was its main representative in Lagos. Nevertheless, his position required him to also carry out other missions on the African continent. Thus, various interlocutors acted as intermediaries between the ICRC and Nigerian government, in particular the Swiss ambassador, Fritz Real, but also Swiss nationals who were well acquainted with government circles. For example, Mr Zollinger, who worked for Nestlé in Lagos, sometimes acted as an ICRC correspondent.[32] In February 1968 the ICRC set up a delegation in Lagos led by Jean-René Pierroz. This delegate was unable to cope with the expansion of operations in the spring of 1968. He was replaced by a Swiss national from outside the ICRC, Robert Hitz, who was chosen for his management skills and knowledge of Africa. He too was overwhelmed by the magnitude of the challenge, and in the end the ICRC called on Gerhart Schürch, a member of the Grand Council and the City Council of Bern, who had carried out several missions for Le Don Suisse in 1947 and 1949.[33] The organisation's decision to turn to people from outside of it, and even from outside of the Red Cross world, was emblematic of its recruitment policy for senior positions during the conflict. Schürch was later replaced by Hans Egli, who had led Swiss Post's Personnel Department before becoming August Lindt's deputy.[34] In May 1969 he too was replaced by H. G. de Smit, director of the Lloyd shipping company.[35] In the final months of the conflict the position was filled by Jean-Pierre Hocké, a Swiss national recruited directly in Lagos.

In July 1968 the ICRC finally entrusted the management of the entire operation to an outsider of stature capable of taking it in hand, as pressure was growing on the organisation to find solutions and improve its efficiency. Fearing that the operation would be taken away from it because of the severe criticism it received, it turned to the Swiss Confederation, whose representatives were themselves particularly concerned about the quagmire it found itself in and its repercussions on Switzerland's image in the world.[36] The ICRC had no difficulty in getting the Swiss diplomatic service to make available the Swiss ambassador to Moscow, August Lindt, who had been, among other things, the ICRC's special delegate to Berlin and the UN High Commissioner for Refugees. In July 1968 he was appointed commissioner general for the action in Nigeria–Biafra, for which he had full responsibility. The Swiss government made Lindt available to the ICRC provided the Committee would give him complete freedom of action. He had a representative to the Committee, Swiss Army Lieutenant-Colonel Hans Schaedler, who was thus in charge of the Nigeria–Biafra office in Geneva. His deputies – François Pictet and then Jean-Pierre Zehnder – were selected from among the young recruits of the Swiss diplomatic corps.[37] At first, Lindt's appointment appeared to be a success as he temporarily broke the deadlock on the delivery of relief supplies to Biafra by launching the INALWA operation and setting up regular airlifts from the island of Fernando Poo. He also managed to bring order to the intervention on the federal side, improving the ICRC's credibility with the Nigerian government. Finally, he gave crucial impetus to the operations, insisting on the need to keep them going, plan them and maintain their course, at a time when some Committee members deemed them too onerous.[38] Overall, over the period of one year, he made it possible for the ICRC to engage fully in a large-scale action during which he co-ordinated the management of over 100,000 tonnes of food aid.[39]

Thus, from the summer of 1968 the key staff involved in the humanitarian operation – the commissioner general and heads of delegation in Nigeria and Biafra – were not ICRC delegates but Swiss nationals from the political and economic spheres, who were recruited for the occasion. After Lindt's resignation in June 1969, the ICRC once again brought in someone from outside the organisation. The negotiations with the FMG were entrusted to Enrico Bignami, Vice-President of Nestlé-Alimentana, which he had helped establish in Nigeria.[40] The fact that two prominent Committee members, Jacques Freymond and Max Petitpierre, sat on Nestlé's Board of Directors may well have had something to do with this appointment. This practice was not only in response to a crisis situation, it was also seen as a more general solution to the staff shortage that the ICRC had been facing since the 1950s. Thus, for the two most important relief actions it carried out during this period – in Hungary and Yemen – it preferred to use people from outside the ICRC. As noted by Françoise Perret and François Bugnion, "this situation reflected the lack of qualified managers and the fact that the institution trusted outside figures more than it did its own staff".[41]

In the late 1960s the organisation considered turning more systematically to the Confederation to alleviate its problem in recruiting delegates. Thus, in July 1968 the ICRC director went to Bern to share his difficulties with the Swiss Federal Political Department. He wanted the ICRC to be able to use some of the Department's officials on delegate missions lasting a few months, and the Public Economy Department to be approached for the purpose of encouraging large Swiss companies to make some of their staff temporarily available to the ICRC.[42] This second avenue was particularly pursued by the ICRC, which approached the Vorort (Swiss Union of Commerce and Industry), a grouping of commercial and industrial employers' associations. In September 1968 this organisation together with the Central Union of Swiss Employers' Associations, Swiss Union of Arts and Crafts, Swiss Farmers' Union and Swiss Bankers' Association sent a circular to their members relaying the request of the ICRC. The latter explained that in order to recruit temporary staff it had to "appeal to the management of Swiss companies who have highly qualified and diverse executives with experience in public relations, travelling, and international relations, and to ask them very urgently to invite a certain number of their executives to volunteer to work for the ICRC should the need arise".[43] It further used patriotic arguments which were taken up by the circular's signatories: "The ICRC performs an important role for Switzerland. However, it can only fulfil its role in a manner commensurate with the international reputation of our country if it is provided with the additional forces it needs".[44] It is also on the basis of this argument that the Swiss Confederation made members of its diplomatic corps available to the ICRC.

While the ICRC needed personnel, it also had to find the necessary funds to carry out an action which, because of the airlifts, quickly proved to be extremely costly. The ICRC had an extraordinary budget to cover the costs of the relief operations. Until 1967 it was relatively small and often underused because of the ICRC's policy – mentioned earlier – of avoiding large-scale actions. Most of the funds came from an annual collection of donations from the Swiss people. During the 1950s and 1960s the extraordinary budget fluctuated between two and three million Swiss francs per year, except in 1957, during the action in Hungary, when it reached nine million – the highest amount until 1968. In the 1960s the ICRC's activities in Nepal and Yemen already showed the limitations of this formula since the budget was unable to cover the expenses incurred by these operations, forcing the ICRC to draw on its reserves. But it was really the Nigeria–Biafra action, because of the size of its cost, that led the ICRC to rethink its policy in this regard. As noted by Freymond, Willemin and Heacock, the organisation's extraordinary budget was twenty times higher in 1969 (in real terms) than the average of previous years (since the early 1950s), and nine tenths of it were allocated to the Nigeria–Biafra operation.[45]

Quite soon after the start of the conflict in Nigeria the extraordinary budget was no longer enough and donations were slow in arriving. The ICRC therefore drew on its regular budget, which was theoretically intended for the organisation's usual activities, namely its running costs, activities promoting international humanitarian law, as well as visits to prisoners of war. From the early 1950s to the Nigeria–Biafra war it had not exceeded four million Swiss francs (in real terms). In the mid-1960s the budget was made up almost equally of contributions from governments and those from National Societies in the form of annual membership fees. The Swiss Confederation was the main contributor since, in addition to its regular contributions, it also made extraordinary contributions in the form of credit lines whose repayment was not always required. These enabled the organisation to cope with the expansion of its activities in the late 1960s. Indeed, in March 1968, at the request of the ICRC, which at the time was carrying out four parallel actions (Yemen, Vietnam, the Middle East and Nigeria–Biafra), the Federal Council allocated it a loan of ten million Swiss francs. The organisation used just under three million francs from this amount for its operation in Nigeria–Biafra, before setting up a special fund for it. This was necessary due to the exponential increase in costs incurred in 1968. According to an internal report by Edmé Regenass, the expenditure associated with the Nigeria–Biafra operation – the overheads related to field delegations, personnel, delivery, distribution and purchase of relief supplies – increased considerably in the summer of 1968.[46] In the space of three months (July–September 1968) the ICRC spent the equivalent of two thirds of what it had spent in the previous year (July 1967–July 1968) (see Table 9.2). These figures did not include the significant costs that

Table 9.2 ICRC expenditure on the Nigeria–Biafra action, July 1967–October 1968

Period	ICRC expenditure on the Nigeria–Biafra action
July–December 1967	CHF 828,000
January–June 1968	CHF 700,000
July–September 1968	CHF 10,500,000

were borne directly by the National Red Cross Societies or other voluntary agencies (such as chartering some planes or funding medical teams).

As pointed out by Regenass, the massive sudden expansion of the operation required the deployment of human and material resources on a scale that went beyond what the ICRC and National Societies could provide. And the expenses forecast for the following months in the event that the military situation remained the same would be even more substantial. It was therefore necessary to come up with solutions to reduce costs and above all find new sources of funding. Indeed, Regenass forecast an expenditure of between 10 and 20 million Swiss francs per month from October 1968 onwards. In November 1968 32 million Swiss francs had to be found to cover the budget until the end of February 1969.[47]

To raise these funds, the ICRC turned to National Societies and especially governments. In the autumn of 1968 three Committee members approached Washington, London and Bonn to seek funding. The former president of the Swiss Confederation, Max Petitpierre, took on the task of pleading the ICRC's cause with the US government, while Paul Ruegger and Hans Bachmann went to the United Kingdom and the Federal Republic of Germany respectively. They received the support of Swiss diplomatic representatives abroad, in addition to the ICRC's appeals to other governments and National Societies. These initiatives enabled it to raise 36,076,480 Swiss francs in 1968 for the Nigeria–Biafra operation. State donations accounted for 79 per cent of the total (CHF 28,361,158) and came from the United States, the Federal Republic of Germany, Switzerland, the Netherlands, Italy, the United Kingdom, Finland, Ethiopia, Jamaica, Denmark, Turkey and Botswana. The National Red Cross Societies contributed CHF 4,102,867, representing 11 per cent of the donations.[48] The remaining 10 per cent was divided between contributions from the IUCW, Oxfam, the World Council of Churches, UNICEF and Catholic Relief Services, amounting to CHF 2,806,482 (8 per cent), and donations from other organisations and individuals which came to CHF 805,972 (2 per cent). Whilst contributions came from all five continents and from a variety of organisations, the financial contributions from the American and West German governments were the most substantial, accounting for more than two thirds of the total amount (the Americans provided CHF 15,552,000, representing 45 per cent of the total amount raised; the West Germans, CHF 5,423,825, representing 15 per cent of the total amount raised). Their magnitude raised the question of the ICRC's independence from its donors. Whilst the latter did not seem to interfere directly in the conduct of the operation, nevertheless, the ICRC was careful to give these partners a special role in organising the relief effort. The minutes of a Directorate meeting held in the summer of 1968 stated: "since the Americans have made considerable donations, it will be necessary to earmark some important posts for them".[49]

These various payments enabled the ICRC to resolve the financial impasse in 1968. Thus, whilst in the last six months of 1968 the organisation spent 36 million Swiss francs, the figures for the following year were higher still. Indeed, in 1969 the ICRC spent three times as much, namely CHF 106,706,069. Two thirds of this amount went to the operation in Biafra, not least because of the extraordinary costs incurred by the air bridge. Funds were once again secured from governments, National Societies and various organisations.[50] Once the Nigeria–Biafra action was over, the assessment report devoted to it put the total expenditure handled by the ICRC at 162,563,000 Swiss francs.[51] As the study by Freymond, Willemin and Heacock has shown, this was a particularly remarkable increase in ICRC expenditure compared to the cost of other operations conducted at that time.

And this amount did not represent the full cost of the action, since it included neither contributions in kind (food, medicines) nor services (meeting some of the operating costs of the airlifts, funding teams on the ground etc.), which were provided directly by governments, National Societies and other organisations. According to ICRC estimates, these contributions amounted to 76,300,000 Swiss francs for services provided, and 347,500,000 Swiss francs for donations in kind. These estimates allowed the ICRC to assess the total value of the relief effort it had co-ordinated (see Table 9.3).[52] Despite the planning efforts made from 1969, managing an operation on this scale was particularly testing for the organisation, and whilst it did manage to find the funds, there were times when it faced the prospect of bankruptcy.[53]

Table 9.3 Estimated value of the relief actions coordinated by the ICRC in Nigeria and Biafra, 1967–70

Cash contributions (total: CHF 239,200,000)	Participation in special projects	CHF 91,200,000
	Cash donations	CHF 148,000,000
Contributions in kind (total: CHF 347,500,000)	Medicines	CHF 246,600,000
	Food	CHF 100,900,000
Contributions in the form of services (total: CHF 76,300,000)	Personnel	CHF 17,800,000
	Vehicles	CHF 5,300,000
	Chartering of ships	CHF 2,100,000
	Air transport	CHF 51,100,000
Total		**CHF 663,000,000**

In the autumn of 1968, when the operations had barely started, their sheer scale led the ICRC to try to share its responsibilities with other organisations. This decision sparked debates in Geneva. The Directorate first suggested that a joint commission be considered, bringing together the ICRC, the League, the National Societies most involved and the Nigerian Red Cross. This solution would follow the model of the Joint Relief Commission established during the Second World War. A debate soon ensued on the role to be assigned in this process to the other organisations which operated separately in Biafra but took part in ICRC operations in Nigeria. Pierre Gaillard suggested bringing them together in an advisory committee which would work with this commission, whereas Jean Pictet was in favour of a commission in which the Red Cross and the main charities would be on an equal footing. He pointed out that the delivery and distribution of relief supplies were not the ICRC's primary tasks and came after its traditional activities: "The Committee is not responsible for the lives of entire populations whose neglect is the fault of irresponsible authorities. This is a worldwide problem. It is a governmental task which is completely beyond the material capabilities of a private organisation like the ICRC".[54] On the basis of these arguments, in late November 1968 the members of the Presidential Council approved the principle of setting up a joint commission comprising the National Societies, the League, the ICRC and other charities.

A plan was then submitted to Committee members. It proposed establishing a joint commission, based in Geneva in premises provided by the municipality, which would take over the management of all of the ICRC's assets in the Nigeria–Biafra action, as well as its undertakings up to that point.[55] The supreme body of this commission would be a council made up of two representatives from the League, two representatives from the ICRC, one representative from the Nigerian Red Cross and one representative from each National Society wishing to participate directly in the action by making a regular contribution, sending aid or providing personnel paid by it. The ICRC and the League could veto any decisions taken.

The possibility of including agencies from outside the Red Cross was dismissed fairly quickly. It was argued that these could not accept the ICRC's and the League's right of veto. Moreover, by including the other organisations, the Red Cross could give the impression that it had partially given up. On the other hand, sharing responsibilities with National Red Cross Societies and the League had several advantages. It would allow the ICRC to gradually withdraw from operations that it found too burdensome and concentrate on its traditional tasks. This solution would also allow it to "present a united broad front" in the face of criticisms that were likely to be levelled at it at the Istanbul conference.[56] Moreover, engaging more closely with the Societies that had been vehemently critical of it could be a good way to neutralise them, at a time when the organisation's role within the Movement was being challenged.[57] Indeed, since the early 1960s discussions had been taking place with the most active National Societies and the League to revise the 1951 agreement which governed, among other things, the co-ordination of relief in the event of armed conflict.[58]

In early December 1968 the Committee unanimously decided to find a "successor" for the Nigeria–Biafra operation on the basis of the plan mentioned above.[59] However, implementing this solution proved to be fraught with pitfalls. August Lindt, who did not think that the ICRC should be replaced as leader of the action, objected. He put forward four arguments. Firstly, such a decision could be interpreted as the ICRC shirking its responsibilities. Secondly, now that the operations were running in a satisfactory manner, changing the organisation would be inopportune. Thirdly, it would probably be more difficult to obtain donations since potential donors would be less willing to provide funds to an unknown organisation. Fourthly, the action would risk being less effective due to the division of responsibilities. Despite the fact that the decision to find a successor to the ICRC had been taken unanimously a few days earlier, it seems that these arguments were not lost on the members of the Presidential Council.[60]

The crisis in Santa Isabel in early 1969 also helped postpone taking a decision on this plan. By the end of January 1969 it was still dormant and the main parties concerned were not persuaded by it. Lindt threatened to withdraw if responsibilities were to be divided, and the League's Secretary General, Henrik Beer, was not particularly enthusiastic about inheriting responsibility for this action. Even within the ICRC positions seemed to be changing. The events in Santa Isabel cast a light on the tensions that could arise at the heart of the ICRC's action, namely between the Committee and the commissioner general.[61] The need to take decisions quickly was also emphasised, something which an increased number of partners did not always allow for. A shift was emerging within the Presidential Council where it was made clear that this committee would be responsible for the technical aspects of the operation, but not for political or diplomatic ones.[62] However, some Committee members were still considering appointing a successor to the ICRC:

> Other members are concerned about the ICRC getting too involved in a single part of the world. Figures are becoming astronomical and it is a dangerous spiral. Moreover, the ICRC no longer has the time to deal with other issues. The question of succession therefore has become pressing. We need to, on the one hand, deliver as much aid as possible and, on the other, adhere to the ICRC's rule of intervening when others are not able to act.[63]

In the end, a compromise solution prevailed. The ICRC made provisions to continue the action by adopting a funding plan for the following six months.

At the same time it continued its efforts to co-ordinate it together with the other organisations so that it could disengage from the food-distribution operation as soon as possible, and concentrate on medical activities and its traditional tasks. Paradoxically, it was not until Henrik Beer put forward a proposal to the League that a commission bringing together various partners finally materialised. In late February Beer proposed setting up an advisory commission consisting of one member of the ICRC and the League, and two representatives from the National Societies.[64] As its name indicates, this commission only had an advisory role and the ICRC remained in charge of the action. Unlike the previous plan, it did get set up and met once a month from March 1969. It usually brought together the Vice-President and Deputy Director of the ICRC, Jacques Freymond and Pierre Basset, Commissioner General August Lindt, the Secretary General of the League Henrik Beer and representatives of the Scandinavian Red Cross societies.[65]

These various episodes show the ICRC's ambivalence towards its responsibilities. Despite its clearly expressed desire to free itself from an action it considered too onerous, it nevertheless ended up remaining in charge of it. Lindt seems to have played a significant part in that respect since he had insisted on it. Other Committee members were probably also convinced that, whilst better co-ordination was needed, the ICRC should not abandon its responsibility for the operation. The organisation's 1968 activity report, which included a foreword by Jacques Freymond, made specific reference to the ICRC's involvement with the civilian population in the Nigeria–Biafra operation. Thus, Freymond wrote that "this action should not necessarily be seen as an exceptional case, but rather as a new type of engagement which the ICRC may have to undertake as a result of the evolution of contemporary international relations".[66] Such a comment not only meant that the ICRC fully assumed its responsibilities in this action, but that it might also have to conduct similar actions in the future. Indeed, the publication of this text gave rise to a debate within the Committee. Those who were most fervently in support of the plan for a joint commission, Jacques de Rougemont and Jean Pictet, "made it clear that, whilst the Committee accepts this new type of engagement, it does not accept the conditions imposed on it by the parties to the conflict and by events, which have led it, in spite of itself, to feed a population of more than two million by plane".[67] Nevertheless, the report was accepted by the Committee as a whole. These hesitations and changes of course illustrate the ICRC's ambivalence at a time when it sought to redefine its place in the humanitarian field. They also explain why, when the Nigerian government decided to remove the ICRC from its role as co-ordinator in the federal area and forced it to suspend its nightly airlifts, it did not put up any fierce resistance. Instead, this reinforced its belief that lessons had to be learned from the Nigeria–Biafra experience in order to be able to deal with similar crises in the future.

"Organising the unpredictable"

As the previous chapters have shown, the ICRC's record at the end of the war was mixed. Although it did conduct a major operation, it was forced to partially terminate it before the conflict ended and was the target of much criticism in Europe and Africa. Afterwards when the operation was assessed, the solutions found during the war showed their limitations and confirmed the need for in-depth restructuring at various levels if the organisation was to maintain its role in providing relief to war victims.

Firstly, the costs involved in the Nigeria–Biafra operation led the ICRC to develop a more active fundraising policy, particularly for the extraordinary budget. This budget, which until then had been relatively small, increased after the Nigeria–Biafra conflict and never returned to its original level. This reflected a deeper change within the ICRC. This fund no longer drew solely on collections from the Swiss people but also, as with the regular budget, on contributions from National Societies and governments. Furthermore, the ICRC developed a more active policy of responding to the various conflicts in which it may be called upon to act. Whereas previously it had made its interventions conditional on the resources at its disposal, beginning with Nigeria–Biafra the trend was reversed. It would first commit to an action and then find ways to obtain the necessary funds. This way of doing things had an impact on the extraordinary budget, and donors could now specify for which operation their money should be used. While this new practice limited the ICRC's freedom to allocate funds to a certain extent, it did allow it to undertake actions on a larger scale. To this end, the organisation also developed a more dynamic fundraising policy which included improving communications in general and especially with donors.[68] This was all the more necessary since the increase in the volume of the organisation's activities also led to an increase in its regular expenditure and therefore regular budget. As pointed out by Jacques Freymond, whilst up until then the ICRC had been content to appeal to governments and National Societies for contributions by sending out letters, from the 1970s its representatives went to meet with donors in order to plead the organisation's cause directly and promote its activities. This recognition of the need to strengthen its canvassing policy was also reflected in its reorganisation, since in 1974 a fundraising post was created under the direct supervision of the head of the finance department.

Secondly, as far as personnel was concerned, the solutions tested by the organisation during the conflict – using volunteers for short missions via other organisations or Swiss political and economic circles – also showed their limitations. They did not remove the need for the ICRC to put in place a real policy for recruiting, managing and training field personnel.

Following his experience as head of delegation in Lagos, Schürch shared his observations on the impact of the ICRC's system for recruiting and managing personnel on the effectiveness of relief operations.[69] He pointed out several shortcomings. First of all, he found the time spent on a field mission (three months) too short, not least because of the time needed to adapt to the situation on the ground, which Schürch estimated to be at least one month. Moreover, it led to excessive staff turnover which posed the problem of recruiting new personnel at the end of each mission and jeopardised the continuity of the action. The situation of the delegation in Lagos in late 1968 was again symptomatic. As Schürch was due to complete his mandate at the end of December, at the beginning of the month no replacement had yet been found. He was therefore unable to properly prepare his succession with the authorities in Lagos.[70] The conflict also demonstrated that it was impossible to send the same person to the different belligerents, whether it was the commissioner general, delegates or medical teams. Switching from one side to the other in order to make progress in negotiations or maintain a level of continuity for patients mainly created a climate of suspicion towards the Red Cross. This inconclusive experiment was therefore never repeated. Finally, Schürch underscored the lack of professional experts among the volunteers sent into the field:

> The system for recruiting volunteers, which I agree is necessary, has some serious flaws in that you will always find adventurers of no professional worth, and idealists who are certainly worth something in terms of their intentions, but who in actual practice don't fit the bill.[71]

This problem was compounded by the fact that volunteers were not properly selected and trained. The procedure, which consisted of undergoing an interview at headquarters before their departure, did not seem satisfactory, especially since the delegates' trip to Geneva was not systematic. These shortcomings led the Lagos delegation to set up a selection and training system on the ground.[72] As Chapter 6 has shown, this amateur approach to managing human resources in the field helped fuel the Nigerian authorities' criticism of the conduct of humanitarian organisations.

Thus, the Nigeria–Biafra operation cruelly highlighted the need for the ICRC to professionalise its personnel, particularly its delegates, and to better manage its commitments and the duration of its missions. From 1970 it embarked on a more elaborate recruitment process, selecting candidates on the basis of applications and interviews, supplemented by three-to-five-day training courses in Cartigny, near Geneva. Delegates were now hired for missions lasting around six months which could be renewed. Furthermore, the ICRC realised that it could no longer operate on a purely voluntary basis and that, if it wished to work with competent personnel, it needed to retain them. In 1974 it began recruiting some thirty permanent delegates over a period of five years, making this a general measure at the end of the 1970s,[73] which was a real break with previous decades in terms of personnel management.

Thirdly, the increasing role played by the media and the presence of more and more organisations seeking to respond to humanitarian crises led the ICRC to look at its relationship with these different actors. Until the 1960s informing the latter about its operations had not been a priority. It therefore devoted relatively few resources to communication management, all the more since it continued to pursue the ideal of acting discreetly. When the conflict in Nigeria–Biafra started there was no real information policy, but some timid efforts were made to improve the ICRC's external relations, as shown by the introduction in February 1968 of a system of monthly press conferences about its activities.[74] However, the lack of a clear policy in this respect and dedicated information personnel led to the conclusion that public relations were not managed seriously enough.[75]

First of all, the intense media coverage the humanitarian crisis received from the summer of 1968 onwards contrasted with the lack of information from the ICRC during this period. While its difficulties in setting up its operation in Biafra earned it much criticism, some Committee members pointed out that promoting what it had already done in the conflict could help improve its image. In addition, the increase in the number of humanitarian actors involved in civilian relief placed significant pressure on the ICRC who, in order to maintain its position as a key player in the humanitarian field, had to emphasise its ability to act. It therefore needed to assert its role and credibility, which required that progress be made in terms of, for example, communicating with the press.[76] Its silence about the steps it was taking or the state of negotiations did not only affect its relations with the media, but also with its potential partners who did not appreciate the way they were treated.[77] Better communication on its part could improve its image, while at the same time help solve some of its funding and human-resource problems. Indeed, in order to recruit competent personnel, the Committee needed to make its activities better known among the Swiss population. This required judicious use of the media as well as launching radio and television campaigns, as suggested by the head of the international organisations division of the Federal Political Department with whom Roger Gallopin had discussed the issue.[78]

Overall, the Nigeria–Biafra experience made the organisation realise that it was imperative for it to rethink its external relations.[79] In practice, this was reflected from 1970 by the strengthening of the information service, which was now directly attached to the Presidential Council.[80] Thus, at the end of 1969 President Naville decided on a "new-look" policy for the

ICRC's relationship with the media in order to make the institution better known to journalists.[81] Whilst reaffirming its desire to act discreetly, the ICRC strove to improve the way in which information was disseminated from the organisation's headquarters as well as the field.[82] This need was part of a wider trend which led humanitarian organisations to examine their relationship with public opinion and the media. This was the case within the Red Cross Movement where, as early as 1967, a meeting was held between representatives of the information services in order to "take a fresh look at the whole crucial problem of the Red Cross's public relations".[83] A second similar meeting took place in 1970 and dealt with the subjects of "information in an emergency" and relations with the "mass media".[84] The question of the relationship with the media was also central to the concerns of the new humanitarian actors who emerged in the 1970s.

These various measures were part of a gradual process of restructuring the ICRC which affected its functioning as a whole. This had already started prior to the Nigeria–Biafra war but the latter particularly underlined the need for it. Indeed, Lindt's taking over the Nigeria–Biafra action did not entirely solve its management and organisational problems. The scale of the operation and the setting up of Lindt's office, which was accompanied by the arrival of new employees in Geneva, caused considerable friction at headquarters. These tensions clearly showed the limitations of using outside personnel to run the operation. Furthermore, the belligerents' growing animosity towards Lindt showed the problems that came with personifying such an operation. The commissioner general, who was responsible for negotiating with the two conflicting parties, could not but arouse suspicion on both sides because of his very position.

The difficulties and criticisms the organisation faced when it took over the negotiations in the summer of 1969 once again underscored the fact that it could not avoid a deep re-examination. In September 1969 an article published in London in the British Sunday newspaper *The Observer* by the journalist John de St Jorre was highly critical of the ICRC. He described the Committee as "the least international grouping in the world, as it is dominated by French-speaking, professional Genevans".[85] He emphasised the primarily honorary nature of membership in the organisation, comparing it to receiving the British Order of Merit. According to the journalist, this explained the prestige enjoyed by the Committee at a national level, but also its lack of effectiveness and recognition in the countries that had recently become independent. The organisation, who came across as arrogant and incompetent to its interlocutors, was also criticised for the way it worked.

These negative remarks were echoed to a certain extent on the Swiss national stage, which put the ICRC in an uncomfortable position not least because of its financial dependence on the Confederation. Indeed, Bern's contribution alone accounted for two thirds of governmental contributions to the organisation's regular budget, which in turn accounted for more than 50 per cent of that same budget. Whilst the Federal Council had no say in the use of the funds it provided, their size made the ICRC particularly sensitive to its wishes. Thus, in late 1969 it wanted the Committee, which was dominated by French-speaking Swiss, to be more representative of the various Swiss cantons and rejuvenated. There were also specific criticisms of the organisation's handling of the Nigeria–Biafra operation and in particular its failure to act at the end of 1969:

> Mr Graedel has noted that we are under a kind of pressure that we cannot but yield to, since we are to a large extent dependent on the Confederation. It is therefore necessary to act and act quickly because it would be extremely unfortunate if a debate were to take place in the Chambers on the subject of the Committee before certain measures relating to the rejuvenation and representativeness of the Committee were taken.[86]

The ICRC restarted a co-option procedure in late 1969 and made changes within the Committee beginning with the early 1970s, as two members died in 1968 and six members (four in 1969, and two in 1970) left office or became honorary members. In addition to the six members recruited in 1967, three were co-opted in 1969, 1970 and 1971 (Harald Huber, Victor H. Umbricht and Pierre Micheli), followed by seven new recruits in 1973.[87] Thus, in the decade from 1965 to 1975 the Committee underwent a complete renewal. There was also a growing need to take a closer look at the institution's decision-making and management bodies. Between 1968 and 1970 the ICRC had to deal with the resignation of its president as well as one of its directors general, which led to the dissolution of the Directorate at the end of 1969. The Committee hired a new member of staff under the title of Secretary General, whose duties included diagnosing problems in the way the ICRC operated and proposing improvements.

These different elements pointed to several conclusions which the ICRC drew at the end of the action. It needed to reorganise in order to be able to manage the difficulties involved in large-scale operations, particularly when these were running in parallel. With this in mind, various measures were taken. A new structure was set up in 1970 which brought together "the support services involved in overseas activities in an Operations Department".[88] This was in line with the creation of a delegation service, already mooted in 1968, and was part of a wider process of restructuring the ICRC.[89] It reflected the need to better co-ordinate and conduct the growing number of overseas operations. There were also the changes in terms of personnel, information and funding mentioned above. Humanitarian professionals played a gradually increasing role in setting the ICRC's policy, and the distinction between the responsibilities of the Committee and those of the Presidential Council became clearer in the first half of the 1970s. However, this shift was not self-evident and was coupled with questions about the overall direction of the Committee. The tensions within the latter, which led to Jacques Freymond's resignation as vice-president in the spring of 1971, are a particularly good example of this. An article published in the *Journal de Genève* shed light on the dividing lines running through the organisation:

> There are also two opposing traditions: the legal ICRC which drafts, defends, and promotes humanitarian conventions; and the operational ICRC which gets involved day after day to save human lives, upholding the conventions and the Red Cross ideal like a guiding star, but whose sole criterion for its day-to-day conduct is efficiency.[90]

The presence of many legal experts in the Committee probably influenced the direction taken by the ICRC, which continued to seek to develop humanitarian law. Drawing on its experiences in internal conflicts in the late 1960s, the ICRC stressed the importance of extending humanitarian law to civil conflicts, a process that led to the Additional Protocols of 1977.[91] Nevertheless, its subsequent development also attests to efforts made towards professionalisation, which would provide it with the means to be operational in multiple and varied contexts and thus maintain a predominant place in an increasingly competitive humanitarian field. The measures taken did not really bear fruit, as noted by the Tansley report of 1975. Whilst the road to becoming the ICRC of today would be long and there would be other significant moments in the organisation's development, the moment of realisation in the early 1970s played a decisive role.[92]

Thus, in the late 1960s an increase in the number of theatres of operation laid the foundations for a profound transformation of the Geneva-based institution. In this context, the operations conducted during the Biafran war shook up the ICRC in several ways. They posed many challenges for an organisation whose resources remained limited. In particular, they highlighted the need for multiple reforms, some of which had been envisaged but were slow in being implemented. The simultaneous existence of other areas of engagement, such as the Middle East, accentuated this need. The 1970s clearly started with this imperative, in order to enable the ICRC to "organise what is unforeseeable in advance".[93] These changes translated into a structural reorganisation of the ICRC that was made all the more necessary by the fact that the Nigeria–Biafra operation marked an increase in the organisation's activities, which was reflected in a rise in its budget that would never return to its pre-1968 level. Assistance activities would account for an increasingly large part of it, even if the Committee was somewhat reluctant about this new approach.

An analysis of what played out in the late 1960s and early 1970s also provides an opportunity to delve into the workings of an unique organisation like the ICRC. In particular, it helps highlight its dependence on the Swiss Confederation, but also on Swiss economic and political elites. Whilst this close relationship was not particularly advertised, it was not denied either. Despite its international status, the ICRC remained an exclusively Swiss organisation, employing primarily Swiss staff, not least because of its conception of neutrality. Moreover, the fact that the ICRC was seen as one of Switzerland's representatives in the world confirmed these links. Indeed, the special relationship between the organisation and its country of origin was a source of criticism and tension during the conflict. In this context, the reforms undertaken in the late 1970s can also be seen as the organisation's way of becoming more independent.[94]

Notes

1 This chapter is a reworked version of M.-L. Desgrandchamps, "'Organising the Unpredictable': The Nigeria–Biafra War and Its Impact on the ICRC", *International Review of the Red Cross*, 94:888 (2012), 1409–32.

2 J. Freymond, "Nigeria–Biafra, l'aide aux victimes de la guerre civile", *Preuves*, 1 (1970), 70–83; Forsythe, *The Humanitarians*, p. 62; C. Moorehead, *Dunant's Dream: War, Switzerland and the History of the Red Cross* (London: HarperCollins, 1993), p. 614; S. Delorenzi, *Face aux impasses de l'action humanitaire internationale. La politique du CICR depuis la fin de la guerre froide* (Geneva: CICR, 1997), p. 21; D. Palmieri, "Une institution à l'épreuve du temps, retour sur 150 ans d'histoire du Comité international de la Croix-Rouge", *Revue internationale de la Croix-Rouge*, 94:4, sélection française (2012), 85–111.

3 J.-M. Bornet, *Entre les lignes enemies. Délégué du CICR, 1972–2003* (Georg: Geneva, 2011), p. 87.

4 Forsythe, *The Humanitarians*, p. 51.

5 J. Freymond, G. Willemin & R. Heacock, *Le Comité international de la Croix-Rouge* (Geneva: Georg, 1984), p. 83.

6 Freymond, Willemin & Heacock, *Le Comité international de la Croix-Rouge*, pp. 61–72 and p. 134.

7 Freymond, Willemin & Heacock, *Le Comité international de la Croix-Rouge*, p. 128.

8 C. Rey-Schyrr, *De Yalta à Dien Bien Phu. Histoire du Comité international de la Croix-Rouge, 1945–1955* (Geneva: Georg, 2007), pp. 43–8. See also I. Vonèche-Cardia, *Neutralité et engagement*, and J.-C. Favez, *Une mission impossible*.

9 Most of them were paid. Of these 146 people, 23 worked for the Central Research Agency, which dealt with research requests on past conflicts, including

the Second World War; Freymond, Willemin & Heacock, *Le Comité international de la Croix-Rouge*, p. 139.

10 See, for example, the operation set up for the Hungarian refugees; Freymond, Willemin & Heacock, *Le Comité international de la Croix-Rouge*, p. 89.

11 F. Perret & F. Bugnion, *De Budapest à Saigon. Histoire du Comité international de la Croix-Rouge, 1956–1965* (Geneva: Georg, 2009), p. 309.

12 Perret & Bugnion, *De Budapest à Saigon*, p. 601.

13 Forsythe, *The Humanitarians*, pp. 62–78.

14 On the ICRC's activities in Sub-Saharan Africa, see M.-L. Desgrandchamps, "Éthiques irréconciliables ou suspicions réciproques? Le CICR et les mouvements de libération en Afrique lusophone (1961–1976)", in J.-F. Fayet, M.-L. Desgrandchamps, M. Cugnet & D. Hasler (eds), *La Croix face à l'étoile rouge. Humanitaire et communisme au XXe siècle* (Geneva: Georg, 2025), pp. 266–91; M.-L. Desgrandchamps, "Entre ambitions universalistes et préjugés raciaux", *Histoire@Politique*, 41 (2020), https://doi.org/10.4000/histoirepolitique.313; A. Thompson, "'Restoring Hope Where All Hope Was Lost': Nelson Mandela, the ICRC and the Protection of Political Detainees in Apartheid South Africa", *International Review of the Red Cross*, 98:3 (2016), 799–829; A. Thompson, "Humanitarian Principles Put to Test: Challenges to Humanitarian Action during Decolonization", *International Review of the Red Cross*, 97:897/898 (2016), 45–76; Perret & Bugnion, *De Budapest à Saigon*, pp. 259–329; M.-L. Desgrandchamps, "Africa, the Africans, and the Red Cross: Assessing the Impact of the Long Second World War (1935–1950)", in M.-L. Desgrandchamps, L. Humbert, B. Taithe & R. Balu (eds), *Medical Care, Humanitarianism and Intimacy in the Long Second World War, 1931–1953* (Manchester: Manchester University Press, 2025), 84–108; Y. Pringle, "Humanitarianism, Race and Denial: The International Committee of the Red Cross and Kenya's Mau Mau Rebellion, 1952–60", *History Workshop Journal*, 84 (2017), 89– 107; F. Klose, "The Colonial Testing Ground: The International Committee of the Red Cross and the Violent End of Empire", *Humanity*, 2:1 (2011), 107–26; R. Baudendistel, *Between Bombs and Good Intentions: The Red Cross and the Italo-Ethiopian War, 1935–1936* (New York: Berghahn Books, 2006); Herrmann & Palmieri, "Humanitaires et massacres", p. 237.

15 AICRC, plenary session of the Committee, 5 January 1967.

16 Freymond, *Guerres, Révolutions, Croix-Rouge*, pp. 3–35.

17 Perret, Bugnion, *De Budapest à Saigon*, p. 38; Freymond, Willemin & Heacock, *Le Comité International de la Croix-Rouge*, pp. 126–7. R. Gallopin is responsible for the Executive and Administrative Divisions, while J. Pictet is in charge of all permanent tasks, apart from assistance to victims of conflicts.

18 AICRC, plenary session of the Committee, 1 November 1967.

19 *Revue internationale de la Croix-Rouge*, 589, January 1968. The new coopted members were D. Bindschedler-Robert, M. Naville, J.-F. de Rougemont and W. Jucker.

20 AICRC, plenary session of the Committee, 1 November 1967.

21 AICRC, B AG 12-044, critical note by P. Basset, November 1970.

22 AICRC, plenary session of the Committee, 29 August 1968.
23 Hentsch, *Face au blocus*, p. vii.
24 AICRC, Directorate briefing note, 14 July 1967.
25 AICRC, Directorate briefing note, 5 September 1967.
26 In the spring of 1968, after the ICRC had postponed the dispatch of medical teams to Biafra several times, a doctor from the Church of Scotland finally decided to leave with the airlift of religious operations; AICRC, B AG 202 147-001, letter from Rev. Bernard, 26 March 1968.
27 AICRC, Directorate briefing note, 24 July 1968.
28 Perret & Bugnion, *De Budapest à Saigon*, p. 599.
29 Freymond, Willemin & Heacock, *Le Comité International de la Croix-Rouge*, pp. 136–8.
30 AICRC, Presidential Council meeting, 17 August 1967.
31 AICRC, Directorate briefing note, 15 December 1967.
32 AICRC, Directorate briefing note, 12 September 1967.
33 C. Zürcher, "Gerhart Schürch", *in Dictionnaire historique de la Suisse*, 23.08.2011.
34 Page, *Le Nigeria et la Suisse*, p. 258.
35 AICRC, Directorate briefing note, 22 April 1969.
36 DDS, file "Actions d'entraide au Nigéria (1967–1969)", letter from the Swiss ambassador to Nigeria to the Head of the International Organisations Division, 5 June 1968 (dodis.ch/33767); file "Actions d'entraide au Nigéria – Biafra – Handakten de M. l'Ambassadeur Thalmann (1967–69)", Aktennotiz of the Head of the International Organisations Division, 17 July 1968 (dodis.ch/33790).
37 Page, *Le Nigeria et la Suisse*, p. 258.
38 AICRC, plenary session of the Committee, 7 November 1968.
39 AICRC, B AG 280 147-016, "International Committee of the Red Cross Relief Operations in Nigeria", trustee report by Peat, Marwick, Mitchell & Co., 1 July 1970, pp. 17–23. This figure represents the total food relief managed by ICRC-co-ordinated operations over the period 1967–70 in Nigeria and Biafra (the majority of relief for the war zones passing through Nigeria).
40 Enrico Bignami is also the founder of the IMEDE (Institut pour l'enseignement des méthodes de direction de l'entreprise) in Lausanne; G. Marion, "Enrico Bignami", in *Dictionnaire historique de la Suisse*, 30.09.2004.
41 Perret & Bugnion, *De Budapest à Saigon*, p. 600.
42 DDS, vol. 24, doc. 92 note for the file, interview between the ICRC's Director and the Head of the International Organisations Division, 3 July 1968 (dodis.ch/32824).
43 AICRC, Directorate briefing note, 10 September 1968, letter from the Vorort, 4 September 1968.
44 AICRC, Directorate briefing note, 10 September 1968, letter from the Vorort, 4 September 1968.
45 On the ICRC's budget during the 1960s, see Freymond, Willemin & Heacock, *Le Comité International de la Croix-Rouge*.

46 AICRC, B AG 280 147-015, "Action de secours au Nigeria. Rapport sur la mission d'étude financière effectuée du 7 au 21 September par M. Regenass, délégué administratif", 25 September 1968.
47 AICRC, Directorate briefing note, 12 November 1968.
48 The contribution ranged from 835,000 CHF to 165.50 CHF and came from the national societies of Switzerland, Britain, Canada, West Germany, the Netherlands, Ireland, Sweden, the USA, Australia, Finland, Ethiopia, Liberia, Tanzania, Austria, Japan, Denmark, Luxembourg, Monaco, New Zealand, Italy, South Africa, Liechtenstein, Jamaica, Ivory Coast, Spain, Zambia, Philippines, Syria, South Korea, Cameroon, Kenya and Portugal; AICRC, Directorate briefing note, 8 January 1969, "Action Nigeria–Biafra. Somme des dons reçus en espèce du 1er janvier au 31 décembre 1968".
49 AICRC, B AG 280 147-002, Directorate meeting, 19 August 1968.
50 CICR, *Rapport d'activité 1969* (Geneva: CICR, 1970), p. 116.
51 AICRC, B AG 280 147-016, "International Committee of the Red Cross Relief Operations in Nigeria", trustee report by Peat, Marwick, Mitchell & Co., 1 July 1970. This amount does not include expenditure on special projects.
52 CICR, *Rapport d'activité 1970* (Geneva: CICR, 1971), p. 133.
53 AICRC, plenary sessions of the Committee, 3 October 1968, 7 November 1968; Presidential Council meeting, 29 November 1969.
54 AICRC, Presidential Council meeting, 21 November 1968.
55 AICRC, Directorate briefing note, 3 December 1968, "Mise sur pied d'une commission mixte de secours à la population civile du Nigeria–Biafra", 25 November 1968.
56 AICRC, Directorate briefing note, 3 December 1968, "Mise sur pied d'une commission mixte de secours à la population civile du Nigeria–Biafra", 25 November 1968.
57 AICRC, plenary session of the Committee, 3 October 1968, letter from the President of the Swedish Red Cross, E. von Hofsten, to the President of the Standing Commission of the International Red Cross, 5 August 1968.
58 Freymond, Willemin, Heacock, *Le Comité International de la Croix-Rouge*, pp. 145–52.
59 AICRC, plenary session of the Committee, 4 and 5 December 1968.
60 AICRC, Presidential Council meeting, 12 December 1968.
61 AICRC, plenary sessions of the Committee, 9 and 14 January 1969.
62 AICRC, Presidential Council meeting, 26 January 1969.
63 AICRC, plenary session of the Committee, 6 February 1969.
64 AICRC, Presidential Council meetings, 13 and 20 February 1969.
65 Minutes of these meetings, AICRC, B AG 280 147-004.
66 CICR, *Rapport d'activité 1968* (Geneva: CICR, 1969), p. 5.
67 AICRC, plenary session of the Committee, 3 April 1969.
68 Freymond, Willemin & Heacock, *Le Comité International de la Croix-Rouge*, pp. 159–72.
69 AICRC, plenary session of the Committee, 9 January 1969, report by G. Schürch.
70 AICRC, B AG 121.147-001, letter from G. Schürch, 3 December 1968.

71 AICRC, plenary session of the Committee, 9 January 1969, report by G. Schürch.
72 AICRC, plenary session of the Committee, 6 February 1969.
73 Freymond, Willemin, Heacock, *Le Comité international de la Croix-Rouge*, p. 138.
74 AICRC, Directorate briefing note, 28 February 1968.
75 AICRC, Presidential Council meeting, 18 July 1968; plenary session of the Committee, 23 October 1968, report by K. H. Jaggi.
76 AICRC, plenary session of the Committee, 8 August 1968; Presidential Council meeting, 22 August 1968.
77 Jacobs, *The Brutality of Nations*, p. 52. See also the open letter from the President of the Danish Red Cross, Johannes Frandsen, published in the *Journal de Genève*, 31 October 1968, p. 5.
78 DDS, vol. 24, doc. 92 note for the file, meeting between the ICRC's Director and the Head of the International Organisations' Division, 3 July 1968 (dodis.ch/32824).
79 AICRC, B AG 12-044, critical note by P. Basset, November 1970.
80 Freymond, Willemin, Heacock, *Le Comité International de la Croix-Rouge*, pp. 131–2.
81 AICRC, Directorate briefing note, 12 January 1970.
82 Freymond, Willemin, Heacock, *Le Comité International de la Croix-Rouge*, pp. 199–201.
83 CICR, *Rapport d'activité 1967* (Geneva: CICR, 1968), p. 83.
84 CICR, *Rapport d'activité 1970* (Geneva: CICR, 1971), p. 125.
85 "M. Naville: 'le CICR un instrument au service d'une cause'", *Journal de Genève*, 8 September 1969.
86 AICRC, plenary session of the Committee, 6 November 1969.
87 Fiscalini, "Des élites au service d'une cause humanitaire", annex II.
88 Freymond, Willemin, Heacock, *Le Comité International de la Croix-Rouge*, p. 128.
89 AICRC, Presidential Council meeting, 25 January 1968; plenary session of the Committee, 21 October 1970, "Rapport du secrétaire général sur l'état d'avancement de ses travaux en matière d'organisation". See also the ICRC organisation charts for 1969 and 1970 in Freymond, Willemin & Heacock, *Le Comité international de la Croix-Rouge*, pp. 131–2.
90 C. Monnier, "Où va le CICR maintenant", *Journal de Genève*, 6 April 1971.
91 "Croix-Rouge: Les résultats d'Istanbul", *Journal de Genève*, 30 September 1969.
92 According to D. Forsythe, J. Freymond's ideas are ahead of their time and will take some time to spread within the CICR; Forsythe, *The Humanitarians*, p. 226.
93 AICRC, plenary session of the Committee, 3 April 1969.
94 Forsythe, *The Humanitarians*, pp. 182–92.

Conclusion

This book has sought to approach the Nigeria–Biafra conflict not so much as the birthplace of a "new kind of humanitarianism" as a window on the world of humanitarian action in the late 1960s. It has highlighted the issues, main themes, influences and tensions that shaped the making of this humanitarian crisis and the responses provided to it. Shedding light on the multiplicity of actors involved and the diversity of their practices allows reflection on their room for manoeuvre and on the way they understood the crisis, rather than binding them to legal, prescriptive or moral principles. The aim has also been to reintegrate into this history of humanitarianism – insofar as this is possible – the "fields" in which the action took place and the varied forms that the relationship between those who designed the aid, those who implemented it and those for whom it was intended could take. In the end, the ambition of this study has been to offer a history of the intervention in Nigeria–Biafra whose examination is not limited to the achievements or failures of a particular operation or organisation, but is grounded in a global history of the 1960s. The contribution of this approach is twofold.

Biafra as a humanitarian laboratory ...

This study contributes to the history of humanitarian organisations in the twentieth century by showing how they interacted, co-existed and influenced each other during a specific emergency. Seeing Biafra only as the place that saw the creation of Médecins Sans Frontières – even though MSF has become a key and influential player of the humanitarian sphere – does not shed enough light on the complexity of the humanitarian world inhabited by missionaries, religious and secular NGOs, Red Cross societies, the ICRC, UN agencies and governments. It was at the crossroads of local, national and international imperatives that these actors' action was developed on a daily basis. The study of the interplay of these scales produces a more complex analysis than the one in terms of a confrontation of principles or values. Indeed, it is not possible to understand the relationship between the French doctors and the ICRC without placing it in the context of the French executive's policy of supporting Biafra, the violence experienced on the ground and the role played by the ICRC on the international stage. The history of the ICRC, which is often approached in a compartmentalised manner, particularly benefits from this perspective. The policy followed by this organisation was the result of a synthesis of different, sometimes contradictory influences. Indeed, its decision to intervene in late summer 1968 without the Nigerian government's formal agreement was not so much a matter of principle as a response to competition from the League and the churches, encouragement from other organisations and governments, and criticism from public opinion. The end of its operations in the summer of 1969 shows the ambivalence of an ICRC who wanted to continue to be active on the ground but was overwhelmed internally by the scale of a relief effort that threatened not only its relations with West Africa but also its own survival.

Increasing the number of viewpoints helps shed light on the dynamics of co-operation and rivalry within the humanitarian world. This is particularly evidenced by organised movements such as the Red Cross Movement, or those that arose from the specific circumstances of the Biafran crisis, such as the bodies co-ordinating between the churches. As far as the Red Cross Movement is concerned, the competition crystallised in the conflicting relationship between the ICRC and the League. This was reflected both in the field, where the former had to assert itself as the main interlocutor of the Nigerian Red Cross, and within the Movement, where it had to assert each one's role in co-ordinating the aid. Tensions also arose between the ICRC and the Red Cross societies that were most involved in the relief effort, namely the National Societies of northern Europe, which were under pressure from public opinion. Despite these obvious problems, the members of the Red Cross Movement managed to work together since, except for the French Red Cross, all of them took part in the operations co-ordinated by the ICRC in Biafra as well as the federal area.

Among religious aid organisations tensions manifested differently. While they did co-ordinate themselves at an international level, as evidenced by the setting up of Joint Church Aid, they sometimes found it more difficult to work together on the ground. This situation stemmed from the fact that the organisations who implemented the humanitarian aid on the ground – particularly the Catholic and Protestant missions, the Catholic Secretariat and the Nigerian Christian Council – were and would continue to work in Nigeria after the conflict. Comparing to the ones who collected and delivered the relief supplies through the airlift, the one who distributed them daily faced an additional challenge. Their influence and prestige were locally at stake, in the distribution of aid. Indeed, for them it was not only a question of demonstrating to a Western audience that they were able to mobilise to alleviate the suffering of remote populations, but also of being effective and visible and accepted on the ground with a view to a medium- and long-term presence.

This point raises another issue: that of assessing the consequences of international relief operations for the conflict in general and local structures in particular. Indeed, the Nigeria–Biafra war is a particularly good example of the impact of humanitarian aid on conflict situations. By providing visibility and resources to the Biafran regime, it enabled it to resist the federal offensive longer and to maintain an intransigent position during negotiations over relief and peace. But from here to stating that the living conditions of the civilian population would have been better without the humanitarian mobilisation would be a risky leap to make. And that is probably why in most cases relief organisations stood by their decision to intervene. Yes, the duration of the conflict might have been reduced and the living conditions of the civilian population might have returned to normal more quickly. But this was far from certain. The Biafran regime could have found other ways to survive. It is worth recalling its determination and the support it received from other states. Besides, how could one have made sure in 1968 that there would not be a greater number of famine victims in the absence of any relief operations, even if the conflict had stopped earlier? And would the Nigerian government have paid less attention to the behaviour of its troops if it had not had to demonstrate that no genocide had taken place?

As for the impact of the operations on local relief structures, the case of the Nigerian Red Cross in the last months of the conflict illustrates the special place occupied by National Societies in the countries of the Global South, particularly after independence, at the interface between the local, the national and the international. As a Nigerian organisation member of the International Red Cross Movement, it was in a position to play a specific role when the Nigerian government reasserted its sovereignty in relation to the relief operations. Further work is needed to better understand the longer-term impact of the conflict on this Society. On the same vein, the archives of the Catholic Secretariat of Nigeria suggest promising clues to better gauge the influence of the conflict on the way the missions viewed their social and medical work.[1] Despite the churches' involvement in Biafra, the social work done by the missions was still appreciated by the Nigerian government in the areas that needed rebuilding. This led to compromises enabling the progressive return of the Spiritan missionaries to the regions that went back under federal control. These questions therefore deserve to be explored further. More generally, they remind us of the difficulty in grasping the reception of humanitarian aid on the ground, as well as the complexity of the arrangements between local authorities or institutions and Western organisations in a postcolonial context.

… of postcolonial reconfigurations

Before it could be seen as a "May child",[2] humanitarian action in the 1960s was still essentially marked by the colonial paradigm. The interventions in Biafra were developed in the context of European societies adapting to the decolonisation process. Humanitarian aid thus became one of the components of the reconfiguration of relations between the West and the South. The Biafran case is particularly emblematic of this process. The relief operations resulted from the encounters of representations, knowledge and practices inherited from the colonial era with Western humanitarian structures that had developed in the context of European emergencies from the nineteenth century onwards.

The crucial role played by Catholic and Protestant missionaries – most of whose missions had been set up in the nineteenth century – is one of the manifestations of this encounter. They acted as essential links between the West and Nigeria. By travelling back and forth between Europe and Biafra they helped publicise the crisis: they spread stories about the suffering of the people and helped Western journalists come to the province, a practice that would later be institutionalised by the Biafran authorities. They also played a decisive role on the ground, acting as "mediators" in the process of internationalising the conflict. Furthermore, their involvement was crucial in the setting up and deployment of the relief operations. Indeed, Western Catholic and Protestant charities relied on the network of missions covering eastern Nigeria to distribute humanitarian aid. They entrusted missionaries with managing operations, as shown by the appointment of two Spiritan missionaries (Anthony Byrne and Desmond Byrne) in charge of the activities of Caritas Internationalis. Thanks to their knowledge of the region they were also invaluable intermediaries to organisations such as the ICRC wishing to set up their own operations. Finally, the missionaries' activism put some pressure on traditional relief organisations to act.

Colonial legacies also influenced the way humanitarians perceived their area of operation and the relationships between Nigerian leaders and their Western interlocutors. They were particularly evident in the federal government's propensity to see Western relief organisations in neocolonial terms, and to use this argument to explain all the difficulties in their relations. Conversely, the ICRC, just like the British representatives, essentialised their Nigerian interlocutors and analysed their behaviour through the prism of their status as "Africans". The lasting association in the Western collective imagination between "Africa" and "famine", as well as the attribution of "victim" status to African populations are other significant examples. Indeed, the representations of suffering populations were linked to the relief organisations that used them to obtain moral and financial support in the West. The use of photographs by humanitarian agencies is far from being specific to Biafra and has a long tradition.[3] It worked particularly well during this conflict since it promoted representations that were a continuation of those of the colonial period. During the latter, African populations were already depicted as being dependent on Western input in order to become "civilised". Insisting on their "victim" status once again implied the need for Western action to help them out. According to Didier Fassin, this lack of the victims' subjectivity extended to the practice of bearing witness which involved speaking on behalf of "voiceless victims" unable to express themselves.[4] During the Biafran conflict the secessionist authorities contributed to this process since they saw the humanitarian crisis as a means to advance their cause on the international stage, a cause which, as long as it was presented as a struggle for independence, garnered little support. Insisting on the especially "civilised" nature of the Biafran population allowed victimhood representations to work all the better as they were linked to the "modernity" of the Biafran people, which was implicitly seen as an illustration of the prior success of the "civilising mission".

According to Philippe Ryfman, in the late 1960s humanitarianism gained "the status of a major component of the international handling of armed conflicts or natural disasters, at the same time as it became deeply rooted in the civil societies of both Western and Southern countries".[5] Research shows that this evolution needs to be understood as part of the reconfigurations that took place with the end of empires. During the Biafran war, investing in humanitarian aid became a legitimate political option for Western governments. At a time when relations between former colonies and metropoles were changing, this investment was made not only in the name of a moral imperative to help civilians, but also for different reasons that varied with each government. In the British case, supporting the relief effort and showing concern for the victims allowed the UK government to continue to supply Nigeria with weapons, even though this attitude was widely questioned in Parliament and by public opinion. In the United States, the financial and political commitment to humanitarian aid was clearly seen as a way of sticking to a policy of not intervening in the resolution of the conflict while keeping public opinion happy at home. For the Swiss Confederation, supporting the relief operations was a way to satisfy national public opinion, but also position itself in relation to newly independent countries by asserting its "humanitarian role". Contributing to the ICRC's reputation and activities in the postcolonial world was a key component of this policy, as the Swiss attitude in independent Angola confirmed a couple of years later.[6] Finally, in the French case, humanitarian aid was seen as a foreign-policy tool. It was used to support the cause and independence of Biafra. These examples illustrate particularly well the movement towards "humanitarianising the management of international crises".[7] In the Nigeria–Biafra case, it was made possible by the absence of a strong East–West antagonism thanks to the belligerents not really adopting a revolutionary rhetoric. This "humanitarianisation" also took place within a context where former empires were reassessing their material and financial aid policies. At a time when metropoles could choose whether or not to respond to demands for expertise and capital from their former colonies,[8] sending aid during humanitarian crises was less costly but far more spectacular than setting up major "development aid" programmes.

Non-governmental actors benefited from this reconfiguration which translated into an assertion of their role on the international stage. On the one hand, states' interest in humanitarian aid provided these organisations with space and helped them find resources. These actors – whether the ICRC or NGOs – were able to carry out their operations partly thanks to the support they received from governments, who were important sources of funding as well as logistical and diplomatic assistance.[9] Above all, by running humanitarian actions on the ground from the West, these actors confirmed or developed their capacity to intervene in areas located far from their headquarters, to the point that they were even blamed for prolonging the hostilities. The responsibilities they were given at the time of the Biafran crisis and the difficulties they faced in their interventions led them to examine ways in which they could become more autonomous. On the other hand, the gradual success of "humanitarian" NGOs in civil societies can be explained by the fact that these actors proved to be suited to the reconfiguration of relations between Western societies and newly independent states. Kevin O'Sullivan shows that the aid provided to postcolonial countries via NGOs was a way – especially for British and Irish societies – to re-examine their responsibilities and their relationship with the former empires.[10] Similarly, in the case of the Red Cross and then MSF in France, several volunteers reinvested their experiences in new structures that were better adapted to the age of independence, while continuing to rely on colonial knowledge. In this respect, the "French doctors" are a particularly good example of how investing in humanitarian aid became a way of rethinking France's role in the world and even, as Bertrand Taithe notes, of developing a new conception of French universalism.[11]

Biafra was a seminal experience for a generation of humanitarians who went on to pursue a career in humanitarian organisations, whether they were French doctors, members of Africa Concern or ICRC delegates.

Tony Farmar recalls, for example, that in 1972, during relief operations in Bangladesh, international volunteers in the country's capital, Dhaka, regularly reminisced about the Biafran experience in which many of them had taken part.[12] It is true that this was not yet the humanitarian enthusiasm that would characterise the 1980s, but the response to the conflict by huge parts of public opinion already demonstrated the potential of mobilising in support of "victims". With communism becoming more and more synonymous with humanitarian disasters, the radicalisation of extra-parliamentary left-wing movements in the 1970s, which led to the "Years of Lead" in Italy and Germany, and the gradual disintegration of *tiers-mondisme*, humanitarianism emerged as a new form of engagement. In France, *sans-frontiérisme*, whose identity was gradually built around a type of political activism that involved taking risks and "bearing witness", was a particular beneficiary of this evolution.[13] But the latter affected the whole humanitarian world, with commitment to the "victims" becoming one of the features of evolving Western sensibilities to the countries of the Global South.

Notes

1 NAN, Roman Catholic Missions, 1/174, "Report of the Social Welfare Department of the Catholic Secretariat of Nigeria for the period of June 1 to September 30, 1970".

2 This expression cames from P. Ryfman, "L'humanitaire, enfant de Mai?", in P. Artières & M. Zancarini-Fournel (eds), *68, une histoire collective (1962–1981)* (Paris: La Découverte, 2008), pp. 736–45.

3 Fehrenbach & Rodogno (eds), *Humanitarian Photography*.

4 Fassin, *La raison humanitaire*, pp. 265–6.

5 Ryfman, "L'humanitaire, enfant de mai?", pp. 736–45.

6 S. Widmer, *Switzerland and Sub-Saharan Africa in the Cold War, 1967–1979* (Leiden: Brill, 2021).

7 Fassin, *La raison humanitaire*, p. 288.

8 F. Cooper, "Writing the History of Development", *Journal of Modern European History*, 8:1 (2010), 5–23, at 15.

9 For an example of the ambiguous autonomisation of these actors, see Y. Denéchère "Diplomaties privées et autonomisation des ONG humanitaires dans l'espace de la cause des enfants", *Monde(s)*, 1:1 (2014), 119–35.

10 K. O'Sullivan, "Humanitarian Encounters: Biafra, NGOs and Imaginings of the Third World in Britain and Ireland, 1967–70", *Journal of Genocide Research*, 16:2–3 (2014), 299–315, at 304.

11 Taithe, "Reinventing French Universalism".

12 Farmar, *Believing in Action*, p. 51.

13 Davey, *Idealism Beyond Borders*.

Index

Printed by Libri Plureos GmbH in Hamburg,
Germany

9 781526 190246